Psalms Breathing:

Meditating the Psalms with Music,
Movement
and Silence

Psalms Breathing:

Meditating the Psalms with Music, Movement and Silence

Louis N. Gruber, M.D.

Psalms Breathing: Meditating the Psalms with Music, Movement and Silence.
Copyright © Louis N. Gruber, 2000. [Version 5.0]

All rights reserved, including public performance of the music or movements, or the making of sound or visual recordings. No part of this book may be reproduced or transmitted in any form or by any means, electronic or mechanical, except for brief quotations embodied in critical articles or reviews, without permission in writing from the publisher

ISBN: 1-58721-585-3

1stBooks - rev. 10/16/00

About the Book

Psalms Breathing is not another book *about* the psalms, of which there are many, but a companion for those who would go deep within the psalms, abandon all preconceived notions, and hear them, hear through them, to the voice of God. It is a practice that I call *walking* the psalms, going beyond the intellect, beyond words, toward listening, surrender, poverty in spirit, wisdom. In the book I teach three special methods for this walk, namely music, movement, and the practice of intentional silence. Brief commentaries to each of the psalms bring out some of the deeper meanings and applications to life.

Acknowledgements

Acknowledgement is made to Baker Book House for the quotations from *Gesenius' Hebrew-Chaldee Lexicon to the Old Testament Scriptures*; to the Church Hymnal Corporation for material from *The Book of Common Prayer*; to the American Bible Society for permission to quote from *The Good News Bible*; for Mesorah Publications, Ltd. for permission to quote from the Artscroll *Tehillim (Psalms)*; to Thomas Nelson, Inc., Publishers, for permission to quote from the *New King James Bible* (Psalms 68, 74, 140; and all Biblical references marked NKJ); to Zondervan Bible Publishers for permission to quote Romans 13:11 and Matthew 17:5 from *The Holy Bible, New International Version*, copyright 1973, 1978, 1984, by International Bible Society (NIV); acknowledgement is also made to Cowley Publications for permission to quote Psalm 58:1 from *Meditating on the Word* by David McI. Gracie, copyright 1986. And to Michael V. Carlisle for permission to quote from *Chaos* by James Gleick.

Step One (*Alcoholics Anonymous*, p. 59) is reprinted with permission of Alcoholics Anonymous World Services, Inc. (A.A.W.S.). Permission to reprint Step One does not mean that A.A.W.S. has reviewed or approved the contents of this publication, or necessarily agrees with the views expressed herein. A.A. is a program of recovery from alcoholism *only*. Use of this Step in connection with programs and activities which are patterned after A.A., but which address other problems, or in any other non-A.A. context, does not imply otherwise. Although Alcoholics Anonymous is a spiritual program, it is not a religious program, and use of A.A. material in the present connection does not imply A.A.'s affiliation with or endorsement of any sect, denomination, or specific religious belief.

Thanks to Rev. Robert Pratt, Brother Bede Healy, Raymond Brock, Lowell Saunders for reviewing the manuscript and for helpful suggestions. Special thanks to the Episcopal Church of St. Simon and St. Jude, and to the Tuesday night Bible class, for support and encouragement.

Table Of Contents

About the Book v

Acknowledgements vii

Introduction (1) xi

Introduction (2) xiv

Introduction (3) xvi

Book One   (Psalms 1-41) 1

Book Two   (Psalms 42-72) 117

Book Three   (Psalms 73-89) 201

Book Four   (Psalms 90-106) 247

Book Five   (Psalms 107-150) 297

Afterword 429

Appendix (1) 431

Appendix (2) 434

Appendix (3) 437

About the Author 439

x

Introduction (1)
Walking The Psalms: A Way To Meditate

The purpose of this book is to help you on your spiritual journey. If you follow it, it will be your spiritual companion, a daily help on the path. It is built upon the premise that Scripture is the living Word of God. But this will be true for you only if you *walk* the Scriptures, that is live them, breathe them, and make them your own story.

It is especially true for the psalms, those intimate and emotional hymns, for every thing human is in them—every emotion, every suffering; victory and defeat. Here you will learn to walk them as living Word, with the help of three special methods—music, movement, and silence. It is not an analytical or scholarly process. It is becoming as close to the Word as breathing. It is what we call meditation.

Each of these methods—music, movement, silence—is meant to draw you away from the intellect, from "your own understanding," from words—toward listening, surrender, poverty in spirit, wisdom. This may seem strange at first, but soon you will find it charming and refreshing.

Do not attempt to read quickly through this book. Use it as a part of your daily devotions, praying the psalms appointed for each day. Meditate them, that is read them reflectively, ponder them, let them echo within you. The music will deepen your experience, the movements will energize you, and the experiences of silence will transform your consciousness. You will not understand all that you read in a precise way, but you will allow it to change you. It will penetrate deep within you and it will begin to transform your thinking.

Meditate the psalms morning and evening. Begin with formal prayer (I use the "Daily Devotions" in the *Book of Common Prayer**), then read (sing, chant, walk, dance) the psalms for that day. Conclude—always—with silence. Ask God what he wants you to learn from these verses. Listen and stay as alert as you can. Sometimes you may receive a clear message, more often not. More than anything you will experience a growing sense of his presence, his guidance, his manner of thinking.

Such is the basic plan. These simple thoughts of mine will be repeated over and over, in many ways, as you work your way through the book. You will learn some new ways of reading Scripture, such as slowing, whispering, bowing, walking, lifting the hands, singing that alternates with reading, dancing. You will learn to use the drum in your praying. You will begin to experience what Scripture calls *new song*.

Most important of all is the experience of silence. Always conclude your studies with silence. And in this silence, stop everything —thoughts, words, memories, anticipations, restless movements. Clear your mind as completely as you can. In a few seconds it will

---

*The Book of Common Prayer and Administration of the Sacraments and Other Rites and Ceremonies of the Church. According to the Use of the Episcopal Church. The Church Hymnal Corporation, New York, 1979 (the Prayer Book), pp. 136-140.

be busy again. Clear it again. Sit comfortably in an upright position. Other than this, no special posture is required, no special techniques, no *mantra*; just silence, eyes open, learning to listen.

Begin with five to ten minutes of silence, keeping the time constant from day to day. Gradually increase the time as it feels comfortable. In your silent time do not consciously think about the verses you have read or try to analyze them. Let them work on you from within, without words.

No instructor is required, no *guru*, for your instructor is the Holy Spirit. Ask God to teach you and he will teach you. Ask him to show you his will and he will show you. Seek his guidance and his presence. Use the materials in this book as you find them useful; adapt them to your own personal style. Set aside a regular time and place for your meditation, but keep them flexible. You can meditate anywhere, at any time. Always begin with prayer and end with silence. This will be your path of life.

Suggestions For Psalm Walking

Make the decision that these Scriptures are in fact the Word of God, that is, a way for God to speak to you. What is God trying to teach you in these readings? Put aside for now the historical and literary background of the psalms. Scholarly disputes about the text are not important to you at this moment. Rather, think of the *experiences* in the psalms as your own. How does this text relate to you personally?

Read the psalms for each day, not only those that appeal to you. Read regularly, setting aside the same time and place each day for your study. Read slowly, aloud if possible, in a deliberate, rhythmic way, as explained below. If you still find yourself perplexed, read again, more slowly, one or two verses at a time.

Intersperse your readings with silence, as described above. Always conclude with silent reflection. As soon as possible, begin to add music and movement, using the instructions given below. As you gain confidence, experiment on your own. Do not expect perfection, but enjoy as best you can.

The psalms may be used for individual or group study. When you study in groups, remind one another that we are all experts, no one is an authority. Do not be intimidated by scholars or clergy. Ask the Holy Spirit to interpret for you, and let these beautiful Scriptures speak to you.

Suggested Reading

Thomas R. Hawkins: *The Unsuspected Power of the Psalms*, The Upper Room, Nashville, TN, 1985.

C.S. Lewis: *Reflections on the Psalms*, Phoenix Press, Walker & Company, New York, 1985.

What Are The Psalms?

Poems (songs, dances) composed in the Hebrew language many years before Christ. Scholars continue to debate their age and authorship. Their subject matter is varied: hymns for public worship; outpourings of private grief; moments of despair, pain, anger, elation. What has made them so powerful and so beloved? At first they appear forbidding. Their language is often harsh. They speak of hate and revenge. The writers seem to lose faith. They question God and his power. As we become accustomed to the harsh imagery, we begin to identify with these writers. We realize that they understand our feelings. They have walked the spiritual path before us, and they know its difficulties. Slowly, in the most remarkable way, they come to speak for us. Whatever the words may have meant to the first writers, they are soon overlaid with second, third, fourth layers of meaning. And so they are no longer ancient hymns. They are songs about our own experience.

The central image of the psalms for me is that of a walk or path. It is the spiritual path, the way of surrender. Walking on this path I give up control and go where God takes me. It is a path that goes up a hill, through many and varied experiences, to a high and holy place. To a temple, a place of silence. This simple metaphor will be your roadmap as you walk with me.

The psalms belong to a continuous tradition going back to Abraham. My own experience is rooted in two branches of this tradition. Born and raised in Judaism, I became a Christian in adult life. Now I find myself comfortably at home in the Episcopal Church. It has been for me a happy blending of two cultures with common roots, for each has something that has been partly forgotten in the other. I am convinced that each branch has much to learn from the other, much to share.

The psalms are common to both branches. Jesus lives in them, as he said in Luke 24:44. He used them to express his innermost feelings, for they reflect his manner of thinking. He was a man of my people; a man so humble that he called himself only "son of man." You will find him in the psalms if you seek him and listen for his voice. And if you have never been introduced to him with love and respect, this book will help you to find him. It is a book for Jews, Christians, everyone. No one is excluded. Study with an open mind. This is not the work of an Old Testament scholar, pastor or theologian. The author is a seeker like yourself, a disciple on the road.

Notes: The text of Psalms is largely taken from the Prayer Book, occasionally from the King James Version (KJV) or the New King James Version* (NKJ), or the author's own translation (LNG). I have made a few modifications in the division of lines or punctuation, rarely in the text itself, indicated by (*). The superscriptions or Hebrew titles of the psalms have been omitted. For an excellent overview of the Psalter and psalmody, consult the Prayer Book, pp. 582-584.

Suggestions: Begin with the psalms for the First Day. Continue to the end of the month, then begin over at the First Day. Read the psalms themselves, let the commentaries stir up your thinking, try the suggestions, experiment with the music and movement. Books that I have found helpful are mentioned throughout this work. Whenever possible study in groups and support one another.

---

*Holy Bible. The New King James Version. Thomas Nelson Publishers, Nashville, 1982.

Introduction (2)
Meditating The Psalms With Music

Scripture cannot be fully grasped with the intellect alone. The psalms in particular must connect with deeper levels, with breathing and the emotions, to be truly understood. Music helps make the connection. The music presented here should not be considered primarily as art or religious music. It is an aid to meditation, a bridge to those deeper levels. Its purpose is to direct and redirect the attention, to lead you from the surface to the deeper meaning.

Singing builds upon reading aloud, reading aloud rests upon breathing. Let us begin with Psalm 3, which is read with sung refrains. Consider verse 3:1, which is meant to be read. Notice that the verse is divided into two sections (lines) by an asterisk. The entire verse corresponds to a breath, while the asterisk indicates a *caesura* or pause. Now inhale sharply through the nose, read in a slow and deliberate manner to the asterisk, pause silently for up to one second, read the second half in the same way.

[Inhale] LORD, how many adversaries I have: * [pause]
how many there are who rise up against me.

And similarly, v.2:

[Inhale] How many there are who say of me, * [pause]
"There is no help for him in his God."

Practice this method of reading, until it begins to feel natural. Learn to read slowly, giving each word its full value. At the pause, let your mind be silent.

Verse 3:3 is marked for singing:

But you, O LORD, are a shield a | bout me;
you are my glory, the one who lifts up my | head.

You will notice no asterisk, but two vertical marks (Tone markers). These will indicate where to change pitch. Begin by inhaling sharply through the nose, sing on the first note to the first marker, sing on the second note to the end of the line. In the same way, sing the second line to the third and fourth notes.

[Inhale] (first note) | (second note)
(third note) | (fourth note).

Illustration:

But you, O LORD, are a shield a | bout me;

You are my glory, the one who lifts up my | head.

Each Tone contains a number of simple musical figures (Orders). Each Order has its own characteristic marker (| / \ +, and others), and is sung to the measure(s) of music bearing that marker. As these simple figures follow each other in sequence, a cyclical or wave-like pattern may be created. Hebrew verse does not have stanzas of a fixed length. Therefore, Orders may be omitted or repeated. Each wave is unique.

Certain psalms are sung in their entirety; others are read with sung refrains; or reading and singing alternate in other ways. These contrasts will also deepen the understanding. Sung refrains, as well as each first line of a recurrent cyclical pattern, are generally indicated in boldface type. Always sing deliberately, maintaining a steady pace. Each note should be held for roughly the same time. The music should be gently flowing, guided by the Spirit.

The guiding principle is balance — the balancing of contrasting qualities. Rising tones are balanced with descending; music with speech; music and speech with silence; silence with movement. Nothing is taken to extremes; every tendency is balanced with another; the attention is constantly challenged and redirected.

Pronounce the words naturally, as you would say them. The pitch always changes on the first stressed syllable of a word. The words flow like natural speech. Further material will be found in the Appendix.

Note: The names of the Tones are taken from the Hebrew names of musical instruments and other terms found in the Bible. Some of these terms are found in the superscriptions to the psalms, thought to represent musical instructions. Of course, these Tones are not the actual instructions, and are not of biblical origin.

Suggested Reading

The Psalms: Singing Version. A New Translation from the Hebrew Arranged for Singing to the Psalmody of Joseph Gelineau. A Deus Book Edition of the Paulist Press, 1968. Paperback by William Collins and Sons & Co. Ltd., Glasgow.

Kay Gardner: *Sounding the Inner Landscape. Music as Medicine.* Caduceus Publications, Stonington, ME. 1990.

Introduction (3)
Meditating The Psalms With Movement

My remarks on music apply also to movement. The psalms speak often of movement —of walking, dance, processions, lifting and bowing. Movement, like music, is a bridge to those other levels of being, a way to expand my understanding beyond the verbal. Movement awakens me, engages me at a deeper level of meaning, and keeps me alert. Movement brings me out of religious trance.

An informal method of movement is simply to carry out the actions described. Walk when the verses speak of walking, lift when they speak of lifting, bow deeply from the waist when you read of bowing or worshiping.* Move with the psalms as you yourself interpret them, led by the Holy Spirit.

You may wish to begin by standing. Sense the rhythm of the psalm and breathe with it, as explained earlier. If you find yourself getting light-headed, read or sing more slowly. As you gain confidence, allow your body to sway with the rhythm, or let your feet step with it. Shift your weight from side to side, in a stepping or treading movement. Let your movements portray the emotion of the psalm. Professor Clynes has shown that each emotion has its characteristic form or shape.** Now as you breathe and move, see if you can sense what the writer is experiencing. What is God saying to you?

A more formalized system of movements is given in Appendix (2). Begin from a comfortable seated position unless otherwise instructed. Key elements are the praise gesture, in which the extended hands, palms up, are lifted a little higher than the heart; and the heart gesture, in which the arms are folded across the chest, hands on the shoulders. Somewhat more elaborate is the wave gesture for thank offerings: beginning with the praise gesture, lift and lower the hands on one line of text, move them gracefully leftward and rightward, ending in the original position, on the next line. Like everything in this book these and all the movements described are my suggestions; use them as you find them useful, adapt them to your own needs.

Suggested Reading

Doug Adams & Diane Apostolos-Cappadona (eds.): *Dance as Religious Studies*. Crossroad, New York, 1990.

---

*See *Aspects of Nonverbal Communication in the Ancient Near East* by Mayer I. Gruber, Biblical Institute Press, Rome, 1980, especially pp. 182-200.
**Manfred Clynes: *Sentics: the Touch of the Emotions*, Doubleday, 1977.

Book One

The Way: Introduction And Commentary To Psalm 1

Scholars consider this psalm the introduction to the Psalter. Here, as in a number of psalms, the writer speaks of walking a path or way. In a few psalms the expression is of climbing a mountain. It is a beautiful metaphor for the spiritual life, the life of surrender. Psalm 1 will be your introduction to that way.

.ASHREY HÁ.IYSH .ASHER LO. HÁLAKH*
v.1a Happy is the man who has not walked.

Happy or blessed is the one who has not walked (lived), for the way begins with little choices. He or she has chosen not to live in the counsel (advice) of the wicked; popular advice that is taken by many good people as wisdom. Such advice as *It's not what you know, it's who you know*, or, *Look out for number one*. Happy or blessed is the one who no longer lives by such advice.

And he has chosen not to stand with the sinners. She has decided not to take her stand, shall we say, with those who "miss the mark." Better to say they miss the point, like arrows flying past the target altogether. They are trying to steer themselves, and so they speed through life missing the point. They fly with great energy but they have nowhere to land. Happy is the one who does not fly with them, but chooses this path.

He or she has also decided not to associate with scorners (scoffers, cynics, those who make fun of things). For though they are often amusing, their wit is negative, and its effects destructive. Hurtful to the individual, the family, the fellow workers. Happy is the one who does not sit with them, who does not scorn or ridicule anyone else.

The way begins with a change of direction, a new way of thinking. This is the preparation for the way. Now, for the way itself:

UV:THORÁTHOW YEH:GEH YOMÁM WÁ<u>LAY</u>LÁh*
v.2b and in his *Torah* he begins to meditate day and night.

In the *Torah* or teaching of the LORD, he immerses himself, he begins to meditate, day and night. She talks to herself about it. He thinks of it, listens, hears, reflects in silence. He does this "day and night," which I take in two ways. First, he meditates morning and evening: he practices formal meditation twice a day. Second, she meditates all day long: informal meditation, for a moment or a few seconds, at intervals throughout the day.

He goes from walking to standing to sitting to meditating. He learns to be silent and listen. She chooses this humble path. No special techniques are needed, only this.

v.3 And he has become like a tree planted by streams of water,
     who gives his fruit in its season.

He has become like a healthy organism, controlling nothing but perfectly controlled, self-regulating. A healthy tree, fresh and green, she brings forth fruit, that is, natural, spontaneous outgrowth of her being. Of that natural outgrowth, Jesus said, "You will know them by their fruits" (Matthew 7:16, NKJ), for it reflects the innermost heart and cannot be dissembled. I think it is what we call fruit of the Spirit—*love, joy, peace, patience, gentleness* (Galatians 5:22). Those who practice this meditation and walk this path will be like trees bearing such fruit. This will be their evidence of spiritual progress.

> v.3   and all that he begins to do begins to succeed.

It will be fruitful, it will bring forth good results. Good for the person, the family, the fellow workers. Nourished from the Mind of God, she begins to bear this fruit—not constantly, but often; unexpectedly, unplanned. He begins to live a life of wisdom, without knowing how.

LO. KHÉN HÁR:SHÁ"IM*

> v.4   Not so the wicked.

In the short run the wicked may experience striking success. In the longer view their lives are meaningless, like something blown away by the wind. In spite of their apparent importance and their appearances on talk shows, the wicked have no real future. And the sinners who fly about without direction will also be left out. There is nothing moralistic about this. Like plants with shallow roots, they will soon dry up and blow away.

> v.6   For the LORD knows the way of the righteous,
>   but the way of the wicked shall perish.

To know in Hebrew means to know intimately, as a husband knows his wife. The LORD knows the path of the righteous, for he is intimately involved in it. It doesn't matter where one goes on such a path, because the path itself is life-giving. But the way of the wicked is a road that perishes, a road to nowhere. The spiritual path of the psalms is a simple path. As always, God begins with the small, and requires what is possible. It almost seems too easy.

<u>Suggestions</u>:   Begin your walk today with this lesson. Sing Psalm 1 to the Tone *Alphabet*, four notes to one verse, one measure. Meditate the psalms day and night (morning and evening). Read or sing the psalms for each day. Reflect on the readings prayerfully and let God speak to you through them. Listen without analyzing and let the message sink deep within you. Always follow your readings with silence. Cultivate that silence, for a moment or a few seconds, whenever you can throughout the day.

---

*Selected words and verses are provided in the original Hebrew, transliterated by the author, for the student who is interested. Consult Appendix (3) to learn the method of pronunciation.

Psalm 1 (BCP)

First Day: Morning Prayer **Tone:** *Alphabet*

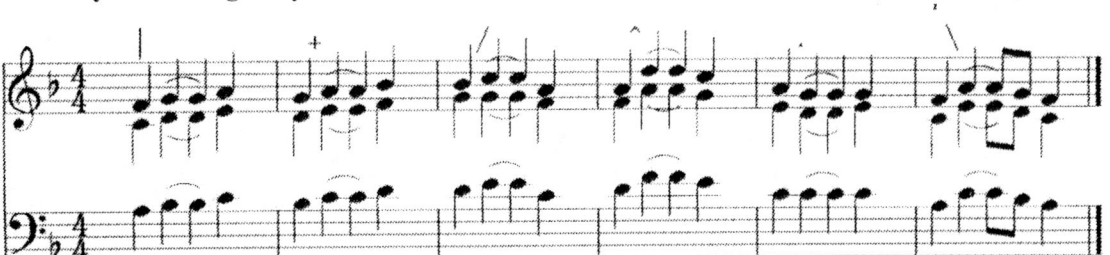

1 **Happy are they who have not walked in the counsel of the | wicked,**
   nor lingered in the way of sinners,
   nor sat in the seats of the | scornful!
2 Their delight is in the law of the + LORD,
   and they meditate on his law day and + night.
3 They are like trees planted by streams of water,
   bearing fruit in due season, with leaves that do not / wither;
   everything they do shall / prosper.
4 It is not so with the ^ wicked;
   they are like chaff which the wind blows a^way.
5 Therefore the wicked shall not stand upright when . judgment comes,
   nor the sinner in the council of the . righteous.
6 \For the LORD knows the way of the \ righteous,
   but the way of the \ wicked is \ doomed.

By What Authority? Commentary To Psalm 2

Psalm 2 is also considered part of the introduction. You might wish to open your morning paper and glance at the headlines as you study it.

        LÁMMÁH RÁG:SHUW GOYIM   UL:.UMMIM YEH:GGU-RIYQ

v.1 Why have the nations created such a tumult? And why do the peoples continue murmuring and meditating emptiness? Why are the nations in an uproar? Why am I? Why do the peoples murmur and meditate what is foolish and empty? And why do I? Like the outer world of the newspaper, so is my inner world: a world of tumult, noise, confusion, pointless conflict and meaningless competition; anger and disappointment; anxiety, suspicion, the sense of futility, and the feeling of despair.

In the world of the newspaper, groups and their leaders are struggling for illusory power. Leaders who really lead no one, but reflect the consciousness of their people, arise and try to exert control. They align themselves in shaky alliances to carry out futile schemes, betray each other, regroup and try again, always cloaked in idealistic language. And all of it ends in futility. Commentators and pundits tell us what all this means, but the meaning changes daily. What the pundits told us yesterday is now called "conventional wisdom," discredited by the onrush of new happenings.

In my inner world, thought leads to thought and emotion to emotion. Thoughts and emotions sweep over me, tides of panic, resentment, emptiness, and fleeting elation. I sense that I should somehow be in control as life rushes away from me. I begin my walk in darkness, confusion; in a world at war with God. One thought leads to another thought, emotion to emotion. The peoples rush off to war or to kill; to whatever has caught their attention. Like those arrows flying past the target in Psalm 1. I shake my head in bafflement, wondering why problems cannot be solved.

        WA.aNIY NÁSAKHTI MALKIY   "AL-3IYYON HAR-QODSHIY

v.6 But as for me, I have anointed my king

    on Zion my holy mountain. I (God) have already established my government. Forget the newspaper and the pundits, for they are missing the real story. My administration is already in place!

v.7 "I will announce," says the king, "what the LORD has declared. He said to me, 'You are my son; today I have become your father'" (Good News Bible).

Fold up the newspaper and put it away. The real news is that God is in control. At the heart of the universe is a Person with authority, a Father, and you are his child. The walking of the way, the spiritual path, is a walk to him, under his authority. It will take you and me from confusion and darkness to meaning, coherence and wisdom; not by our thoughts, by reasoning; but by surrender, by willingness; by the discipline of meditation; by walking the psalms each day with music, movement, and silence.

It is not a difficult walk. The steps are easy and small. Only the willingness may be difficult; staying the course. Remembering to be silent. Remembering to meditate morning and evening, and to practice silence through the day. It is easy to begin this path, but hard to continue; and yet, if it is hard to continue on this path, it is easy to start again, at any and every moment.

"IVDUW .ETH YHWH B:YIR.ÁH   W:G̲IYLU BIR:"ÁDÁH

v.11 Serve the LORD with fear,
     and rejoice with trembling!   Serve the LORD with a clear understanding of his power. Rejoice, even as you tremble, for that power belongs to your Father. It is no light thing to begin this walk, for it will take you and change you. The spiritual path is a path of surrender, a path you cannot control. As you meditate the words of God day by day, they will penetrate within you and change your way of thinking, your outlook and your priorities. It will be like asking God, your heavenly Father, to take direction of your life. It is an awesome commitment. A willing commitment, freely chosen. Chosen again, each morning, each evening, each moment, again and again. Are you ready to begin?

v.13 Happy are they all
    who take refuge in him!
Real happiness is found in giving up, completely, the search for control. All control, in the world and in your family. In moving beyond that world of thoughts and emotions, beyond human means. You cannot solve the problems of this world by reasoning; not by manipulating or intimidating others. Not by self-control or self-improvement or will power. Give up the power games. Find safety *in him*. Find your security, your answers, in the power and protection of God. These concepts, so well intentioned and so hard to grasp, will become real to you as you work your way through this book. They are not abstract concepts, but experiential realities. But where they will ultimately take you, neither of us can say. Are you ready to begin?

Notes: "Why are the nations in an uproar?" (v.1), compare Acts 4:25-26. "You shall crush them with an iron rod" (v.9), see Revelation 2:26-27, 12:5 and 19:15.

Suggestions: Sing the refrains indicated in boldface type to the Tone #a3O3:ROTH (*trumpets*), two notes to a measure, one measure to a line of poetry. Note how the writer changes his focus as he moves through the verses: from the tumult of "the peoples," to the power of the king, to trust. As you read the news each day, watch yourself reacting. Notice how thought leads to thought, slogan to slogan, emotion to emotion. Why are the nations in an uproar? Why am I?

In your spiritual practice, submit yourself to higher authority. Take this path as a discipline and practice faithfully. Seek God and his will at every step of the path. Ask God to teach you how to meditate. Put yourself under religious authority as well: congregation, pastor, rabbi, priest, bishop. Practice respect for authority in all your affairs. Seek guidance on your spiritual path.

Psalm 2

Tone: #a3O3:ROTH

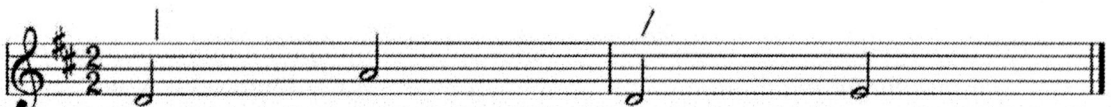

1 Why are the nations in an uproar? *
    Why do the peoples mutter empty threats?
2 Why do the kings of the earth rise up in revolt,
    and the princes plot together, *
    against the LORD and against his Anointed?
3 "Let us break their yoke," they say; *
    "let us cast off their bonds from us."
4 He whose throne is in heaven is laughing; *
    the Lord has them in derision.
5 Then he speaks to them in his wrath, *
    and his rage fills them with terror.
6 **"I myself have set my | king**
    /upon my holy hill of / Zion."
7 Let me announce the decree of the LORD: *
    he said to me, "You are my Son; this day have I begotten you.
8 Ask of me, and I will give you the nations for your inheritance *
    and the ends of the earth for your possession.
9 You shall crush them with an iron rod *
    and shatter them like a piece of pottery."
10 And now, you kings, be wise; *
    be warned, you rulers of the earth.
11 **Submit to the LORD with | fear,**
    /and with trembling bow be/fore him;
12 Lest he be angry and you perish; *
    for his wrath is quickly kindled.
13 Happy are they all *
    who take refuge in him!

How Many Troubles: Commentary To Psalm 3

YHWH MÁH-RABBUW 3ÁRÁY

v.1 LORD, how many are my troubles (problems, stresses). The root means to compress, squeeze, or constrict. Like the English word *anxiety* it implies suffocating confinement. It is everything that hems me in and squeezes the breath from me. I have so much to learn about troubles.

Troubles are inherently many. They will not be over when I eliminate some "basic problem" or "root cause"; every problem has replacements. When one is solved, more are coming. Problems rise up against me when I least expect them. They rise up taller than I and they overshadow me. And they set themselves against me all around, they surround me so that I cannot escape. More importantly, they undermine my very self.

RABBIM .OMRIM **L:NAPHSHIY** .EYN Y:SHU"ÁTHÁH LLO VE.LOHIM

v.2 Many are saying *to my soul*, "There is no help for him in his God."

Many are saying this to my NEPHESh (*soul*). This fascinating word can be interpreted on many levels. Like the Greek *psuché* the root meaning is breath. So we read, "And the LORD GOD formed man of the dust of the ground, and breathed into his nostrils the breath of life; and man became a living soul" (Genesis 2:7, KJV). So the man became a human breathing. And the soul (breath, breathing, life) is the actual man, not some ghostly entity that inhabits the man.

The word is often used in the psalms as of a person, my self personified, my inner Other, the inner person I talk to when I talk to myself. I talk to her fondly and protectively, as to a child who lives within me (my "precious little self"); or to an intimate friend, or to an inner spouse (feminine gender), more intimate than my spouse.

How remarkable that I can be divided like this, that I can also be "me" or "myself," as though there were an Other within me. We are so used to having this companion, this Other, that we take her for granted. And the horror of this verse is that *they*—the adversaries, the troubles — are speaking to my Other, my most intimate companion, and turning her against me.

They are turning my soul against *me*! And so they undermine me from within and destroy my ability to resist. Even as I struggle against my troubles, they have already gotten through to my inner self; they are telling her that the struggle is hopeless.

And that makes it really hopeless. They have infiltrated my defenses. The enemy is within me as well as without, replicating like a virus. A virus that turns me against myself so that I destroy myself.

After that realization, there is no solution, no therapy, no insight, no problem-solving strategy. Silence (see discussion on *selah*). Then like a shining column of light piercing the darkness comes v.3. A quantum leap to a radical new perspective.

"But you, O LORD, are a shield about me." Craigie* explains the transformation brilliantly. The battle is lost, the situation is hopeless, and then that sudden leap. The problems are never solved, but they are transcended, leaped over. I lift my vision to a new level of understanding. Conversion!

"But you, O LORD." I turn from the situation and I am talking to the LORD the Solution. Only then, "I begin to call with my voice upon the LORD, and he begins to answer me from his holy hill." Silence again. I sleep and wake, knowing the LORD is in control. The troubles have not changed, but the situation has changed completely.

v.7 Surely you have struck all my enemies ... you have broken the teeth of the wicked. Deliverance (salvation, freedom, victory) is already accomplished.

This is a traditional morning psalm (see Craigie). When I first wake up—at three, four, or five in the morning—an awareness of troubles comes flooding in. This is for me the most vulnerable time of the day. As I come up out of sleep my mind is already churning with problems and grasping at solutions. I toss and turn, trying to hold on to sleep for a few more minutes, but it never happens. "LORD, I really don't want to go to work today." Then I turn my vision to God. He has already worked out the solutions. He has already defeated the enemies. Freedom and victory are of him, and of him alone. Silence.

Suggestions: Sing refrains, verses 3-4 and 7-8, to the Tone GITTITH (*of Gath*), two notes to a measure, one measure to a line.

When you waken in that vulnerable state, when the troubles, the "enemies" come flooding in, do this: Interrupt that cycle of thoughts and emotions. You might, for example, take a deep breath through the nose; or say a quick mental prayer of one or two words; or breathe the sweet Name of Jesus; and then be silent. Clear your mind of all thoughts, *all*, however briefly. Turn your attention to God, with or without words; focus your attention toward him, and be silent. The enemies are already defeated. This practice will be referred to throughout the book as a "moment of silence." It will be your informal meditation, and a constant help to you on the path.

---

*Peter C. Craigie: *Word Biblical Commentary* Vol. 19: Psalms 1-50. Word Books, Waco, Texas, 1983, pp. 72-75.

Psalm 3 (BCP)

Tone: GITTITH[1]

1 LORD, how many adversaries I have! *
  how many there are who rise up against me!
2 How many there are who say of me, *
  "There is no help for him in his God."
        [Silence...]
3 **But you, O LORD, are a shield a | bout me;**
  you are my glory, the one who lifts up my | head.
4 \I call aloud upon the \ LORD,
  and he answers me from his \ holy hill;
        [Silence...]
5 I lie down and go to sleep; *
  I wake again, because the LORD sustains me.
6 I do not fear the multitudes of people *
  who set themselves against me all around.
7 **Rise up, O LORD; set me free, O my | God;**
  surely, you will strike all my enemies across the | face,
  \you will break the teeth of the \ wicked.
8 Deliverance belongs to the \ LORD.
  /Your blessing be upon your / people!
        [Silence...]

Silence Is A Window To Eternity: A Note About *Selah*

RABBIM .OMRIM L:NAPHSHIY .EYN Y:SHU"ÁTHÁH LLO VE.LOHIM SEL<u>Á</u>h
3:2 Many are saying to my soul,
"There is no help for him in his God." [Silence...].

There are almost as many explanations of *selah* as there are commentators. Many consider it impenetrable, of indeterminate meaning, or perhaps as some lost musical or liturgical instruction. A few commentators suggest a pause of some kind either in words or music. Some of the Jewish commentators render it as "forever." Gesenius* interprets it as "rest, silence ... a short pause in singing the words of the psalm." He notes that the Greek Septuagint renders it as *diapsalma*, an interlude. His suggestion is the one I find most plausible.

Selah is usually found at a transition point. There is a leap from one line of thought, mood, or attitude to another. Time to stop and reflect. Less often it will be found in the middle of a thought. Stop. Listen to this.

I have rendered *selah* as [Silence...] in this work, and my suggestion is to observe it as a silent pause. When it appears, stop everything—words, music, thoughts, restless movements. Be completely silent for ten to fifteen seconds. Then continue. It is not easy to still that internal chatter, but it can be done for a few seconds. Let the words you have just read reverberate within you. Watch yourself breathe.

There is no need to hurry on, for the spiritual path is a path of eternity. Silence takes us, momentarily, out of the rush of time. [Silence...] is a tiny window to eternity. [Silence...] transforms our walk with the psalms from reading to meditation. In group study [Silence...] is especially powerful, for it dissolves self-consciousness.

<u>Suggestions</u>: Begin and end your studies with silence. When you study in a group, allow time for silence. After every break, resume with a minute (or more) of silence. Let go of that need to control, to explain. Let go of that need to fill every silence with words. Let the Holy Spirit speak to you.

Conclude your meditation always with a period of silence. At first you may conclude your practice with five to ten minutes of silence at each session; gradually increase the time as you feel directed by the Spirit. In your silence, let your inner world be still. No words. No lengthy intercessions. No analysis. Keep your eyes open, be relaxed but alert. Let the verses you have just read echo within you.

Observe silence in daily life as well. When you find yourself rushing and worrying, stop everything. Just for a moment, be silent. Practice moments of silence at every opportunity throughout the day.

---

*H.W.F. Gesenius: *Gesenius' Hebrew-Chaldee Lexicon to the Old Testament Scriptures* (Translated by Samuel Prideaux Tregelles), Baker Book House, Grand Rapids, MI, 1979, p.588.

In Peace All Together: Commentary To Psalm 4

A psalm for bedtime. Snatches of conversation are heard, their meaning elusive, as I drift into sleep.

BA33ÁR HIR#AVTÁ LLIY

v.1 In stress (constraint, confinement) you have enlarged me. In straits you have set me free. "In stress," paradoxically, you have freed me from stress.

RIGZUW W:.AL-TE#etÁ.UW

v.4 Tremble—or be angry—and do not sin. Compare Ephesians 4:26. I come home agitated and upset. I'm going over what happened during the day, what I should have said, but didn't; what I said that I shouldn't have; how exasperated and humiliated I feel. My wife asks me, "Do you want to talk about it?"

"No!" I mutter, "I just need to be alone for a while and calm down."

"Is it something I've done?" she asks.

"No. Just let me be alone for a while."

So I lie there fretting and feeling miserable. And that's acceptable. But, "Do not sin." Do not go off on your own path. Mostly I sin when I decide to do something about my feelings. I become convinced that I know enough to act on them. I have decided who is to blame. Or I pretend I don't have these feelings. "I must calm down," I say; or, "I must stay in control."

Tremble—or be angry, agitated, upset—but do not sin. Speak within your heart(s) upon your bed(s). Think about it, talk about it with your beloved spouse, talk about it within your heart. Experience every emotion—anger, hate, grief, love, joy—and do nothing. Lie quietly in your home, in your bed, and be completely silent [Silence...].

B:SHÁLOM YA#DÁW .ESHK:VÁH W:.IYSHÁN

v.8a In *shalom* (wholeness, completeness, harmony) all together, I begin to lie down, and I fall asleep. The inner dualism of *I* and *myself* begins to fade away. A kind of passive attention takes over; thoughts come and go. Whatever I am is just happening now, breathing regular and slow. I turn myself over to the LORD, and I thank him, and I am at peace. Whole and complete and all together. For you, LORD, alone, restore me to (or make me dwell in) safety.

Speak within your hearts upon your beds, and be silent [Silence...]. The heart of all spiritual practice is silence. First, outward silence; then inward silence. Practicing silence I begin to bear fruit, that is *love, joy, peace, patience* and all the rest (Galatians 5:22). I begin to have gladness in my heart. I can sleep.

Suggestions: Sing refrains to the Tone N:GINOTH (*stringed instruments*). Practice silence as you prepare yourself for sleep. Clear your thoughts again and again. There is nothing you can think about that will be more restful than this. And if you cannot fall asleep, get out of your bed, pray these psalms, practice silence again.

Psalm 4 (BCP)

Tone: N:GINOTH

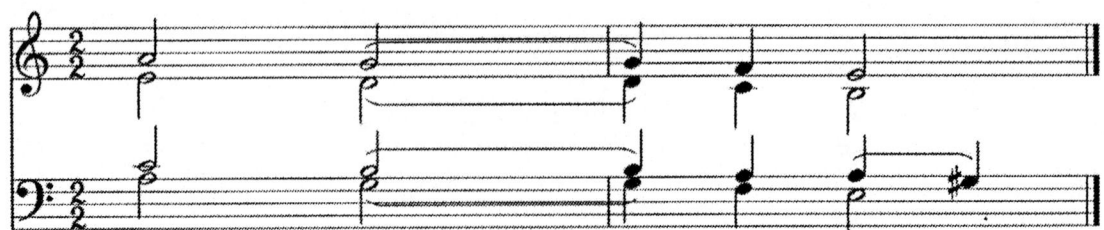

1 Answer me when I call, O God, defender of my cause; *
    you set me free when I am hard pressed;
    have mercy on me and hear my prayer.
2 "You mortals, how long will you dishonor my glory; *
    how long will you worship dumb idols
    and run after false gods?"
                    [Silence...]
3 Know that the LORD does wonders for the faithful; *
    when I call upon the LORD, he will hear me.
4 **Tremble then, and do not | sin;**
    speak to your heart in | silence upon your | bed.
                    [Silence...]
5 Offer the appointed sacrifices *
    and put your trust in the LORD.
6 Many are saying,
    "Oh, that we might see better times!" *
    Lift up the light of your countenance upon us, O LORD.
7 You have put gladness in my heart, *
    more than when grain and wine and oil increase.
8 **I lie down in peace; at once I | fall asleep;**
    for only | you, LORD, make me dwell in | safety.

Early In The Morning: Commentary To Psalm 5

I slept well, but now it is morning again. Preparing to go to work in a harsh and competitive world. It really is "a jungle out there."

BOQER .E"eRÁKH-L:KHÁ WA.a3APPEH
v.3   In the morning I begin to prepare myself for you and I begin to keep watch.

I prepare myself, interestingly, for you—God—and not so much for the job. The job which seemed so important when I left last night, may not be there when I arrive this morning. All may have changed before the day is over. My real job is working for you. I remind myself what kind of God you are: a moral God, a God who hates dishonesty and cruelty. A God who despises all boasting. Watch over me today, LORD. Protect me from the wicked and their wickedness. Protect me from myself! Keep me straight, LORD, keep me honest. Don't let me fall into their treacherous ways.

v.7   But as for me ... I will go into your house;
   I will bow down toward your holy temple.

Again and again in the psalms I encounter this abrupt shift: from a world of boasting, lying and cruelty, to the silence of "your holy temple." I will not find my bearings in the world where I go to work today. The more I try to make sense of it the more I become confused and discouraged. But in your temple I see clearly. For your temple is not a building but a state (John 4:23)—spirit and truth.

vv.9-10   For there is no truth in their mouth ...
   they flatter with their tongue.

I will go to work today with *them*, whoever they are. I will try to do what is asked of me and more. I will try to be a positive influence. But I will put no reliance on them. I will not yearn for their approval or fear their condemnation. There is nothing I can rely on in them.

v.13   But all who take refuge in you will be glad ...

You will shelter them ... bless the righteous ... defend them ... as with a shield. Almost ready now. Sheltering in you, working for you, seeking my approval from you and you alone, I will make it through this day and all days. Whether I am working, technically, for state government or Great Evangelist, I will keep my eyes on you. I will work for you. Now I'm ready. Time to go!

Note: Verse 9 ("there is no truth in their mouth"), compare Romans 3:13.

Suggestions: Sing the refrains standing. Bow deeply from the waist on v.7b ("I will bow down"). Traditional Jews bow repetitively, rhythmically, during prayer, perhaps continuing this ancient gesture of worship. Establish a regular place for your formal meditation, a regular time, and a regular bit of liturgy. Keep these things as constant as you can. Always meditate with your attention directed to God.

Psalm 5 (BCP)

Tone: GITTITH

1 Give ear to my words, O LORD; *
    consider my meditation.
2 Hearken to my cry for help, my King and my God, *
    for I make my prayer to you.
3 In the morning, LORD, you hear my voice; *
    early in the morning I make my appeal and watch for you.
4 For you are not a God who takes pleasure in wickedness; *
    and evil cannot dwell with you.
5 Braggarts cannot stand in your sight; *
    you hate all those who work wickedness.
6 You destroy those who speak lies; *
    the bloodthirsty and deceitful, O LORD, you abhor.

7 **But as for me, through the greatness of your mercy I will**
    go into your | house;
    I will bow down toward your holy temple in | awe of you.
8 \Lead me, O LORD, in your \ righteousness,
    because of those who lie in \ wait for me;
    /make your way straight be/fore me.

9 For there is no truth in their mouth; *
    there is destruction in their heart;
10 Their throat is an open grave; *
    they flatter with their tongue.
11 Declare them guilty, O God; *
    let them fall, because of their schemes.
12 Because of their many transgressions cast them out, *
    for they have rebelled against you.

13 **But all who take refuge in you will be glad;**
    they will sing out their joy for | ever.
14 You will shelter them,
    so that those who love your Name may | exult in you.
15 \For you, O LORD, will bless the \ righteous;
    you will defend them with your favor as with a \ shield.

Dark Thoughts In The Night: Commentary To Psalm 6

The "wee hours of the morning" and I can't sleep. Time for dark thoughts and deep questions. My defenses are down. My suit is hanging in the closet. I am undressed and helpless. Now I ask if my life has any meaning at all. The enemies seem to be gaining. I haven't been feeling well lately. Is it just another virus, or is it the beginning of the end? How much longer do I have? Is there anything for me beyond the grave?

    R:PHÁ.ÉNI YHWH KI NIVHaLUW "a3ÁMÁY   W:NAPHSHIY NIVHaLÁH M:.OD
vv. 2-3   Heal me, O LORD, for my bones are shaking,
and my soul (breath, breathing) is terrified.

The verb implies shaking, trembling, and sudden dissolution. My bones are shaking (with fear? with fever?), and my soul (my breathing) is agitated, shaking. My breathing is rapid, shallow and ineffective. Panic sweeps over me.

Tradition calls this a penitential psalm (along with 32, 38, 51, 102, 130 and 143). It is also a song of desperate illness. I am not just philosophizing now as I toss and turn. I know what a hopeless case I am. People have been tolerant up to now, but I sense they are losing patience with me. My wife is sleeping beside me, unaware of my agitation. Is even she about to lose patience with me?

More importantly, has God lost patience? He has been gentle with me till now. Has he reached his limit? O God, please not! Scold me, yes, but not in your anger. For who could stand that? And who deserves it more? No, I haven't robbed a bank or killed anyone, because I never had the opportunity. I am inhibited, but do I really have a conscience? LORD, don't give up on me yet, for in death there is no remembrance of you. From SH.OL (*Sheol*, the Pit) — whatever shadowy place that may be — there is no praising you; no one can draw strength from remembering your goodness, once they are dead.

    YÁGA"TI V:.AN#ÁTHIY
v.6   I grow weary with my sighing and groaning, sinking ever deeper into despair and resentment. My energy drains away as I sigh and groan this way. I am going down in this emotional storm.

v.8   for the LORD hath heard the voice of my weeping.

A turning point; crisis past. Somehow I know that God has heard my weeping. God continues to receive my prayers. Forgiveness has come, unexplained, undeserved. The forces of darkness turn back in defeat, and, as so often with miracles, it happens in a moment.

<u>Suggestions</u>: When panic sweeps over you, take a deep breath through your nose, and be silent. Clear your thoughts, all thoughts, and turn your attention to God. Do this again and again. For God has already heard your weeping and accepted your prayer.

Psalm 6 (KJV)

First Day: Evening Prayer   **Tone: SH:MINITH**

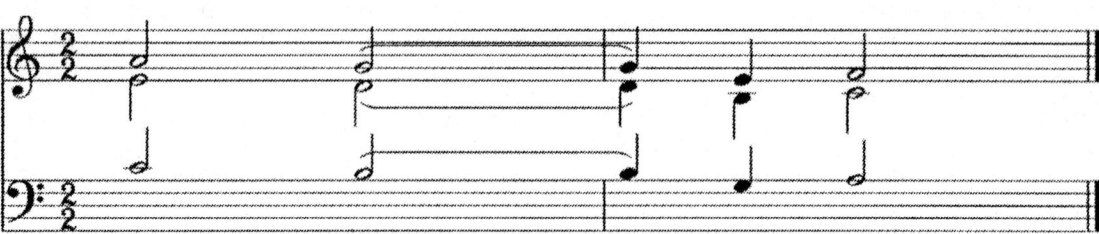

1 O LORD, rebuke me not in thine anger, *
   neither chasten me in thy hot displeasure.
2 Have mercy upon me, O LORD; for I am weak; *
   O LORD, heal me; for my bones are vexed.
3 My soul is also sore vexed: *
   but thou, O LORD, how long?
4 **Return, O LORD, deliver my | soul:**
   oh | save me for thy | mercies' sake.
5 For in death there is no remembrance of thee: *
   in the grave who shall give thee thanks?
6 I am weary with my groaning; *
   all the night make I my bed to swim;
   I water my couch with my tears.
7 Mine eye is consumed because of grief; *
   it waxeth old because of all mine enemies.
8 **Depart from me, all ye workers of in | iquity;**
   for the | LORD hath heard the voice of my | weeping.
9 The LORD hath heard my supplication; *
   the LORD will receive my prayer.
10 Let all my enemies be ashamed and sore vexed: *
   let them return and be ashamed suddenly.

Tearing Like A Lion My Soul: Commentary To Psalm 7

It is the experience of persecution. It can happen to anyone, at school or at work. Terrible persecutions take place in schoolyards every day. Someone is picked to be the odd one, the victim; how is not clear. And from that moment on, he or she can do nothing right. There is no escape, no way to fight back, no clever retort that will deflect the torment. Such is the experience of the writer in this psalm. Implacable persecutors who tear at him/her without mercy. The victim actually feels torn in pieces.

        PEN-YItROPH K:.ARYÉH NAPHSHIY   PORÉQ W:.EYN MA33IYL

v.2   Lest he (who chases after me) tear like a lion my soul (breath, life), dismembering, and no one is rescuing. Lest he tear; the Hebrew means to pull, tear in pieces, as a wild animal its prey.

v.3   O LORD my God, if I have done these things; if there is any wickedness (depravity) in my hands ... then let the enemy chase down my soul (inner self, breath, life), pursue and trample my life to the ground. The victim sinks into self-questioning and then self-blame. "Did I bring it on myself?" the victim asks. "What is wrong with me?" Many will support these doubts. "He brought it on himself," they will say. "It was her own fault." For a victim is always alone in that helpless state.

The persecutors may be within as well as without. Like the internal persecutors of my patients, these enemies are implacable; they tear and dismember from within. Some patients experience them as "voices"; others as condemning thoughts. Some Christians think of them as demonic. To me they are powerful thoughts, learned in childhood from abusive parents. They pull and tear from within, as implacable as the schoolyard bully or the office tormentor.

On the practical level, there are no good answers. Do I fight? Run? Ingratiate? Confront? Tell the teacher? Call the police? Tormentors have uncanny power, the power to intimidate, to confuse, to destroy self-confidence. They work in darkness, conditioning their victims to startle, to lose hope, to question themselves. Soon the victim is cowed and shaken, yet no one can see the persecution. And these things can happen to anyone, anywhere, under the right conditions.

After [Silence...], I turn to God. "Stand up, O LORD ... rise up against ... my enemies ... decree justice." The answers are not within myself. The answers will not be found by taking thought or consulting lawyers. I ask God to rise up against my enemies, but more importantly to restore my self, my sense of worth. Give judgment for me, I cry, according to my righteousness ... my innocence. For you test the mind and heart. I plead with him to heal those inner wounds, more damaging than any visible scars.

<u>Suggestions</u>: Meditate the psalms in terms of your own experiences and emotions. Speak not of David but of yourself. Who is tearing your soul? Make yourself aware of persecution, the tearing of souls, in everyday life. Give no encouragement to persecutors, no matter how benign or humorous they may appear. Give no advice to victims, but listen to them. Be ready to help when they need you.

Psalm 7 (BCP)

Tone: N:GINOTH

1 **O Lord my God, I take | refuge in you;**
　　save and de | liver me from all who pur | sue me.
2 \Lest like a lion they tear me in \ pieces
　　and snatch me away with none to de\liver me.
3 **O Lord my God, if I have | done these things;**
　　if there is any | wickedness in my | hands,
4 \If I have repaid my friend with \ evil,
　　or plundered him who without cause is my \ enemy;
5 Then let my enemy pursue and over\take me,
　　trample my life into the ground, and lay my \ honor in the dust.
　　　　　　[Silence...]
6 **Stand up, O Lord, in your | wrath;**
　　rise | up against the fury of my | enemies.
7 \Awake, O my God, decree \ justice;
　　let the assembly of the peoples gather \ round you.
8 Be seated on your lofty throne, O Most \ High;
　　O Lord, judge the \ nations.
9 **Give judgment for me according to my righteousness, O | Lord,**
　　and according to my | innocence, O Most | High.
10 \Let the malice of the wicked come to an \ end,
　　but establish the \ righteous;
　　for you test the mind and heart, O \ righteous God.
11 \God is my shield and \ defense;
　　he is the savior of the true in \ heart.
12 God is a \ righteous judge;
　　God sits in judgment every \ day.
13 \If they will not repent, God will whet his \ sword;
　　he will bend his bow and make it \ ready.
14 He has prepared his \ weapons of death;
　　he makes his arrows shafts of \ fire.
15 \Look at those who are in labor with \ wickedness,
　　who conceive evil, and give \ birth to a lie.
16 They dig a pit and make it \ deep
　　and fall into the \ hole that they have made.

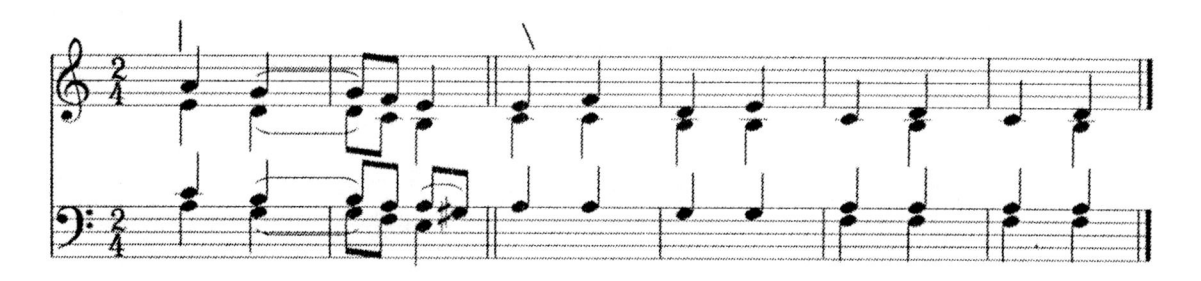

17 \Their malice turns back upon their own \ head;
    their violence falls on their own \ scalp.
18 **I will bear witness that the L**ORD **is | righteous;**
    I will | praise the Name of the LORD Most | High.

When I Consider Thy Heavens: Commentary To Psalm 8

Can anyone look up at those stars and not realize there is a God? Yes. It's easy. Most people don't see God in the stars, or in you! Most people don't see much of anything. They are too preoccupied. School is over for them. If there is something in the sky worth seeing, someone will tell them. Mostly, they don't even look. They have too much to worry about.

Some people look at the stars and fantasize. Space ships crossing the galaxy. Aliens from distant worlds. Someone is coming who will teach us how to live. *They say* they are already among us, they kidnap people into their ships. *They say it happened near here. I saw it in the news.* Some people worship the stars. Not many, but a few. The moon and stars are awesome and mysterious. They seem to be alive with power. They control our destiny. If only I knew their secrets.

                    MIPPIY "OL:LIM W:YON:QIM YIS*SAD*:TÁ "OZ
v.2 Out of the mouth of babes and sucklings hast thou ordained strength.

Strangely enough we learn more about God from babies than from the stars. From babies nursing at the breast you have established strength. From the tiny ones we pretend to raise and to teach, unfolding in a way we could never imagine.

Man, the insignificant, you remember; and BEN-.ÁDÁM (*son of man*), the child of red earth, you visit. You made us just short of god-like beings. You put us in charge of creation. You begin with the small and bring glory out of weakness. You made me, LORD, weak yet marvelous. How do I know this? Not from the stars.

There is no word for Nature in Hebrew, but .ERE3 (*the earth*) comes close. Earth is feminine in Hebrew, the mother side of creation. Earth is the nurturing matrix for sheep and oxen, beasts of the field, fowl of the air, and fish of the sea. And I look at all this and wonder what it means. Until I know you.

First we must know the Star-Maker, then the stars. We come to know God by intention, by commitment. We know him because we ask, seek, and knock. We come to know the Artist, then his art. We find his signature in stars, earth, sheep, oxen, babies.

Notes: Verse 2 ("out of the mouths of infants"), compare Matthew 21:16. From the mouths of infants, tiny but perfectly formed human persons who study the world around them, look searchingly at me, smile, frown, take note of everything, all without words. Verse 4 ("What is man?"), compare 144:3 and Job 7:17-18.

Suggestions: Stand. Sing to the Tone GITTITH (*of Gath*).
Meditate the psalms with the idea that God is speaking to you. There are many interpretations, all correct. Ask the Holy Spirit to guide your study. As often as you can, clear your thoughts and look around you, at stars, earth, trees, animals, babies. Look at these things without naming them or commenting, just see them, amazing works of God. Compare 67.

Psalm 8 (KJV)

Tone: GITTITH

1 **O Lord our | Lord,**
   how excellent is thy name in all the | earth!
   \who hast set thy glory above the \ heavens.
2 Out of the mouth of babes and sucklings hast thou ordained
   strength because of thine \ enemies,
   /that thou mightest still the enemy and the a/venger.
3 **When I consider thy heavens, the work of thy | fingers,**
   the moon and the stars, which thou hast or|dained;
4 \What is man, that thou art \ mindful of him?
   and the son of man, that thou \ visitest him?
5 **For thou hast made him a little lower than the | angels,**
   and hast crowned him with glory and | honor.
6 \Thou madest him to have dominion over the works of thy \ hands:
   thou hast put all things under his \ feet:
7 /All sheep and oxen, yea, and the / beasts of the field;
8 /The fowl of the air, and the fish of the sea, and whatsoever passeth
   through the / paths of the seas.
9 **O Lord our | Lord,**
   how excellent is thy name in all the | earth.

Alphabet Of The Streets: Commentary To Psalm 9

Psalms 9 and 10 are the first alphabetic psalms. In Hebrew alphabetic poetry, the verses or stanzas are regular in form and length; each begins with the next successive letter of the alphabet. A mysterious sense of order is conveyed, though its logic may not be obvious. The letters of the alphabet have profound meaning in Hebrew thought. Their order represents the orderly way of God.

Once we learn it in childhood, the alphabet comes to symbolize learning itself. To progress through the alphabet is to master a series of lessons. It becomes a metaphor for spiritual growth. So each alphabetic psalm carries a sense of instruction or wisdom. This learning, however, is not acquiring knowledge, but learning to surrender.

    .ODEH YHWH B:KHOL-LIBBIY   .aSAPP:RÁH KOL-NIPHL:.O<u>TH</u>EYKHÁ
v.1 I begin to thank you, O LORD, with my whole heart;
I begin to tell of all your marvelous works. Heading into dangerous times I begin by giving thanks. The root in Hebrew means hand, suggesting a movement or gesture. The verse actually portrays a two-fold movement: *I will give thanks* and *I will tell*. An inward movement of the heart, an outward movement of telling, praising. See also 50:14, 92:1, 138:1. The alphabet begins with grateful affirmation, regardless of circumstance. Knowing that thought leads to thought and emotion to emotion, I will begin with this thought: Thank you. And I will do so with my whole heart. That is the difficult part, for in spiritual matters, words tend to drive out realities. The words *thank you* replace the thankful attitude.

Things in the city are going from bad to worse. Many are oppressed, afflicted, needy and poor. Those who have a little power abuse it, taking advantage of those who cannot protect themselves. We do not begin by defining the problem, but by giving thanks. Behind the corruption of the city, God is ruling in righteousness. And the wicked are starting to drop back, stumble, and fall into their own traps.

v.16 The LORD is known by his acts of justice,
the wicked are trapped in the works of their own hands.
[Meditation-Silence...]. Think about these things. Let the peoples know, for everyone is involved in the economics of evil. The power to amass wealth by exploiting the poor is fleeting. Let people begin to realize that they are only human [Silence...].

<u>Suggestions</u>: Sing verses 1, 5, 9, 13, 19, to the Tone *Alphabet*. Observe [Meditation-Silence...] with a prolonged silence. Sing verse 1 with the wave gesture for thank offerings (see the Introduction). Be attentive in your meditation and practice always with your whole heart. Always begin with thanks and praise. The inward movement of gratitude; the outward movement of telling, sharing and praise. Carry this teaching into your study of the news. The wicked are already trapped in their own misdeeds. The needy shall not always be forgotten.

Psalm 9 (BCP)

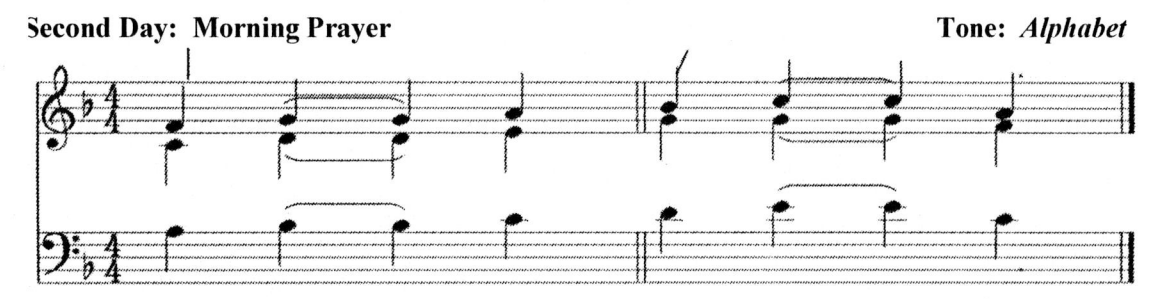

Second Day: Morning Prayer Tone: *Alphabet*

1 **I will give thanks to you, O L<small>ORD</small>, with my whole | heart;**
 I will tell of all your marvelous | works.
2 I will be glad and rejoice in you; *
 I will sing to your Name, O Most High.
3 When my enemies are driven back, *
 they will stumble and perish at your presence.
4 For you have maintained my right and my cause; *
 you sit upon your throne judging right.
5 **/You have rebuked the ungodly and destroyed the / wicked;**
 you have blotted out their name for ever and / ever.
6 As for the enemy, they are finished, in perpetual ruin, *
 their cities ploughed under,
 the memory of them perished.
7 But the L<small>ORD</small> is enthroned for ever; *
 he has set up his throne for judgment.
8 It is he who rules the world with righteousness; *
 he judges the peoples with equity.
9 **The L<small>ORD</small> will be a refuge for the op | pressed,**
 a refuge in time of | trouble.
10 Those who know your Name will put their trust in you, *
 for you never forsake those who seek you, O L<small>ORD</small>.
11 Sing praise to the L<small>ORD</small> who dwells in Zion; *
 proclaim to the peoples the things he has done.
12 The Avenger of blood will remember them; *
 he will not forget the cry of the afflicted.
13 /Have pity on me, O L<small>ORD</small>;
 see the misery I suffer from those who / hate me,
 O you, who lift me up from the gate of / death;
14 So that I may tell of all your praises
 and rejoice in your salvation *
 in the gates of the city of Zion.
15 The ungodly have fallen into the pit they dug, *
 and in the snare they set is their own foot caught.
16 The L<small>ORD</small> is known by his acts of justice; *
 the wicked are trapped in the works of their own hands.

[Meditation-Silence...]

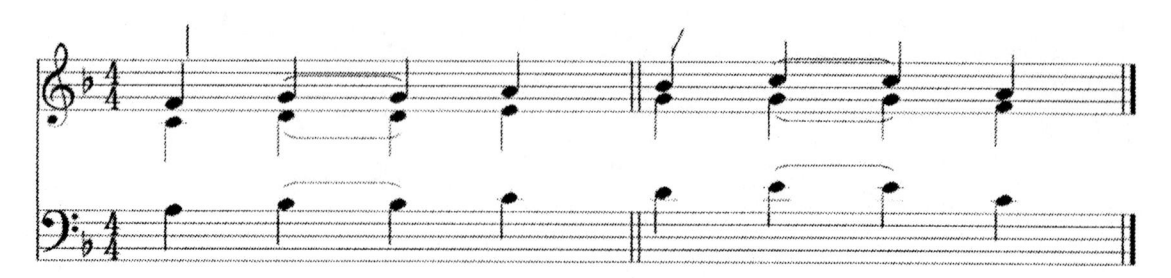

17 The wicked shall be given over to the grave, *
    and also all the peoples that forget God.
18 For the needy shall not always be forgotten, *
    and the hope of the poor shall not perish for ever.
19 /Rise up, O LORD, let not the ungodly have the upper / hand;
    let them be judged be/fore you.
20 Put fear upon them, O LORD; *
    let the ungodly know they are but mortal.
                [Silence...]

Alphabet Of The Streets, Part II: Commentary To Psalm 10

Craigie* speaks here of "practical atheism" — life lived as if, for all practical purposes, "God does not matter." God may exist in theory, but to the practical atheist he is irrelevant, for "God has forgotten ... he will never notice."

Meanwhile, as now, the city is in chaos. The wicked run the streets; they have only contempt for a legal system gone berserk. They can well say, "No harm shall happen to me, ever." Lofty principles are debated in the courts, while in the streets, "the innocent are broken and humbled ... the helpless fall." People have a pervasive sense of injustice. There is still a concept of justice, but the system of justice is seen as a sham. A system of empty formalities does not protect the innocent.

QUMÁH YHWH .ÉL N:SÁ. YÁDEKHÁ   .AL-TISHKA# "aNÁWIM
v.12 Rise up, O LORD;
lift up your hand O God;
do not forget the afflicted.

We have already encountered "Rise up, O LORD" in 3, 7 and 9. What can it mean, giving a command such as this to the LORD? Does God need to be told about the poor and needy? And if so, what good will it do for us to tell him? Because if we, the sinners, have to tell him, perhaps he doesn't really care. Perhaps the practical atheist is right.

As I began to think about "Rise up, O LORD," it seemed to embody a basic tension of the faith community, social action versus mysticism. Some disciples are social activists. If God has to be told, "Rise up, O LORD," perhaps it is for us to rise up. Organize the people, raise funds, change the laws. Eliminate social injustice by social action. "Faith by itself, if it does not have works, is dead" (James 2:17, NKJ).

Other disciples see all this as a waste of energy. The more problems we solve by social action the more we create. Social engineering is worse than useless. *It's a spiritual problem*, they like to say. It will only be solved by spiritual renewal. Admit things are hopeless, turn inward, pray and meditate. "Unless the LORD watches over the city, in vain the watchman keeps his vigil" (127:2).

Most disciples, most churches, lean toward one or the other. Putting them together is difficult. Rise up, O LORD, in us. Let us be your hands. Show us what to do and what not to do. Not our program but yours, your agenda. Rise up in us, O LORD, work through us.

Suggestions: Sing the verses indicated to the Tone *Alphabet*, reciting alternate verses. Notice the sharp contrast between singing and reading.

When you pray for your community, ask God for direction. Ask him to rise up and lift his hand; remember that you yourself may be his hand in this situation. Meditate the psalms day after day, immersing yourself in God's way of thinking.

---

*Peter C. Craigie: *Word Biblical Commentary* Vol. 19: Psalms 1-50. Word Books, Waco, Texas, 1983, pp. 126-128.

Psalm 10 (BCP)

Tone: *Alphabet*

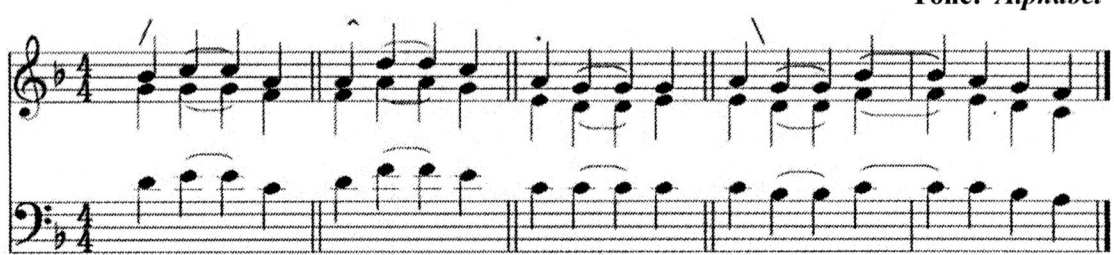

1 Why do you stand so far off, O LORD, *
   and hide yourself in time of trouble?
2 The wicked arrogantly persecute the poor, *
   but they are trapped in the schemes they have devised.
3 The wicked boast of their heart's desire; *
   the covetous curse and revile the LORD.
4 The wicked are so proud that they care not for God; *
   their only thought is, "God does not matter."
5 Their ways are devious at all times;
   your judgments are far above out of their sight; *
   they defy all their enemies.
6 They say in their heart, "I shall not be shaken; *
   no harm shall happen to me ever."
7 Their mouth is full of cursing, deceit, and oppression; *
   under their tongues are mischief and wrong.
8 They lurk in ambush in public squares
   and in secret places they murder the innocent; *
   they spy out the helpless.
9 They lie in wait, like a lion in a covert;
   they lie in wait to seize upon the lowly; *
   they seize the lowly and drag them away in their net.
10 The innocent are broken and humbled before them; *
   the helpless fall before their power.
11 They say in their heart, "God has forgotten; *
   he hides his face; he will never notice."
12 /Rise up, O LORD; lift up your hand, O / God;
   do not forget the af/flicted.
13 Why should the wicked revile God? *
   why should they say in their heart, "You do not care"?
14 ^Surely, you behold trouble and ^ misery;
   you see it and take it into your own ^ hand.
15 The helpless commit themselves to you, *
   for you are the helper of orphans.
16 .Break the power of the wicked and . evil;
   search out their wickedness until you . find none.

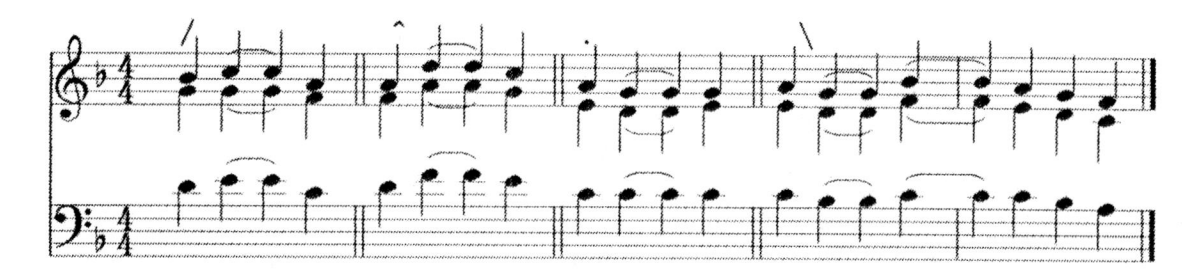

17 The Lord is King for ever and ever; *
    the ungodly shall perish from his land.
18 \The Lord **will hear the desire of the \ humble;**
    you will strengthen their heart and your ears shall \ hear;
19 To give justice to the orphan and op\pressed,
    so that mere \ mortals may strike terror no \ more.

Fly To Your Mountain, Bird: Commentary To Psalm 11

v.1 In the LORD have I taken refuge;
how then can you say to my soul (breath, life),
"Fly to your mountain, Bird."

My soul (breath, life) is like a fluttering bird (compare 124), sensitive and fearful; quick but all too vulnerable. Again *they* are talking to my soul, my inner Other, life, breathing—and they are alienating her from me. They are trying to separate me from my life.

They talk to my life contemptuously, "Fly to your mountain," they say. The pronoun *your* is plural. To the mountain of "your kind" or "your people," wherever it is that "you people" belong. My value as an individual means nothing to them.

When the foundations are being destroyed, even the very foundations of my being, what indeed can the righteous do? Nothing. Total change of perspective. The LORD is in his holy temple. Yet, after all, I have taken refuge in the LORD. How then, can they say these things? How shall I really look at my situation?

Craigie's* commentary is helpful: a time of testing. I have good reason to fear. That fluttering bird, my life, may fall this time. Should I flee to the mountains? Or should I stand and face them, though they shoot with deadly aim from ambush? There are no easy answers.

>   YHWH B:HEYKHAL QODSHOW   YHWH BASSHÁMAYiM KIS.OW
v.4 The LORD is in his holy temple;
the LORD's throne is in heaven ...
v.6 The LORD continues to test the righteous and the wicked,

and those who love violence, his soul hates! The LORD who reigns in eternity is found in a temple. In a place of silence. We may take this in a historical sense, a temple built of stones on a great hill. In a deeper sense we may take it as silence itself, the place where we listen to God. Beyond the noise and turbulence, we encounter another world, a foundation that cannot be destroyed. A reality that never changes, moral reality. The very life of the LORD, his inner self, his breathing, as it were, hates those who love violence.

v.8 For the LORD is righteous;
he loves righteous deeds. On one level, the wicked are about to shoot down my life, and no one cares. On a higher level, God cares intensely. Right and wrong are so clear at his level.

<u>Suggestions</u>: Sing refrains to the Tone GITTITH (*of Gath*). In the time of peril, step into his temple; take a deep breath through your nose and clear your thoughts. Lift your attention to God and listen for his guidance.

---

*Peter C. Craigie: *Word Biblical Commentary Vol. 19: Psalms 1-50*. Word Books, Waco, Texas, 1983, pp. 131-135.

Psalm 11 (BCP)

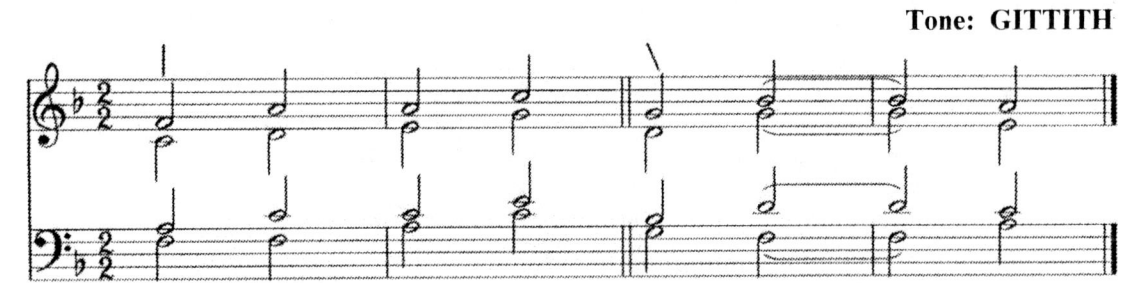

Tone: GITTITH

1 In the LORD have I taken refuge; *
    how then can you say to me,
    "Fly away like a bird to the hilltop;
2 For see how the wicked bend the bow
    and fit their arrows to the string, *
    to shoot from ambush at the true of heart.
3 When the foundations are being destroyed, *
    what can the righteous do?"
4 **The LORD is in his holy | temple;**
    the LORD's throne is in | heaven.
5 \His eyes behold the inhabited \ world;
    his piercing eye weighs our \ worth.
6 The LORD weighs the righteous as well as the wicked, *
    but those who delight in violence he abhors.
7 Upon the wicked he shall rain coals of fire and burning sulphur; *
    a scorching wind shall be their lot.
8 **For the LORD is righteous;**
    he delights in righteous | deeds;
    and the just shall see his | face.

A Heart And A Heart: Commentary To Psalm 12

A psalm of disillusionment. Talking about evil is one thing, but seeing everyone around you turn slippery and dishonest is another. It is part of growing up to give up our illusions about others and to realize that all are sinners. Yes, every one of us is hopeless, a hopeless case, in his or her own way.

>   SHÁW. Y:DABB:RUW .IYSH .ETH-RÉ"ÉHU   S:PHATH #aLÁQOTH
> v.2 Falsely do they speak, (each) man with his neighbor,
> smooth, slippery words (literally a lip or tongue of smooth slipperies).

>   B:LÉV WÁLÉV Y:DABBÉRU
> v.2 with a heart and a heart they speak.

We learn ideals and values, we try to live up to them, we fail, and we learn that everyone else fails too. The important people, the experts and therapists we see on television have failed as well. And so we speak dishonestly with our friends and associates, with a smooth tongue and a double heart. Yes, "a heart and a heart," as the Hebrew says: one heart for public comment, another for our real thoughts and feelings.

Indeed we dare not do otherwise. We become comfortable with a smooth tongue, with high-sounding words, with rationalizing. The wicked prowl on every side, but they do not consider themselves wicked; we hear their pompous words every day in church and in government. They say what they think we want to hear, and think of themselves as leaders. They boast of their leadership, yet the needy continue to be oppressed and the poor to cry out in misery. We may criticize these leaders, but they only reflect ourselves. They will not vote for the cause if I will not pay for it.

For I too speak with a heart and a heart, but not by design. I am simply inconstant, blowing with the wind. I live by feelings and think they are values, or faith. I am moved by words and phrases. I like to think of myself as scrupulously honest. I follow the rules to the letter. I argue with compliments. On a deeper level my duplicity is astounding. My feelings change with the weather; I hear myself saying what will please. What do I really believe? It depends who is asking. With a heart and a heart I speak, convincing myself as I talk. O LORD, watch over me, and save me from this generation (from me) forever.

<u>Suggestions</u>: Sing refrains to the Tone SH:MINITH (*eighth*).

Do not judge others for their duplicity, but become aware of your own, how you speak with a heart and a heart. Do not waste time trying to decide what you "really" think and feel, for it changes constantly. One thought leads to another, emotion leads to emotion, and the human breathing blows with the wind. In your practice of meditation, listen to the voice of God and seek his constancy.

Psalm 12 (BCP)

Second Day: Evening Prayer Tone: SH:MINITH

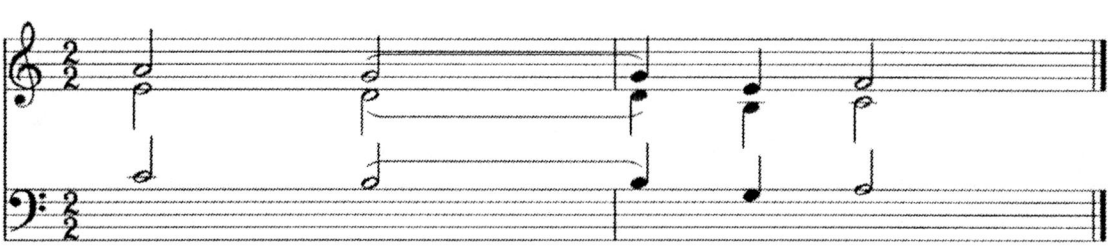

1 Help me, LORD, for there is no godly one left; *
 the faithful have vanished from among us.
2 **Everyone speaks falsely with his | neighbor;**
 with a | smooth tongue they speak from a | double heart.
3 **Oh that the LORD would cut off all | smooth tongues,**
 and | close the lips that utter proud | boasts!
4 Those who say, "With our tongue we will prevail; *
 our lips are our own; who is lord over us?"
5 "Because the needy are oppressed,
 and the poor cry out in misery, *
 I will rise up," says the LORD,
 "and give them the help they long for."
6 **The words of the LORD are | pure words,**
 like silver refined from | ore
 and purified seven times in the | fire.
7 O LORD, watch over us *
 and save us from this generation for ever.
8 The wicked prowl on every side, *
 and that which is worthless is highly prized by everyone.

Counsel In My Soul: Commentary To Psalm 13

"AD-.ÁNÁH YHWH TISHKÁ#ÉNI NE3A#

v.1 How long, O Lord
will you forget me for ever?

People in our day are likely to say, "Why is this happening to me?" The biblical writers asked, "How long?" How long will God forget me in oblivion? When I experienced his presence, I felt such peace! But now he is silent, and he leaves no messages. All I can do is wait, in emptiness. Time flies when I'm happy; now it has slowed to a crawl. Sometimes in deep depression, it stops completely. That is the experience of hell, despair that cannot end.

v.2 How long shall I take counsel in my soul (KJV)?

In my inner world thought leads to thought, the same thoughts over and over. How long shall I take counsel (advice) within my soul (breath, inner self)? I say *Cheer up* or *Calm down* or *Don't be a jerk*, while grief resides in my heart, unmoving. How long will I go on brooding these repetitive thoughts? Without that enlivening relationship to God the inner relationship becomes dead and meaningless. I give inane advice to myself, but my soul no longer answers.

And as that inner relationship goes still, I find I cannot relate to anyone else. "How long shall my enemy triumph over me?" Not enemy in the military sense, but everyman, anyone, my competitor, someone who breaks into my line at the store. Those "enemies" are as wary of me as I of them. Not outwardly hostile, they just don't care about me. If they heard of my sudden death, they would say "How awful," but in their hearts they would say, "Thank God it was him, not me."

v.3 Lighten my eyes lest I sleep the sleep of death. My eyes are dull, they stare into yours without recognition. Like death or living death. Put some light back into my eyes, O Lord, that I may live. "Give light to my eyes" lest I fall into oblivion. Help me to wake up.

v.5 But as for me. Another abrupt transition: my enemies are already rejoicing at my downfall, but as for me I have trusted (perfective verb) in your mercy. I have already made the decision to trust, and my heart begins to be joyful. I begin to sing praises to the Lord, for I realize that he has indeed rewarded me richly.

<u>Suggestions</u>: Sing vv. 1-2 with exquisite slowness, taking 40 to 50 seconds, yet flowing smoothly from word to word. Hand gestures are given in the Appendix.

If your spiritual practice is correct you will be increasingly alert. Avoid practices that lead to dullness. Meditate with eyes open, but do not stare at any one spot. If you find yourself falling asleep, take a deep breath through your nose, kneel or stand. In grief or perplexity, be aware of those "counsels" in your inner world: *Cheer up. Calm down. Get a grip on yourself. Try harder. You did your best. You should have been more careful.* Observe those thoughts and let them go. Clear your thoughts as often as you can. Be silent and listen.

Psalm 13 (BCP)

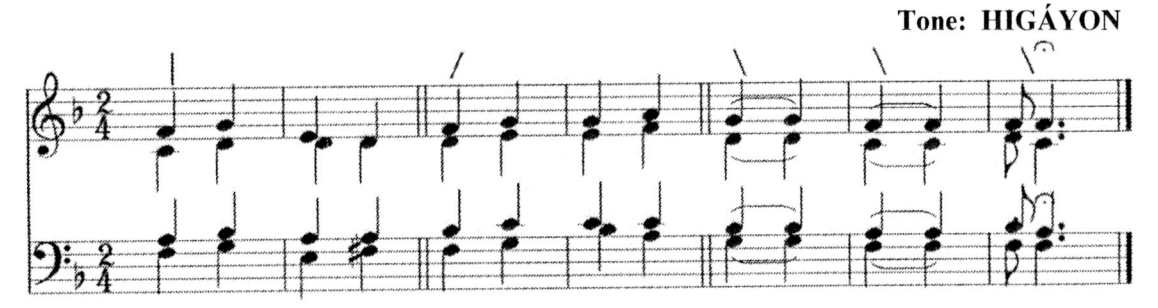

Tone: HIGÁYON

[Slowly]

1 **How long, O Lord**
   will you forget me for | ever?
   how long will you hide your | face from me?
2 **How long shall I have perplexity in my mind,**
   and grief in my heart, day after | day?
   how long shall my enemy triumph | over me?
          [Normal tempo]
3 /Look upon me and answer me, O Lord, my / God;
   give light to my eyes lest I sleep in / death;
4 \Lest my enemy say,
   \ "I have prevailed over him,"
   and my foes rejoice that I have \ fallen.
5 /But I put my trust in your / mercy;
   my heart is joyful because of your / saving help.
6 \I will sing to the Lord, for he has dealt with me richly;
   \I will praise the Name
   of the Lord Most \ High.

The Fool Has Said: Commentary To Psalm 14

.ÁMAR NÁVÁL B:LIBBOW   .EYN .eLOHIM

v.1 The fool has said in his heart, "There is no God." The fool has said (perfective verb, completed state): his final statement. The fool seldom questions his own judgements. They are final and he takes them to be profound truth. So the first word here is .ÁMAR (*he has said*). He has said it in his heart, the inner psychological space where he orders his approach to life. In his basic, fundamental attitude he has said—what?

.EYN means there is not, the word of negation. The word sounds like ain't. The fool has said in his heart, "There ain't no God." That is his judgment on the matter, a judgment of negation and negativity. There ain't no such thing as... I never heard of... No way, Josè.

The fool in Hebrew—NÁVÁL—is not merely misinformed or even unwise. Scripture describes him as aggressively wrong-headed, determined to have his own way, no matter if it leads to destruction. A wonderful portrait of a NÁVÁL is the man named Nabal in 1 Samuel 25. Such a fool is not merely wrong, which would be excusable, but he refuses to learn. If they didn't teach it in the first grade, he never heard of it.

If God is the Great Yes, if following him is learning to say yes, whatever the cost, then the way of the fool is to say no. His negativism is as typical as his dogmatism. I don't have to be very bright, if I have an open heart. If I can listen and try new things there is hope for me. But if all I can say is no, I am really doomed.

This psalm about the fool is written in a light-hearted way, like a little dance. How foolish of the fool to be so sure of himself, so wrong and so negative. How silly and sad for anyone to be so dogmatic as he heads for destruction. How fortunate that God has a sense of humor. Perhaps even a fool like me can be saved.

The psalm goes on to say that we all have a lot of the fool in us. I am doggedly sure of myself, even as God says, "There is none who does good, no, not one!" Yet God is in the company of the righteous. Who are they? Are they smarter than the fools? Not at all, but "the LORD is their refuge," they ask for help.

Right spiritual practice leads to increasing but faithful uncertainty, a kind of wondering innocence. Incorrect practice, in any tradition or religion, leads to increasing dogmatism, certainty, and a sense of righteousness. That in turn fosters the illusion of self-sufficiency. God is no longer necessary, and the student is lost.

<u>Suggestions</u>:   Compare 51, 53. The movement suggested is Twirling Dance (see Appendix). Sing to the Tone MÁ#OL (*dance*), two measures corresponding to each verse. Note that the fourth measure (second measure of second Order) is repeated in verses of three lines (vv. 2,4,7).

When you hear yourself speaking dogmatically, absolutely certain of anything, stop for just a moment and be silent. Listen to the other person. Ask God for direction.

Psalm 14 (BCP)

Tone: MÁ#OL

1 **The fool has | said in his | heart,**
   "There is no | God."
   \All are corrupt and commit abominable \ acts;
   there is none who does any \ good.
2 \The LORD looks down from heaven upon us \ all,
   to see if there is any who is \ wise,
   if there is one who seeks after \ God.
3 \Every one has proved \ faithless;
   all alike have turned \ bad;
   there is | none who does | good;
   no, not | one.
4 \Have they no knowledge, all those \ evildoers
   who eat up my people like \ bread
   and do not call upon the \ LORD?
5 /See how they tremble with / fear,
   because God is in the company of the / righteous.
6 \Their aim is to confound the plans of the \ afflicted,
   but the LORD is their \ refuge.
7 \Oh, that Israel's deliverance would come out of \ Zion!
   when the LORD restores the fortunes of his \ people,
   Jacob will rejoice and Israel be \ glad.

Walking Simply: Commentary To Psalm 15

Who may advance on the spiritual path? Compare 24. The incomparable Spurgeon* refers to this psalm as The Question and The Answer. The Question (vv. 1,2) is directed to God. The rest of the psalm is God's Answer, and it is simple:

HOLÉKH TÁMIM UPHO"ÉL 3EDEQ W:DOVÉR .eMETH BIL:VÁVOW

v.2 Whoever walks simply (in wholeness, integrity); and does what is right (does righteousness). He walks in TÁMIM—a word we will encounter many times. The meaning of the root is wholeness, completeness. I think integrity is a good translation, innocent simplicity better still. He has no complex strategy for success. He is simple and straight.

A psychiatrist might say he is congruent: he is what he says he is, at every level. He does not say one thing with his lips and another with his eyes. I instinctively trust her, she has no hidden agendas. He speaks the truth in his heart—*thinks* the truth. He thinks what is constant, reliable, unchangeable. And she herself is constant and reliable.

Progress on the spiritual path is based upon morality; but not a morality of rules, regulations, forbidden foods and self-deprivation. It is a simple and humble morality which is never moralistic. If it is hard to describe such a moral life, the writer attempts to portray it in broad strokes. More than anything it is the life of humility, life lived without much concern about self. The individual pictured here does not give self-effacing speeches, or make a point of being the last one in line. One simply lives without making a great issue of oneself. And because one's self is not a big issue, one is not forced to aggrandize one's self, to steal from others, or to put others down. There is no need to make others look inferior.

Because there is no need to put others down or to make oneself look better than others, there is no need for guile, hurtful remarks, heaping contempt, or passing on scandalous rumors. It is all based upon humility, but humility does not come easy to a human breathing. See 131. We might ask if these qualities are requirements for the spiritual path or the results from the path. In a sense they are both. I could not start this path without a little humility, simplicity; or at least the desire for them. And I quickly find that they do not come naturally to me. They are gifts. I do not achieve them by effort. I must search for them, ask for them, give them a home when they appear, develop them further as I pursue the spiritual path.

LO.-RÁGAL "AL-L:SHONOW

v.3 He does not run around, shall we say (from the same Hebrew root as foot), with his tongue. He does not go about saying negative things about others. He does not gossip. He does not say things "jokingly" about the man who just left his office, to the man who just walked in. He does not say these little things about his fellow workers, like I do.

I had to be almost fifty years old before I realized how destructive that can be. I used to hate the way my mother and father would sit at the kitchen table for hours, criticizing people we knew. Yet I do the same thing. But he, the one who can dwell in your tabernacle, does not cause harm with his tongue; he doesn't pick up and pass along accusations against one who is close to him. Everyday recreational gossip is not his obstacle to spiritual progress.

He also doesn't hurt anyone with legal or financial tricks. He doesn't wriggle out of a bad contract. He doesn't take advantage. He practices 3EDEQ (*justice* or *righteousness*). It means that he looks after those who cannot look after themselves—orphans, widows, strangers passing through town. Compare 72. He will not manipulate the system to hurt anyone even if it is technically his right. Some people will take advantage of him, but he can live with himself.

"OSÉh .ÉLLEh LO.-YIMMOt L:"OLÁM

v.7 Whoever is doing these things will not be moved—shaken, toppled—to eternity.

Who is advancing on the spiritual path? Again, we will know them by their fruits. *Love, joy, peace, patience, kindness* ... most of all *humility*, described here in slightly different terminology. First, a little spiritual practice, a little silence, then the fruit comes almost immediately. And if it does not, the practice is a waste of time.

Suggestions: Stand. Sing to the Tone #a3O3:ROTH (*trumpets*).

Practice moments of silence throughout the day; clear your thoughts and walk in simplicity. In all the struggles and temptations of life, return, again and again, to this foundation. The spiritual path of the psalms is elegantly simple, but remember that the way is narrow, and it is easy to go astray. Be ever watchful for the tendency to hurt and condemn, to speak ill of neighbors, and to take advantage of fellow workers. When you find yourself doing these things, do not condemn yourself, but step back, reflect, return to silence. Ask God for direction. Return, again and again, to the path of simplicity.

---

*C.H. Spurgeon: *The Treasury of David*, containing an original exposition of the Book of Psalms; a collection of illustrative extracts from the whole range of literature; a series of homiletical hints upon almost every verse; and lists of writers upon each psalm. In Three Volumes. Hendrickson Publishers, Peabody, MA, Vol. I, p. 176.

Psalm 15 (BCP)

Third Day: Morning Prayer Tone: #a303:ROTH

1 LORD, who may dwell in your | tabernacle?
   /who may abide upon your holy / hill?
2 **Whoever leads a blameless life and does what is | right,**
   /**who speaks the truth from his / heart.**
3 +There is no guile upon his + tongue;
   he does no evil to his / friend;
   he does not heap contempt upon his \ neighbor.
4 +In his sight the wicked is + rejected,
   but he honors those who fear the / LORD.
5 He has sworn to do no wrong
   and does not take back his \ word.
6 +He does not give his money in hope of + gain,
   nor does he take a bribe against the / innocent.
7 Whoever does these things
   shall never be \ overthrown.

Song Of Resurrection: Commentary To Psalm 16

The text is obscure and the translation difficult, yet certain themes come through clearly. I take refuge in God, I am satisfied with God, I bless God, and I take counsel from him. I study the instructions of God day by day, and I grow into fullness of joy. Compare 17, 25.

v.7 I will bless the LORD who hath given me counsel:
my reins also instruct me in the night season (KJV).

I do not learn God's ways with a murmured prayer or a sentimental bow toward religion or with years of intellectual study. At night, when I sleep, he instills his teaching into me, not through my intellect but through—literally—my kidneys! Perhaps it is a biblical way of saying the Unconscious. The kidneys are silent, hidden deep within me, and they work day and night without consulting me (that is, my thoughts). They purify me from within, without words. What I learn is not intellectual, not theology. I cannot put it into words. It is direction and grounding. It is wisdom for the daily walk.

SHIW<u>WI</u>THI YHWH L:NEGDIY THÁMIYD
v.8 I have set the LORD always before me.

The word SHIW<u>WI</u>THI means I have leveled out or balanced. Compare 131. But surely I do not balance or level out the LORD, or make myself equal to the LORD. Perhaps it implies a balanced relationship with him. More likely, I balance myself—I keep myself on a level, in balance, with the LORD always before me. My thoughts and emotions in balance—*aequanimitas*. It is another way of describing those fruits of the Spirit: *peace, patience, gentleness, self-control*.

v.9 My heart, therefore, is glad, and my spirit rejoices;
my body also shall rest in hope.

I respond to this wonderful instruction from all levels of my being. From my heart, that place where I formulate my basic approach to life, my attitude. And from K:VODIY (*my glory*), my higher self or me at my best. See 51, 57. A profound sense of well-being wells up within me, at least on occasion, and my higher self, my best self, "is elated" (Feuer*). My body also (my flesh) shall dwell in safety, for this teaching restores and stabilizes my health. Everything I do, from my breathing to the way I walk, becomes balanced, steady, calming and life-supporting.

KI LO.-THA"aZOV NAPHSHIY LISH.OL
v.10 For you will not leave my soul in hell. Compare Acts 13:35.

You will not abandon my soul (breath, breathing, life) to SH.OL (*Sheol*, the Pit of emptiness). Not in this life and not in the next life. That which you have taught me silently in the night has made me happy. I do not understand resurrection or life after death, but I know that what I am is information. I know, for example, that the code for what I am is written down, in a substance called DNA. The formula for all that I am—my temperament, my way of thinking, even the way I walk—is something that can be known. And I know that God knows it. I understand that death is not the end. I do not know the details. I only need know that

v.11 You will show me the path of life. Not some exotic revelation about past or future, not some secret advice for anyone else, but the path of life. My own life. You will show me how to live, one step at a time. Again and again I will complete this cycle of instruction. I seek you as my portion and my cup. I take refuge in you. I receive your instruction in the night. And I follow the path you have showed me. And I experience fullness of joy. It is the core teaching of this book on the psalms. I am learning to listen to God and receive his instruction.

At another level this seems to be a teaching about that other life, the next life. You will show me the path of that life as well. You will not abandon me to oblivion. What do I learn about that other life? No details at all. No visions of the tunnel or the Light. Only the assurance that I will not be abandoned. I will not be discarded in the Pit where all is forgotten. I do not understand the resurrection or the life after death. I do not need to know anything more than this. You will not abandon my soul to the Pit. You will show me the path of life.

Suggestions: Sing refrains, vv. 1b and 8. Lift arms in the praise gesture at v.7 ("I will bless"), fold them in the heart gesture at "my heart teaches me." Repeat this gesture at v. 9 ("my heart therefore") and return to the praise gesture at "my body also." Point into the distance with the extended right arm, at v. 11 ("You will show me the path"), return to the heart gesture at "in your presence"; extend the right arm as before at "and in your right hand."

Practice moments of silence (informal meditation) as you settle down to sleep. Ask the LORD, always, to instruct you. Daily, in every situation of your life, seek direction from God. Ask him precisely what he wants you to learn from every situation,exactly where he wants you to go. Follow the directions you are given, learn what you can, take it to heart, seek further instruction, follow the path.

---

*Rabbi Avrohom Chaim Feuer: *Tehillim (Psalms)/ A New Translation with a Commentary Anthologized from Talmudic, Midrashic and Rabbinic Sources.* Mesorah Publications, Ltd., Brooklyn, NY, 1977, p. 197.

Psalm 16 (BCP)

Tone: N:GINOTH

1 Protect me, O God, for I take refuge in you; *
  I have said to the LORD "You | are my Lord,
   my | good above all | other."
2 All my delight is upon the godly that are in the land, *
   upon those who are noble among the people.
3 But those who run after other gods *
   shall have their troubles multiplied.
4 Their libations of blood I will not offer, *
   nor take the names of their gods upon my lips.
5 O LORD, you are my portion and my cup; *
   it is you who uphold my lot.
6 My boundaries enclose a pleasant land; *
   indeed, I have a goodly heritage.
7 I will bless the LORD who gives me counsel; *
   my heart teaches me, night after night.
8 **I have set the LORD be|fore me;**
   because he is at my | right hand I shall not | fall.
9 My heart therefore is glad, and my spirit rejoices; *
   my body also shall rest in hope.
10 For you will not abandon me to the grave, *
    nor let your holy one see the Pit.
11 You will show me the path of life; *
    in your presence is fullness of joy,
    and in your right hand are pleasures for evermore.

I Shall Be Satisfied: Commentary To Psalm 17

It comes after battles and struggles, trying to hold on and do right in a world ruled by injustice. The wicked surround me, telling lies about me. I have tried to defend myself, forgetting that the only safety is "under the shadow of your wings."

.aNIY B:3EDEQ .E#eZEH PHÁ<u>NEY</u>KHÁ .ESB:"ÁH V:HÁQIY3 T:MUNÁ<u>THE</u>KHÁ
v.16 But at my vindication I shall see your face;
when I awake, I shall be satisfied, beholding your likeness.

I in righteousness shall see your face, your presence; I shall be satisfied when I awaken, with your likeness. Of the many profound images in the psalm, I am struck by this one: when I awake, I shall be satisfied. Satisfied! That wonderful state that comes between one spoonful and the next, when I know I have had enough. Compare 103. When I stop and sigh with contentment. In truth I am rarely satisfied, usually discontented. I have so much but it is never quite enough. I have gone through life with a long face, wishing for—who knows what?

Awakening here might be taken metaphorically. Wakening from foolishness or dullness. From the fog of self-centered complaining, wishing I were somewhere else or another person. Spiritual life is a series of little awakenings—to acceptance, to graceful surrender. To knowing when enough is enough.

BÁ#ANTÁ LIBBIY PÁ<u>QA</u>D:TÁ <u>LAY</u>LÁh
v.3 You have tested my heart, you have visited by night.

Life in the Spirit begins in the darkness, in confusion, when I know I know nothing. When I turn to God in the night (compare 16:7) and let him test me. When I let him teach me in the night, insomnia time.

When I awake in the morning, let me be a little more content. Satisfied at last with the world and with my life. Let me be a little more satisfied to be me as you have made me. When I awake a little bit more from trance, from wishing and dreaming. When I begin to live in the present, here and now, not anticipating or re-living.

When I awake from knowing better and from trying to improve things. Above all, from improving myself. Let me awaken to praise you and thank you. With your image in my heart when I awake, I shall be satisfied, satisfied at last. When I awake to life everlasting. Like 11 and 16, the psalm hints at immortality. When I awaken in the resurrection or in heaven. As always no details, no theology. Only the assurance that I shall be satisfied.

<u>Suggestions</u>: Meditate the psalms wakefully, staying fully alert. Keep your attention present, here and now, not a minute ahead of yourself or a minute behind. And each time you do this, note how that dissatisfied, restless feeling falls away. If you should find yourself drifting into sleep or trance, inhale sharply through the nose. Open your eyes, stand, or kneel.

Psalm 17 (BCP)

Tone: N:GINOTH *irregular*

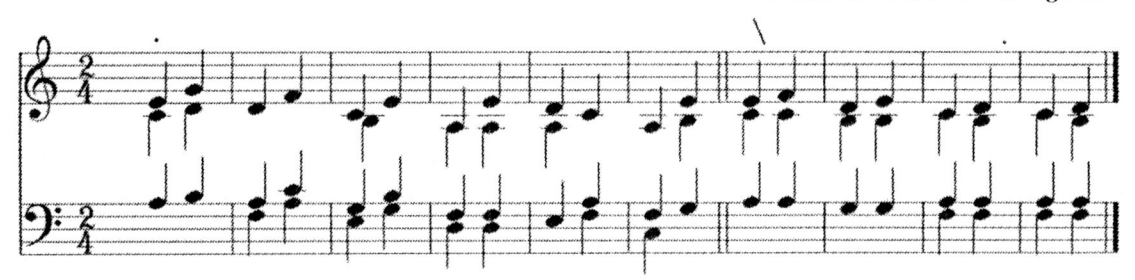

1 Hear my plea of innocence, O LORD; give heed to my cry; *
   listen to my prayer,
   which does not come from lying lips.
2 Let my vindication come forth from your presence; *
   let your eyes be fixed on justice.
3 Weigh my heart, summon me by night, *
   melt me down; you will find no impurity in me.
4 I give no offense with my mouth as others do; *
   I have heeded the words of your lips.
5 My footsteps hold fast to the ways of your law; *
   in your paths my feet shall not stumble.
6 I call upon you, O God, for you will answer me; *
   incline your ear to me and hear my words.
7 .Show me your marvelous loving . kindness,
   O Savior of those who take refuge at your right . hand
   from those who rise up . against them.
8 Keep me as the apple of your . eye;
   hide me under the shadow of your . wings,
9 From the wicked who assault me,
   from my deadly enemies who . surround me.
10 They have closed their heart to pity, *
   and their mouth speaks proud things.
11 They press me hard, now they surround me, *
   watching how they may cast me to the ground,
12 Like a lion, greedy for its prey, *
   and like a young lion lurking in secret places.
13 \Arise, O LORD; confront them and bring them \ down;
   deliver me from the wicked by your \ sword.
14 Deliver me, O LORD, by your \ hand
   from those whose portion in life is this \ world;
15 \Whose bellies you fill with your \ treasure,
   who are well supplied with \ children
   and leave their wealth to their \ little ones.
16 But at my vindication I shall see your face; *
   when I awake, I shall be satisfied, beholding your likeness.

By You I Can Run: Commentary To Psalm 18

v.1 I love you, O LORD my strength.

My stronghold ... crag ... haven ... rock ... shield ... refuge. With many different expressions the writer brings out his teaching. God is my strength. And it slowly dawns on me, over a period of years, that this is far more than a metaphor. The LORD really is my strength. I accomplish nothing out of my own skills and abilities, the abilities that belong to my concept of self. All real strength comes when I call for help; when I reach beyond myself, to him.

v.21 The LORD begins to do good to me in accordance with my righteousness; according to the cleanness of my hands he begins to make return to me.

The righteousness and cleanness are also not mine. As I begin to be straight with God, at once my life begins straightening out. As I begin to be pure with God, my life begins to be pure. With each tiny step of simplicity, I enjoy more of his goodness.

WÁ.eHIY THÁMIM "IMMOW

v.24 And so I become TÁMIM (*innocently simple*) with him. The word suggests wholeness, straightforward simplicity, integrity. I have no layers of meaning or hidden agendas. What I say I say as a whole person. I no longer try to manipulate God, or anyone else, with flowery prayers or pious behavior. My prayers contain no secret messages.

v.26 With the faithfully devoted, you are faithfully devoted; with the innocently simple you show innocent simplicity.

Looking into your eyes, I see myself. That is the way of intimacy, the way of relationship. I learn who I am by what you see in me. It takes courage to look, for I don't always like what I see. Having seen the worst, I am always surprised. For that gleam in your eyes, that love-light, tells me there is more. Finding myself in you I find more and better, I change and grow. I do not find God by looking into myself. I find myself by looking into God. In intimacy with God, as in a mirror, I learn who I am. And I begin to change. I find myself growing to be what you see in me.

v.30 For by you I can run against a troop,
and by my God I can leap over a wall (NKJ).

Improving myself is death and deception. Having improved myself for years I felt lost and helpless. Finding myself in you is finding life. The "me" I see in you can do all things. In you, I can run against a(ny) troop. I can leap over a(ny) wall!

Note: The psalm appears entire in 2 Samuel 22:2-51. Vv. 3 and 5, compare 116. Verse 34, compare the Psalm of Habakkuk (3:19).

Suggestions: Do not try to improve yourself or find yourself. In your practice of meditation, search for God, and let God find you.

Third Day: Evening Prayer Psalm 18 (BCP) Tone: KINNOR

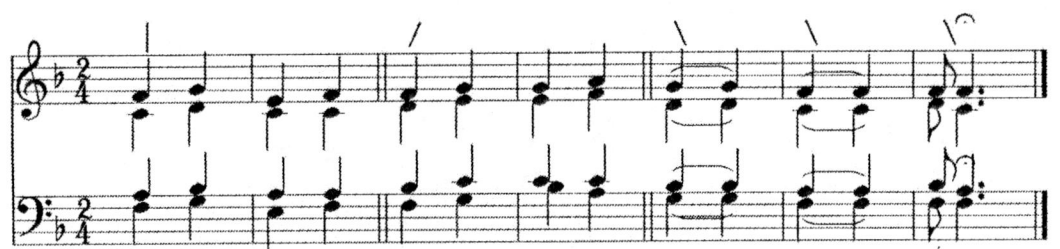

1 I love you, O LORD my strength, *
  O LORD my stronghold, my crag, and my haven.
2 My God, my rock in whom I put my trust, *
  my shield, the horn of my salvation, and my refuge; you are worthy of praise.
3 **I will call upon the | LORD,**
  and so shall I be saved from my | enemies.
4 The breakers of death rolled over me, *
  and the torrents of oblivion made me afraid.
5 The cords of hell entangled me,*
  and the snares of death were set for me.
6 **I called upon the LORD in my dis|tress**
  and cried out to my God for | help.
7 He heard my voice from his heavenly dwelling; *
  my cry of anguish came to his ears.
8 The earth reeled and rocked; *
  the roots of the mountain shook; they reeled because of his anger.
9 Smoke rose from his nostrils
  and a consuming fire out of his mouth; *
  hot burning coals blazed forth from him.
10 He parted the heavens and came down *
  with a storm cloud under his feet.
11 He mounted on KRUVIM and flew; *
  he swooped on the wings of the wind.
12 He wrapped darkness about him; *
  he made dark waters and thick clouds his pavilion.
13 **/From the brightness of his presence, through the / clouds,**
  burst hailstones and coals of / fire.
14 The LORD thundered out of heaven; *
  the Most High uttered his voice.
15 **/He loosed his arrows and / scattered them;**
  he hurled thunderbolts and / routed them.
16 The beds of the seas were uncovered,
  and the foundations of the world laid bare, *
  at your battle cry, O LORD, at the blast of the breath of your nostrils.
17 He reached down from on high and grasped me; *
  he drew me out of great waters.

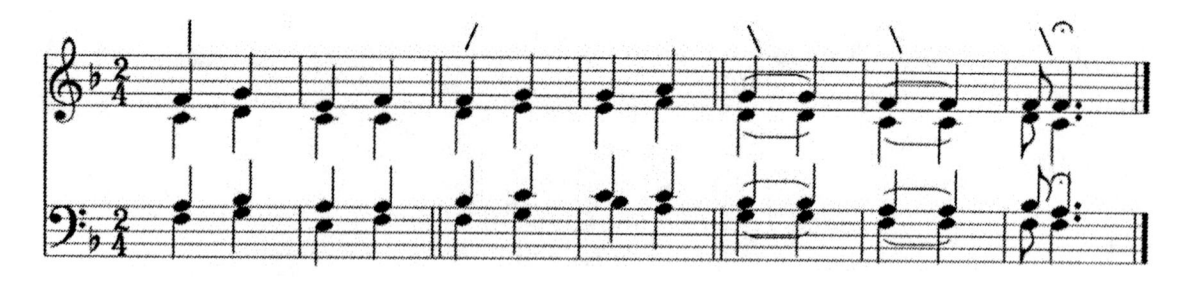

18 He delivered me from my strong enemies
 and from those who hated me; *
 for they were too mighty for me.
19 They confronted me in the day of my disaster; *
 but the Lord was my support.
20 He brought me out into an open place; *
 he rescued me because he delighted in me.

Part II

21 **The Lord rewarded me because of my righteous | dealing;**
 because my hands were clean he re | warded me;.
22 For I have kept the ways of the Lord *
 and have not offended against my God;
23 For all his judgments are before my eyes, *
 and his decrees I have not put away from me;
24 For I have been blameless with him *
 and have kept myself from iniquity;
25 Therefore the Lord rewarded me according to my righteous | dealing,
 because of the cleanness of my hands in his | sight.
26 With the faithful you show yourself faithful, O God; *
 with the forthright you show yourself forthright.
27 With the pure you show yourself pure, *
 but with the crooked you are wily.
28 You will save a lowly people, *
 but you will humble the haughty eyes.
29 You, O Lord, are my lamp; *
 my God, you make my darkness bright.
30 With you I will break down an enclosure; *
 with the help of my God I will scale any wall.
31 **As for God, his ways are | perfect;**
 the words of the Lord are tried in the | fire;
 he is a shield to all who trust in him.
32 For who is God but the Lord? *
 who is the Rock, except our God?
33 **It is God who girds me about with | strength**
 and makes my way | secure.
34 He makes me sure-footed like a deer *
 and lets me stand firm on the heights.

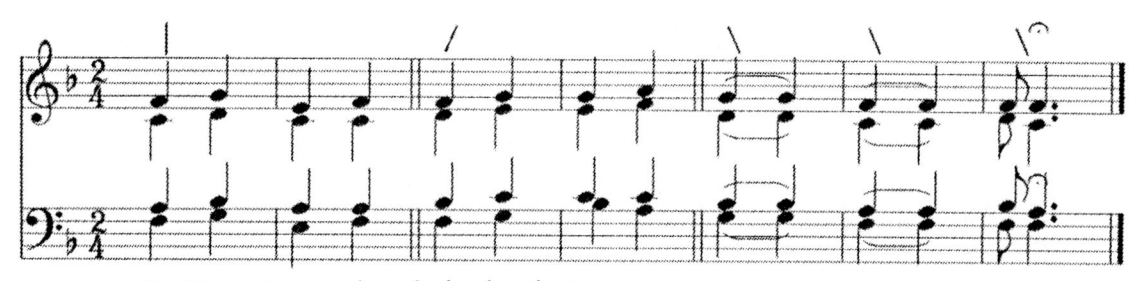

35 He trains my hands for battle *
    and my arms for bending even a bow of bronze.
36 You have given me your shield of victory; *
    your right hand also sustains me; your loving care makes me great.
37 You lengthen my stride beneath me, *
    and my ankles do not give way.
38 I pursue my enemies and overtake them; *
    I will not turn back till I have destroyed them.
39 I strike them down, and they cannot rise; *
    they fall defeated at my feet.
40 You have girded me with strength for the battle; *
    you have cast down my adversaries beneath me;
    you have put my enemies to flight.
41 I destroy those who hate me; they cry out, but there is none to help them; *
    they cry to the LORD, but he does not answer.
42 I beat them small like dust before the wind; *
    I trample them like mud in the streets.
43 You deliver me from the strife of the peoples; *
    you put me at the head of the nations.
44 A people I have not known shall serve me;
    no sooner shall they hear than they shall obey me; *
    strangers will cringe before me.
45 The foreign peoples will lose heart; *
    they shall come trembling out of their strongholds.
46 **The LORD lives! Blessed is my | rock!**
    Exalted is the God of my | salvation!
47 /He is the God who gave me / victory
    and cast down the peoples / beneath me.
48 \You rescued me from the fury of my enemies;
    \you exalted me above those who rose against me;
    you saved me from my deadly \ foe.
49 /Therefore will I extol you among the / nations, O LORD,
    and sing praises to your / Name.
50 \He multiplies the victories of his king;
    \he shows loving-kindness to his anointed,
    to David and his descendants for \ ever.

Their Line Goes Out: Commentary To Psalm 19

    B:KHOL-HÁ.ÁRE3 YÁ3Á. QAWWÁM UVIQ3ÉH THÉVÉL MILLEYHEM
v.4 Their line goes out in(to) all the earth,
and their words to the end of the world.

 Mysterious lines of communication link the universe. From one end to another, particles commune with particles and stars with stars. Although they do not speak English or Hebrew, all things influence all things. Imperceptible changes in the beginning can have vast and unforeseen consequences in the end. Some have called it "the Butterfly Effect—the notion that a butterfly stirring the air today in Peking can transform storm systems next month in New York."*

 A similarity that never repeats itself exactly is found at every level, from galaxies to atoms. A profound yet unpredictable orderliness animates all. Closer to human experience, the sun makes his daily run across the sky—as a bold young man, a newlywed, does his daily run in our neighborhood.

    TORATH YHWH T:MIMÁH M:SHIVATh NÁPHESh
v.7 The law of the LORD is perfect
and revives the soul.

 The *Torah* or teaching of the LORD is perfect (complete, whole, innocent), reviving or restoring the soul (breath, breathing, life). The law that orders the universe supports my life. It is a law of exquisite simplicity, yet its application generates infinite complexity. This law or teaching not only restores life; it is faithful (constant), makes the simple wise, rejoices the heart and puts light into the eye. I do not think of this law as the six-hundred-thirteen commandments of Jewish orthodoxy, or as "the law" so burdensome to Paul. I think of it as the teaching of God, a teaching that may appear in many guises. It is the teaching of Scripture, but it is also the teaching of tradition. It has been revealed many times to many peoples, never completely grasped by anyone, available now to anyone who will pray for it and ask for it.

v.11 By them also is your servant enlightened.

 From the galaxy to the sun to generic humankind to your servant—me—the law(fulness) of God amazes me. For it guides the careening stars at their level and enlightens me at mine. It penetrates into the deepest levels of my existence and knows my secret thoughts. It cleanses me and keeps me pure. The law of God gives me free will, the power to make choices; and saves me from possibly fatal deviations. This cosmic law is also your teaching, *Torah*, your guide for my life.

<u>Suggestions</u>: Compare 119. Sing verses 7-13 to the Tone <u>NÉ</u>VEL (*lyre*). Sing the first Order (first two measures) three times, the second Order once.

---

*James Gleick: *Chaos: Making a New Science*, Viking, New York, 1987, p.8, by permission, Michael V. Carlisle.

Psalm 19 (BCP)

Fourth Day: Morning Prayer Tone: NEVEL

1 The heavens declare the glory of God, *
   and the firmament shows his handiwork.
2 One day tells its tale to another, *
   and one night imparts knowledge to another.
3 Although they have no words or language, *
   and their voices are not heard,
4 Their sound has gone out into all lands, *
   and their message to the ends of the world.
5 In the deep he has set a pavilion for the sun; *
   it comes forth like a bridegroom out of his chamber;
   it rejoices like a champion to run its course.
6 It goes forth from the uttermost edge of the heavens
   and runs about to the end of it again; *
   nothing is hidden from its burning heat.
7 **The law of the L ORD is | perfect**
   and re|vives the | soul;
   the testimony of the L ORD is | sure
   and gives | wisdom to the | innocent.
8 The statutes of the L ORD are | just
   and re|joice the | heart;
   \The commandment of the L ORD is \ clear
   and gives \ light to the \ eyes.
9 **The fear of the L ORD is | clean**
   and en|dures for | ever;
   the judgments of the L ORD are | true
   and | righteous alto|gether.
10 More to be desired are they than | gold,
   more than | much fine | gold,
   \sweeter far than \ honey,
   than \ honey in the \ comb.
11 **By them also is your servant en|lightened,**
   and in | keeping them there is | great reward.
12 Who can tell how often he of|fends?
   cleanse me from my | secret | faults.

13 Above all, keep your servant from presumptuous | sins;
    let them | not get dominion | over me;
    \then shall I be whole and \ sound,
    and \ innocent of a great of\fense.
                    [Read]
14 Let the words of my mouth and the meditation of my
    heart be acceptable in your sight, *
    O LORD, my strength and my redeemer.

Accept Your Offering: Commentary To Psalm 20

v.3 (May the LORD) remember all your offerings
and accept your burnt sacrifice.
[Silence...]

Literally it means anoint your burnt sacrifice with oil, as in 23. Anointing with oil is a way of dedicating a thing to some exalted use. God does not need my offering, but may he use it, may he exalt it.

He was having deep trouble with his church. He wanted to offer a certain ministry in the church, but no one seemed to care. He felt ignored and unappreciated because no one was asking him to do it. He became more and more sensitive. He was leaving church in a terrible mood every Sunday. He prayed about this for a long time without (apparently) receiving an answer. As husband and wife talked about their relationship to the church they fell deeper into resentment. They were feeling like uninvited guests. Adding insult to injury, their twelve year old child felt very much a part of this church and didn't hesitate to point out their bad attitude!

After some months he was drawn to Psalm 20:3. One morning in church, that verse lit up for him. He was not to offer this ministry to a person or to "the church," but to God. He asked God if he would receive it. What kind of offering would he accept? Immediately his thoughts leaped to Genesis 4:5-7 (NKJ):

"But He did not respect Cain and his offering. And Cain was very angry and his countenance fell. So the LORD said to Cain, 'Why are you angry? And why has your countenance fallen? If you do well, will you not be accepted?'" Like Cain, my friend had been lifting up his offering in the wrong spirit, to the wrong person. In that instant he experienced healing. A few words were exchanged after church, and the ministry began to take shape.

We tend to think of sacrifice as a primitive form of worship, and it is. We may also think of it as a spiritual discipline. It is the outward practice and inward grace of lifting up and letting go. Taking something I enjoy, lifting it up to God, and letting it go. Trusting that God will give me what I need. The word "OLÁH (*burnt offering*) means going up—for in lifting that portion up on a raised altar, I have lifted my enjoyment to a higher level. I am learning to enjoy without attachment. In giving up control, I begin to rise from addiction.

Sacrifice is both powerful and dangerous. It must be done in the right way, at the right time, in the right place, and with the right attitude. Freely, cheerfully, without resentment, without competitiveness, without demanding a reward.

<u>Suggestions</u>: Sing to the Tone "ÁSOR (*ten-string*) and observe [Silence...] where so directed.

Offer everything you do to God. Practice lifting it up to God, and letting it go. Do not expect praise or encouragement from human breathings. Do not look for results or try to control the outcome. Ask God to accept your offering. In just this way, when you pray, lift up and let go. Lift up your thoughts, your prayers, to God; let them go and be silent.

Psalm 20 (BCP)

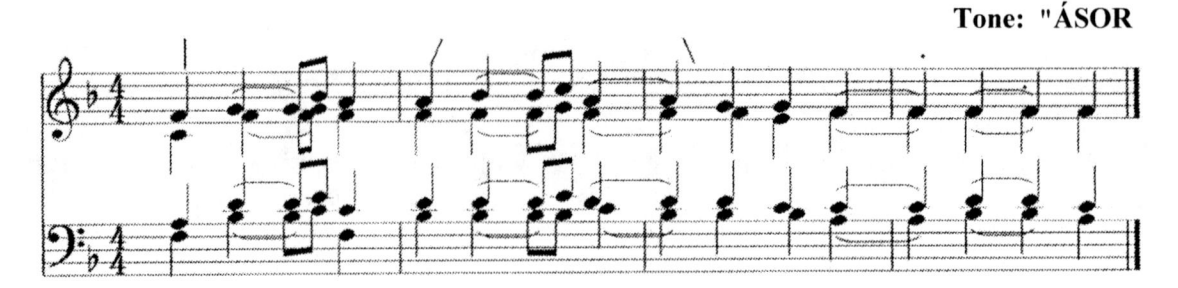

Tone: "ÁSOR

1 **May the LORD answer you in the day of | trouble,**
 the | Name of the God of Jacob de | fend you.
2 /Send you help from his / holy place
 and / strengthen you out of / Zion;
3 \Remember all your \ offerings
 and accept your burnt \ sacrifice;
   [Silence...]
4 .Grant you your heart's . desire
 and prosper all your . plans.
5 \We will shout for joy at your \ victory
 and triumph in the Name of our \ God;
 .may the . LORD grant all your re.quests.
6 \Now I know that the LORD gives victory to his a\nointed;
 he will answer him out of his holy \ heaven,
 .with the victorious . strength of his right . hand.
7 **Some put their trust in chariots and some in | horses,**
 but | we will call upon the Name of the | LORD our God.
8 /They collapse and fall / down,
 but / we will arise and stand / upright.
9 \O LORD, give victory to the \ king
 and answer us when we \ call.

The King Rejoices: Commentary To Psalm 21

YHWH B:"ÁZZ:KHÁ YISMA# MELEKh

v.1 The king rejoices in your strength, O LORD.

Continuing a thought from 20:9—O LORD, give victory to the king. We have some difficulty thinking seriously about kings in our time. Most kings and queens today are museum figures; they perform ceremonial functions but have little authority. Yet the real meaning of kingship or queenship is authority—the socially recognized power to command obedience. One way to think about "the king" is the person in authority. The supervisor or the boss. Whoever has authority over me.

The authorities in my life do not wear robes or crowns, but they can make my life pleasant or miserable. They can support my work or interfere with it. They can come into my office and interrupt me whenever they wish. If they so choose they can have me discredited, humiliated, and deprived of my livelihood. I am tempted to be afraid of these authorities and to think of them as larger than life.

Most of the kings in my life are ill prepared to be kings. They are not well trained in management. Their own kings give them great responsibility but little authority to carry it out. Their "subjects" look to them for help, but often they have little help to offer. More often than not the subjects have little respect for them, and they in turn treat the subjects with intimidation and abuse.

I like to consider these kingship psalms as a way of thinking about authority. Real authority comes from God alone. His authority is a blessing that comes with grace and joy. God blesses his king, so that the king can bless his subjects. And the subjects in turn bless and uphold the king. The king or queen is an ordinary person, a sinner like myself, anointed (commissioned) for a special role. There is no training or power that can prepare for such a role. It can only come from God, and when it does it will be joyful and fruitful.

If God has given me authority over others, let me turn to him, moment by moment, for direction. Let me be a blessing to his people, empowering them with his power. When I am wrong, let my people have the courage to tell me, face to face. And if God has put authorities over me, let me pray for them and uphold them. Let me not go around complaining about them. Realizing that they are sinners like myself, let me pray for their health and safety at all times, and praise God for placing them where they are. And if the king is wrong, let me have the courage to tell him.

Suggestions: Sing to the Tone "ÁSOR (*ten-string*) and observe the [Silence...].

In every impossible situation and difficult relationship turn to God and accept his authority. Pray for all who have authority over you. Clear your thoughts and be silent. And "though they intend evil against you ... yet they shall not prevail."

Psalm 21 (BCP)

Tone: "ÁSOR

1 The king rejoices in your strength, O Lord; *
    how greatly he exults in your victory!
2 You have given him his heart's desire; *
    you have not denied him the request of his lips.
                [Silence...]
3 **For you meet him with blessings of pros | perity,**
    and set a | crown of fine | gold upon his head.
4 He asked you for life, and you gave it to him: *
    length of days, for ever and ever.
5 His honor is great, because of your victory; *
    splendor and majesty have you bestowed upon him.
6 **For you will give him everlasting fe | licity**
    and will make him | glad with the | joy of your presence.
7 For the king puts his trust in the Lord; *
    because of the loving-kindness of the Most High, he will not fall.
8 Your hand will lay hold upon all your enemies; *
    your right hand will seize all those who hate you.
9 **\You will make them like a fiery \ furnace**
    at the time of your appearing, O \ Lord;
10 You will swallow them up in your wrath, *
    and fire shall consume them.
11 You will destroy their offspring from the land *
    and their descendants from among the peoples of the earth.
12 Though they intend evil against you
    and devise wicked schemes, *
    yet they shall not prevail.
13 **\For you will put them to \ flight**
    and aim your \ arrows at them.
14 .Be exalted, O Lord, in your . might;
    we will sing and praise your . power.

Be Not Far: Commentary To Psalm 22

.ÉLIY .ÉLIY LÁMÁH "aZAV<u>T</u>ÁNI RÁ#OQ MIYSHU"ÁTHIY

v.1 My God, my God, why hast thou forsaken me? Why art thou so far from helping me? (KJV).

For Christians this is sure to evoke one image: the agonized last words of Jesus, his Aramaic dialect passed down by witnesses. "And about the ninth hour Jesus cried out with a loud voice, saying, '*Eli, Eli, lama sabachthani?*' that is, 'My God, My God, why have you forsaken me?'" (Matthew 27:46, NKJ).

My God, my God, why? — and as always there is no answer. *Why are children abused? Why is there war? Why does cancer happen? Why do we have to die? Why do you let... ?* And there is only stillness. God is not answering why. I tell my patients that God doesn't answer *why?* questions. Psychologically *why?* means You owe me an explanation! I might say, "I just want to know why," or, "Just give me one reason." The reason explains nothing, but I think it will make me feel better. At least you will be talking to me. At least for a moment, you won't be so far away. I cry out not for explanation, really, but for you. For intimacy. For the sense of your presence, that now seems so remote. You owe me no explanation, God (friend, lover, spouse, child), but be not far. Talk to me. Touch me.

Now is the final surrender. Jesus has given up everything: family, friends, disciples, healing, miracles. Now as he draws his last tortured breaths, he has given up even his closeness to the Father. Abandoned, he dies alone, like any human breathing. He dies pleading for that Presence.

v.2 There is no silence for me. I am overwhelmed with thoughts, emotions, pain, noise, dirt, flies. My brain is racing and cannot quiet itself. All I have learned in meditation is forgotten, inaccessible. I cannot be still. My patients complain bitterly of this: their racing thoughts will not stop. That turbulent misery we might call noise or entropy. It is the very essence of suffering.

v.3 Yet you are (the) Holy (One),

enthroned upon the praises of Israel (our community). A sudden disjunction. Conversion moment. Change of perspective. But as for you, LORD, you are found in praise. Still no explanation, but in praising you, I find you.

v.6 But as for me, I am a worm and no man.

An equally sharp transition back to myself. Grief comes in terrible waves. You comfort me, I feel better, then more pain. You must understand this if you would minister to me. I cry out not for explanation, but for presence. I must come out of myself, and turn to God. And I must also go back in to my pain.

.AL-TIR#AQ MIM<u>ME</u>NNI KI-3ÁRÁH Q:ROVÁH KI .EYN "OZÉR

v.11 Be not far from me, for trouble is near,
and there is none to help.

Do not abandon me, O LORD, when trouble comes. When hard times come and the fierce wild bulls are pawing the earth. When the dogs are closing in. When all I have is taken away. Do not abandon me (friend, lover, spouse, child), do not be far away.

W:.ATTÁH YHWH .AL-TIR#AQ   .eYÁLUTHIY L:"EZRÁTHIY #USHÁh

v.18 Be not far away, O LORD;
you are my strength; hasten to help me. But as for you, LORD, be not far away. It is not really death we fear, but abandonment. To suffer alone, with no one who will tell the truth, or touch, or look at me. I cry out not for explanation, LORD (friend, lover, spouse, child), but for your presence.

I must remember this as therapist. When my patients cry out in distress and ask me, "Why?" When fierce bulls of Bashan are surrounding them and my wonder drugs seem to do nothing for them. I must remember that they cry out from abandonment. Not for an explanation but for presence. Sometimes I can help my patients actively, and how exciting that is. Sometimes I can only stand by their crosses, and be not far.

v.21 I will declare your Name to my brethren;
in the midst of the congregation I will praise you.

A new series of images begins here, almost like a different psalm. More and more now I rise up out of my suffering into praise, and out of praise I come into a longer perspective. The view of community and history, where "my descendants shall serve him." I do not reach this point easily or quickly, but with time, with patience, with acceptance.

v.25 The poor shall eat and be satisfied.

The afflicted or miserable ones shall begin to eat; more importantly, they shall begin to be satisfied. They shall come to that state of enlightenment where enough is really enough and blessings are enjoyed. Compare 17.

Note: (*) Verse 28 is modified from KJV.

Suggestions: Stand, vv.22-30. Bow deeply from the waist at v.26b ("and all the families") and again at v.28 ("All who are fat on the earth shall eat and worship").

When there is "no silence" for you, when the racing thoughts will not stop, you may need help to move from thoughts to silence. A word or phrase or a short prayer, like "Help, LORD," or *Abba*; or the Jesus Prayer or a breath prayer.* Sometimes it helps to walk in a smooth, rhythmic pace, or to close the eyes. Any of these methods can help the transition from thought to no-thought. Remember, though, that helps and methods are not meditation. The heart of meditation is the silence; nothing more.

---

*Ron DelBene with Herb Montgomery: *The Breath of Life. Discovering Your Breath Prayer*. Harper & Row, San Francisco, 1981.

Psalm 22 (BCP)

Fourth Day: Evening Prayer Tone: "UGÁV

1 My God, my God why have you forsaken me? *
   and are so far from my cry
   and from the words of my distress?
2 O my God, I cry in the daytime, but you do not answer; *
   by night as well, but I find no rest.
3 Yet you are the Holy One, *
   enthroned upon the praises of Israel.
4 Our forefathers put their trust in you; *
   they trusted, and you delivered them.
5 They cried out to you and were delivered; *
   they trusted in you and were not put to shame.
6 But as for me, I am a worm and no man, *
   scorned by all and despised by the people.
7 All who see me laugh me to scorn; *
   they curl their lips and wag their heads, saying,
8 "He trusted in the LORD; let him deliver him; *
   let him rescue him, if he delights in him."
9 Yet you are he who took me out of the womb, *
   and kept me safe upon my mother's breast.
10 I have been entrusted to you ever since I was born; *
    you were my God when I was still in my mother's womb.
11 **Be not far from me, for trouble is | near,**
    and there is none to | help.
12 Many young bulls en|circle me;
    strong bulls of | Bashan sur|round me.
13 They open wide their jaws at me, *
    like a ravening and a roaring lion.
14 I am poured out like water;
    all my bones are out of joint; *
    my heart within my breast is melting wax.
15 My mouth is dried out like a pot-sherd;
    my tongue sticks to the roof of my mouth; *
    and you have laid me in the dust of the grave.
16 Packs of dogs close me in,
    and gangs of evildoers circle around me; *

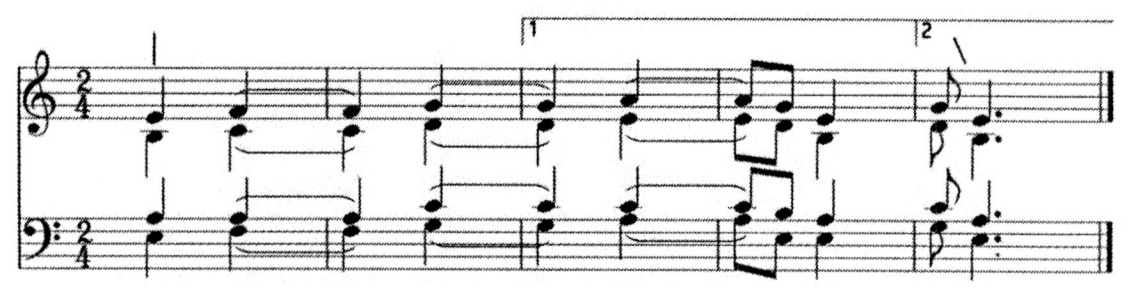

    they pierce my hands and my feet;
    I can count all my bones.
17 They stare and gloat over me; *
    they divide my garments among them;
    they cast lots for my clothing.
18 **Be not far away, O | L**ORD**;**
    you are my strength; hasten to | help me.
19 Save me from the | sword,
    my | life from the | power of the dog.
20 Save me from the lions's mouth, *
    my wretched body from the horns of wild bulls.
21 I will declare your Name to my brethren; *
    in the midst of the congregation I will praise you.
                    [Stand]
22 Praise the LORD, you that fear him; *
    stand in awe of him, O offspring of Israel;
    all you of Jacob's line, give glory.
23 For he does not despise nor abhor the poor in their poverty;
    neither does he hide his face from them; *
    but when they cry to him he hears them.
24 My praise is of him in the great assembly; *
    I will perform my vows in the presence of those
    who worship him.
25 **The poor shall eat and be | satisfied,**
    and those who seek the LORD shall | praise him:
    "May your \ heart live for ever!"
26 All the ends of the earth shall remember and turn to the LORD, *
    and all the families of the nations shall bow before him.
27 For kingship belongs to the LORD; *
    he rules over the nations.
28 **All who are fat on the earth shall eat and | worship; (*)**
    all who go down to the dust shall bow be|fore him;
    but \ none can keep alive his own soul.
29 My soul shall live for him;
    My descendants shall serve him; *
    they shall be known as the LORD's for ever.
30 They shall come and make known to a people yet unborn *
    the saving deeds that he has done.

Song Of The Sheep: Commentary To Psalm 23

Here I am the sheep, that woolly and not-so-bright animal grazing the hillsides. I am the sheep; the LORD is my shepherd. And the Good Shepherd is also the Lamb—the shepherd who lived as a sheep, who knows how a sheep thinks.

The sheep-shepherd relationship is one of trusting but at times resentful dependency. Does the shepherd answer the prayers of a sheep? Not always in the form requested. The shepherd is always thinking of the sheep, but the sheep might not agree. Often the sheep thinks it knows better. Sometimes the sheep wanders off and gets into trouble, as in 119:176.

NAPHSHIY Y:SHOVÉV

v.3 He restores my soul (breath, life). Breath by breath he keeps returning my breath to me. He keeps me alive, renews and refreshes me. And having restored me, refreshed me, he guides me in the paths of 3EDEQ (*righteousness, justice*). He restores me, physically and morally.

TA"aROKH L:PHÁNÁY SHUL#ÁN   NEGED 3OR:RÁY

v.5 You prepare a table before me
in the presence of those who trouble (confine, constrain) me.

Here we shift metaphors. No longer a four-legged sheep, I am still in that dependent relationship. The LORD prepares lunch for me in the presence of those who trouble me—my problems. In the presence of those I would rather not deal with, in the presence of my troubles, he offers me lunch. He invites them and brings them to my table. All that I would rather run away from he brings into my presence.

Raymond Brock does a beautiful visualization on this. A lovely banquet spread on the grass. The depression or pain is brought to the edge of the tablecloth, it is faced, and then it slowly fades away. I cannot run away from my troubles. As my former patient once said, lifting a heavy glass ashtray from my desk, "Reality is like this ashtray, it don't go away." Reality comes to the table, and I face it with God, and it changes—or I do.

vv. 6-7 Goodness and mercy shall pursue me or chase after me. Indeed they have pursued me; they chased after me and found me even when I was hiding. Now they seem to find me more easily. And I will dwell, literally *I have dwelt*, or, *I have returned*. The Hebrew says "for length of days." I have committed my life to living in his house, all my days. I will practice silence and listening, in my everyday life, all the days of my life.

<u>Suggestions</u>: Sing softly to the Tone KINNOR (*harp*). Hand movements for this Tone are given in the Appendix.

Think of yourself as the sheep in this psalm. Notice those sheep-like traits in yourself: the tendency to follow any thought or emotion; to wander off the path and get lost; to do things your own way; to follow other sheep no matter where they are going. As you pray this psalm, keep your attention focused on the Shepherd.

Psalm 23 (KJV)

Tone: KINNOR

1 **The LORD is my | shepherd;**
   I shall not | want.
2 **He maketh me to lie down in green | pastures:**
   he leadeth me beside the still | waters.
3 /He restoreth my / soul:
   he leadeth me in the paths of righteousness for his /
   Name's sake.

4 \Yea, though I walk through the valley of the shadow of death,
   \I will fear no evil; for thou art with me;
   thy rod and thy staff, they \ comfort me.

5 **Thou preparest a table | before me**
   in the presence of mine | enemies;
/Thou anointest my head with / oil;
   my cup runneth / over.

6 \Surely goodness and mercy shall follow me all the days of my life:
   \and I will dwell in the house
   of the LORD for \ ever.

Doorways Of Eternity: Commentary To Psalm 24

LAYHWH HÁ.ÁRE3 UM:LO.ÁH' TÉVÉL W:YOSHVEY VÁH'
v.1 Of the LORD is the earth and her fullness,
the inhabited world, and those who dwell in her.

Of the LORD is all and everything. The world, things, people, me. Everything comes from God and belongs to God. Nothing belongs to anyone else—to me, or to the government, or even to Satan. For God has founded her (the earth) upon oceans, and continues to establish her upon rivers. Her apparently solid structure is built upon chaos and turbulence. Out of self-organizing yet unpredictable complexity he continues to structure trees, rocks, stars and the human brain.

v.3 Who can ascend the hill of the LORD
and who can stand up in his holy place?

v.4 (The) clean of hands and pure of heart,
who has not lifted up his soul to falsehood.

Who is advancing on the spiritual path? Compare 15. The answer is simple. Whoever has clean hands and a pure heart. His hands are not stained with innocent blood; his heart (attitude) is pure (clear, clean), free of deception and self-deception. He has not lifted up his soul (breath, breathing, life) to what is empty and useless. His hands are not stained with innocent blood because he has not entertained murderous thoughts or said condemning words. His heart is pure because he has lived in simple integrity, without hidden agendas and complicated schemes. He has not lifted up his soul to what is empty and useless because he is not carried away by thoughts and emotions. What is this picture? It is fruit of the Spirit—*love, joy, peace, patience* — the spontaneous, natural, almost unconscious living out of Galatians 5:22.

S:.UW SH:"ÁRIM RO.SHEYKHEM W:HINNÁS.UW PITH#EY "OLÁM
v.7 Lift up, O gates, your heads;
and be lifted up, O doorways of eternity,

and the King of glory shall come in. What are these doorways? What does it mean for this King to enter his kingdom? Scholars propose elaborate ceremonies in which, perhaps, the ark was brought into the temple. I would rather think of those doorways as the doorways of my inner world; those gates as the gates of perception; and the King coming in to rule my life. Who is this King of glory? He is strong and mighty, mighty in battle, the LORD of armies. Why is God "mighty in battle," and, "the LORD of armies"? Because he is Lord of all forces and energies, and Lord of all conflict. He is there, in conflict and turmoil, and he is in control. [Silence...].

Suggestions: Stand. Sing to the Tone #a3O3:ROTH (*trumpets*). The movement Standing Drum is suggested for vv. 7-10 (see Appendix).

Continue your meditation, even in conflict and turmoil. The evidence of success will be fruit of the Spirit—*love, joy, peace*... Look for this evidence, but only in yourself. For Jesus teaches that we should never judge the spiritual progress of another.

Psalm 24 (BCP)

Fifth Day: Morning Prayer Tone: #a3O3:ROTH

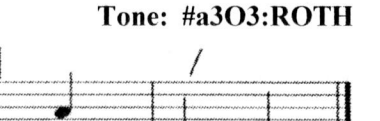

1 +The earth is the LORD's and all that is + in it,
    the world and all who dwell / therein.
2 For it is he who founded it upon the \ seas
    and made it firm upon the rivers of the \ deep.
3 "Who can ascend the hill of the | LORD
    /and who can stand in his / holy place?"
4 +"Those who have clean hands and a pure + heart,
    who have not pledged themselves to / falsehood,
    nor sworn by what is a \ fraud.
5 **They shall receive a blessing from the | LORD**
    /and a just reward from the God of their / salvation."
6 **Such is the generation of those who | seek him,**
    /of those who seek your face, O God of / Jacob.
                [Silence...]
7 Lìft up your hèads, O | gàtes; `
    lift them hìgh, O èverlasting | dòors; `
    /and the Kìng of glòry shall come / ìn.`
8 **"Whò is this Kìng of | glòry?" `**
    "The LÒRD, stròng and | mìghty,`
    /the LÒRD, mìghty in / bàttle."
9 Lìft up your hèads, O | gàtes; `
    lift them hìgh, O èverlasting | dòors; `
    /and the Kìng of glòry shall come / ìn. `
10 **"Who is hè, this Kìng of | glòry?" `**
    "The LÒRD ` of | hòsts, `
    /hè is the Kìng of / glòry."

Alphabet Of Prayer: Commentary To Psalm 25

As a new Christian, my ideas on prayer were somewhat magical. LORD, please do this. LORD, please do that. Don't let the telephone ring tonight. Let me find a parking place. Heal me! Such prayer has a deservedly bad reputation, even if it occasionally seems to work. Psalm 25 is different.

.ÉLEYKHÁ YHWH NAPHSHIY .ESSÁ.

v.1 To you, O LORD, my soul I lift up.

To you alone, O LORD. I begin by directing my attention to whom. Not to myself, or to the universe, but to Someone. To you, O LORD.

My soul, my inner Other. The person I talk to when I talk to myself. The partner in my inner dialogue. At a deeper level my breath (breathing, life). The tide of breath that flows in and out of me, and which perhaps is the real me. This NEPHESh I lift up; I bring my inner Other into relationship with you, into the vertical. I lift up my very life and offer it to you. I lift up my breath, inhaling sharply and filling my lungs. As I do so I become alert; lifting my eyes ever so slightly heavenward I direct my consciousness to you.

A wealth of teaching is packed into these words. Preparation for prayer. First a relationship. Then, a direction. Then my inner self, or breath, I lift up, that is, I bring it into that vertical relationship. See also 86.

D:RÁKHEYKHÁ YHWH HODI"ÉNI .OR#OTHEYKHÁ LAMM:DÉNI

v.3 Your ways, O LORD, show me;

your paths, teach me.

And in v. 4, "Lead me in your truth and teach me." The heart of prayer in four verbs: Show me. Teach me. Lead me. Teach me.

I began to understand prayer after I had been a Christian for some time. I had been deeply involved in Transcendental Meditation (TM), but I realized it was taking me nowhere. In my dream I was on a train, going nowhere. The conductor kept assuring the passengers of progress; then we discovered that our train was—had been for years—parked on a siding. Where was I to go now for that rest and silence? I began to use the short liturgical forms in the Prayer Book, pp. 136-140, together with the psalms for each day. Then I would sit quietly and ask God, "What do you want to teach me today? What do you want me to learn from these Scriptures?" And I began to experience his guidance.

Not in voices or visions or clear-cut answers; rather, in a subtle, growing sense of being under direction. A growing sensitivity to the needs of others and of total situations. A growing ability to say yes to the demands made on me, and to put my own personal wishes in second place.

I began to receive suggestions. Sometimes in Scripture; sometimes a word from my wife; sometimes an unexpected whisper that I sensed infused into my deepest self. An understanding that could lead to unexpected solutions.

I never found it helpful to present God with a wish list. I don't get answers when I ask God to please let this happen and don't let that happen. Or when I run through long lists of intercessions that people have asked me to pray. I never get answers to *why?* questions. But when I ask him to teach me, he teaches me. When I ask him what he wants me to do this minute, this hour, this day, he shows me. When I ask him how he wants me to deal with this problem, he shows me the next step. Sometimes I don't even know what he has showed me or taught me, because it is nonverbal. It is a faint but steadying sense of what to do the very next step. God doesn't give long dissertations; he tells me only what I need to know.

In v.7 we learn that being a sinner is no obstacle to prayer, but that

YADRÉKH "aNÁWIM BAMMISHPÁt WIYLAMMÉD "aNÁWIM DARKOW
v.8 The afflicted (lowly, humble) he guides in judgment,
and teaches the afflicted (lowly, humble) his way.

Whom does he teach and guide? The surrendered ones who know they are powerless. Not the perfect who know all the answers; not the great preachers and theologians. As often as not the sinner. Always the humble (lowly). No expert can teach you to pray. My experience is that God will teach you how to pray if you sincerely ask him. Ask him to take direction of your life, but don't tell him how; be humble and listen. Ask God what he wants you to learn, what he wants you to do; and how.

And then, having taught us to pray, God takes us on a strange journey indeed. From "They shall dwell in prosperity," to "I am left alone and in misery," and, "the sorrows of my heart have increased." What is going on here? — I might well ask. Not the abundant life as I might have pictured it, not life on the pink cloud of happiness. Everyday life. Real life, with its ups and downs, joy and disaster. And prayer. Real life, with its real harshness, and this: relationship with God.

<u>Suggestions</u>: Sing reverently to the Tone *Alphabet*. When you feel sure you have heard from the LORD, do not boast. Tell no one. Keep listening, keep listening, be sure you have heard correctly. Keep going back to Psalm 25: Show me. Teach me. Lead me. Teach me.

Notice the subtle variations of silence. There is a silence in which you are aware of your surroundings; you see things around you with unusual clarity, without thoughts. There is a silence in which you are aware of your inner self, the *feeling* of silence. And there is a silence in which your attention is directed toward God. It is like silence lifted up, like praying without words or thoughts. Lift up your soul, as it were, to God, and practice this prayer of silence whenever you can.

Psalm 25 (BCP)

Tone: *Alphabet*

1 **To you, O LORD, I lift up my | soul;**
   my God, I put my | trust in you;
   let me not be + humiliated,
   nor let my enemies triumph + over me.
2 Let none who look to you be put to / shame;
   let the treacherous be disappointed in their / schemes.
3 Show me your ways, O ^ LORD,
   and teach me your ^ paths.
4 Lead me in your truth and . teach me,
   for you are the God of my salvation;
   in you have I trusted all the day . long.
5 **Remember, O LORD, your compassion and | love,**
   for they are from ever | lasting.
6 Remember not the sins of my youth and my trans+gressions;
   remember me according to your love
   and for the sake of your goodness, O + LORD.
7 Gracious and upright is the / LORD;
   therefore he teaches sinners in his / way.
8 He guides the humble in doing ^ right
   and teaches his way to the ^ lowly.
9 All the paths of the LORD are love and . faithfulness
   to those who keep his covenant and his . testimonies.
10 \For your Name's sake O \ LORD,
   forgive my \ sin, for it is \ great.
11 **Who are they who fear the | LORD?**
   he will teach them the way that they should | choose.
12 They shall dwell in pros+perity,
   and their offspring shall inherit the + land.
13 The LORD is a friend to those who / fear him
   and will show them his / covenant.
14 My eyes are ever looking to the ^ LORD,
   for he shall pluck my feet out of the ^ net.
15 Turn to me and have . pity on me,
   for I am left alone and in . misery.

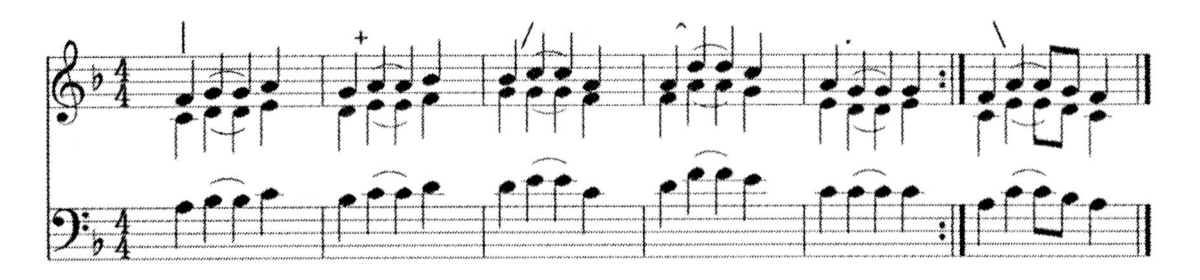

16 **The sorrows of my heart have in | creased;**
   bring me out of my | troubles.
17 Look upon my adversity and + misery
   and forgive me all my + sin.
18 Look upon my enemies, for they are / many,
   and they bear a violent hatred a/gainst me.
19 Protect my life and de^liver me;
   let me not be put to shame for I have ^ trusted in you.
20 Let integrity and uprightness pre.serve me,
   for my hope has been in . you.
21 \Deliver Israel, O \ God,
   out of \ all his \ troubles.

Walking Simply: Commentary To Psalm 26

KI-.aNIY B:THUMMIY HÁLAKHTI

v.1 For I have walked with integrity(*). Forms of the word HÁLAKH are rendered here as *walk*. Walking in Hebrew means living, the way you live your life.

I remember from my first Christian community the way people talked about their Christian walk or spiritual journey. I learned that no one is born a Christian, although some friends refer to themselves as "cradle-born" Episcopalians. I used to wonder how they were born in a cradle! Christianity is not an identity but a way. Christian life is a walk, always in process. Sometimes this is overdone. Perhaps we talk a little too much about our spiritual journeys. Perhaps we think too hard about our personal histories and look too hard for spiritual experiences and turning points.

My Jewish experience was different. I was Jewish because I was born Jewish, period. I might choose to become "religious" or "a good Jew," or I might not. I don't remember much discussion about a "Jewish walk." For the Jewish community of my childhood, survival and continuity were major issues; spiritual journeys were not.

Here in Psalm 26 we are all back to walking. This is an unusual kind of walk, for I never actually go anywhere. Walking itself is the whole point of the walk. What matters is how I walk, and whom I follow. And so the writer says in v. 1, "I have walked with integrity (simplicity, innocence, wholeness), and I have trusted in the LORD." (Therefore), "I will not falter." And in v. 4, "I have walked in your faithfulness." Not in "faith" or "my faith," but rather "in your faithfulness." That is, I have trusted in you, LORD, and I have walked confident in your steadiness, constancy, reliability.

This is not a walk where I will get better and better or go higher and higher. If anything I may be going round and round. It is a walk of surrender. The longer I walk this walk, the less I try to decide where I should be going. I learn to give up control and take direction. I'm learning to simplify my life and appreciate my blessings. I'm learning that I don't know better than everyone else. I also forget this daily and learn it again. I'm not getting better or wiser. I will probably never be "enlightened" and I have doubts whether I will even "grow up."

I walk simply, trusting that you are reliable. I walk in simplicity, learning to be grateful. Sometimes I recall what Jesus said to Peter: "When you were younger, you girded yourself and walked where you wished; but when you are old, you will stretch out your hands, and another will gird you and carry you where you do not wish" (John 21:18, NKJ). That scares me, of course, but surrender is surrender. Keep walking.

<u>Suggestions</u>: Form a large circle and read this psalm as walking meditation. Let each (`) represent a footstep. Start each line on the left foot, and maintain a slow but steady rhythm. Walk in balance, with smooth, flowing steps, the left side balancing the right. Feel yourself walking without thoughts, without that consciousness of self. Practice this walk in daily life as well. This will be one of your informal meditations: a human breathing walking in simplicity, in silence.

Psalm 26 (BCP), modified*

Tone: **KINNOR (1)**

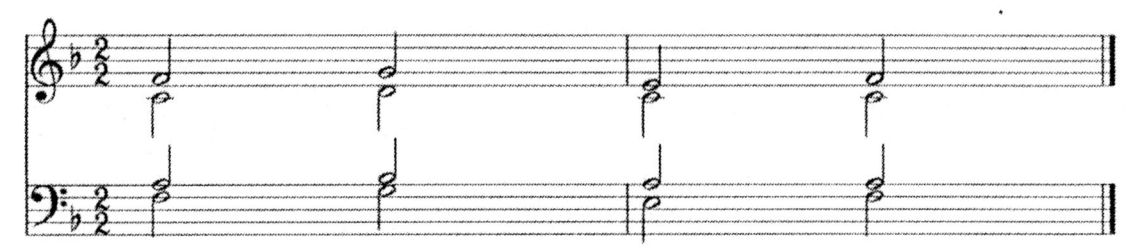

1 **Give jùdgment for me, O LÒRD, for I have wàlked with in | tègrity;`` (*)**
   ànd I have trùsted in the LÒRD, I will not | fàlter. ```
2 Tèst me, O LÒRD, and try` me; `
   exàmine my hèart and my mìnd. `
3 For your lòve is befòre my èyes; `
   and I have wàlked in your fàithfulness. `` (*)
4 Ì have not sàt with the wòrthless, `
   nòr do I consòrt with the decèitful. `
5 I have hàted the còmpany of èvildoers; `
   I will nòt sit dòwn with the wìcked. `
6 I will wàsh my hands in ìnnocence, O LÒRD, `
   that I may gò in procèssion round your àltar, `
7 Singing alòud a sòng of thanksgìving `
   and recòunting all your wònderful dèeds. `
8 LÒRD, I love the hòuse in which you dwèll `
   and the plàce where your glòry abìdes. `
9 Do not swèep me awày with sìnners, `
   nor my life with those who thìrst for blòod, `
10 Whose hànds are full of èvil plòts, `
   and their rìght hand fùll of brìbes. `
11 **As for mè, I will wàlk with in | tègrity. ` (*)**
   redèem me, O LÒRD, and have | pìty on mè. ``
12 My fòot stands on lèvel gròund; `
   in the full assèmbly I will blèss the LÒRD. `

Seek My Face: Commentary To Psalm 27

YHWH .ORIY W:YISH"IY MIMMIY .IYRÁ.

v.1 The LORD is my light and my salvation;
whom then shall I fear?

A lady was consulting me for anxiety, and I recommended a simple exercise to her. It consists of repeating a little phrase, like "I am relaxed," with passive attention. You inhale, thinking "I am... " and you exhale thinking "relaxed." You do this over and over, without concentration or effort. "I am... relaxed... I am... relaxed... I am... relaxed."

It is a simple technique from a system called autogenic training. This lady, who had many problems, an unhappy marriage, but a teachable heart, went home and practiced the exercise. As she did so, she "heard a voice" deep within herself: "Psalm 27, Psalm 27." Feeling puzzled what this might mean, she went to her Bible and found these words:

The LORD is my light and my salvation;
whom then shall I fear?

I don't know what may have happened to this lady over the years, but her story affected me profoundly. God was teaching me through her experience. A teaching about anxiety. Can anyone actually say, "Whom then shall I fear?" Can anyone actually say, "Though an army should encamp against me, yet my heart shall not be afraid"? Perhaps, but not by repeating "I am... relaxed."

Frank Herbert, in his *Dune* books, often refers to something called the Litany against Fear. The adepts of the *Bene Gesserit* Order learned it in their training, and repeated it, like a mental prayer, when they were in danger. I loved his books, but I never found the Litany believable. Even his characters did not seem to find it convincing, though they repeated it stoically as terror closed in on them.

Some Christians use 2 Timothy 1:7 as their Litany against Fear: "For God has not given us a spirit of fear, but of power and of love and of a sound mind" (NKJ). They use it, but they still suffer with anxiety. They find they cannot control anxiety with Scripture. It ought to work, it seems to, but then it doesn't. If it seems to help at first, it is soon making things worse.

.A#ATH SHÁ.ALTI MÉ.ETH YHWH   .OTHÁH' .aVAQQÉSH

v.5 One thing have I asked of the LORD;
one thing I seek;
 that I may dwell in the house of the LORD
 all the days of my life.

Not to be calm or safe or cured, not to be mature or fulfilled; not to be anything at all, but to live with God, where God lives, in his house. I will no longer ask to be relaxed... relaxed... but to be sent where he needs me and go where he tells me.

L:KHÁ .ÁMAR LIBBIY BAQQ:SHUW PHÁNAY .ETH-PÁNEYKHÁ YHWH .aVAQQÉSH

v.11 You speak in my heart and say, "Seek my face."
Your face, O LORD, will I seek.

Literally, my heart has spoken for you, in your Name as it were, saying, "Seek my face, my presence." Not "Try to calm down," or, "Just relax," but this: Seek my face.

Seek me! And I respond to him, saying, "Your face, O LORD, I will begin to seek." I will not try to relax. I will not constrict my breathing to keep calm. I will seek his face and do what needs to be done.

Slowly I learned there is no magic against anxiety. There is no *mantra* nor Scripture that will overcome all fear. So I rarely teach my patients little exercises to cope with anxiety. I seldom if ever teach them to relax. I enjoyed those methods, and they worked—for a little while. But they didn't help my patients (or myself) to grow up and deal with life. These methods sounded good, but they were based on a delusion: the idea of controlling my self or my anxiety. *Self-control* is quite different. It is a fruit of the Spirit, life under higher direction. Now I am more likely to say, "Anxiety is your best friend." Anxiety is a signal that we are missing the point, that life does not belong to us. We are not in control.

So the writer is not asking for help with anxiety. He seeks but one thing: God. The face, the presence of God. Nothing else. This is what I call radical insecurity. The security of having no security at all. Only God is in control. The humorist James Thurber once wrote, "There is no safety in numbers, or in anything else!"* The answer to anxiety is to give up trying to be safe. Realize there is no escape, no control. Not even prayer. Listen to the little voice in your heart: Seek my face! Seek me! I am indebted to Ogilvie** for this insight. See also 91, 142.

QAWWÉH .EL-YHWH #aZAQ
v.18 Wait for the LORD and be strong.

Suggestions: Sing to the Tone "ÁSOR (*ten-string*). Sing v.18 with exquisite slowness, like 13:1-2. Wait for the LORD and be strong. Wait. Wait. Wait. When you are anxious, clear your thoughts and listen, and wait for instruction.

The suggestions in this book are not relaxation techniques or self-hypnosis. The practice of silence is based on the recognition that my thoughts, even my best thoughts, can only guide me to limited answers. It is only in stepping outside my thoughts, my intellect, even my faith (if I think of it as *my* faith), that I can begin to listen to God, who has all answers. It is my nature to think and reason, thought following thought and emotion following emotion. It is a gift to be able to step outside my thoughts, again and again, and listen to the source of all wisdom. To seek your face.

Fables for Our Time and Famous Poems Illustrated. HarperCollins, New York. Copyright 1940 James Thurber, Copyright 1968 Rosemary A. Thurber. From "The Fairly Intelligent Fly," p,13.
**Lloyd John Ogilvie: *Falling into Greatness*, Guideposts, Carmel, New York, 1984, pp. 59-72.

Psalm 27 (BCP)

Tone: "ÁSOR

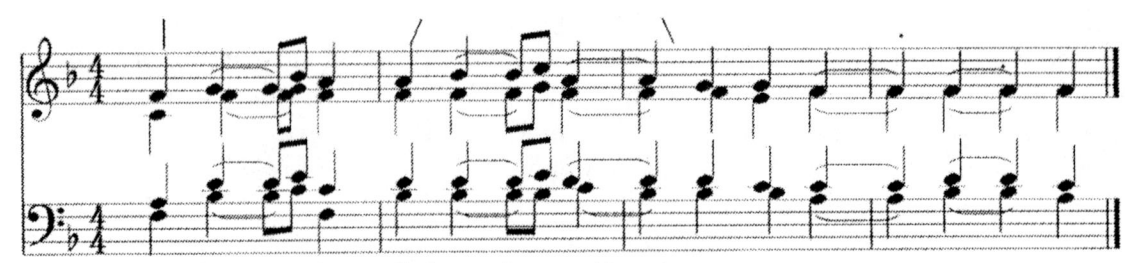

1 **The LORD is my light and my sal | vation;**
   | whom then shall I | fear?
   the LORD is the strength of my / life;
   of / whom then shall I be a/fraid?

2 \When evildoers came upon me to eat up my \ flesh,
   it was they, my foes and my adversaries who stumbled and \ fell.

3 Though an army should encamp a.gainst me,
   yet my heart shall . not be afraid;

4 And though war should rise up a.gainst me,
   yet will I put my . trust in him.

5 **One thing have I asked of the | LORD;**
   one | thing I | seek;
   that I may dwell in the house of the / LORD
   all the / days of my / life;

6 \To behold the fair beauty of the \ LORD
   and to seek him in his \ temple.

7 For in the day of trouble he shall keep me safe in his . shelter;
   he shall hide me in the secrecy of his dwelling
   and set me high upon a . rock.

8 **Even now he lifts up my | head**
   above my | enemies round a | bout me.

9 Therefore I will offer in his dwelling an oblation
   with sounds of great / gladness;
   I will / sing and make music to the / LORD.

10 \Hearken to my voice, O LORD, when I \ call;
   have mercy on me and \ answer me.

11 **You speak in my heart and say, "Seek my | face."**
   Your | face, LORD, will I | seek.

12 Hide not your / face from me,
   nor turn away your / servant in dis/pleasure.

13 \You have been my helper; cast me not \ away;
   do not forsake me, O God of my sal\vation.

14 Though my father and mother for.sake me,
   the LORD will sus.tain me.

15 **Show me your way, O | LORD;**
   lead me on a level | path, because of my | enemies.

16 Deliver me not into the hand of my / adversaries,
    for false witnesses have risen up a/gainst me,
    and also those who speak / malice.
17 \ What if I had not believed
    that I should see the goodness of the \ LORD
    in the land of the \ living!
                    [S l o w l y]
18 O tarry and await the LORD's . pleasure;
    be strong, and he shall comfort your heart;
    wait patiently for the . LORD.

The Voice Of My Prayer: Commentary To Psalm 28

An ordinary sinner am I, going down with millions of others to the Bottomless Pit. Going down with the cheerfully dishonest

v.3 who speak peace with their neighbors (or friends),
while evil (strife, trouble) is in their hearts. Who cheerfully say, "I'll be honest with you," convincing themselves even as they speak. Who, if you question them, grow sullen: "Are you calling me a liar?" They control fate with their words, they believe, even as they fall to oblivion. I am no better than they. I am falling along with them. Do not sweep me away to oblivion with them.

v.2 Hear the voice of my prayer when I cry out to you,
when I lift up my hands to your holy of holies. I turn from the horizontal (where I can do nothing to help myself) to the vertical, to you. I lift up my hands to you, more than a gesture. As a little child lifts up the arms to be held. Lift me up, O LORD, from my level to yours. Hold me. Be my refuge.

v.7 Blessed is the LORD!
for he has heard the voice of my prayer.
How do I know that my prayers have been answered? Mostly there are no voices or visions. Miracles happen, but not every time. Sometimes I feel at peace after prayer, sometimes not. Sometimes nothing at all seems to happen—no results, no answers, no inner peace. And yet I know, because

v.8b my heart has trusted in him, and I have been helped.
I know to the extent I have trusted you. I have given up control of the outcome. I really don't know how you will answer this one. I do not have to tell you what to do or how to do it. I am but a YOR:DI-VOR (*one going down to the Pit*) with millions of others. I lift up my hands to you in worship, in helplessness. I have trusted you to know what I need. Having trusted you, I know you have heard me.

UMISSHIRIY .aHODENNU

v.9b and from my song I begin to praise him. From my inner music, my inner defining rhythm, my way of thinking and moving. Similar, perhaps, to what Professor Clynes* calls the "inner pulse" of music. Every living thing has its "song"; we see it in the spontaneous joy of babies and young animals. My own song is not always so uplifting. All too often my song is a song of complaint and fretful worry; now, listening to God, I can begin to learn a *new song*, as in 33, 96, 98.

<u>Suggestions</u>: Extend arms in the praise gesture, vv. 2a and 7a; raise them heavenward at 2b and 7b. Cross them protectively in front of the body, hands closed, at v. 8 ("the LORD is my strength"), fold them in the heart gesture at "my heart trusts."

---
*Manfred Clynes: *Sentics: the Touch of the Emotions*, Doubleday, 1977.

Psalm 28 (BCP)

Tone: GITTITH

1 O LORD, I call to you;
   my Rock, do not be deaf to my cry; *
   lest, if you do not hear me,
   I become like those who go down to the Pit.
2 **Hear the voice of my prayer when I cry | out to you,**
   when I lift up my hands to your holy of | holies.
3 Do not snatch me away with the wicked or with the evildoers, *
   who speak peaceably with their neighbors,
   while strife is in their hearts.
4 Repay them according to their deeds, *
   and according to the wickedness of their actions.
5 According to the work of their hands repay them, *
   and give them their just deserts.
6 They have no understanding of the LORD's doings,
   nor of the works of his hands; *
   therefore he will break them down and not build them up.
7 **Blessed is the | LORD!**
   for he has heard the voice of my | prayer.
8 \The LORD is my strength and my \ shield;
   my heart trusts in him, and I have been \ helped.
9 /Therefore my heart / dances for joy,
   /and in my song will I / praise him.
10 The LORD is the strength of his people, *
    a safe refuge for his anointed.
11 Save your people and bless your inheritance; *
    shepherd them and carry them for ever.

Voice Upon The Waters: Commentary To Psalm 29

QOL YHWH "AL-HA<u>MÁ</u>YiM

v.3 The voice of the LORD (is) upon the waters:

the God of glory thunders:

the LORD (is) upon many waters!

The waters — power and storm. Compare 93. Creation begins with the waters. Raging, immeasurable waters are divided. Disorderly waters become organized waters — in clouds, in crystals, in my cells, in my veins. What once seemed formless and meaningless is revealed as intelligent, self-organizing complexity. Where once we saw mere disorder now we see chaos, orderly yet never predictable.

A voice calls forth that intelligence. A voice reaches deep into Nothing and calls out chaos. A voice says, "Let there be light!" and it is good. It is the voice we pray to, the voice we hear in the silence. It is the voice we call God.

We trivialize that voice. We talk as if we understood, as if we invented it. Saying, for example, "We believe in a God who... " as though the kind of God we believe in showed how clever we are. Saying, for example, that God is a good God, or a need-meeting God; as if to improve upon that God of mystery. Telling what God will do or never do, and whose prayer God will not hear.

I trivialize that voice when I condemn anyone else's religion. When I feel the slightest bit better, more "saved," than another. When I take the Word of God in a literal, mechanical way; when I claim to know exactly what it means; when I teach that there is only one interpretation. When I persecute anyone in the name of Christ.

The voice of the LORD is upon the waters, calling into being the world. It is the voice that causes to be. It is I Am. It is YHWH — unpronounceable. It is Y<u>ÉSHU</u>a" — Jesus, the humble "son of man." Do not explain. Do not explain. Do not explain.

The psalm has a primitive quality, suggesting the most ancient layers of Hebrew poetry. The powerful rhythmic beat comes through even in translation. It is an experience of primitive worship, not refined, intellectual or pious. The message is coded in the form: "Give unto the LORD," repeated over and over.

<u>Note</u>: (*) Verse 6 is modified based on BCP.

<u>Suggestions</u>: Stand. Sing to the movement Standing Drum (see Appendix). Bow deeply from the waist on v.2 ("worship the LORD"). Each ` is a beat of the drum. Pause at the dash (—). There are many ways to sing this psalm in groups. One way is to divide it between leader and chorus. Let the leader sing the boldface lines, the chorus all the rest. Repeat the psalm if you wish, letting different groups sing. Elaborate the simple movement as you are led by the Spirit. Let this be your worship.

Psalm 29 KJV)

Tone: #a3O3:ROTH

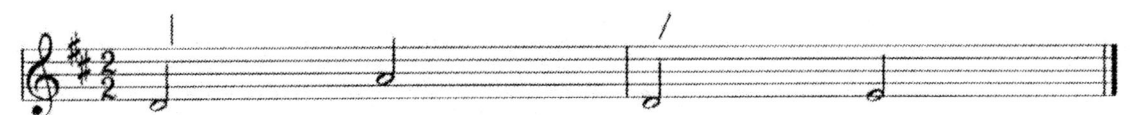

1 ` ` ` ` **Gìve unto the LÒRD, O ye | mìghty,** `
  gìve unto the LÒRD glòry and | strèngth. `
2 /Gìve unto the LÒRD the glory dùe unto his / nàme; `
  wòrship the LÒRD in the beaùty of / hòliness. —

3 **The vòice of the LÒRD is upon the | wàters:** `
  the Gòd of glòry | thùndereth: `
  /the LÒRD is upòn many / wàters. —

4 **The vòice of the LÒRD ìs | pòwerful;** `
  the vòice of the LÒRD is full of | màjesty. `

5 /The vòice of the LÒRD brèaketh the / cèdars; `
  yea, the LÒRD brèaketh the cèdars of / Lèbanon. —

6 **He maketh Lèbanon to skìp like a | càlf;** `
  /and Sìrion like a yòung wild / òx. — (*)

7 **The vòice of the LÒRD divideth the | flàmes of fìre.** `

8 **The vòice of the LÒRD shàketh the | wìlderness;** `
  /the LÒRD shàketh the wìlderness of / Kàdesh. --

9 **The vòice of the LÒRD maketh the | hìnds tò càlve;** `
  and discòvereth the | fòrests: `
  /and in his tèmple doth èveryone spèak of his / glòry. —

10 **The LÒRD sìtteth upon the | flòod;** `
  /yea, the LÒRD sitteth Kìng for / èver. `

11 **The LÒRD will give strèngth unto his | pèople;** `
  /the LÒRD will bless his pèople with / pèace. `

Wailing Into Dancing: Commentary To Psalm 30

A psalm about healing. Like many of the psalms it is a journey—a transforming process. A human breathing is changed from one state of being to another.

v.1 I will exalt you, LORD,
because you have lifted me up.

You have drawn me up like water from a well. You have drawn up my life from the depths. You bring out what is latent but unrecognized within me, and you have not made my "enemies" joyful over me. You do not let me sink into complete degradation. The biblical concept of healing is not so much the curing of disease as the healing, making whole, of persons.

YHWH .eLOHÁY SHIW<u>WA</u>"TI .ÉL<u>E</u>YKHÁ WATIRPÁ.ÉNI

v.2 O LORD my God, I have cried out to you,

and you begin to heal me. That is, you begin to knit me together, from a root that means to sew. You stitch me back together or glue me back together. You do so much more than eradicate viruses or replace failing organs. You make me whole.

YHWH HE"eL<u>I</u>THÁ MIN-SH.OL NAPHSHIY

v.3 LORD, you have lifted up my soul from SH.OL (*Sheol*, the Pit). I have cried and now you begin to heal me. You have raised up my soul (breath, breathing, life) from SH.OL (*Sheol*, the Pit), and restored her to me. In my illness she seemed to fall silent; I was desperately alone. My inner Other was dying, and the inner conversation was stilled. There was no inner voice to encourage or gently laugh at me, only a harsh echo. And as that inner relationship went silent, I could relate to no one else. Even my marriage was in trouble.

So you brought up my soul from SH.OL—that "subterranean place, full of thick darkness," as Gesenius* explains, "in which the shades of the dead are gathered together," from a root that means to ask, "from the idea of its asking for, demanding all, without distinction." From that devouring emptiness, whatever it may be, you brought me up. From death, from hopelessness, from whatever hopeless condition I might have had. The name of the disease is not important.

v.6 At evening weeping comes to spend the night,
but at morning (a shout of) joy!

The night was horrible, the suffering intense, but in the morning the fever broke, the pain was better, the depression lifted, the vomiting stopped. In the morning hormones surge, the patient rallies, What a poignant expression here: weeping moves in for the night, like an unwelcome guest, but we never realize when she moves out. Suddenly, toward morning, I find myself joyful.

v.7 And I (But as for me), I said in my security,
"I will not be moved (shaken, toppled) to eternity."

In my momentary and illusory feeling of security I said—and more foolish words have never been spoken. When I felt good I became proud and overconfident. I thought I would always feel good, and I went around giving advice to others. I was convinced that "me and God" had come up with the answer to my illness. Then I would tell people, "You should do what I did," or, "You should read this book I read," or, "You just need to have faith. That's what helped me." A psychiatrist might say I had a flight into health. I was reluctant to look inward and face the real issues. A false sense of recovery allowed me to flee from treatment.

With God it is so easy to do this. Now I'm saved, now I'm spirit-filled, now I have been healed by Great Evangelist, now I have turned it all over to Jesus, now it's "me and God" and I just have to hold on to my healing. And so, in the name of God, I am back in control. I can do it myself.

HISTARTÁ PHÁNEYKHÁ   HÁYITHI NIVHÁL

v.8 You have hidden your face (presence),
I have become terrified (confounded, shaking).

Soon the flight into health has crashed. My miracle seems to have collapsed. I experience a full-blown relapse, maybe worse than before. I feel more discouraged than ever. And so I come back to God, fearful and shaken. I begin to cry and beg; now I know I don't have the answers. "Will the dust praise you?" I ask. As death becomes a real possibility, I am pleading with God for my life. Pathetically I try to convince him, not knowing he has already healed me.

v.12 He has turned my wailing (mourning, beating the breast) into a dance for me. I am going to live! My grief-stricken wailing and breast-beating has turned into dancing. Joy bubbles up within me; I begin to skip and jump around. I dance and this dance is my praise. I'm no authority now, and I have no advice for your case. I just feel so much better that I have to dance and praise God.

A journey of healing, from the edge of the grave to dancing and singing. Details unknown. We are not told of the physician's work, of medicines or surgeries, of prayers, or even of Great Evangelists casting out demons. These things may have happened, and they would have been important. What we are told is that the person had a long, difficult journey, and suffered much, and was transformed. In some way unique to that individual, God knitted the person together and made him or her whole.

<u>Suggestions</u>: Sing joyfully to the movement Twirling Dance (see Appendix).

There is no greater obstacle to healing than medical dogmatism, the conviction that one knows exactly what needs to be done. When in need of healing, begin with the practice of silence. Ask God for direction. Healing does not always depend upon drugs, upon surgery, or even upon prayer. Often it depends precisely on those things, but not in the way you would have chosen. Be humble and let God choose how to heal you. As physician, pray constantly for direction.

---

*H.W.F. Gesenius: *Gesenius' Hebrew-Chaldee Lexicon to the Old Testament Scriptures* (Translated by Samuel Prideaux Tregelles), Baker Book House, Grand Rapids, MI, 1979, p. 798.

Psalm 30 (BCP)

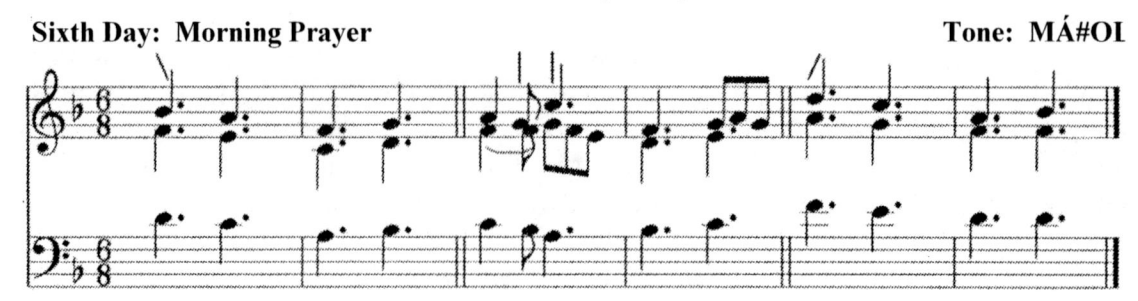

Sixth Day: Morning Prayer   Tone: MÁ#OI

1 \I will exalt you, O LORD,
   because you have lifted me \ up
   and have not let my enemies triumph \ over me.

2 **O LORD my | God, I cried | out to you,**
   and you restored me to | health.

3 \You brought me up, O LORD, from the \ dead;
   you restored my life as I was going \ down to the grave.

4 /Sing to the LORD, you / servants of his;
   give thanks for the remembrance of his / holiness.

5 \For his wrath endures but the twinkling of an \ eye,
   his favor for a \ lifetime.

6 **Weeping may | spend the | night,**
   but joy comes in the | morning.

7 \While I felt secure, I said,
   "I shall \ never be disturbed.
   You LORD, with your favor, made me as strong
   as the \ mountains."

8 /Then you hid your / face,
   and I was filled with / fear.

9 \I cried to you, O \ LORD;
   I pleaded with the LORD, \ saying,

10 / "What profit is there in my blood, if I go down to the / Pit?
   will the dust praise you or declare your / faithfulness?

11 \Hear, O LORD, and have \ mercy upon me;
   O LORD, be my \ helper."

12 **You have turned my | wailing into | dancing;**
   you have put off my | sack-cloth
   and clothed me with | joy.

13 \Therefore my heart \ sings to you
   without \ ceasing.
   O | LORD my | God,
   I will give you thanks for | ever.

Into Your Hands: Commentary To Psalm 31

B:YÁD:KHÁ .APHQIYD RU#IY

v.5 Into your hands I commend my spirit (Luke 23:46, NKJ). Into your hands I entrust my (last) breath ... O God of truth. I entrust my life to you for safekeeping, for you are unchanging and reliable. The word RUa# means breath, wind, or spirit. My spirit is not a permanent part of me, but a gift, like a breath of air, renewed minute by minute.

B:YÁD:KHÁ "ITHOTHAY

v.15 In your hands (are) my times. The word "ÉTH means a time; a moment or season; like the Greek *kairos*, the proper time for something. It is not an abstract concept of time as process. My life is made up of breaths and moments, entrusted into your hand.

When I reflect on my experience I realize it really is but breaths and moments. I like to think of my life as a smoothly flowing process. But when I think back over a day, I remember bits and pieces. I had experiences, then I lost myself re-living those experiences. I sneezed and lost my train of thought. I was anxious or irritable. I made lists of things to do, or drank water or ate something. I answered the telephone and forgot what I was thinking about. I felt bad about things I said earlier. Suddenly the day was over. Then, when you asked me about my day, I could only talk about moments.

My life is made up of breaths. Twenty times a minute I inhale the good air and breathe it out. I cannot save it for later. I just breathe it in and breathe it out. How good it is to take a breath like this. How many more will I have? I take a breath and let it out. Will I have another?

Breaths and moments, entrusted into your hand. What else can I do? I cannot even keep track of my moments; how can I be trusted with my breaths? I could try to stay in control, but I choose to turn over to you, LORD. I surrender these things into your hand. Then of course I take them back again. Over and over.

v.24 Be strong and let your heart take courage,
all you who wait for the LORD.

Suggestions: In meditation, notice your breaths and your moments. Experience each moment as it comes, not thinking of the moment to come or the moment that has passed. Do this in daily life as well, as often as you can. Live the moment now, in silence, then let it go. Breathe slowly.

Follow the spiritual path moment by moment. You will wander off the path hundreds and thousands of times, yet you can start anew at any and every moment. When you find yourself in turmoil, caught up in thoughts and emotions, look at the clock! Come back from the vortex to the moment. What time is it *now*?

Verse 24 may be read s l o w l y, like 27:18.

Psalm 31 (BCP)

Tone: SHÁRIM

1 **In you, O LORD, have I taken | refuge;**
   let me never be put to | shame;
   /deliver me in your / righteousness.
2 Incline your ear to me; *
   make haste to deliver me.
3 Be my strong rock, a castle to keep me safe,
   for you are my crag and my stronghold; *
   for the sake of your Name, lead me and guide me.
4 Take me out of the net that they have secretly set for me, *
   for you are my tower of strength.
5 **Into your hands I commend my | spirit,**
   for you have re|deemed me,
   /O LORD, O / God of truth.
6 I hate those who cling to worthless idols, *
   and I put my trust in the LORD.
7 I will rejoice and be glad because of your mercy; *
   for you have seen my affliction; you know my distress.
8 You have not shut me up in the power of the enemy; *
   you have set my feet in an open place.
9 Have mercy on me, O LORD, for I am in trouble; *
   my eye is consumed with sorrow, and also my throat and my belly.
10 For my life is wasted with grief,
   and my years with sighing; *
   my strength fails me because of affliction,
   and my bones are consumed.
11 I have become a reproach to all my enemies and even to my neighbors,
   a dismay to those of my acquaintance; *
   when they see me in the street they avoid me.
12 I am forgotten like a dead man, out of mind; *
   I am as useless as a broken pot.
13 For I have heard the whispering of the crowd; fear is all around; *
   they put their heads together against me;
   they plot to take my life.
14 But as for me, I have trusted in you, O LORD. *
   I have said, "You are my God.

15 **My times are in your | hand;**
   rescue me from the hand of my | enemies,
   /and from those who / persecute me.
16 Make your face to shine upon your servant, *
   and in your loving-kindness save me."
17 **LORD, let me not be ashamed for having | called upon you;**
   rather, let the wicked be put to | shame;
   /let them be / silent in the grave.
18 Let the lying lips be silenced which speak against
      the righteous, *
   haughtily, disdainfully, and with contempt.
19 How great is your goodness, O LORD!
      which you have laid up for those who fear you; *
   which you have done in the sight of all
      for those who put their trust in you.
20 You hide them in the covert of your presence from those who slander them; *
   you keep them in your shelter from the strife of tongues.
21 Blessed be the LORD! *
   for he has shown me the wonders of his love in a besieged city.
22 Yet I said in my alarm,
      "I have been cut off from the sight of your eyes." *
   Nevertheless, you heard the sound of my entreaty
      when I cried out to you.
23 Love the LORD, all you who worship him; *
   the LORD protects the faithful,
   but repays to the full those who act haughtily.

[S l o w l y]
24 Be strong and let your heart take courage, *
   all you who wait for the LORD.

A Dance Of Forgiveness: Commentary To Psalm 32

.ASHREY N:SUY-PESHA" K:SUY #atÁ.ÁH

v.1 Happy transgression-lifted, sin-covered up!

The Hebrew is compact (and ambiguous) as classical Chinese. Real happiness is called "transgression-lifted." Real happiness is when my deliberate misbehavior is somehow lifted from me. Lifted up off me, into the vertical dimension, where God can perhaps make something good of it. Real happiness is called "sin-covered up." Covered by punishment less than I deserve. Covered by grace. Covered because God considers it no longer. When my sin, my innate tendency to fly off the mark and miss the point is covered, somehow made right.

v.2 Happy the human (whom) the LORD does not think guilty;
and there is not in his spirit deceit.

Real happiness is not when I look clean, but when the LORD considers me clean. When God does not find any guilt in me. When in my spirit (breath) there is no deceit. When I don't breathe falsehood because I have stopped pretending.

v.3 When I kept silent, my bones wasted away,
while I groaned (or, in my groaning) all day long.

Real misery is trying to look good. It is hoping that if I keep my mouth shut and act nice, I will look good. I might impress some casual strangers, but my family is not fooled and God is certainly not fooled. Trying to look good is a fatal malady. Even my bones are crumbling within me. [Silence...].

v.5 Then I acknowledged my sin to you.

Real happiness is giving up the pretense and asking God to forgive me. It is Step One* of Alcoholics Anonymous: "We admitted we were powerless over alcohol — that our lives had become unmanageable." That is what I did as a sinner. I admitted that I was powerless over sin, that my life was a shambles. And you, you lifted up, lifted off me, the guilt of my sin. [Silence...].

Looking good, I sometimes think, is the Christian disease: the tight smile, the exaggerated politeness, the pretense that one never gets angry, the "virtuous" preacher who is never allowed to complain or be tired. And God says here, Don't try to look good any more. Give up your stubborn ways. Be teachable, and I will teach you and guide you. "I will guide you with my eye," he says, in that intimate closeness of teacher and student, where the tiniest flick of an eye will show you where to go. Then you will "be glad ... rejoice ... shout for joy."

Suggestions: Sing to the Tone MÁ#OL (*dance*). Practice the awareness of powerlessness in all situations. You are not in control.

Alcoholics Anonymous, p. 59 (with permission). Obtain and study this book, what A. A. members call "The Big Book" (Alcoholics Anonymous World Services, Inc., New York City, 1976).

Psalm 32 (BCP)

Sixth Day: Evening Prayer

Tone: MÁ#OL

1 \Happy are they whose transgressions are for\given,
   and whose sin is put a\way!
2 \Happy are they to whom the LORD imputes no \ guilt,
   and in whose spirit there is no \ guile!
3 /While I held my tongue, my bones / withered away,
   because of my groaning all day / long.
4 \For your hand was heavy upon me day and \ night;
   my moisture was dried up as in the heat of \ summer.
        [Silence...]
5 **Then I | acknowledged my | sin to you,**
   and did not conceal my | guilt.
6 \I said, "I will confess my transgressions to the \ LORD."
   Then you forgave me the guilt of my \ sin.
        [Silence...]
7 \Therefore all the faithful will make their \ prayers to you
   in time of \ trouble;
   when the great | waters | overflow,
   they shall not | reach them.
8 \You are my hiding place;
   you preserve me from \ trouble;
   you surround me with shouts of \ deliverance.
        [Silence...]
9 \ "I will instruct you and teach you in the way that you
   should \ go;
   I will guide you with my \ eye.
10 **Do not be like | horse and | mule,**
   which have no under|standing;
   who must be fitted with | bit and | bridle,
   or else they will not stay | near you."
11 \Great are the tribulations of the \ wicked;
   but mercy embraces those who \ trust in the LORD.
12 \Be glad, you righteous, and rejoice in the \ LORD;
   shout for joy, all who are \ true of heart.

Learning To Sing A New Song: Commentary To Psalm 33

RAN:NUW 3ADDIQIM BAYHWH LAY:SHÁRIM NÁ.WÁH T:HILLÁH
v.1 Rejoice, you righteous, in the LORD;
it is good for the just to sing praises.

Praise is NÁ.WÁH (*fitting*) for the righteous. Praise sits well on them, from a root meaning rest or quietness. For someone like me, praise must be learned. It was a novel idea for me. Strange at first, I soon find it fits me well; it rests comfortably on me and becomes my greatest delight.

v.2 Praise the LORD with the harp;
play to him upon the psaltery and lyre.

Praise him with different instruments—not just musical instruments, but with all talents and faculties, with every state of mind, every emotion. Praise him with anger, hate, grief, love, joy. Praise him with jokes and with tears.

SHIYRU LO SHIR #ÁDÁSH
v.3 Sing to him a new song.

My old song, my inner world as I experience it, is surprisingly barren. The inner world of my thoughts is not a world of great ideas, but of trivial habits. Phrases and sentences, begun, broken off and repeated, over and over. Most of it complaint and outrage, whining, self-pity and blaming. And silly songs, jingles I made up twenty years ago. Inane jokes about men who walk into bars with ducks under their arms. Bits of today's conversations, as they were and as they should have been. Sometimes a thought stirs up emotion; instantly I'm re-living a scene, gesturing and talking under my breath. I comment on the world situation, the same comments I have made for years, repeated and repeated.

How glad I am that you cannot hear my old song, that my old song is not broadcast on the radio, or printed on your fax machine. Yet I know it is not unique. It is simply the inner world of a sinner, a human breathing. It is the random activity of brain cells firing at will. One thought leads to another thought; emotion leads to emotion. And the human breathing goes where it is taken and says, "I decided to go there."

New song means a new way of thinking. Thoughts of praise, of gratitude, of being satisfied. Thoughts of *How good!* and *How beautiful!* An inner world that is calmer and more balanced. A way of thinking that waits before acting. As I begin to have glimpses of this *new song*, I find it refreshing and delightful. I begin to understand things I never understood and see things I never noticed. I begin to have a grasp of situations I never had before. My inner world is quieter now, my thoughts are fewer, and yet I act more effectively. It is receptive thinking, more like listening than talking. It is learning to listen to God.

New song is a new state of consciousness, a state of novelty and freshness. Seeing things new as though I had never seen them before. A state of spontaneity. Speaking without rehearsal. Not knowing what I will say, but trusting I will say the right thing.

The old songs, the silly songs and the depressing songs will always be part of me. Old thoughts can never be erased. Old thoughts—of blame, rage, self-pity, dreams of fame and fortune, self-improvement — are part of me forever, indelible. But a new thought, a *new song*, is always possible. I can sing a new song now, with my next breath. Do not try to forget the old songs, but start a new song, a new thought, ask a new question, now.

Old thoughts, repeated like *mantras*, make us old. Old songs, old slogans drag us to war and death. New songs renew, set free. Ever so slightly recast, they renew our powers. This reflects a profound biologic law. The healthy heart varies its rhythm, ever so slightly, with every beat. It is the old heart, perfectly regular, that signals approaching death. *New song* means life.

v.16 There is no king that can be saved by a mighty army.

Old thoughts have an air of wisdom. Old solutions seem right because we know them. The horse was considered high technology, but still the battle was lost. Old thoughts will never change old enemies, no matter how loudly or often we repeat them. New thoughts may change old battlefields. New song is praise.

Note: With twenty-two verses of equal length, Psalm 33 is considered alphabetic though not acrostic. For further reflection on *new song*, see 40, 96, 98 and others.

Suggestions: Sing to the Tone *Alphabet*. Use the same music for 33 and 34.

Today perform one action of daily life in a new way, a fresh way. Vary it ever so slightly, discover it, watch what happens. Today see one thing differently, as you never quite saw it before. Look at the one you love in a different way. In a tiresome old conversation today, say something new.

Practice this teaching at every opportunity. Practice those tiny steps of growth, from old song to praise, to silence and listening, to *new song*, new ways of thinking.

Remember this teaching in all hopeless and tiresome situations. In marital conflict, where the same words have been said hundreds of times, say something new. Stop and clear your thoughts, all thoughts. Praise God. Be silent. See something old in a new and fresh way. Sing a new song!

Psalm 33 (BCP)

Tone: *Alphabet*

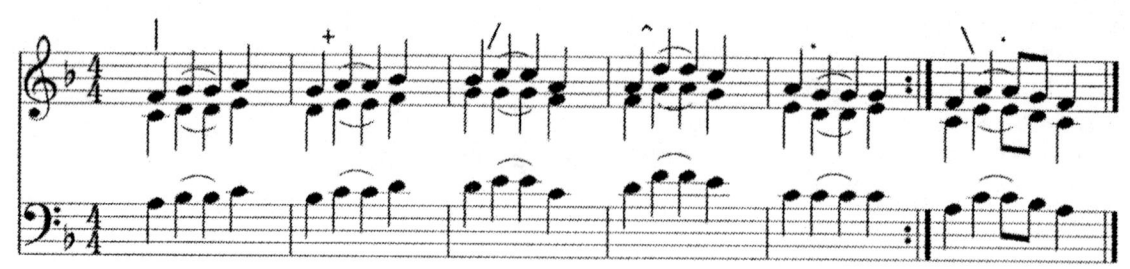

1 **Rejoice in the LORD, you | righteous;**
   it is good for the just to sing | praises.
2 Praise the LORD with the + harp;
   play to him upon the psaltery and + lyre.
3 Sing for him a new / song;
   sound a fanfare with all your skill upon the / trumpet.
4 For the word of the LORD is ^ right,
   and all his works are ^ sure.
5 He loves righteousness and . justice;
   the loving-kindness of the LORD fills the whole . earth.
6 **By the word of the LORD were the | heavens made,**
   by the breath of his mouth all the heavenly | hosts.
7 He gathers up the waters of the ocean as in a + water-skin
   and stores up the depths of the + sea.
8 Let all the earth fear the / LORD;
   let all who dwell in the world stand in / awe of him.
9 For he spoke, and it came to ^ pass;
   he commanded, and it stood ^ fast.
10 The LORD brings the will of the . nations to naught;
   he thwarts the designs of the . peoples.
11 \But the LORD's will stands fast for \ ever,
   and the designs of his \ heart from age to \ age.
12 **Happy is the nation whose god is the | LORD!**
   happy the people he has chosen to be his | own!
13 The LORD looks down from + heaven,
   and beholds all the people in the + world.
14 From where he sits enthroned he turns his / gaze
   on all who dwell on the / earth.
15 He fashions all the ^ hearts of them
   and understands all their ^ works.
16 There is no king that can be saved by a mighty . army;
   a strong man is not delivered by his great . strength.

17 **The horse is a vain hope for de | liverance;**
    for all its strength it cannot | save.
18 Behold, the eye of the LORD is upon those who + fear him,
    on those who wait upon his + love,
19 To pluck their lives from / death,
    and to feed them in time of / famine.
20 Our soul waits for the ^ LORD;
    he is our help and our ^ shield.
21 Indeed, our heart re.joices in him,
    for in his holy Name we put our . trust.
22 \Let your loving-kindness, O LORD, be u\pon us,
    as \ we have put our \ trust in you.

Alphabet Of Blessing: Commentary To Psalm 34

.aVÁR:KHÁH .ETH-YHWH B:KHOL-"ÉTH TÁMIYD T:HILLÁTHOW B:PHIY
v.1 I will bless the LORD on every occasion,
always his praise in my mouth.

An alphabetic psalm. This alphabet begins with gratitude as in 9:1. I will bless the LORD in every moment, and his praise will be continually in my mouth. When the telephone rings, when the traffic is heavy. In each of these moments, praise in my mouth, instead of complaint. In my mouth, sub-vocal speech, before it comes out of my mouth. Thank God for the telephone! Praise God for the traffic! Is it possible? Yes, but not easy. In the LORD my soul (my inner self, breath, life) is boasting, losing herself in praise. Affirmation has become part of my very breathing. My inner self overflows with gratitude, and my thoughts follow.

It is a completely new way of thinking, the transformation of my inner world. Little by little those muttered curses, cutting retorts, fragmented sentences and phrases, advertising jingles and half-remembered jokes will be replaced. It will not happen overnight, but slowly, one blessing at a time. Little by little that cloud of negative thought and emotion begins to lift. I have moments of clarity, sometimes hours or even days. My song, my *new song*, begins to bubble up within me.

v.3 Make great the LORD with me;
and let us exalt his name together.

Overflowing, it must be shared. Affirmation. The yes. The gift of receiving. My patients struggle with it, and so do I. Show them their goodness and they shake their heads. Show them their strength, their own value, and they don't want to hear it. If I could teach them one letter of the alphabet, it would be this: to receive, to say yes and thank you.

v.5 Look upon him and be radiant,
and your faces, let them not be ashamed.

No more sour looks, no more worried looks. Look at God and you will stream or flow, like an energy source, like little rivers. Like the lamp set high on a lamp-stand (Matthew 5:15) so that it can give light to human breathings. Let the light shine through me, flow through me and out of me. Let it shine in my face and my eyes. I'm not there yet, but I'm learning. When it happens, I am always surprised. The light shines out of me, unexpectedly, and people who pass me in the halls shine back at me.

v.8 Taste and see that the LORD is good.

Taste life, taste fresh water, taste milk, taste chocolate, taste home-made bread, taste the one who loves you. Taste these things and be grateful, and see that the LORD is good. Taste and see; experiment with prayer. You have heard about God second hand; now taste for yourself.

v.9 Fear the LORD, you that are his saints,
for those who fear him lack nothing.

Fear the LORD. That difficult concept called the beginning of wisdom (compare 112). Not an emotion, we will learn, but a kind of insight, understanding how things really are. One aspect of fearing the LORD is fearing *only* the LORD. Not to be in awe of the boss, the official, the celebrity, or you. The other is being vulnerable, having no defenses. Knowing that God can say no. Understanding that all I have, everything, I have but for this moment, by his pleasure. Understanding these things, a certain reticence with God, a certain reserve. Learning not to boast, not to say what God will do or will not do. Not to be overly familiar with God.

v.13 Keep your tongue from evil speaking.

A new way of thinking, speaking and living. I begin to understand, really understand, how evil speaking affects me. How my cutting remarks and sarcastic comments affect those around me; how the atmosphere I create with my thoughts comes back to hurt me. How I perpetuate subtle dissension in my workplace. At first it is hard to believe and I can only detect the most obvious examples. With time I become sensitized: a negative word or phrase crosses my mind and immediately I feel the nervous agitation. I begin to let go of those thoughts, so entertaining and so hurtful. I let go of those critical perceptions. Perhaps I don't after all know more than all my associates. I am learning to seek peace and pursue it.

v.19 Many are the troubles of the righteous,
but the LORD will deliver him out of them all.

The righteous will have many troubles. Do not say to him, "If you had faith you would not have these troubles," or, "If you were not in sin, you would not have these troubles." Do not tell the broken-hearted that her discouragement is "of the devil"; do not tell the righteous not to cry. For the LORD hears that cry and is close to that discouraged one. In some ultimate way which we do not fully understand, the LORD will deliver them (the righteous, the broken-hearted, the spirit-crushed) from all their troubles and will redeem their soul (breath, life).

Fearing the LORD means never blaming others for their troubles; for you are as vulnerable as they. Take a deep breath and enjoy it and let it fill your mouth with blessing and thanks. You did not earn this breath and you may not have another. But the LORD does, ultimately, ransom the soul (breath, life) of his servants. None will be blamed who seek refuge in him.

Notes: Verse 8 ("taste and see") compare 1 Peter 2:3. Verse 20 ("He will keep safe all his bones") see John 19:36.

Suggestions: Bless the LORD at all times; at every moment and every opportunity. When the telephone rings, when the traffic is stalled, when the door will not open, when you are wrongly attacked. In good news and bad, let his praise be in your mouth, sub-vocally. "Bless you, LORD," and, "Thank you, God!" Practice this way of responding as often as you can. Sing this psalm cheerfully, to the Tone *Alphabet*.

Read *Prison to Praise* by Merlin Carothers (Escondido, California, 1970).

Psalm 34 (BCP)

1 **I will bless the L**ORD **at all | times;**
   his praise shall ever be in my | mouth.
2 I will glory in the + LORD;
   let the humble hear and re+joice.
3 Proclaim with me the greatness of the / LORD;
   let us exalt his Name to/gether.
4 I sought the LORD and he ^ answered me
   and delivered me out of all my ^ terror.
5 Look upon him and be . radiant,
   and let not your faces be . ashamed.
6 **I called in my affliction and the L**ORD **| heard me**
   and saved me from all my | troubles.
7 The angel of the LORD encompasses those who + fear him
   and he will de+liver them.
8 Taste and see that the LORD is / good;
   happy are they who / trust in him!
9 Fear the LORD, you that are his ^ saints,
   for those who fear him lack ^ nothing.
10 The young lions lack and suffer . hunger,
   but those who seek the LORD lack nothing that is . good.
11 \Come, children, and \ listen to me;
   I will \ teach you the fear of the \ LORD.
12 **Who among you loves | life**
   and desires long life to enjoy pros|perity?
13 Keep your tongue from evil + speaking
   and your lips from lying + words.
14 Turn from evil and do / good;
   seek peace and pur/sue it.
15 The eyes of the LORD are upon the ^ righteous,
   and his ears are open to their ^ cry.
16 The face of the LORD is against those who do . evil,
   to root out the remembrance of them from the . earth.

17 **The righteous cry and the Lord | hears them**
    and delivers them from all their | troubles.
18 The Lord is near to the broken + hearted
    and will save those whose spirits are + crushed.
19 Many are the troubles of the / righteous,
    but the Lord will deliver him out of them / all.
20 He will keep safe all his ^ bones;
    not one of them shall be ^ broken.
21 Evil shall slay the . wicked,
    and those who hate the righteous will be . punished.
22 \The Lord ransoms the souls of his \ servants,
    and \ none will be punished who \ trust in him.

Fight Those Who Fight Me: Commentary To Psalm 35

RIYVÁH YHWH .ETH-Y:RIVAY L:#AM .ETH-LO#aMÁY
v.1 Strive, LORD, against those who strive with me;
Fight those who are fighting me!

My father had few interests outside his ministry of teaching and preaching. Suddenly one day he found himself enmeshed in The Controversy. I'm not sure what The Controversy was about. In fact, I don't think it was *about* anything at all. My father had been rabbi of that little congregation for a long time. A whole generation had grown up under his ministry. He had bruised some feelings. There was a restlessness in the air, vague accusations, disputes that could never be resolved, nameless enemies. There was nothing he could do to defend himself. After a year things seemed to settle down, but the knives were put aside for later. How well I remember my father's perplexity, outrage and helplessness.

Director has worked for the state for years, developing and defending his institution. He is a skilled administrator who understands state politics. But new leadership comes in, and he finds himself fighting for survival. He can't defend himself, for the rules keep changing. Lies take on a life of their own, and his network of powerful friends has melted away. Old enemies sharpen their knives, those whose feelings he hurt years ago. A tenacious fighter, he determines not to be pushed aside. But finally he decides to step down graciously, so the institution can continue under someone new. A lovely ceremony takes place, speeches are given in his honor. The next day, those Director has long protected find the knives sharpened for them.

Here in Psalm 35 the writer is fighting against just such faceless enemies. They have plotted his downfall with exquisite cunning, patiently waiting for him to make the fatal misstep. Working skillfully to manipulate public opinion, they have goaded him to a futile self-defense, and pushed him ever closer to that misstep. False witnesses come out of nowhere to accuse him. He finds his position becoming hopeless.

How does he handle it? About as well as my father or Director. Waves of self-pity come over him, alternating with outrage, disbelief, self-doubt and self-defense. *How could they do this to me? I never did those things they say I did!* Sometimes he takes heart; for a few days things look better. "I will give you thanks in the great congregation!" Then more doubts. The enemies are again on the move. Finally, in exhaustion, he turns to God. *I can't fight any more.* You "fight those who fight me, O LORD."

He says many things that are not "nice." He asks God to do terrible things to the enemies. Sometimes he feels sorry for himself. The low point for me comes in vv. 13-14. "But when they were sick ... I prayed (for them)." Our hero is learning painful lessons here. Good deeds are not always rewarded here on earth. Prayer does not always solve real-life problems. There is no real justice in this world, no help in powerful friends or anyone. Ultimately the cause is hopeless. And perhaps it is meant to be hopeless. We identify with a cause, an institution, a constituency, friends. We are given these things and then we have to let them go. And if we do anything meaningful in life at all, we will come to this place.

Victory is not guaranteed. Being a believer does not assure a life free of problems, or fairness, or good health. I am not entitled to any particular success. My part in God's plan may be defeat or apparent failure. It is right, or at least understandable, for me to pray for salvation, for rescue; to pray that the enemies go down to ruin, that they "fall into the pit they dug." But I am not entitled to any of it. "If it is possible, let this cup pass from me," Jesus prayed, "nevertheless, not as I will, but as You will" (Matthew 26:39, NKJ).

.eMOR L:NAPHSHIY Y:SHU"ÁTHÉKH ÁNI
v.3 Say to my soul, "I am your salvation."

Say to my soul (breath, breathing, life), "I (God) am your salvation (liberation, victory)." Say this, God, not to me, my restless thinking, the part of me that is ever saying "Yes, but," or, "but as for me." Say it to my breathing, my biological self. She can accept and surrender, as I cannot.

My salvation is not success nor victory, at least not this time. I will not win this battle on the battlefield. I am not in control any more. And perhaps I can begin to understand that I never really was. It was all illusion. You let me have my moment of glory and you let me taste defeat. Now you have something to say that I will never understand or accept. Say it to my soul, my real self, my breathing. "You will not win this battle on the battlefield but by conversion. I am your victory!"

W:NAPHSHIY TÁGIYL BAYHWH TÁSIYS BIYSHU"ÁTHOW
v.9 And my soul shall rejoice in the LORD;
she shall be glad in his salvation (victory).

After my father died, the little congregation continued its communal life. Families passed from the scene and new families joined. There were ups and downs, controversies and conflict, but "the Temple" survived and continues. After Director retired, his institution went through many changes. There were some who predicted its demise; but though it moved in new directions it continued to serve the state well. There will always be troubles, conflict, division, false witnesses, teeth gnashing—always. But my soul (breath, breathing, life) shall rejoice.

<u>Suggestions</u>: Continue your practice of meditation through the battles and conflicts of life. Formal meditation morning and evening; moments of silence throughout the day; especially in the difficult times. The practice you are learning is wakeful practice for everyday life. Keep your eyes open and practice silence when you are driving to work, when you sit in meetings, when you deal with the boss or the client or the customer. There will be conflicts, enemies without cause, false accusations, problems that are never resolved. Draw on the infinite reserves of God and keep fighting.

Psalm 35 (BCP)

Seventh Day: Morning Prayer
Tone: N:GINOTH

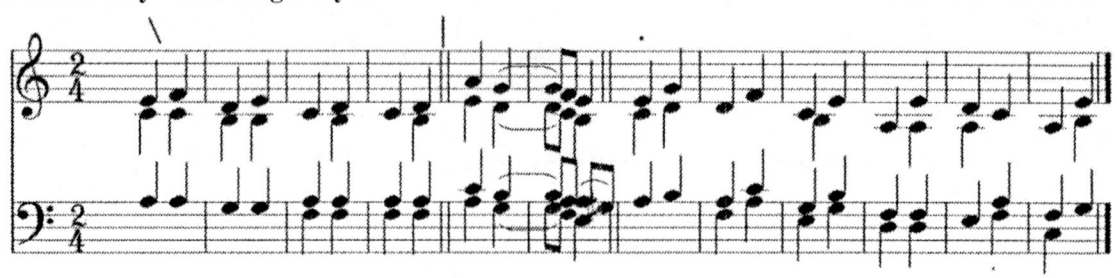

1 \Fight those who fight me, O \ Lord;
   attack those who are at\tacking me.
2 Take up shield and \ armor
   and rise up to \ help me.
3 \Draw the sword and bar the \ way
   against those who pur\sue me;
   say to my \ soul,
   "I am your sal\vation."
4 **Let those who seek after my life be shamed and | humbled;**
   let those who plot my | ruin fall back and be dis|mayed.
5 \Let them be like chaff before the \ wind,
   and let the angel of the Lord drive them a\way.
6 Let their way be dark and \ slippery,
   and let the angel of the Lord pur\sue them.
7 \For they have secretly spread a net for me without a \ cause;
   without a cause they have dug a pit to \ take me alive.
8 **Let ruin come upon them una|wares;**
   let them be caught in the net they | hid;
   let them fall into the pit they | dug.
9 .Then I will be joyful in the . Lord;
   I will glory in his . victory.
10 My very . bones will say,
   "Lord, who is . like you?
     You deliver the poor from those who are too . strong for them,
     the poor and needy from those who . rob them."
11 \Malicious witnesses rise up a\gainst me;
   they charge me with matters I know \ nothing about.
12 They pay me evil in exchange for \ good;
   my soul is full of de\spair.
13 .But when they were sick I dressed in . sack-cloth
   and humbled myself by . fasting;
14 I prayed with my whole . heart,
   as one would for a friend or a . brother;
     I behaved like one who mourns for his . mother,
     bowed down and . grieving.

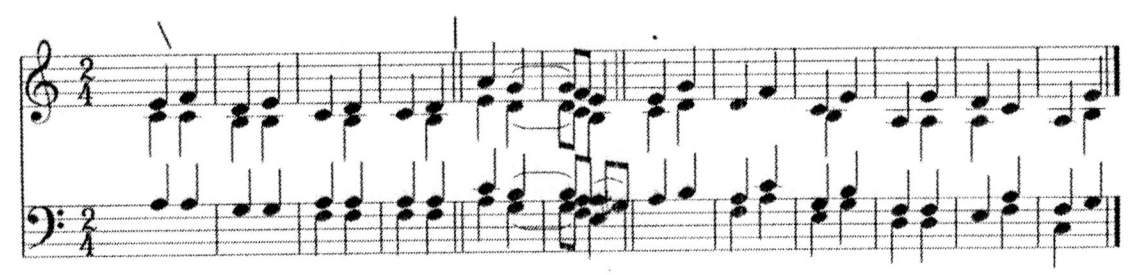

15 \But when I stumbled, they were glad and gathered together;
   they gathered a\gainst me;
     strangers whom I did not know tore me to pieces and
     \ would not stop.
16 They put me to the test and \ mocked me;
   they gnashed at me with their \ teeth.
17 **O Lord, how long will you look | on?**
   rescue me from the roaring | beasts,
   and my life from the young | lions.
18 .I will give you thanks in the great congre.gation;
   I will praise you in the mighty . throng.
19 Do not let my treacherous foes rejoice . over me,
   nor let those who hate me without a cause wink at each . other.
20 For they do not plan for . peace,
   but invent deceitful schemes against the . quiet in the land.
21 \They opened their mouths at me and \ said,
   "Aha! we saw it with our own \ eyes."
22 You saw it, O Lord; do not be \ silent;
   O Lord, be not \ far from me.
23 \Awake, arise, to my \ cause!
   to my defense, my God and my \ Lord!
24 Give me justice, O Lord my God,
   according to your \ righteousness;
   do not let them triumph \ over me.
25 \Do not let them say in their \ hearts,
   "Aha! just what we \ want!"
   Do not let them say, "We have swallowed him \ up."
26 **Let all who rejoice at my ruin be ashamed and dis | graced;**
   let those who boast a | gainst me be clothed with
   dismay and | shame.
27 \Let those who favor my cause sing out with joy and be \ glad;
   let them say always, "Great is the \ Lord,
   who desires the prosperity of his \ servant."
28 And my tongue shall be talking of your righteousness
   and of your praise all day \ long.

A Word About The Sin Of The Wicked: Commentary To Psalm 36

Two striking pictures in sharp contrast.

N:.UM-PESHA" LÁRÁSHÁ" B:QEREBh LIBBIY
v.1 An oracle of sin for the wicked, deep within my own heart.

I know only too well how the wicked slides into evil. An ordinary man, with a heart like mine, lacking one thing. "There is no fear of God before his eyes." Fear of everything else: of the devil, the communists, the humanists, the boss, the environment, cholesterol. Fearing such things, I act. Something has got to be done, and I will do it. Pride.

First, there is no fear of God before my eyes. Second, I flatter myself in my own eyes. Third, the words of my mouth are wicked and deceitful; soon after that, I have left off acting wisely and doing good, and before long I am actively thinking up "wickedness upon my bed." I no longer even pretend to be good. And this sequence of events can happen to anyone, at any level of spiritual development. It can happen, and usually does, with the finest motives, the highest ideals, and the loftiest goals. Always framed in idealistic language.

YHWH B:HASSHÁMAYiM #ASDEKHÁ .eMUNÁTH:KHÁ "AD-SH:#ÁQIM
v.5 O LORD, your love is in the heavens; your faithfulness (reaches) to the clouds.

Man is unreliable. But God! His love pervades the universe, and his faithfulness reaches up endlessly. They are infinite and infinitely reliable. To us, who flicker like candles, his constancy is beyond understanding. And his righteousness is like mountains of power; and his judgments like the vasty deep. Your (fierce, protective) love is "precious." Your people "feast upon ... abundance." More than enough, they feast on the fat, the choicest part of the banquet.

KI-"IMM:KHÁ M:QOR #AYYIM   B:.OR:KHÁ NIR.EH-.OR
v.9 For with you is the well of life,
and in your light we see light.

You are the source of this breathing and seeing. Yours is the light. All I am is drawn up from you and all depends on you. As for the wicked and evildoers (vv.11-12), their brief reign is already over. They are cast down and shall not be able to rise. Go back to verse 1.

<u>Suggestions</u>: Omit hand gestures. Stand beginning at v.5. When your best intentioned plans are not working, when things are going badly, look to your source. Is it really God? Or something that looks like God: a church, a movement, a leader, or (most likely) your own thoughts? Stop. Do nothing. Listen. Turn your attention back to God.

Psalm 36 (BCP)

Tone: KINNOR

1 **There is a voice of rebellion deep in the heart of the | wicked;**
   there is no fear of God before his | eyes.
2 **He flatters himself in his own | eyes**
   that his hateful sin will not be found | out.
3 /The words of his mouth are wicked and / deceitful;
   he has left off acting wisely and doing / good.
4 \He thinks up wickedness upon his bed
     \and has set himself in no good way;
   he does not abhor that which is \ evil.
5 /Your love, O LORD, reaches to the / heavens,
   and your faithfulness to the / clouds.
6 \Your righteousness is like the strong mountains,
     \your justice like the great deep;
   you save both man and \ beast, O LORD.
7 **How priceless is your love, O | God!**
   your people take refuge under the shadow of your | wings.
8 **They feast upon the abundance of your | house;**
   you give them drink from the river of your | delights.
9 /For with you is the well of / life,
   and in your light we see / light.
10 **Continue your loving-kindness to those who | know you,**
   and your favor to those who are | true of heart.
11 /Let not the foot of the proud come / near me,
   nor the hand of the wicked push me / aside.
12 \See how they are fallen, those who work wickedness!
     \they are cast down
   and shall not be \ able to rise.

Do Not Fret: Commentary To Psalm 37

.AL-TITH#AR BAM:RE"IM

v.1 Do not fret yourself, literally *do not heat yourself up*, over those who do wrong. The verb form is reflexive. I heat myself up, and the process is not so mysterious. I just hear myself talking to *them*. In my thoughts I'm telling them off in brilliant, cutting speeches. I use words like *inexcusable, unacceptable, incompetent* and *jerk*! To my bosses, my patients, my colleagues, my wife. Sometimes whole classes of people, whole professions, whole nationalities. The adrenaline flows; I begin to feel energized. If I can share these thoughts with others, I feel even stronger.

And I notice myself breathing in a certain way, exhaling sharply and rhythmically through my nostrils. Then I remember that .APH (*nose*) is also the Hebrew word for anger. Once I start this breathing it's hard to stop; it's a natural high. I feel so righteous! Inside I keep rehearsing: "You idiot! You always... this, you never... that!" while outwardly I breathe those sharp hot breaths through my nose. Sometimes I'm assertive and "make scenes"; other times I fret inwardly and say nothing.

HEREPh MÉ.APH WA"aZOV #ÉMÁH .AL-TITH#AR .AKH L:HÁRÉa"

v.9 Refrain from anger, leave rage alone;
do not fret yourself; it leads only to evil.

HEREPh (*let go*), as in 46:10. Let go of anger. Why? Because I have no control over *them* or anything else. Because anger is life lived backwards, trying to prevent what has already happened. Heating myself up I burn energy and create lasting ill-will. I deplete my lifetime reserves of coping. I shorten my life by so many sharp, hot breaths. It feels good for a moment, but it leaves scars that do not heal. "Do not heat yourself up," repeated three times. Leave rage alone. "For the wrath of man does not produce the righteousness of God" (James 1:20, NKJ).

I do not have control, I have choices. There is nothing I can do about the evildoers and those who do wrong. Their fate is already sealed. But I have choices—to trust, to do good, to dwell in the land and feed on its riches, to take delight, to commit my way. I have a choice to "be still ... wait ... refrain from anger." To rehearse those speeches or not.

I do not control things, people or outcomes. I control my muscles, sometimes my thoughts. I can influence people and sometimes they respond to my wishes. If only I knew a little more, I think, or tried a little harder, I could control them.

It is the delusion of every toddler. "If I scream loud enough and hard enough I can control them!" It is the delusion of self-help books, and "secrets of success." If only I knew a little more, I would really be in control. I could even control myself. Yes, in that infinite regress that Gerald May* calls insanity, "I" could control that mythic entity, my *self*.

It is hard to give this up. It is painful to learn that I cannot control them, I cannot make it happen my way. It feels so right to heat myself up, to make those sharp demands. To think I can control the forces of evil. To control the evildoers. But only God has control. Do not heat yourself up. To a psychiatrist, mental illnesses have many causes. Yet in almost every case this is at least a complication: the wish to control; the belief that one has no choice. The patient asks, "How can I make them listen to me?" He does not want to hear, "You can't. They have a choice." She certainly doesn't want to hear, "You have a choice, to get angry or to let it go."

If I say that I have no control over the evildoers, it seems like giving in to evil. Yet the truth is that I can choose to fall in with the evildoers or to live with integrity. I can go with the evildoers or not, but I cannot control them. Heating myself up into a rage will never change them.

While some disciples claim they never get angry, others boast of their rages. They will tell you proudly that they are Irish or red-headed or "have a temper, just like my Daddy!" They have not yet realized how frightening they are and how they damage the ones they love. Maybe they will realize too late. It feels so good, and it hurts so terribly, often beyond repair. Are you one of them?

<u>Notes</u>: "Do not fret yourself" (v.1), compare Proverbs 24:1,19.

<u>Suggestions</u>: When you are angry, listen for that inner voice that blames and accuses. Perhaps it is speaking sharply to some *you*: "You always... you never... Why don't you... ?" With each rehearsal you find yourself getting hotter. Listen to that rhythmic breathing through the nostrils. Watch how you move, with abrupt, whip-like movements. It is not immoral to do these things, but it hurts you, it is bad for your health. It blocks your spiritual growth. Figure out how you do it, how you generate that burning anger, then, ever so gently, stop.

Much illness begins with anger and there is little value in "releasing" anger. "Be silent before the LORD." The practice of silence is the way to stop the fretting and the anger. When you are angry, do not try to reason with yourself, but practice moments of silence. Inhale sharply through the nose, exhale gently and easily, lift your attention to God and clear your thoughts. Let your mind be completely silent, however briefly. Do this again and again as you ask God to help you with your anger.

Sing this alphabetic psalm slowly to the long version of *Alphabet*, eight notes or two measures to two verses. Only the first, third, fifth and sixth Orders are sung; the alternate verses are to be read.

---

*Gerald May: *Simply Sane. The Spirituality of Mental Health*, Crossroads, New York, 1977. Compare 86, 101.

Psalm 37 (BCP)

Seventh Day: Evening Prayer   **Tone:** *Alphabet*

1 **Do not fret yourself because of | evildoers;**
    do not be jealous of those who do | wrong.

2 For they shall soon wither like the | grass,
    and like the green grass fade a | way.

3 Put your trust in the LORD and do good; *
    dwell in the land and feed on its riches.

4 Take delight in the LORD, *
    and he shall give you your heart's desire.

5 /Commit your way to the LORD and put your / trust in him,
    and he will bring it to / pass.

6 He will make your righteousness as clear as the / light
    and your just dealing as the / noonday.

7 Be still before the LORD *
    and wait patiently for him.

8 Do not fret yourself over the one who prospers, *
    the one who succeeds in evil schemes.

9 .Refrain from anger, leave rage a.lone;
    do not fret yourself; it leads only to . evil.

10 For evildoers shall be cut . off,
    but those who wait upon the LORD shall possess the . land.

11 **In a little while the wicked shall be no | more;**
    you shall search out their place, but they will not | be there.

12 But the lowly shall possess the | land;
    they will delight in abundance of | peace.

13 The wicked plot against the righteous *
    and gnash at them with their teeth.

14 The LORD laughs at the wicked, *
    because he sees that their day will come.

15 /The wicked draw their sword and bend their bow
    to strike down the poor and / needy,
    to slaughter those who are upright in their / ways.

16 Their sword shall go through their own / heart,
    and their bow shall be / broken.

17 The little that the righteous has *
    is better than great riches of the wicked.

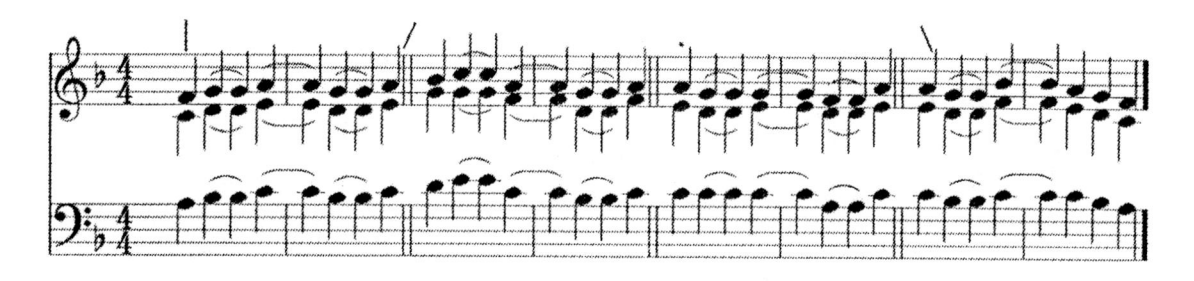

18 For the power of the wicked shall be broken, *
    but the LORD upholds the righteous.

[Part II]

19 .The LORD cares for the lives of the . godly,
    and their inheritance shall last for . ever.
20 They shall not be ashamed in bad . times,
    and in days of famine they shall have e.nough.
21 \As for the wicked, they shall \ perish,
    and the enemies of the \ LORD, like the glory of
    the meadows, shall \ vanish;
    they shall \ vanish like \ smoke.
22 **The wicked borrow and do not | repay,**
    but the righteous are generous in | giving.
23 Those who are blessed by God shall posses the | land,
    but those who are cursed by him shall be | destroyed.
24 Our steps are directed by the LORD; *
    he strengthens those in whose way he delights.
25 If they stumble, they shall not fall headlong, *
    for the LORD holds them by the hand.
26 /I have been young and now I am / old,
    but never have I seen the righteous forsaken,
    or their children begging / bread.
27 The righteous are always generous in their / lending,
    and their children shall be a / blessing.
28 Turn from evil, and do good, *
    and dwell in the land for ever.
29 For the LORD loves justice; *
    he does not forsake his faithful ones.
30 .They shall be kept safe for . ever,
    but the offspring of the wicked shall be . destroyed.
31 The righteous shall possess the . land
    and dwell in it for . ever.

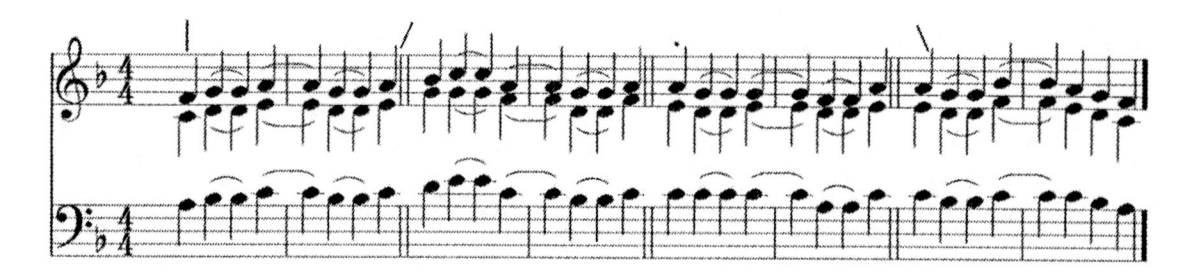

32 **The mouth of the righteous utters | wisdom,**
   and their tongue speaks what is | right.
33 The law of their God is in their | heart,
   and their footsteps shall not | falter.
34 The wicked spy on the righteous *
   and seek occasion to kill them.
35 The Lord will not abandon them to their hand, *
   nor let them be found guilty when brought to trial.
36 /Wait upon the Lord and keep his / way;
   he will raise you up to possess the / land,
   and when the wicked are cut / off, (*)
   you will / see it.
37 I have seen the wicked in their arrogance, *
   flourishing like a tree in full leaf.
38 I went by, and behold, they were not there; *
   I searched for them, but they could not be found.
39 .Mark those who are honest; observe the . upright;
   for there is a future for the . peaceable.
40 Transgressors shall be destroyed, one and . all;
   the future of the wicked is cut . off.
41 \But the deliverance of the righteous comes from the \ Lord;
   he is their stronghold in time of \ trouble.
42 The Lord will help them and \ rescue them;
   he will rescue them from the wicked and \ deliver them,
   because they seek \ refuge in him.

But I Am Like A Deaf Man: Commentary To Psalm 38

The writer is desperately ill, maybe terminal. We cannot be sure of the diagnosis. He may be septic: raging infection is overwhelming the body defenses. His heart is racing, and his eyes have that dulled appearance of one who is near death. As health fails, friends melt away; relatives don't visit; those who always disliked him are waiting for him to die.

v.13 But I am like a deaf man who does not hear,
and like a mute who does not open his mouth.

But as for me. Another sharp disjunction. I am overwhelmed by sickness, infections, pain, racing heart, friends who won't answer my calls, enemies planning the future without me. Thought leads to thought and emotion builds upon emotion. As I reflect upon the meaning of my suffering I suffer more. I am caught up in a vortex of regret, rage, bitterness, despair. My racing thoughts bring me no comfort. Discouragement rolls in upon me in waves. As in Psalm 22, I can get no silence. Then I think, "But as for me... what about me?"

What any good therapist would ask: "But what about you? How do you feel right now?" I cannot change the past, my sins, my failures, *them*, the enemies. I cannot change even my friend. I control nothing now. But as for me. Step back, observe, stop struggling. What I am is what I am this moment, *now*, in absolute present, as I look into your eyes. They continue to attack me but somehow I no longer react. They accuse me but I no longer defend myself. I am like Jesus who "answered him not one word" (Matthew 27:14, NKJ). My only defense is no defense at all.

v.15 For in you, O LORD, I have fixed my hope;
You will answer me, O LORD, my God.

I do not heal myself from within. I do not call on powers or spirit guides. "I" is but a thought: Step back in silence, *see*, give up control. The answer within is that the answer is not within me at all. The answer lies outside my world of thoughts. But as for me... I look within, and then I turn to you.

.AL-TA"AZVÉNI YHWH .eLOHAY .AL-TIR#AQ MIMMENNI

v.21 Do not abandon me, O LORD, my God;
be not far from me.

It is the first and last prayer of a human breathing. Be not far. Do not abandon me as I lie dying.

Notes: A penitential psalm. Verse 6, compare "verily every man at his best state is altogether vanity" (KJV), and, "Certainly every man at his best state is but vapor" (NKJ). The psalm has twenty-two verses, suggesting the Hebrew alphabet, but is not acrostic.

Suggestions: Psalms 38 and 39 are sung to the same music. As comforter or therapist, remember: There are no magic words. Give no advice. Just be not far. Be present with me, in absolute here and now.

Psalm 38 (BCP)

Eighth Day: Morning Prayer

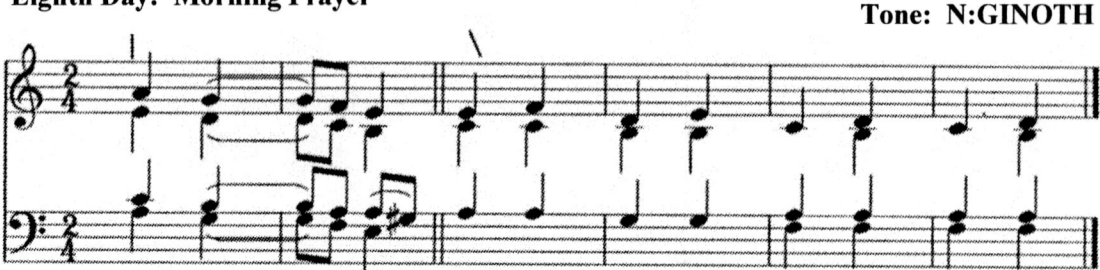

Tone: N:GINOTH

1 **O Lord, do not rebuke me in your | anger;**
    do not | punish me in your | wrath.
2 \For your arrows have already \ pierced me,
    and your hand presses hard u\pon me.
3 There is no health in my flesh,
    because of your \ indignation;
    there is no soundness in my body, because of my \ sin.
4 \For my iniquities over\whelm me;
    like a heavy burden they are too much for me to \ bear.
5 My wounds stink and fester
    by reason of my \ foolishness.
6 **I am utterly bowed down and | prostrate;**
    I go about in | mourning all the day | long.
7 \My loins are filled with searing \ pain;
    there is no health in my \ body.
8 I am utterly numb and \ crushed;
    I wail, because of the groaning of my \ heart.
9 \O Lord, you know all my \ desires,
    and my sighing is not \ hidden from you.
10 My heart is pounding, my strength has \ failed me.
    and the brightness of my eyes is \ gone from me.
11 \My friends and companions draw back from my af\fliction;
    my neighbors stand afar \ off.
12 **Those who seek after my life lay | snares for me;**
    those who strive to hurt me speak of my | ruin
    and plot treachery all the day | long.
13 \But I am like the deaf who do not \ hear;
    like those who are mute and do not open their \ mouth.
14 I have become like one who does not \ hear
    and from whose mouth comes no \ defense.
15 \For in you, O Lord, have I fixed my \ hope;
    you will answer me, O Lord my \ God.
16 For I said, "Do not let them rejoice at my ex\pense,
    those who gloat over me when my \ foot slips."

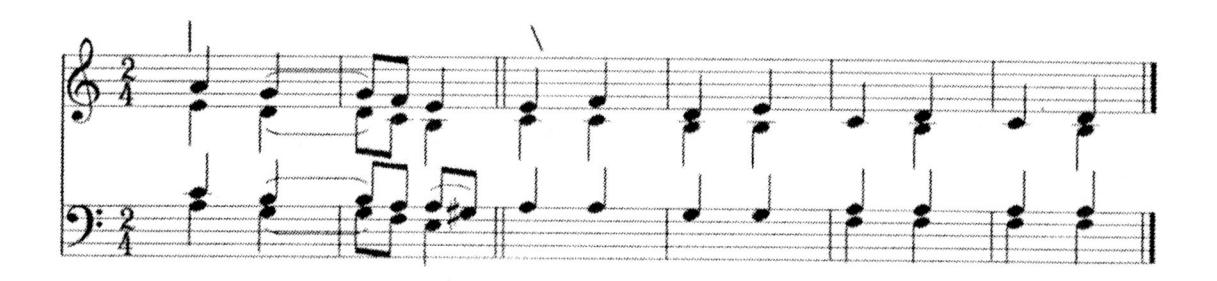

17 **Truly I am on the verge of | falling,**
    and my pain is always | with me.
18 I will confess my iniquity
    and be sorry for my | sin.
19 \Those who are my enemies without cause are \ mighty,
    and many in number are those who wrongfully \ hate me.
20 Those who repay evil for good \ slander me,
    because I follow the course that is \ right.
21 \O Lord, do not for\sake me;
    be not far from me, O my \ God.
22 Make haste to \ help me,
    O Lord of my \ salvation.

So I Held My Tongue: Commentary To Psalm 39

.ÁMARTI .ESHM:RÁH D:RÁKHAY MÉ#atOW. VIL:SHONIY
v.1 I have said: "I will start to keep watch upon my ways;
so as not to sin with my tongue." When I was training in psychiatry, we talked a lot about assertiveness. Don't hold the anger in. Tell them how you feel. If people upset you, confront them. Like every false idea it has a grain of truth. Better to come right out and say what you want than to whine and sulk. State your position, so the other person can say yes or no.

We believed in anger. That we go through life generating this mystical fluid. That it must have a place to flow or something will burst. Hold it in and it's sure to explode, like my mother's pressure cooker. Tomatoes on the ceiling!

In the years that followed I expressed a lot of anger. I had tantrums and confrontations, some in writing, with copies to a dozen individuals. I said things that hurt many people, even people I loved. They were not accidental; I rehearsed and polished them and felt very self-righteous. None of this made me a better person, or gained me respect. It was exciting to rattle those cages, but it left scars.

By the age of fifty I was learning to muzzle my mouth and watch my tongue. Not to make those brilliant cutting remarks. I was learning that there is no value in hurting another person's feelings no matter how wrong they are. No matter how good it would feel, for a few seconds, to "confront" them. There is no victory, no issue worth hurting my life-partner or crushing the feelings of my child.

v.3 So I held my tongue and said nothing ...

but my pain became unbearable. You see, I cannot do this. I get so terribly angry, and I'm always certain that I'm right. I ask God to help me with it continually. Bottling it up is not enough; I must learn not to produce it. So I'm learning not to dwell on those thoughts, not to rehearse them. Step back and think. Is this really important? Am I really the only one who understands? And I praise God. Praise you for this situation. For making these people as they are. For someone being as abrasive as I used to be. Praise you, for so-and-so speaking up that way. And I ask him: LORD, help me with this. Help me let go.

.AKH- B:3ELEM YITHHALLEKH-.IYSH .AKH-HEVEL YEHeMÁYUWN
v.7 Man walks about in shadow, and in vain (like a puff of wind) they sigh and moan. I am a stranger here, passing like a shadow. Help me let go.

<u>Suggestions</u>: The management of anger is not easy. Refer back to 37. Replace the angry thoughts with praise thoughts, then with moments of silence. The popular concept of mental well-being centers on assertiveness, the ability to ask, or demand, what one needs. The biblical concept of mental health is more like self-control. Anger is increasingly muted and modulated. Look for this in yourself. As you advance on the spiritual path, less and less will you be controlled by anger.

Psalm 39 (BCP)

1 **I said, "I will keep watch upon my | ways,**
 so that I do not offend with my | tongue.
2 I will put a muzzle on my mouth
 while the wicked are in my | presence."
3 \So I held my tongue and said \ nothing;
 I refrained from rash \ words;
 but my pain became un\bearable.
4 \My heart was hot with\in me; while I pondered, the fire burst into \ flame;
 I spoke out with my \ tongue:
5 \ LORD, let me know my \ end
 and the number of my \ days,
 so that I may know how short my \ life is.
6 **You have given me a mere handful of | days,**
 and my lifetime is as nothing in your | sight;
 truly, even those who stand erect are but a | puff of wind.
  [Silence...]
7 \We walk about like a \ shadow, and in vain we are in \ turmoil;
 we heap up riches and cannot tell who will \ gather them.
8 \And now, what is my \ hope?
 O Lord, my hope is in \ you.
9 Deliver me from all my trans\gressions
 and do not make me the taunt of the \ fool.
10 \I fell silent and did not open my \ mouth,
 for surely it was you that \ did it.
11 Take your affliction \ from me;
 I am worn down by the blows of your \ hand.
12 **With rebukes for sin you | punish us;**
 like a moth you eat away all that is | dear to us;
 truly, everyone is but a | puff of wind.
  [Silence...]
13 \Hear my prayer, O \ LORD, and give ear to my \ cry;
 hold not your peace at my \ tears.
14 \For I am but a so\journer with you,
 a wayfarer as all my \ forebears were.
15 Turn your gaze from me, that I may be \ glad again,
 before I go my way and am no \ more.

Waiting I Have Waited: Commentary To Psalm 40

QAWWOH QIWWITHI YHWH

v.1 Waiting I have waited upon the LORD

and he begins to lean toward me, and to listen to my cry for help, and to lift me up out of the desolate pit, out of the mire and clay, and to stand my feet upon a rock, establishing my steps.

Waiting expectantly I have waited. QÁWWÁH from QÁW (*a rope*), hence to bind fast, hence to be strong; also to wait, to expect, and to hope (Gesenius*). The notion of waiting and that of strength are intimately related. It makes sense psychologically as well. Maturation is learning to wait instead of acting. It is learning to bind the impulse; to inhibit all responses except the one needed, till the moment needed.

The infant startles, jerks, flails; the child wiggles and fidgets; the adolescent boy is in constant movement — punching, jabbing, shaking or tapping. With maturation there are fewer movements, yet more effective. With maturity we learn to wait—for minutes, hours or years—until the moment for action.

Waiting may be strength, but it feels like weakness. In a crisis we want to act—now! We want to strike, throw, punch or shoot. Ask me a question, I want to answer. Insult me, I want to retaliate—now! We do not admire waiting in our time. We admire the driven, the man who gets angry at stop-lights. Myself, I hate to wait. When I'm hungry I want to eat—now! I begin to feel faint. If I don't eat soon something awful is sure to happen.

Yet we know that waiting may be strength. Let your heart beat slowly, like the heart of a trained athlete, and live long. Eat slowly. Breathe slowly. Bind the impulse, slow the rhythm, make each movement powerful and perfect. Speak slowly, waiting for the Spirit to direct you. Waiting is relating to God. As I wait patiently, he leans his ear toward me and listens, and he begins to lift me up.

v.3 And he begins to put in my mouth a new song, a new way of thinking. Out of waiting I listen and learn. Out of waiting I learn a new relationship to time. My pointless rushing and hurrying is slowly transformed into the effective use of time, to graceful movement. I move slowly, yet skillfully, and I begin to see things in a remarkable new way. Ordinary things become beautiful.

Suggestions: Sing vv. 1-2a with exquisite slowness (like 13:1-2 or 27:18). Today do one thing, one action of daily life, with that same exquisite slowness, like a sacred ritual. Watch it happening. Watch for that remarkable fruit of the Spirit, *patience*, to make its appearance. When everything is going wrong, practice waiting. Stop what you are doing for a moment. Walk slowly. Act slowly. Breathe slowly. Think before speaking. Note that verses 14-19 correspond to Psalm 70.

---

*H.W.F. Gesenius: *Gesenius' Hebrew-Chaldee Lexicon to the Old Testament Scriptures* (Translated by Samuel Prideaux Tregelles), Baker Book House, Grand Rapids, MI, 1979, p. 726.

Psalm 40 (BCP)

Tone: N:GINOTH

[Slowly]

1 \I waited patiently upon the \ LORD;
   he stooped to me and heard my \ cry.
2 He lifted me out of the desolate \ pit,
   out of the mire and \ clay;
               [Normal tempo]
   \he set my feet upon a high \ cliff
   and made my \ footing sure.
3 \He put a new song in my \ mouth,
   a song of praise to our \ God;
   many shall see and stand in \ awe,
   and put their trust in the \ LORD.
4 .Happy are they who trust in the . LORD!
   they do not resort to evil spirits or turn to false . gods.
5 Great things are they that you have done, O LORD my . God!
   how great your wonders and your . plans for us!
   there is none who can be com.pared with you.
6 Oh, that I could make them known and tell them!
   but they are more than I can . count.
7 \In sacrifice and offering you take no \ pleasure
   (you have given me ears to \ hear you);
8 Burnt-offering and sin-offering you have \ not required,
   and so I said, "Behold, I \ come.
9 \In the roll of the book it is written con\cerning me:
   'I love to do your will, O my \ God;
   your law is deep in my \ heart.'"
10 .I proclaimed righteousness in the great congre.gation;
   behold, I did not restrain my . lips;
   and that, O LORD, you . know.
11 Your righteousness have I not hidden in my . heart;
   I have spoken of your faithfulness and your . deliverance;
   I have not concealed your love and faithfulness from the great congre.gation.
12 **You are the LORD;**
   do not withhold your com | passion from me;
   let your love and your | faithfulness keep me safe for | ever.

13 \ For innumerable troubles have crowded u \ pon me;
　　　my sins have overtaken me, and I cannot \ see;
　　　they are more in number than the hairs of my \ head,
　　　and my heart \ fails me.
14 \ Be pleased, O Lord, to de \ liver me;
　　　O Lord, make haste to \ help me.
15 **Let them be ashamed and altogether dismayed**
　　　who seek after my life to de | stroy it;
　　　let them draw back and be dis | graced
　　　who take pleasure in my mis | fortune.
16 \ Let those who say "Aha!" and gloat over me be con \ founded,
　　　because they are \ ashamed.
17 \ Let all who seek you rejoice in you and be \ glad;
　　　let those who love your salvation continually \ say,
　　　"Great is the \ Lord!"
18 \ Though I am poor and af \ flicted,
　　　The Lord will have re \ gard for me.
19 You are my helper and my de \ liverer;
　　　do not tarry, O my \ God.

Hospital Psalm: Commentary To Psalm 41

As the writer lies in his hospital bed, he hears only bad news. He can no longer tell friend from enemy, for even his friends are whispering in the corridors. If we understand the power of suggestion, we know that, without even realizing it, they are planting suggestions for his death. Fortunately he knows that his recovery does not depend on friends, or even doctors.

.ASHREY MASKIYL .EL-DÁL
v.1 Praiseworthy is he who cares wisely for the sick (Feuer*).

The word DÁL signifies something hanging down, weak or thin, hence sick; someone too weak to stand. MASKIYL has connotations of wisdom, learning or study. Real happiness is found in caring for the sick, studying them and learning from them.

The LORD will deliver them in the time of trouble. Does the LORD deliver the sick, or the one who cares for the sick? Note the ambiguity. The caretaker today may be in sickbed tomorrow. Suffering patient may become wounded healer. So it is a wise physician who learns from his or her patients, listens, tries to understand them. It is a wise patient who finds redemption in the illness and reaches out to help other patients. It is an even wiser patient who realizes that the doctor cannot heal. It is a wise physician and patient who listen to each other, open each other up to healing. That patient who sits in front of me may have come to teach me or change me.

Meanwhile, in the visitors' lounge and the hospital corridors, the "enemies" are full of sly condemnation. How easy—and how evil—it is to blame the patient for being sick. *He never watched his diet. She should have stopped smoking. He didn't exercise. I warned him. I told her.*

How much worse when we add moral condemnation. *It's the result of sin. It's spiritual. It's demonic. We prayed for her but she didn't have faith.* A deadly thing has fastened on him—D:VAR-B:LIYA"AL—a repulsive, disgusting thing. Perhaps, even, a demonic thing. Jesus taught us that illness is not the result of sin (John 9:2-3), but we forget. Even the patient is halfway convinced.

In the closing prayer, vv. 10-12, our patient seems to say, "Don't let me sink into degradation. Even as a patient, let me have dignity. Let me know that you are still pleased with me."

<u>Suggestions</u>: When you pray for the sick or treat the sick, begin always with silence. Be present to the sick patient, but give no advice. Be aware of your tendency to condemn the sick person or blame the sick person for the illness.

When you yourself need healing, go with an open mind and a teachable heart. Do not give religious tests to your healer or dispute with your healer about his or her beliefs. For God can heal you through anyone.

---

*Rabbi Avrohom Chaim Feuer: *Tehillim (Psalms)/ A New Translation with a Commentary Anthologized from Talmudic, Midrashic and Rabbinic Sources.* Mesorah Publications, Ltd., Brooklyn, NY, 1977, p. 515.

Psalm 41 (BCP)

Eighth Day: Evening Prayer Tone: N:GINOTH

1 **Happy are they who consider the poor and | needy!**
   the LORD will de|liver them in the time of | trouble.
2 \The LORD preserves them and keeps them a\live,
   so that they may be happy in the \ land;
   he does not hand them over to the will of their \ enemies.
3 \The LORD sustains them on their \ sickbed
   and ministers to them in their \ illness.
4 **I said, "LORD, be | merciful to me;**
   | heal me, for I have | sinned against you."
5 \My enemies are saying wicked \ things about me;
   "When will he die and his name \ perish?"
6 \Even if they come to see me, they speak empty \ words;
   their heart collects false \ rumors;
   they go outside and \ spread them.
7 \All my enemies whisper together a\bout me
   and devise evil a\gainst me.
8 "A deadly thing," they say, "has \ fastened on him;
   he has taken to his bed and will never get \ up again."
9 \Even my best friend, whom I \ trusted,
   who broke \ bread with me,
   has lifted up his heel and turned a\gainst me.
10 But you, O LORD, be | merciful to me
   and | raise me up,
   and I shall re|pay them.
11 \By this I know that you are \ pleased with me,
   that my enemy does not triumph \ over me.
12 In my integrity you hold me \ fast,
   and shall set me before your face for \ ever.
13 Blessed be the LORD God of | Israel,
   from age to | age. Amen. A|men.

Book Two

Why Do I Feel So Bad? Commentary To Psalms 42 And 43

MAH-TISHTO#a#IY NAPHSHIY WÁTEHeMIY "ÁLÁY

v.6 Why are you so crushed down, so oppressed, O my life,
and why do you moan so pitifully within me?

I hear myself breathing in deep, sighing breaths. Long, sharp inhalations through my nose, and long, heavy, sighing expirations. My breathing is mournful and sorrowful. A crushing sense of heaviness overwhelms me. Swimming in two contrary streams, I am lost and confused. My soul (breath, breathing, life) is moaning and thirsting for God; And *I* swim in words and concepts, worrying what *they* might be saying. What are they thinking of me now? I am sad and depressed. I feel that heaviness in my stomach, while they seem to ask me, "Where now is your God?" Who are they? Anyone. Everyone. Friend, stranger, patient, wife, daughter.

Why do I feel so bad? I have asked this question all my life. For a minute or an hour I was content, then that heaviness rolled in. When I was in high school I began to call it depression. I ask my soul (breathing) "Why?" but my soul cannot answer. My soul is sensitive but inarticulate. My soul can only cry in wordless moaning.

I sense that heavy feeling always in relation to an other. A human breathing is hopelessly dyadic, made to be bonded to an other. That heaviness rolls in when one of us moves away. Someone is disappointed in me. Someone doesn't like me. I had a chance to do something for this person and I refused. I had my critical four minutes of small talk and could not connect. I tried to make a joke but it wasn't funny. I was trying to impress you but your eyes were miles away. Even if I never see you again, I will re-live the disappointment.

It may be someone I have never met, someone I have read about. He is the same age as I, but he is president of a company. He has published three books, while I have done nothing. He is a justice of the Supreme Court, but I consider myself to be nobody.

Even on the weekend I experience it. I was looking forward to this day off, but something is missing. I feel I should be doing more. I sense that I am letting someone down. Colleagues are making money in their big practices, while I delegate whatever I can, and turn away referrals. I planned a romantic weekend with my wife, but now we are quarreling, and the weekend is ruined. Was it really all my fault?

My thoughts have many plans, but my soul is yearning for closeness, relatedness. My soul may not fully understand she is yearning for God. My soul (breath, breathing, life itself) is moaning for God as a thirsty woodland animal moans for water. My real life is moaning for God, my source, while *I* wander around in confusion, listening to *them*; and what are they saying? "Where now is your God?"

I pour out my breath in deep sighs as I think about these things: even in church I feel that heaviness, as I wonder how *they* feel about me, and whether they accept me. Even there, where I go to be with God, I find myself yearning for approval.

v.4 I remember these things.

I remember how I went with the multitude, how I led that dancing procession into the house of God, how we sang songs of praise. I remember the highs, the peak experiences. I long for those times, those highs, but I cannot bring them back. "Put your trust in God."

    v.8 My soul is heavy within me;
therefore I will remember you.
    I begin to turn my attention—heavily, painfully—from myself, my heaviness, to you. It is the secret of relationship. I turn to you. And not to the idea of you, or my need for you, but you yourself, your presence, here and now. And I will speak to you, simply and humbly:

    v.11 I will say to God my rock,
why have you forgotten me?
    Why do I walk in darkness (murk, confusion) in the pressure of the enemy? As always, it is not explanation I seek, but presence. The actual presence of God (friend, lover, spouse, child). Intimacy with you (God) or you (friend). I am yearning for that bond with other that makes me whole. That need for relationship, says Paul Tournier, is what is spiritual in a person.*
    For God created humankind "so that they should seek the LORD in the hope that they might grope for him and find him" (Acts 17:27, NKJ). And so I go back and forth—from them, the friends, false friends, enemies, rivals—to God; and from God, to them. Restless and searching for them, I search for God. Yearning for that intimacy with you, I yearn for him.

        HO#IYLI LÉ.LOHIM KI "OWD .ODENNU Y:SHU"OTH PÁNÁY
    v.15 Wait hopefully for God, for I will continue to thank him,
O the salvation (help, victories) of my face!
    Another conversion moment. Suddenly and without explanation, I rise to his presence (his *face*). And I must do this again and again. I will never be self-sufficient and I will never have God in a box. As long as I breathe on this earth, I will yearn for relation. My life will depend on a sacred, fragile bond.

    <u>Suggestions</u>: Begin heavily, head bowed or kneeling. Rise slowly to a standing position on v.7 ("Put your trust") and lift your arms to heaven on "who is the help." Kneel again at v.8 ("My soul is heavy") and rise to a standing position at v.15 ("Put your trust"). Lift the arms again at "who is the help." Similarly in Psalm 43, remain bowed or kneeling up to the last half of v. 5 ("Put your trust"). The music is the same for these two psalms.

    Do not pretend to be eternally cheerful. Be aware of the lows, the heaviness, separation. Give up control in your relationship with God; in all relationships.

---

*Paul Tournier: *A Listening Ear*, Augsburg, Minneapolis, 1986, p. 53.

Psalm 42 (BCP)

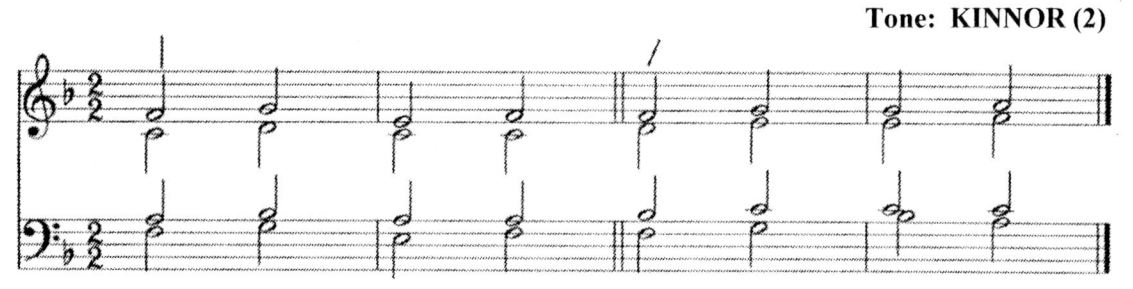

Tone: KINNOR (2)

1 As the deer longs for the water brooks, *
    so longs my soul for you, O God.
2 My soul is athirst for God, athirst for the living God; *
    when shall I come to appear before the presence of God?
3 My tears have been my food day and night, *
    while all day long they say to me,
    "Where now is your God?"
4 I pour out my soul when I think on these things: *
    how I went with the multitude and led them into the house of God,
5 With the voice of praise and thanksgiving, *
    among those who keep holy-day.
6 **Why are you so full of heaviness, O my | soul?**
    and why are you so disquieted with | in me?
7 /Put your trust in God;
    for I will yet give / thanks to him,
    who is the help of my countenance, and my / God.
8 My soul is heavy within me; *
    therefore I will remember you from the land of Jordan,
    and from the peak of Mizar among the heights of Hermon.
9 One deep calls to another in the noise of your cataracts; *
    all your rapids and floods have gone over me.
10 The LORD grants his loving-kindness in the daytime; *
    in the night season his song is with me,
    a prayer to the God of my life.
11 **I will say to the God of my strength,**
    "Why have you for | gotten me?
    and why do I go so heavily while the enemy op | presses me?"
12 While my bones are being broken, *
    my enemies mock me to my face.
13 All day long they mock me *
    and say to me, "Where now is your God?"
14 **Why are you so full of heaviness, O my | soul?**
    and why are you so disquieted with | in me?
15 /Put your trust in God;
    for I will yet give / thanks to him,
    who is the help of my countenance, and my / God.

Psalm 43 (BCP)

1 Give judgment for me, O God,
    and defend my cause against an ungodly people; *
    deliver me from the deceitful and the wicked.
2 **For you are the God of my strength;**
    why have you put me | from you?
    and why do I go so heavily while the enemy op|presses me?
3 Send out your light and your truth, that they may lead me, *
    and bring me to your holy hill
    and to your dwelling;
4 That I may go to the altar of God,
    to the God of my joy and gladness; *
    and on the harp I will give thanks to you, O God my God.
5 **Why are you so full of heaviness, O my | soul?**
    and why are you so disquieted with|in me?
    /Put your trust in God;
    for I will yet give / thanks to him,
    who is the help of my countenance, and my / God.

For I Do Not Trust In My Bow: Commentary To Psalm 44

KI LO.-V:QASHTIY .EVtA# W:#ARBIY LO. TOSHI"ÉNI
v.6 For I do not trust in my bow,
and my sword will not save me.

The success is not mine, and I accept that, at least superficially. "The LORD gets the credit, not me." I say this with a warm, good feeling. It sounds humble and feels religious. Rarely do I ask, "Why me?" or think how unfair it all is. In the time of success I am glowing. I must have done something right.

The failure is also not mine, but I accept it badly. I experience outrage. Who can I blame or sue? I did what I thought was right. I tried to be a good man. Now it is easy to ask, "Why me?" and to think how unfair it all is. I go over and over what happened, in my thoughts. Where did I go wrong? How did I fail?

In victory time it is easy to be humble. "It was nothing," I say, "I owe it all to..." In failure I suffer alone. There is no one to share my humiliation, and no one wants to hear my explanation. I turn to God, but I don't like what I hear. I thought we had a covenant, LORD. I have prayed and worshiped you daily; I have never forgotten. I have listened to you in my heart and studied your Word. And now that I need your help, I get no answers. Where are the miracles now?

"URÁh LÁMMÁH TIYSHAN YHWH
v.23 Awake, O Lord, why are you sleeping?

A cry of outrage, saying the unthinkable. And I think it is acceptable to him. I think he would rather hear an honest "Why are you sleeping?" than a false "Thy will be done." Success and disaster are both in his control, both unexplained. Theologians have theories that give no comfort. One thing seems clear about God: he gives no explanations.

As a therapist perhaps I can learn from this. Listen to the cry of outrage; have no explanations. Listen and try to understand, but give no answers. I do not know why bad things happen. I do not know what lies ahead for you. I cannot speak for God. I will listen and try to understand. I will try to get inside your inner world, your feelings. I will not tell you what to do. If you rage at God and ask, "Why are you sleeping?" — I will listen. I think that is what God does.

Suggestions: Sing refrains to the Tone #a3O3:ROTH (*trumpets*) and observe [Silence...] where indicated.

Be aware that you cannot rely on your "bow" or your "sword" — your own abilities — for anything. Read Psalm 44 as a story, a process of transformation from one state of being to another. We might see it as the painful evolution from religious boasting to outraged complaining to the cry of desperation. From flattering and manipulating God to the acceptance of helplessness. Now read Psalm 44 as your own story.

Psalm 44 (BCP)

Ninth Day: Morning Prayer Tone: #A3O3:ROTH

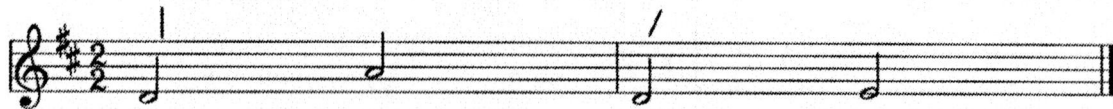

1 We have heard with our ears, O God,
   our forefathers have told us, *
   the deeds you did in their days, in the days of old.
2 How with your hand you drove the peoples out
   and planted our forefathers in the land; *
   how you destroyed nations and made your people flourish.
3 **For they did not take the land by their | sword,**
   /nor did their arm win the victory / for them;
   but your right hand, your arm, and the light of your countenance,
   because you favored them.
4 You are my King and my God; *
   you command victories for Jacob.
5 Through you we pushed back our adversaries; *
   through your Name we trampled on those who rose up against us.
6 **For I do not rely on my | bow,**
   /and my sword does not give me the / victory.
7 Surely, you gave us victory over our adversaries *
   and put those who hate us to shame.
8 Every day we gloried in God, *
   and we will praise your Name for ever.
             [Silence...]
9 Nevertheless, you have rejected and humbled us *
   and do not go forth with our armies.
10 You have made us fall back before our adversary, *
   and our enemies have plundered us.
11 You have made us like sheep to be eaten *
   and have scattered us among the nations.
12 You are selling your people for a trifle *
   and are making no profit on the sale of them.
13 You have made us the scorn of our neighbors, *
   a mockery and derision to those around us.
14 You have made us a byword among the nations, *
   a laughing-stock among the peoples.
15 My humiliation is daily before me, *
   and shame has covered my face.
16 Because of the taunts of the mockers and blasphemers, *
   because of the enemy and avenger.

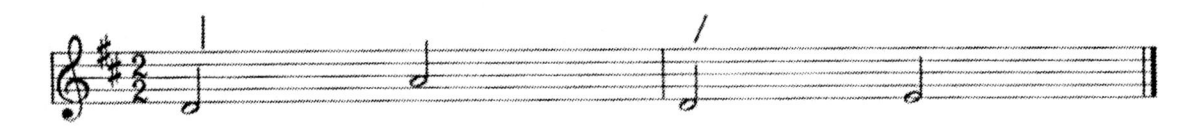

17 All this has come upon us; *
    yet we have not forgotten you,
    nor have we betrayed your covenant.
18 Our heart never turned back, *
    nor did our footsteps stray from your path;
19 Though you thrust us down into a place of misery, *
    and covered us over with deep darkness.
20 If we have forgotten the Name of our God, *
    or stretched out our hands to some strange god,
21 Will not God find it out? *
    for he knows the secrets of the heart.
22 Indeed, for your sake we are killed all the day long; *
    we are accounted as sheep for the slaughter.
23 **Awake, O Lord! why are you | sleeping?**
    /Arise! do not reject us for / ever.
24 Why have you hidden your face *
    and forgotten our affliction and oppression?
25 We sink down into the dust; *
    our body cleaves to the ground.
26 **Rise up, and | help us,**
    /and save us, for the sake of your steadfast / love.

Royal Wedding: Commentary To Psalm 45

> Therefore shall a man leave his father and his mother, and shall cleave unto his wife; and they shall be one flesh (Genesis 2:24, KJV).

Today I'm invited to a royal wedding. The groom is someone I truly admire and respect, my dearest friend. I think I would follow him anywhere. And today in his moment of glory, there is also a sadness. Every wedding is a mixture of leaving and cleaving, of joy and that strange sadness. Something precious is gained, something given up. I remember my bachelor apartment, decorated in a black and white zebra motif. Zebra pillows and a fake zebra rug, pictures of zebras and shiny black tables created an ambience, a life-style. Living there my life was empty and lonely. I would never go back to it; yet I was scared to surrender it. I found my life companion, but it was hard to give up my zebras.

Covenant means one path chosen, every other path given up. And the chosen path will be followed, come what may. Not to be tried for a while, but to be lived. Like Mooch, who appeared at our wedding and stayed to be our cat. We threw him out the back door but he came back in at the front, climbed on the judge's lap and stayed for the ceremony. And stayed with us till he died. I never knew much about cats or intimacy; I am still learning.

TA#ATh .aVOTHEYKHÁ YIH:YUW VÁNEYKHÁ
v.17 In place of your fathers there shall be your sons.

You will be known more and more by your fruits and not your roots. Your parents did what they could and are resting. Now it is you who ride forth, "ride high on truthfulness" (v.4, Feuer*). In every great moment of life, something is chosen, something given up. A road less traveled is taken to the end. That is what it means to grow up. It is the glory of adulthood.

v.11 and forget your people and your father's house. Speaking now to the bride in "cloth of gold." Something beautiful gained, something given up. A people, family, identity, perhaps even a language. What will she remember from this day of excitement and confusion? The guests from Tyre? That gown of cloth of gold? Myrrh, aloes, and cassia? Or me, my hand cold and trembling in that covenant moment?

<u>Suggestions</u>: Read v.1, sing vv. 2-18, paying close attention to the Tone markers, as the music does not always follow the division of lines and verses.

Ponder this psalm on its many levels. Think of those moments of choice in your life, in the life of your father and your mother. Think of those covenant moments in the life of Jesus. Renew your own covenants daily.

---

*Rabbi Avrohom Chaim Feuer: *Tehillim (Psalms)/ A New Translation with a Commentary Anthologized from Talmudic, Midrashic and Rabbinic Sources.* Mesorah Publications, Ltd., Brooklyn, NY, 1977, p.565.

Psalm 45 (BCP)

Tone: "ÁSOR

1 My heart is stirring with a noble song; let me recite what I have fashioned for the king; *
   my tongue shall be the pen of a skilled writer.
2 **You are the fairest of men; grace flows from your | lips,**
   because God has | blessed you for | ever.
3 Strap your sword upon your thigh, O mighty / warrior,
   in your / pride and in your / majesty.
4 \ Ride out and conquer in the cause of \ truth
   and for the sake of \ justice.
5 Your right hand will show you marvelous . things;
   your arrows are very sharp, O mighty . warrior.
6 The peoples are falling at your . feet,
   and the king's enemies are losing . heart.
7 **Your throne, O God, endures for ever and | ever,**
   a scepter of righteousness is the | scepter of your | kingdom;
   you love righteousness and hate / iniquity.
8 Therefore God, your / God, has an/ointed you
   \ with the oil of gladness above your \ fellows.
9 All your garments are fragrant with myrrh, aloes, and \ cassia,
   and the music of . strings from ivory . palaces makes you glad.
10 **Kings' daughters stand among the ladies of the court; on your right hand is the | queen,**
   adorned with the | gold of | Ophir.
11 "Hear, O daughter; consider and listen / closely;
   forget your / people and your / father's house.
12 \ The king will have pleasure in your \ beauty;
   he is your master; therefore do him \ honor.
13 The people of Tyre are here with a . gift;
   the rich among the people seek your . favor."
14 **All glorious is the princess as she | enters;**
   her | gown is cloth of | gold.
15 In embroidered apparel she is brought to the / king;
   after her the / bridesmaids / follow in procession.
16 \ With joy and gladness they are \ brought,
   and enter into the palace of the \ king.

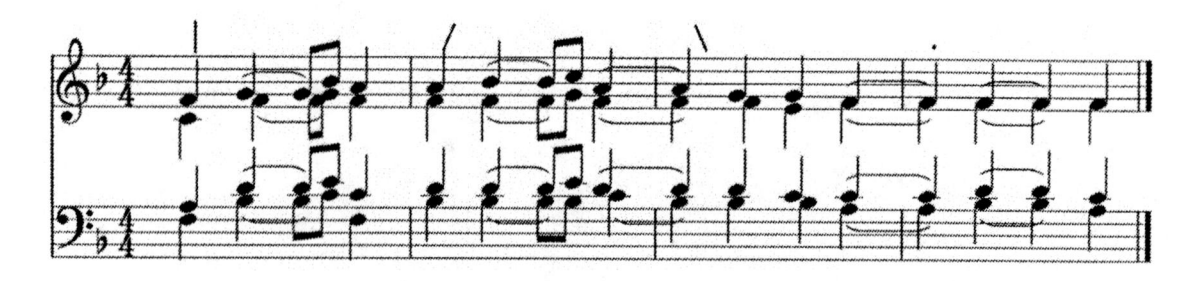

17 "In place of fathers, O King, you shall have . sons;
   you shall make them princes over . all the earth.
18 **I will make your name to be remembered from one generation to an | other;**
   therefore nations will | praise you for | ever and ever."

Found, Very Much: Commentary To Psalm 46

.eLOHIM L̲ÁNU MA#aSEH WÁ"OZ "EZRÁH V:3ÁROTH NIM3Á. M:.OD

v.1 God is for us a sheltering-place and strength,
a help in troubles he is found, very much.

God does not provide but *is* that place of shelter, hiding place, and strength. Not like a back yard shelter I could go when I wish; he himself is the place. Likewise the help he does not send, but is, hard to accept. Not so I could choose when to use it or keep it for emergencies. I find him when all has failed, at the point of desperation.

Miracles come at the moment of need, to be used, not saved for later. Every miracle is an elegant solution to an unsolvable problem, yet though I may admire it and think, "How obvious!" I can never learn how it's done. The only thing I learn from a miracle is to trust him—hard to accept.

Harder still, he is our help in troubles. Almost the same word in Hebrew as the "enemies" of Psalm 1. Stress. The forces that hem me in, compress me, and smother me. From a root that means narrow or compressed, like the word *anxiety*. If God is found in stress, why worry about stress?

Because he is my help, my room to breathe, my stress-relief, in troubles. In stress. Not just in church or in meditation, but when it seems that everyone is screaming at me, having me paged, and blaming me. He is there in the troubles, not around, behind, or beyond them. There, where I said, "I can't stand it any more," or, "I am stressed out." There will I find him. He is found there M:.OD (*very much*). Not by accident but by design. Hard sayings, how will I live them? How can I grasp that God is in the problem; that conflict and stress are not the detour but the path? That God has placed me in a world of conflict, but he is here in the midst of it?

v.2 Therefore we will not fear though the earth change. Though everything change. Though in truth I am afraid when anything changes. Though change is difficult, even if good.

HARPUW UD:"UW KI-.ÁNOKHIY .eLOHIM

v.11 Let go, then, and know that I am God. Give up control, and know. Let go, relax, release, give up control of the outcome and accept the moment. This verse is not about silent meditation, but surrender. True spirituality is this: a life-long process of positive, active, willing, enlightened surrender. Letting go and letting go and letting go.

<u>Note</u>: Verse 4. This refrain—"The LORD of hosts is with us"—is not found in the Masoretic text, and may be omitted here if desired.

<u>Suggestions</u>: Practice letting go, moment by moment, as you go through the day. Take each moment as it comes, let go of the moment that has passed. Let go of the last conversation, the last thing that happened at work today. Let go of the next five minutes, the next hour, tomorrow, the results of your work. Let go.

Psalm 46 (BCP)

Tone: TOPH *irregular*

1 God is our refuge and strength, *
 a very present help in trouble.
2 Therefore we will not fear, though the earth be moved, *
 and though the mountains be toppled into the
 depths of the sea;
3 Though its waters rage and foam, *
 and though the mountains tremble at its tumult.
 [Silence...]
4 /The LORD of hosts is / with us; (*)
 the God of Jacob is our / stronghold.
5 There is a river, whose streams make glad the city of God, *
 the holy habitation of the Most High.
6 God is in the midst of her;
 she shall not be overthrown; *
 God shall help her at the break of day.
7 The nations make much ado, and the kingdoms are shaken; *
 God has spoken, and the earth shall melt away.
8 /The LORD of hosts is / with us;
 the God of Jacob is our / stronghold.
 [Silence...]
9 **Còme now and | lòok upon the | wòrks of the | LÒRD,**
 what àwesome thìngs he has dòne on | èarth.
10 It is he who makes war to cease in all the world; *
 he breaks the bow, and shatters the spear,
 and burns the shields with fire.
11 "Be still, then, and know that I am God; *
 I will be exalted among the nations;
 I will be exalted in the earth."
12 /The LORD of hosts is / with us;
 the God of Jacob is our / stronghold.
 [Silence...]

All The Peoples: Commentary To Psalm 47

KOL-HÁ"AMMIM TIQ"U-KHÁPH HÁ<u>RIY</u>"U LÉ.LOHIM B:QOL RINNÁH

v.1 All the peoples, strike the hand (clap hands);
shout to God with a cry of joy.

All the peoples are invited to this celebration, for true praise includes and brings together. No one is excluded. This will be hard for some disciples. No one will be asked to sign a statement of beliefs. Whoever celebrates belongs.

Which is not to say that "all are saved." Or that all may do as they please. God will sift the wheat from the weeds. But those who celebrate God will celebrate together. Including some difficult people. Some who are not saved exactly as we define it, and some who may not think about Jesus exactly as we do. True praise includes. No one is left out.

v.2 For the LORD Most High is to be feared;

For the fear of God eliminates divisions. For to fear God is to fear no one else—no class, nationality, race, or belief. To fear God is to judge no one. So that there are no classes of disciples, no first and second class followers. If you ask to be with us, you are with us. This is your dance. Compare 122.

vv. 3-4 He subdues the peoples under us ... under our feet ... chooses our inheritance ... the pride of Jacob (our family).

He subdues whom he wishes to subdue, and chooses as he chooses. We (our kind, our group, our denomination, our non-denomination), we neither subdue nor choose. Our unique role in his plan is given to us for a time and place; then it is handed to another. The people of God have always struggled with this tension—the sense of being set apart; the imperative of inclusion. I have chosen to emphasize the latter, the radical inclusiveness of the psalms. I know this will upset some readers. I find nothing here about excluding anyone, anyone at all, from fellowship, from worship, from communion, from ordination, from anything.

v.9 The nobles of the peoples have gathered together.

Recognizing the true source of authority, the leaders of nations are coming together. Just as all that is negative creates division, so praise brings together, even in the most difficult situations. The rival governments of Earth, long in deadly competition, begin drawing together, in praise, with the people of our family. As they do so, they find common interest with all who praise him. No longer shall they say, "the enemy of my enemy is my friend," but, "whoever affirms my God affirms me!"

<u>Suggestions</u>: Sing to the movement Marching and Swaying Dance, or Standing Drum (see Appendix). Practice the teaching of not judging (Matthew 7:1) in its most radical form: Do not judge (exclude) even those who judge others. Do not judge (exclude) even those who boast of their intolerance.

Psalm 47 (BCP)

Ninth Day: Evening Prayer Tone: SHOPHÁR

1 ` ` ` `**Clàp your hànds, all you | pèoples;** `
   shout to Gòd with a cry` of | jòy. `
2 /For the LÒRD Most Hìgh is to be / fèared; `
   he is the grèat King òver all / the èarth. `
3 \He subdues the peoples \ under us,
   and the nations under our \ feet.
4 He chooses our inheritance \ for us,
   the pride of Jacob whom he \ loves.
               [Silence...]
5 **Gòd has gone ùp with a | shòut,** `
   the LÒRD with the sòund of the | ràm's-horn. `
6 /Sing pràises to Gòd, sing / pràises; `
   sing pràises to our Kìng, sing / prài`ses. `
7 \For God is King of all the \ earth;
   sing praises with all your \ skill.
8 God reigns over the \ nations;
   God sits upon his holy \ throne.
9 **The nòbles of the pèoples have gàthered to | gèther** `
   with the pèople of the Gòd of | Àbraham. `
10 /The rùlers of the èarth belong to / Gòd, `
   and hè is hìghly ex/àltèd.

A Dance Of Holiness: Commentary To Psalm 48

Is this the city that is called "the perfection of beauty, the joy of the whole earth"? Lamentations 2:15 (NKJ).

There is a chilling undertone to this beautiful dance of Jerusalem. Even as we dance we hear whispers of doom. There is still a city called Jerusalem, but that Jerusalem is gone forever.

v.1b In the city of our God is his holy hill. Holiness for God is universal. Holiness for us is always local. It is found in special things and particular places. In real neighborhoods. In a city, a temple, or a place called holy of holies. Untouched, set apart and special, it leads us heavenward. Holiness, in particular things, is our channel to God.

DIMMIYNU .eLOHIM #ASDEKHÁ B:QEREBh HEYKHÁLEKHÁ
v.8 We have waited in silence,
on your loving-kindness, O God,
in the midst of your temple.

God is not limited to a temple or a city. Yet that room set apart in that reverential way, that no one could enter, was a place where men once found him. Strangely enough, they found him in that silent place by not going in. It was a teaching in the form of a building, silence made visible. Made holy by meticulous observance and sacred boundaries.

We have waited in silence, O God, in the infinitesimal space between thought and thought. Not in doing or trying, but in the practice of silence. Moments not used to accomplish but to wait, to listen. Surrender and constancy, that is spirit and truth. We have waited in silence, O God, in a temple of great stones. We have waited in silence in the places we find ourselves. Just silence, here and now [Silence...].

v.11 Make the circuit of Zion;
walk round about her;
count the number of her towers.

Remember all holy things. Search them out and study them. Seek holiness in all things, and keep them holy. Protect all holy traditions—those of your family and those of all families. The holiness of God is absolute, beyond space and time. What is holy here on earth is holy by intention. By protecting, keeping apart, remembering.

Suggestions: Sing to the movement Twirling Dance (see Appendix). There are three Orders (musical phrases) to this music, each of two measures. In a verse of three lines, like 1, 6, 8, you will repeat the second measure of the indicated Order. Note that several verses have been modified by the author (*), to reflect the Hebrew more accurately as well as to enhance the rhythm.

Study Psalm 79 and the Book of Lamentations. Continue to practice your meditation, morning and evening. Create a sacred space for it, and sacred times. Continue your moments of silence, all through the day. These things will be your temple.

Psalm 48 (BCP), modified*

Tone: MÁ#OL

1. \Great is the LORD, and highly to be \ praised;
    in the city of our \ God
    is his \ holy hill.
2. \Beautiful and lofty, the joy of all the \ earth,
    is the hill of \ Zion,
    /the very center of the / world
    and the city of the / great King.
3. **God is | in her | citadels;**
    he is known as her | stronghold. (*)
4. \Behold, the kings of the earth \ assembled
    and marched forward \ together.
5. \They looked and were a\stounded;
    they retreated and fled in \ terror.
6. /Trembling / seized them there;
    they writhed like a woman in / childbirth,
    like ships of the sea when the east wind / shatters them.
7. **As we have heard, | so we have | seen,**
    in the city of the | LORD of hosts,
    \in the city of God, our \ God; (*)
    he established her for \ ever. (*)
                    [Silence...]
8. /We have waited in / silence,
    on your loving-/ kindness, O God,
    in the midst of your / temple.
9. \Your praise, like your \ Name, O God,
    reaches to the \ world's end;
    your right hand is full of \ justice.
10. \Let Mount Zion be \ glad
    and the daughters of \ Judah rejoice, (*)
    because of your \ judgments.
11. /Make the circuit of / Zion;
    walk round / about her;
    count the number of her / towers.

12 \Consider well her \ bulwarks;
   examine her \ strongholds;
     that you may tell those who come \ after.
13 **For this is | God our | God, (*)**
   for ever and | ever;
     he shall guide us for | ever. (*)

Death Is Their Shepherd: Commentary To Psalm 49

As a college student I was intrigued by "The Seventh Seal," Ingmar Bergman's symbolic drama of life and death. An aging knight, played by Max von Sydow, returns from the crusades to face a personalized encounter with Death. All is emptiness, Bergman proclaims in a series of harsh vignettes. Life is cruel and meaningless.

The knight has a chance to play chess with Death. If he wins Death will spare him. Although the game goes on for days, there is no doubt of its outcome. At least our hero manages some dignity when Death comes to his home to take him. The last scene will always remain with me: the silhouetted figures of the knight and his friends following Death along a distant ridge. Death leads them dancing to oblivion.

I think of this haunting picture when I read Psalm 49. I think of that gaunt, gray knight to whom life is indeed empty. Empty because, as far as I can tell, it has been without meaning. Its high point is a chess game with Death. He seems to relish the contest; for one brief moment he convinces himself that he can win. Then he confides his winning strategy, in the confession booth, to a "priest" who in fact is Death. Well, if Death is cheating at chess, to whom can one complain?

<u>MÁWETh YIR"ÉM</u>

v.13 Death is their Shepherd (literally *Death shepherds them* or *grazes them*) and definitely not the Good Shepherd. This shepherd does not lead his flock to green pastures but to SH.OL (*Sheol*, the Pit) — the place of oblivion. I picture him dancing along the ridge that leads to emptiness, his followers straggling behind. And who are his followers? The rich, the wise, the learned, the old families, all who think they know a thing or two, all who like to hear themselves talk, just about everyone. The best and the brightest and everyone else will be walking that Trail of Tears.

v.15 But God will ransom my life;
he will snatch me from the grasp of death.

No details. God, like the Army, operates on a need-to-know basis. Somehow, through this relationship with Jesus, I belong to eternity. That is my only hope. I do not even begin to understand this. I still find myself playing chess with Death, looking for meaning in meaningless contests. Just a little more recognition, just a little more experience, just one more esoteric book, just one more technique of enlightenment, just one more publication. Then I remember — again — that my life has no meaning that I can give it or find for it. It is meaningless except as I surrender it. It is the Shepherd who finds meaning in the sheep.

Many years later, I saw "The Seventh Seal" again. Somehow the haunting magic of the movie had faded. Now it was all too clear why the characters brooded about emptiness and romanticized Death. There were symbols of Christianity in that bleak Swedish landscape, but no God. In a world of thoughts and emotions the old knight wandered hopelessly, untouched by God.

<u>Suggestions</u>: Sing the refrains. Do not search for the meaning of life. Seek God. Spend time in silence, listening for his voice.

Psalm 49 (BCP)

Tone: N:GINOTH

1 Hear this, all you peoples;
   hearken, all you who dwell in the world, *
   you of high degree and low, rich and poor together.
2 My mouth shall speak of wisdom, *
   and my heart shall meditate on understanding.
3 I will incline my ear to a proverb *
   and set forth my riddle upon the harp.
4 Why should I be afraid in evil days, *
   when the wickedness of those at my heels surrounds me,
5 The wickedness of those who put their trust in their goods, *
   and boast of their great riches?
6 We can never ransom ourselves, *
   or deliver to God the price of our life;
7 For the ransom of our life is so great, *
   that we should never have enough to pay it,
8 In order to live for ever and ever, *
   and never see the grave.
9 For we see that the wise die also;
   like the dull and stupid they perish *
   and leave their wealth to those who come after them.
10 Their graves shall be their homes for ever,
   their dwelling places from generation to generation, *
   though they call the lands after their own names.
11 **Even though honored, they cannot | live for ever;**
   they are | like the beasts that | perish.
12 Such is the way of those who foolishly trust in themselves, *
   and the end of those who delight in their own words.
              [Silence...]
13 Like a flock of sheep they are destined to die;
   Death is their shepherd; *
   they go down straightway to the grave.
14 Their form shall waste away, *
   and the land of the dead shall be their home.
15 But God will ransom my life; *
   he will snatch me from the grasp of death.
              [Silence...]

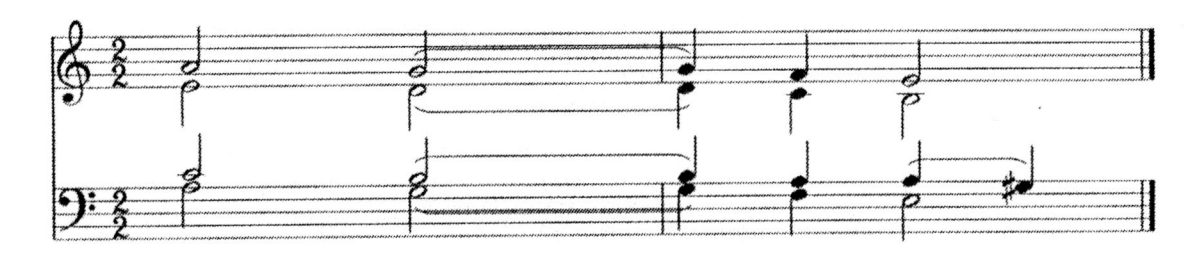

16 Do not be envious when some become rich, *
    or when the grandeur of their house increases;
17 For they will carry nothing away at their death, *
    nor will their grandeur follow them.
18 Though they thought highly of themselves while they lived, *
    and were praised for their success,
19 They shall join the company of their forebears, *
    who will never see the light again.
20 **Those who are honored, but | have no understanding,**
    are | like the beasts that | perish.

Not Because Of Your Sacrifices: Commentary To Psalm 50

v.8 I do not accuse you because of your sacrifices;
your offerings are always before me.

Think of sacrifice as a spiritual practice. I give my life to God and he gives it back to me. I take something I need and enjoy, lift it up to God, let it go, give up control of it. And God gives it back to me many times over. Like any spiritual practice it can become ritualized, practiced as if it were important in itself. To my beloved Episcopal Church, for example, he might say: "I do not accuse you because of your Eucharists.

"Because in fact you are doing very well with these. You are having eucharistic services morning, noon, and night, every Sunday, with and without music, Rite I and Rite II, high Mass with incense, folk Mass with guitars, family Eucharist and services for children. But, you see, I do not need Eucharists. I do not eat communion wafers or drink wine mixed with water. And if I did, I would not need these things from you."

God does not need our offerings and sacrifices. We ourselves need them. He allows us to observe these practices because of what they can do for us. Because they can liberate us from the endless pursuit of more and better. They can lift our awareness to him. Unfortunately we soon forget why we do them. We make our offerings out of habit, out of guilt; resentfully or proudly. We do it because we learned to do it.

v.14 Offer to God (a sacrifice of) thanksgiving. What God really wants from me, the offering that may be most difficult, is thankfulness itself. Gratitude. Sometimes easy, sometimes almost impossible. Not to deprive myself of something, but to share it with him. What God really wants from me is a relationship of affirmation. I offer him thanksgiving, and I call upon him, and he delivers me, and I honor him.

v.20 You are always speaking evil of your brother ... your own mother's son. I always stumble on this verse. I talk about my brother all the time. It is easy for me to ridicule him because I know him so well. But God doesn't think it funny. Verses 16-23 remind us that religion is not even acceptable to God unless we live in a moral way. "Why do you offer me Eucharists," he might be saying, "while you continue to say terrible things about one another?"

Suggestions: Sing refrains with the wave gesture for thank offerings (see Edersheim*). Beginning with the praise gesture, lift and lower the hands on 14a and 24a, move them from left to right on 14b and 24b, ending in the original position.

Practice thankfulness with your whole heart. God does not need your sacrifices and offerings, but he honors your grateful attitude. Ask yourself this: What are the practices of my religion or denomination that God does not need? He might be saying of those things, even now, "I do not accuse you because of that."

---

*Alfred Edersheim: *The Temple, Its Ministry and Services*. Updated Edition, Hendrickson Publishers, Peabody, MA, 1995, p. 82.

Psalm 50 (BCP)

Tenth Day: Morning Prayer   **Tone: KINNOR (1)**

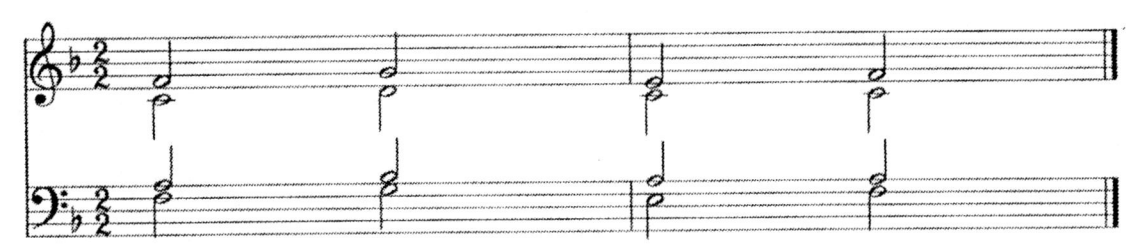

1 The LORD, the God of gods, has spoken; *
   he has called the earth from the rising of the sun to its setting.
2 Out of Zion, perfect in its beauty, *
   God reveals himself in glory.
3 Our God will come and will not keep silence; *
   before him there is a consuming flame,
   and round about him a raging storm.
4 He calls the heavens and the earth from above *
   to witness the judgment of his people.
5 "Gather before me my loyal followers, *
   those who have made a covenant with me and sealed it with sacrifice."
6 Let the heavens declare the rightness of his cause; *
   for God himself is judge.
                  [Silence...]
7 Hear, O my people, and I will speak:
   "O Israel, I will bear witness against you; *
   for I am God, your God.
8 I do not accuse you because of your sacrifices; *
   your offerings are always before me.
9 I will take no bull-calf from your stalls, *
   nor he-goats out of your pens;
10 For all the beasts of the forest are mine, *
   the herds in their thousands upon the hills.
11 I know every bird in the sky, *
   and the creatures of the fields are in my sight.
12 If I were hungry, I would not tell you, *
   for the whole world is mine and all that is in it.
13 Do you think I eat the flesh of bulls, *
   or drink the blood of goats?
14 **Offer to God a sacrifice of thanks | giving**
   and make good your vows to the Most | High.
15 Call upon me in the day of trouble; *
   I will deliver you, and you shall honor me."
16 But to the wicked God says: *
   "Why do you recite my statutes, and take my covenant upon your lips;

17 Since you refuse discipline, *
    and toss my words behind your back?
18 When you see a thief, you make him your friend, *
    and you cast in your lot with adulterers.
19 You have loosed your lips for evil, *
    and harnessed your tongue to a lie.
20 You are always speaking evil of your brother *
    and slandering your own mother's son.
21 These things you have done, and I kept still, *
    and you thought that I am like you."
22 "I have made my accusation; *
    I have put my case in order before your eyes.
23 Consider this well, you who forget God, *
    lest I rend you and there be none to deliver you.
24 **Whoever offers me the sacrifice of thanksgiving | honors me;**
    but to those who keep in my way will I show the sal|vation of God."

Wash Me: Commentary To Psalm 51

v.2 Wash me through and through from my wickedness
and cleanse me from my (state of) sin.

    KI-PH:SHÁ"ÁY .aNIY .ÉDÁ" W:#AttÁ.THIY NEGDIY THÁMIYD

v.3 For I know my (deliberate) transgressions,
and my (state of) sin is ever before me.

There are three levels of moral discomfort. Shame is public, like embarrassment. What I have done is bad because people know about it. If I can hide it, I feel better.

Guilt is more private. What I have done is bad because I myself know. Most of the time I deal with guilt by making excuses or by getting irritable. "Let's not talk about that," I might say. The only thing that really helps is to make it right with the person I hurt (if possible), and for that person to forgive me (if they so choose). See especially Matthew 5:23-24. Some guilt cannot be relieved. What I have done cannot be repaired. Or the victim doesn't choose to forgive. All I can do is ask. When I have really done all I can, forgive myself.

In the practice of psychiatry I often see pathologic guilt. A sense of condemnation, looking for a reason. Some small thing I might have done, years before. I smoked a cigarette. I looked at a woman. Now I am haunted by a sense of damnation. Some patients believe they have committed the unpardonable sin. It is one of the most obscure concepts in Scripture, but they are clear about it. They are convinced that God cannot forgive them.

Perhaps in a sense it's true. If I insist that God cannot help me, perhaps I am committing the sin that cannot be forgiven. God doesn't force forgiveness on anyone. But the patients don't say it like that. It's always in the past tense, and there's nothing they can do about it. "Sometimes," a frustrated pastor once said to me, "you would like to tell them, 'Yes, you are probably going to hell. Go ahead and pack your bags, but don't take any winter clothing!'"

The sense of sin is the most private of all. Maybe no one will ever know, but God knows. The sense of sin is between me and God. Hiding doesn't help. Restitution doesn't help. The only thing that helps is divine laundering. Have mercy on me. Wash me. Cleanse me. Look into me as deep as you will, see how bad I am, clean me.

Shame seems less of a problem as we get older. Guilt is more manageable as we learn the rules of life. But strangely, the sense of sin grows stronger. The farther we go in spiritual life, the more we are aware of it. It is a basic flaw, not a symptom. Our innate, inherited tendency to fly off under our own direction, even though we have no compass, no way to steer, and no place worth going. See Psalm 1. I was born with it and I cannot change it.

Verses 3-7 deal with the diagnosis; 8-13 with the treatment.

    LÉV tÁHOR B:RÁ.-LIY .eLOHIM W:RUa# NÁKHON #ADDÉSH B:QIRBIY

v.11 Create in me a clean heart, O God,
and renew a right spirit within me.

Create in me—B:RÁ. (*create out of nothing*) in me — as you created the world—a new heart. That inner place, where I sort out my thoughts and make hard choices. Perhaps it is best translated as attitude. Create in me, O God, a new and teachable attitude, an attitude of surrender. Compare 73.

And renew a right spirit within me. Renew, restore my breath, my RUa# (*spirit*), that delicate little breath of wind that makes me a living soul. That blows through me but doesn't belong to me. That I do not own nor control, never boast of, seek to follow. Breathe it into me, LORD, now.

Create in me, out of nothing, a new attitude; animate me with a new and right spirit. And support me with your Spirit. Not a self-help operation, but radical surgery. And it works! I want to tell everyone about it and sing about it. If God would let me, I would even offer sacrifices. All he requires is an attitude of helpless surrender; but now, with a new heart and a refreshed spirit I come to him, and he allows me to practice religion. Compare 50.

Personal Reflection

Coming to church that morning I was irritable as usual. Church makes so many demands. If I haven't fought with my family on the way, I'm sure to be irritated before the service is over. I was thinking how the church is like training, like weekend drills, a spiritual discipline that grinds you and shapes you. No pain, no gain.

When the priest said, "Lift up your hearts," we responded, "We lift them to the LORD" (Prayer Book, p. 361). Suddenly I understood that quaint expression. Lift up, elevate your attitude, toward me (God). Lift up your attitude from the earthly to the spiritual, and I will take you and create in you a new and clean attitude. And he did. And I was ready to pray.

<u>Suggestions</u>: Sing the refrains as shown. Do not attempt to create a new heart (attitude) for yourself out of thoughts or words. Not with injunctions or admonitions to do better or try harder. Let God create in you a new heart out of nothing, out of spaces and emptiness. Allow God to do this in your moments of silence. Continue your practice of formal and informal meditation. Clear your thoughts again and again, and listen, so that God can work with you.

Psalm 51 (BCP)

Tone: HIGÁYON

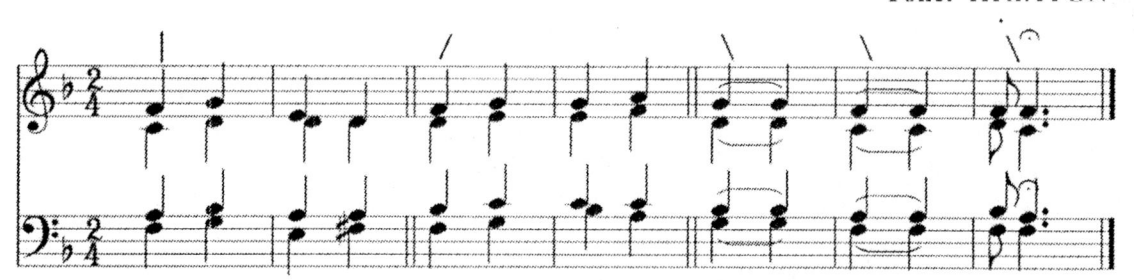

1 Have mercy on me, O God, according to your loving-kindness; *
    in your great compassion blot out my offenses.
2 **Wash me through and through from my | wickedness**
    and cleanse me from my | sin.
3 For I know my transgressions, *
    and my sin is ever before me.
4 Against you only have I sinned *
    and done what is evil in your sight.
5 And so you are justified when you speak *
    and upright in your judgment.
6 Indeed, I have been wicked from my birth, *
    a sinner from my mother's womb.
7 **For behold, you look for truth deep with | in me,**
    and will make me understand wisdom | secretly.
8 Purge me from my sin, and I shall be pure; *
    wash me, and I shall be clean indeed.
9 Make me hear of joy and gladness, *
    that the body you have broken may rejoice.
10 Hide your face from my sins *
    and blot out all my iniquities.
11 Create in me a clean heart, O God, *
    and renew a right spirit within me.
12 Cast me not away from your presence *
    and take not your holy Spirit from me.
13 **Give me the joy of your saving | help again**
    and sustain me with your bountiful | Spirit.
14 /I shall teach your ways to the / wicked,
    and sinners shall re/turn to you.
15 \Deliver me from death, O God,
    \and my tongue shall sing of your righteousness,
    O God of my sal\vation.

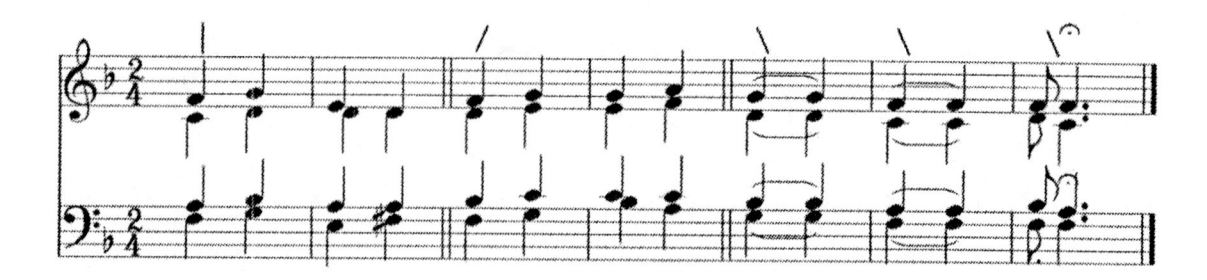

16 Open my lips, O LORD, *
   and my mouth shall proclaim your praise.
17 Had you desired it, I would have offered sacrifice, *
   but you take no delight in burnt-offerings.
18 The sacrifice of God is a troubled spirit; *
   a broken and contrite heart, O God, you will not despise.
19 **/Be favorable and gracious to / Zion,**
   and rebuild the walls of / Jerusalem.
20 \Then you will be pleased with the appointed sacrifices,
      \with burnt-offerings and oblations;
   then shall they offer young bullocks upon your \ altar.

Worker Of Deception: Commentary To Psalm 52

The superscription refers to DO.ÉG (*Doeg*) the Edomite, who betrayed David. Reflecting on DO.ÉG I began to think of Satan.

The subject of Satanism is fascinating to many Christians. They are eager to hear and read about it. Satanism is a sort of negative Christianity, the values and symbols of Christianity turned upside-down. Satanism has no reference point of its own. It is meaningless except as a caricature of the Christian faith.

Yet some Christians seem to define their faith in terms of Satan—fighting, resisting, and rebuking Satan. They look for Satan and Satanism everywhere. To understand these things we must understand a little bit about Satan. Just enough to avoid becoming fascinated with Satan.

v.2 O worker of deception.

The main characteristics of Satan, as I understand them, are deceit, confusion, and intimidation. To act satanically is to create a cloud of confusion and fear. To tell a different story to each person. To deny what you told me earlier and blame me for the confusion. To intimidate me with frightening stories and threats. To entice me into doing wrong and then condemn me.

v.4 You love all words that hurt,
O tongue of deception.

Dealing with satanic behavior you feel "jerked around," torn apart. The whole point is to hurt. Sometimes the language is apparently Christian. There is talk of Jesus and the Holy Spirit, but the talk hurts and confuses. Prayer and deliverance are commended, but the real topic is condemnation. This one *claims to be a Christian* and that one has *a demonic spirit*. This thing is *of the devil* and that group is *a cult*. What about you? Maybe you are of the devil, too! Soon you find yourself choosing your words and concealing your thoughts. You find yourself becoming dishonest to prove you are Christian.

The name DO.ÉG means worrier. He worries and gets others to worry. Lacking internal constancy, he runs about looking for security. Finding it not, he tries to destroy insecurity. He may quote Jesus but he is trusting only in himself. The answer? Only God can deal with Satan. The righteous shall see ... tremble ... laugh ... look on in amazement (vv. 6-7), planted securely ... in the house of God." The righteous are rooted in God and do not concern themselves with Satan.

<u>Suggestions</u>: Sing cheerfully to the Tone MÁ#OL (*dance*) and the movement Twirling Dance (see Appendix). Note that the second measure of the second Order is repeated in the three-line verses, 1, 3, 7 and 9.

Do not concern yourself with Satan; do not communicate in any way with Satan or with demons, even to rebuke them. Do not associate with those who are given to condemnation. Do not condemn or denounce anyone.

Psalm 52 (BCP)

Tone: MÁ#OL

1 \You tyrant, why do you boast of \ wickedness
   against the godly all day \ long?
2 You plot \ ruin;
   your tongue is like a | sharpened | razor,
   O worker of de|ception.
3 \You love evil more than \ good
   and lying more than speaking the \ truth.
                   [Silence...]
4 **You love all | words that | hurt,**
   O you deceitful | tongue.
5 \Oh, that God would demolish you \ utterly,
   topple you, and snatch you from your \ dwelling,
   and root you out of the land of the \ living.
[Silence...]
6 **The righteous shall | see and | tremble,**
   and they shall laugh at him, | saying,
7 \ "This is the one who did not take God for a \ refuge,
   but trusted in great \ wealth
   and relied upon \ wickedness."
8 **But I am like a | green olive | tree**
   in the house of | God;
   I trust in the | mercy of | God
   for ever and | ever.
9 \I will give you thanks for what you have \ done
   and declare the goodness of your \ Name
   in the presence of the \ godly.

The Fool Says No: Commentary To Psalm 53

The minor differences between 53 and 14 need not concern us. Let us take a slightly different approach.

.ÁMAR NÁVÁL B:LIBBOW   .EYN .eLOHIM
v.1 The fool has said in his heart (attitude), "No! There ain't no God!"

It may be the most primitive and powerful thought in the brain: No. We learn it very early. *No I won't. You can't make me. You can't stop me. No.* When our children begin to use it we are amazed. We hear ourselves say it and we are embarrassed. It is the thought that cancels all other thoughts and brings everything to a stop. We cannot reason with it or persuade it. It is the tiny bit of behavior that underlies all rebellion, refusal and stubbornness.

We seem to need that word in our development. By learning to say no I begin to experience myself as a separate being. I begin to understand that others are not extensions of my self and that I am not an extension of anyone else. It is a painful process that psychiatrists call individuation—becoming a human individual. None of this could take place without that ability to say no.

We learn to express it more politely. *I'll try. I'll see. I don't know. I forget. I can't. I don't have time. I wish I could but...* Sometimes we can't bring ourselves to say it at all—we just—don't. We forget. We don't show up. We feel bad about it and we say *I'm sorry*. We may say we *feel terrible about it*. We would like to please you, but we simply can't. It is regrettable, but no is in charge. I would love to, but you can't make me.

Further development, that is, spirituality, is growing beyond the no. It is the growth from no to yes. And not a half-hearted *yeah* or *OK* or *I'll try*, but the real yes, Amen! Real maturity, spirituality, is learning to say yes without knowing all the details; learning to make commitments without completely knowing the cost. It is learning to say yes to God. Yes, there is a God. Better still: Yes, God.

We have been told to *just say no* to drugs, to peer pressure. Say no to unreasonable demands. Be assertive. It is a good beginning. Enough to be a fool. Real happiness is learning to say yes. Whatever it may cost. Whatever I may have to give up. Yes, LORD, here I am.

<u>Suggestions</u>: Just say yes. Practice saying yes—or at least *Let me think about it*—in every situation where you would ordinarily say no. When you are asked to do something, or give of your time, or try something new, or consider a new idea. Practice actually considering it in your heart, responding with a yes tone of voice. Use judgment of course; don't agree to something that is foolhardy or immoral. Ask God for guidance.

Sing this psalm in a lighthearted way, to the movement Twirling Dance (see Appendix).

Psalm 53 (BCP)

Tenth Day: Evening Prayer Tone: MÁ#OL

1 **The fool has | said in his | heart,**
  "There is no | God."
    \All are corrupt and commit abominable \ acts;
    there is none who does any \ good.
2 \God looks down from heaven upon us \ all,
    to see if there is any who is \ wise,
    if there is one who seeks after \ God.
3 \Every one has proved \ faithless;
    all alike have turned \ bad;
    there is | none who does | good;
    no, not | one.
4 \Have they no knowledge, those \ evildoers
    who eat up my people like \ bread
    and do not call upon \ God?
5 /See how greatly they / tremble,
    such trembling as / never was;
    \for God has scattered the bones of the \ enemy;
    they are put to shame, because God has re\jected them.
6 \Oh, that Israel's deliverance would come out of \ Zion!
    when God restores the fortunes of his \ people
    Jacob will rejoice and Israel be \ glad.

Upholding My Soul: Commentary To Psalm 54

v.3 For strangers (foreigners, aliens) have risen up against me,
and the powerful (fierce, violent) have sought after my soul.

Betrayal and treachery. Those I thought I knew have turned against me. They have turned into aliens, with alien values, for they have not set God before them. Their good intentions and mine are of no help to me now, as they pursue me to take away my life.

HINNÉH .eLOHIM "OZÉR LIY   .aDONÁY B:SOM:KHEY NAPHSHIY
v.4 Behold, God is mine helper:
The Lord is with them that uphold my soul (KJV).

The Lord is found, it says, among those who are supporting my soul (breath, breathing, life). I do not always know who they are; I seldom read about them in the newspaper. They are everywhere, keeping me alive by their work and their prayers. I do not know their names or telephone numbers, but God is among them.

They keep me alive on many levels. They maintain the water supply and the food supply. They talk to me on National Public Radio. Sometimes they smile at me in malls, when I need encouragement. At work they surround me with protection, they keep me from making mistakes. Sometimes they support me by their weakness, when they make me feel needed.

Conducting my first retreat, I was suddenly dismayed. I had promised more than I could deliver, and wasn't at all sure what I was doing. I was prepared for all of us to be disappointed, but instead I felt lifted up. I could feel the retreatants' support almost floating me, keeping me aloft like the eagle soaring on thermals.

I tell my patients that God works through community. In the circle of his people, known and unknown, God is present. We do what we never could have dreamed because he works among us. Because we love one another, however inadequately. Because something within us yearns to do his work. Because we encourage one another. Because we pray for one another.

I cannot always tell friend from foe. The one I trust may betray me, and the one I never cared for may save my life. I only know that God knows. He will send whom he chooses and he will save me through his people. His secret agents are everywhere.

Note: See 1 Samuel 23:14-29

Suggestions: Sing verses 3-7. Study the psalms in groups, supporting one another. Form a large circle and let each member read a verse in turn. Remind the group that each member is an expert and every comment is of value.

Support all who work with you, not with flattering speeches, but by simple presence: a word, a smile, a glance, listening, prayer. Support your family in the same unassuming way. God will be found in this work.

Psalm 54 (BCP)

Tone: N:GINOTH

1 Save me, O God, by your Name; *
   in your might, defend my cause.
2 Hear my prayer, O God, *
   give ear to the words of my mouth.
3 \For the arrogant have risen up a\gainst me,
   and the ruthless have sought my \ life,
   those who have no regard for \ God.
                    [Silence...]
4 \Behold, God is my \ helper;
   it is the Lord who sustains my \ life.
5 Render evil to those who \ spy on me;
   in your faithfulness, de\stroy them.
6 \I will offer you a freewill \ sacrifice
   and praise your Name, O LORD, for it is \ good.
7 For you have rescued me from every \ trouble,
   and my eye has seen the ruin of my \ foes.

Fleeing To A Far-off Place: Commentary To Psalm 55

v.7 And I said, "Oh, that I had wings like a dove!
I would fly away and be at rest."

He is overwhelmed by stress, wanting to get away from it all, to a far-off place, to the wilderness. I can relate to this well. From the day I finished school I dreamed of permanent vacation. In each new job I was soon dissatisfied. When our daughter was one year old we made our first trip to the Ozarks; and we fell in love with those hills. After tramping through the woods with a friendly realtor, we bought eighty acres at the top of a mountain. That land became the center of our fantasy. Judy and I would build an underground house on that hill; I would be a footloose writer, doing anything but my profession.

People in the country seemed so friendly. They remembered our names! We invited them to eat in our little vacation cabin; Judy cooked delicious meals out of simple ingredients; we had a marvelous time. We seemed to have more friends in that vacation spot than in the community where we lived and worked. And this all became part of the fantasy.

Partly it was the fantasy that brought us to Tulsa, Oklahoma. There I could work with Great Evangelist, integrating psychiatry with prayer (compare 61, 62, 116); and have the fantasy too. And my oldest and closest friend was living in the nearest town.

Then, piece by piece, the fantasy fell apart. My friend suddenly died. The land had no legal roadway. The economy was impoverished. Our friend the realtor died of cancer. We learned that the backwoods of Arkansas are not that different from the city, where "trouble and misery are in the midst of her," and, "there is corruption at her heart." I subscribed to *Mother Earth News* for one year—long enough to realize I did not have the skills or motivation, really, to go back to the land.

How well I relate to the frustration, to the feelings of pressure and noise and fury. And I do not have wings like a dove and cannot fly away. There will be no permanent vacation. And in truth, no vacation ever solved anything for me. There is no escape.

v.17 But I will call upon God,
and the LORD will deliver me.

It is not to say that God will solve the problems so that I can go back to my vacation. The problems may not be solved on my terms at all. The transformation comes in the calling, turning from my own resources and my own solutions. I will call upon God as in 3, 107, 116, helpless and open, and the LORD, in his own way and timing, will deliver me.

"EREBh WÁVOQER W:3OHoRAYiM .ÁSIHÁh W:.EHeMEH
v.18 In the evening, in the morning, and at noonday,
I will complain and lament.

Or, pray and cry aloud (KJV). Evening and morning and noonday; real time. Real life, going to work. Driving, arriving, hearing the latest bad news. Overwhelmed almost from the beginning. By noonday I am going full speed, but my energies may be flagging. I am solving problems, getting things done, but I am forgetting what I have learned in these lessons. I am forgetting to pray, forgetting to be silent and listen. By noontime there have been too many emergencies, too many bad rumors, too many flash-points of conflict. I have already forgotten who delivers me and who solves every problem. Until I stop and recollect and call upon God. Until I pray for my patients and ask God what needs to be done. Until I stop running and listen.

My prayers at this time may not be graceful or polished. They may be hurried, worried, not grammatical, just calling out to God. Complaining and lamenting. Just *Help, LORD. Or, Father, what do I do now?* Or remembering a verse of these psalms that I memorized earlier. Or breathing the sweet Name of Jesus and lifting up my eyes.

HASHLÉKH "AL-YHWH Y:HÁV:KHÁ W:HU. Y:KHALK:LEKHÁ
v.24 Cast your burden upon the LORD, and he will sustain you.

There is no escape from reality, stress and conflict. I can neither fly from the world nor change it. And I have learned there is no need. God is not out there, in some religious dream or fantasy, but here, wherever I seek him. When I turn to him and cast my burden on him.

Suggestions: Alternate reading and singing as shown. Cast your burdens on the LORD, not in some abstract sense, but specifically. Each specific burden. Each problem, each difficult person. Lift them up to him and ask for his guidance. Ask him what he wants you to do. And then, be silent. This is not a religious or sentimental teaching, but a practical method for life.

Pause in the middle of the day for a time of silence. Find a quiet place if possible, sit quietly for a few moments, direct your attention back to God. If you have the opportunity for formal prayer, use this time to ask for direction in your work. If you can do nothing else, pause for a few seconds, wherever you are, for a moment of silence. If you cannot be alone even for those few seconds, let your eyes rest lightly on the person who is with you, allow yourself to see that person in silence, without internal comment or judgment. As always, direct your attention to God.

Psalm 55 (BCP)

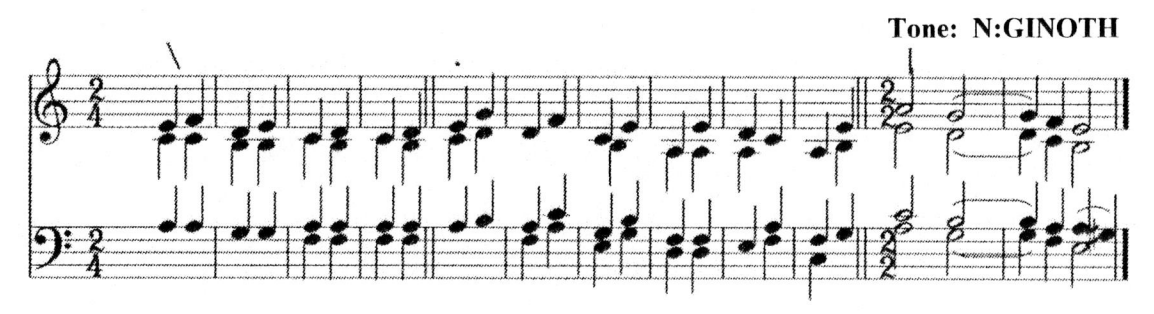

Tone: N:GINOTH

1 Hear my prayer, O God; *
    do not hide yourself from my petition.
2 Listen to me and answer me; *
    I have no peace, because of my cares.
3 \I am shaken by the noise of the \ enemy
    and by the pressure of the \ wicked;
4 For they have cast an evil \ spell upon me,
    and are set against me in \ fury.
5 \My heart quakes with\in me,
    and the terrors of death have fallen u\pon me.
6 Fear and trembling have come \ over me,
    and horror over\whelms me.
7 .And I said, "Oh, that I had wings like a . dove!
    I would fly away and be at . rest.
8 I would flee to a far-off . place
    and make my lodging in the . wilderness.
          [Silence...]
9 I would hasten to es.cape
    from the stormy wind and . tempest."
10 \Swallow them up, O LORD; confound their \ speech;
    for I have seen violence and strife in the \ city.
11 Day and night the watchmen make their rounds upon her \ walls,
    but trouble and misery are in the \ midst of her.
12 \There is corruption at her \ heart;
    her streets are never free of oppression and \ deceit.
          [Read]
13 For had it been an adversary who taunted me,
    then I could have borne it; *
    or had it been an enemy who vaunted himself against me,
    then I could have hidden from him.
14 But it was you, a man after my own heart, *
    my companion, my own familiar friend.
15 We took sweet counsel together, *
    and walked with the throng in the house of God.

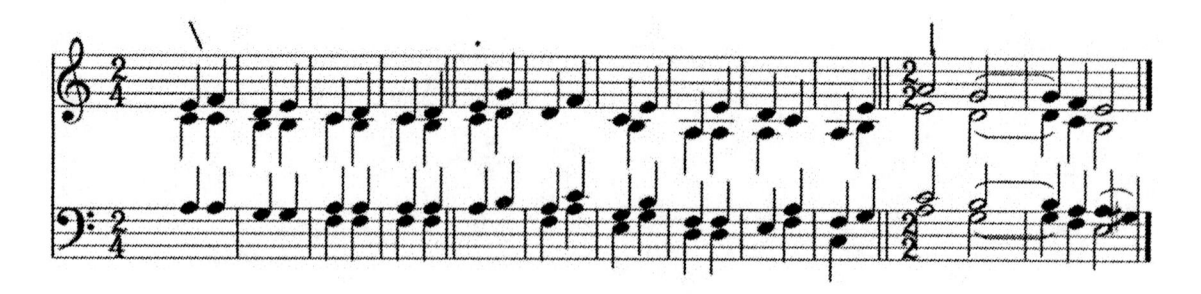

16 **Let death come upon them suddenly;**
    let them go down alive into the | grave;
        for | wickedness is in their dwellings, in their | very midst.
17 \ But I will call upon God,
    and the LORD will \ deliver me.
18 In the evening, in the morning, and at \ noonday,
    I will complain and la\ment,
    and he will hear my \ voice.
19 \ He will bring me back safely from the battle waged a\gainst me;
    for there are many who \ fight me.
20 God, who is enthroned of old, will hear me, and bring them \ down;
                [Silence...]
    they never change; they do not fear \ God.
                [Read]
21 My companion stretched forth his hand against his comrade; *
    he has broken his covenant.
22 His speech is softer than butter, *
    but war is in his heart.
23 His words are smoother than oil, *
    but they are drawn swords.

24 .Cast your burden upon the LORD,
    and he will sus.tain you;
    he will never let the righteous . stumble.
25 For you will bring down the bloodthirsty and . deceitful
    down to the pit of destruction, O . God.
26 They shall not live out half their . days,
    but I will put my . trust in you.

I Trust And Will Not Be Afraid: Commentary To Psalm 56

v.3 Whenever I am afraid,

I will put my trust in you. Sometimes a patient will ask, "How do I know I can trust you?" This is usually a shock to me; I consider myself to be trustworthy, and this comes unexpectedly, out of context. The patient suddenly hesitates to answer a rather ordinary question, or wants to talk but is afraid to sit down. I'm staying late in the hospital trying to be helpful, and he or she is asking, "How do I know I can trust you?"

I remind myself that the patient is feeling vulnerable. The patient's sense of security is shattered, and he wants me to re-establish it. She is asking me to make the world secure, without disappointments. Can I do it? Can I promise not to betray or disappoint? An internist I know likes to wear a button that says, "Trust me, I'm a doctor!" We laugh at the absurdity, yet we trust doctors with our lives every day. My daughter tells me something with the absolute certainty of a teen-ager and says, "Trust me." I respond with an old cliché, "Never trust anyone who says 'Trust me'!"

Psychologically, trust refers to the sense of personal security. We develop it early in life, or not at all. One who grows up in turmoil may never develop it. Victims of child abuse may be permanently vulnerable. When that inner security is missing they may try to find it in others. My patients have difficulty trusting, yet they often trust too much, the wrong persons. Unable to trust, they are victimized over and over.

The writer has reason to fear, and no one he can trust. Yet he says to God, "Whenever I am afraid, I will put my trust in you." What does this mean? If I can't trust my doctor how can I trust an invisible God? He also says, "What can flesh do to me?" In fact, they can do everything to me. My trust is based on radical insecurity, the security of having no security at all. Compare 27. I have given up trying to be safe.

Perhaps this is silly, but then, everyone who would say *Trust me* has been tried and found wanting. There really is no security in the doctor, the lawyer or the banker. God has been trustworthy so far and I have decided to trust him again. The answers are not at all clear; I will get them as I need them.

v.4 In God, whose word I praise,

in God I trust and will not be afraid. First praise—affirmation, thanksgiving—then trust. I am bound by the vow I made to you, O God, and I will present to you thank-offerings. I have committed myself to this relationship of praise. In that covenant I learn to trust. My trust in God is not like other trust, the projected sense of my own security. Not the belief that things will turn out all right, but the decision to accept whatever comes.

v.12 For you have rescued my soul (breathing, life), that I may walk before God in the light of the living.

<u>Suggestions</u>: Lift arms in the praise gesture on the first line of each refrain (vv. 4a and 10a), fold them across the chest, hands on shoulders (heart gesture) on 4b and 10b; return to the praise gesture on 4c and 10c.

Psalm 56 (BCP)

Eleventh Day: Morning Prayer Tone: SHÁRIM

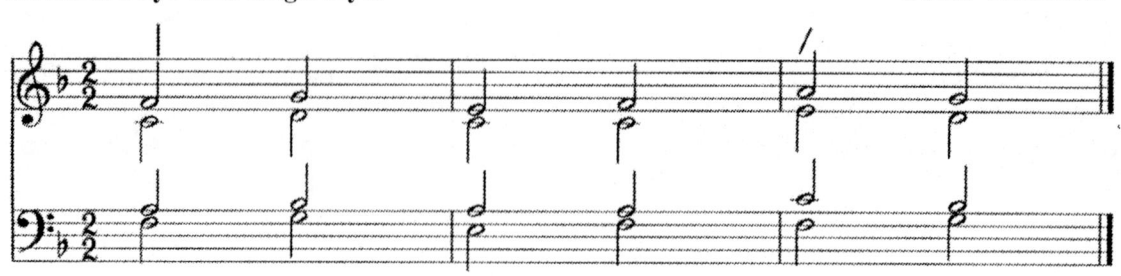

1 Have mercy on me, O God,
 for my enemies are hounding me; *
 all day long they assault and oppress me.
2 They hound me all the day long; *
 truly there are many who fight against me, O Most High.
3 Whenever I am afraid, *
 I will put my trust in you.
4 **In God, whose word I | praise,**
 in God I trust and will not be a | fraid,
 /for what can flesh / do to me?
5 All day long they damage my cause; *
 their only thought is to do me evil.
6 They band together; they lie in wait; *
 they spy upon my footsteps;
 because they seek my life.
7 Shall they escape despite their wickedness? *
 O God, in your anger, cast down the peoples.
8 You have noted my lamentation;
 put my tears into your bottle; *
 are they not recorded in your book?
9 Whenever I call upon you, my enemies will be put to flight; *
 this I know, for God is on my side.
10 **In God the LORD, whose word I | praise,**
 in God I trust and will not be a | fraid,
 /for what can mortals / do to me?
11 I am bound by the vow I made to you, O God; *
 I will present to you thank-offerings;
12 For you have rescued my soul from death and my feet from stumbling, *
 that I may walk before God in the light of the living.

Wake Up, My Glory: Commentary To Psalm 57

And that you put on the new man which was created according to God, in righteousness and true holiness (Ephesians 4:24, KJV).

"URÁh KH:VODIY "URÁh HA<u>NÉ</u>VEL W:KHINNOR .Á"<u>I</u>RÁh <u>SHÁ</u>#AR
v.8 Wake up, my glory! Wake up, lute and harp. I will waken the dawn.

Wake up, K:VODIY (*my glory*), from a root meaning heavy. Hence honor or glory, used poetically as "the heart, the soul ... the more noble part of man" (Gesenius[*]). I think of it as the highest and finest me, me at my very best. A psychiatrist might call it the ego-ideal. There really is such a thing. Moments of greatness, moments of selflessness. Once in a great while I really sense another's need. Once in a great while I have shown real courage. If only I could always be me at my very best.

It always surprises me. I never knew this was in me. My patients are also surprised when they encounter their better selves. What they see clearly in others, they deny in themselves. The new man, Christ within, is the least known part of a human breathing. I think it is the part of me that is directed by the Holy Spirit. I call it "the natural supernatural." It is the part of my inner world that can listen to God, yet its appearances are unobtrusive, almost unnoticed.

Sometimes falling in love awakens it; sometimes marriage; sometimes being a parent. More often than not that conversion comes in relationship. Someone who sees it brings it forth from me. Sometimes a chance encounter is all it takes. A crisis, a need to act, and I responded. Only in looking back do I know what happened. Me at my very best never knows he is there.

Wake up, new man, my better self, me at my best, from trance, from sleep. Images of wakening abound in Scripture: "The hour has come for you to wake up from your slumber" (Romans 13:11 NIV). Hebrew spirituality is not trance or reverie. It is a process of awakening that takes me (and I cannot tell the exact steps) from self-centered, complaining dullness to increasing alertness, awareness of myself and others, awareness of mystery, appreciation of good things, appreciation of all things (even the negative), affirmation, and praise.

<u>Suggestions</u>: Compare 16, 108. Stand at v.6 and sing the verses marked. Learn to recognize your better self, you at your best. However rare they may be, you have moments of greatness. Moments of Christlike behavior. Moments when fruits of the Spirit are clearly present: *love, joy, peace, patience, gentleness...* Do not boast of these moments or call attention to them, but notice them and be grateful.

The meditation you are learning is a practice of waking up. Silence is waking up; coming out of the everyday trance and being fully awake, if only for an instant. Some traditions call it mindfulness. Wake up and keep waking up, as often as you can!

---

[*]H.W.F. Gesenius: *Gesenius' Hebrew-Chaldee Lexicon to the Old Testament Scriptures*(Translated by Samuel Prideaux Tregelles), Baker Book House, Grand Rapids, MI, 1979, p. 382.

Psalm 57 (BCP)

Tone: GITTITH

1. Be merciful to me, O God, be merciful,
    for I have taken refuge in you; *
    in the shadow of your wings will I take refuge
    until this time of trouble has gone by.
2. I will call upon the Most High God, *
    the God who maintains my cause.
3. He will send from heaven and save me;
    he will confound those who trample upon me; *
              [Silence...]
    God will send forth his love and his faithfulness.
4. I lie in the midst of lions that devour the people; *
    their teeth are spears and arrows,
    their tongue a sharp sword.
5. They have laid a net for my feet, and I am bowed low; *
    they have dug a pit before me,
    but have fallen into it themselves.
              [Silence...]
6. **Exalt yourself above the | heavens, O God,**
    and your glory over all the | earth.
7. \My heart is firmly fixed, O God, my heart is \ fixed;
    I will sing and make \ melody.
8. /Wake up, my spirit; a/wake, lute and harp;
    /I myself will / waken the dawn.
9. **I will confess you among the | peoples, O LORD;**
    I will sing praise to you among the | nations.
10. \For your loving-kindness is greater than the \ heavens,
    and your faithfulness reaches to the \ clouds.
11. **Exalt yourself above the | heavens, O God,**
    and your glory over all the | earth.

Evil In Your Hearts: Commentary To Psalm 58

HA.UMNÁM .ÉLEM 3EDEQ T:DABBÉRUWN
MEYSHÁRIM TISHP:tUW B:NEY .ÁDÁM

v.1 Are you then dumb, that you will not speak what is right,
and judge the children of men with equity? (Bonhoeffer[*])

There are as many versions of this difficult verse as there are translators. Whatever the words mean literally, there is no mistaking the tone. Sometimes I must endure a rebuke so harsh, so unexpected, and so accurate that I actually can't hear it at first. It may take a few minutes before I realize that it is myself being rebuked. My mind protects me from the shock by using what a psychiatrist calls mechanisms of defense. For example, *It just isn't true* (denial), or *I won't think about that* (suppression), or *You're the one who does that, not me* (projection).

It's one thing for them to preach about the wicked, quite another to think they are talking about me. I felt so righteous a moment ago; now I feel like a jerk. It is I who have kept silent in the face of evil. I have done nothing in the cause of justice. I am as wicked as they are, I just haven't had the opportunity. Do I want to hear this? No, I would rather stop my ears like the deaf adder. Try to tell me and I don't know what you are talking about. That is often the nature of evil: I don't see it so it isn't true. It isn't my problem.

This is a "hard" psalm, like 109 and 137. We are not used to such open venom. We would like to distance ourselves from it. We may do so by calling it "Old Testament." We choose not to see this harshness in ourselves but project it onto someone else—the Jews or the "Old Testament God." A quick look at today's paper should convince us that we live in the same harsh way, but the language is different. We talk a lot about forgiveness, and we are quite certain who should forgive whom. We see ourselves as controlled and civilized.

v.4-5 like the deaf adder which stops its ear,
which does not hear the voice of the charmer.

We simply don't want to hear it. And so we blame our problems on others: the communists, the hippies, the liberals, secular humanists, the Japanese, welfare recipients, drug abusers, homosexuals, television preachers, and above all, the president. The names of the scapegoats are always changing. Hippies were almost forgotten by the early 1990s. Communists were rapidly becoming obsolete. One thing was constant: the problem was not me!

<u>Suggestions</u>: Sing vv. 2-11 to the Tone SHO.ÁH (*holocaust*).

Do not dismiss Psalm 58, but struggle with it. Listen to it. What is it that you don't want to hear? Practice listening to criticism, even if it is subtle and indirect or takes the form of a joke. When you hear it, do not take offense, and do not defend yourself. Listen and keep listening; ask God what he wants you to learn.

---

[*]Dietrich Bonhoeffer: *Meditating on the Word*, Ed. and Trans. by David McI. Gracie, Cowley, Cambridge MA, 1986, p. 85.

Psalm 58 (BCP), modified*

Tone: SHO.ÁHI

1 Are you then dumb, that you will not speak what is right, *
   and judge the children of men with equity?
2 **No; you devise evil in your | hearts,**
   and your hands deal out violence in the | land.
3 +The wicked are perverse from the + womb;
   liars go astray from their + birth.
4 /They are as venomous as a / serpent,
   they are like the deaf adder which stops its / ears,
5 \Which does not hear the voice of the \ charmer,
   no matter how skillful his \ charming.
6 **O God, break the teeth in their | mouths;**
   pull the fangs of the young lions, O | LORD.
7 +Let them vanish like water that runs + off;
   let them wither like trodden + grass.
8 /Let them be like the snail that / melts away,
   like a stillborn child that never sees the / sun.
9 \Before they bear fruit, let them be cut down like a \ brier;
   like thorns and thistles let them be \ swept away.
10 **The righteous will be glad when they see the | vengeance;**
   they will bathe their feet in the blood of the | wicked.
11 +And they will say,
   "Surely there is a reward for the + righteous;
   surely there is a God who rules in the + earth."

Song Of The Dog: Commentary To Psalm 59

YÁSHUVU LÁ"EREBh YEHEMUW KHAKÁLEBh WIY:SOV:VU "IYR
v.7 They return toward evening, they howl like the dog,

and they go round and round the city. This is no well-fed pet, man's best friend. Feral dogs, hungry and lean, they roam in packs. They scavenge for scraps of food. They are comfortable with man, too comfortable, for they have reverted to the wild. They have no fear of man; and because they have no fear, the streets of the city are not safe.

The image is so powerful that I forget who is meant. Two-legged dogs, human dogs. Restless and irritable they go round and round the city looking for excitement; each responds to the next, till all chase madly after this or that. Like adolescent males who go about surly and swaggering. Or like silver-haired men wearing suits: whatever they see they chase, they run it down, they take, yet they find themselves unsatisfied. They may leave a trail of misery but they do not concern themselves with that, "for who is listening?"

These dogs are restless and driven, they cannot sit still. They drum with their fingers, they stand, they pace, they look at their watches. They curse with their mouths at traffic lights, they worry and fret. They bark because the other dogs are barking, and they run where the other dogs run, but they find no rest. That doggish nature drives us from within. I feel it in myself. I pick up a book, I put it down, I pace, I look at my watch. So much to do, so much pressure, things to accomplish. I run about the city, chasing, more than anything, my tail. I come home exhausted and ask myself, "What did I accomplish?" I may laugh at these two-legged dogs, but I find myself running with them. Driven by thoughts and emotions I go round and round the city.

v.9 But you, O LORD, you laugh at them.

Another sharp disjunction. I can neither win nor escape this chase at the level of the dog. *But you.* But as for you, O LORD. I leap to a higher perspective. I look to you, for you and you alone are my strength.

WA.aNIY .ÁSHIR "UZZEKHÁ

v.18 But as for me, I will sing praise to you for your strength, and as my refuge (place to flee) in straits, anxiety, trouble. When literally *it is narrow for me*. I cannot work my way out of the dog-chase or the rat-race by my own abilities. *But as for me*: a quantum leap, again. From the level of the dog to praise, to the level of singing.

<u>Suggestions</u>: Sing refrains to the Tone "UGÁV (*pipe*).

When you find yourself running in circles, driven by thoughts and emotions, fear of failure and dreams of success, stop. Listen. Practice moments of silence, as often as you can. Turn your attention to God and ask for direction.

Psalm 59 (BCP)

Eleventh Day: Evening Prayer   Tone: "UGÁV

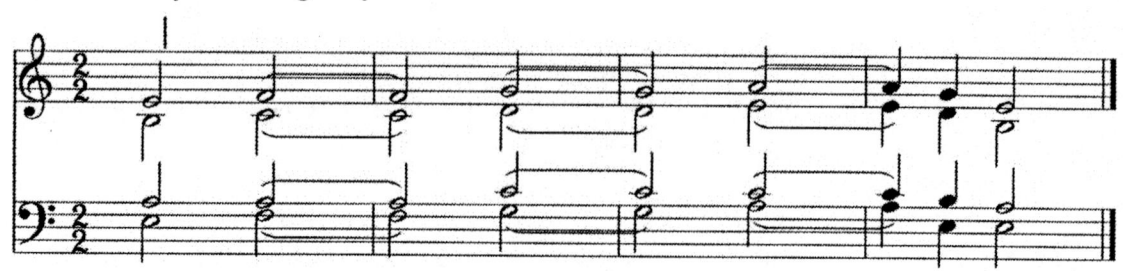

1 Rescue me from my enemies, O God; *
   protect me from those who rise up against me.
2 Rescue me from evildoers *
   and save me from those who thirst for my blood.
3 See how they lie in wait for my life,
   how the mighty gather together against me; *
   not for any offense or fault of mine, O LORD.
4 Not because of any guilt of mine *
   they run and prepare themselves for battle.
5 Rouse yourself, come to my side, and see; *
   for you, LORD God of hosts, are Israel's God.
6 Awake, and punish all the ungodly; *
   show no mercy to those who are faithless and evil.
           [Silence...]
7 **They go to and fro in the | evening;**
   they snarl like dogs and run about the | city.
8 Behold they boast with their mouths, and taunts are on their | lips;
   "For | who," they say, "will | hear us?"
9 **But you, O LORD, you | laugh at them;**
   you laugh all the ungodly to | scorn.
10 My eyes are fixed on you, O my | Strength;
   for | you, O God are my | stronghold.
11 My merciful God comes to meet me; *
   God will let me look in triumph on my enemies.
12 Slay them, O God, lest my people forget; *
   send them reeling by your might and put them down, O Lord our shield.
13 For the sins of their mouths, for the words of their lips,
   for the cursing and lies that they utter, *
   let them be caught in their pride.
14 Make an end of them in your wrath; *
   make an end of them, and they shall be no more.
15 Let everyone know that God rules in Jacob, *
   and to the ends of the earth.

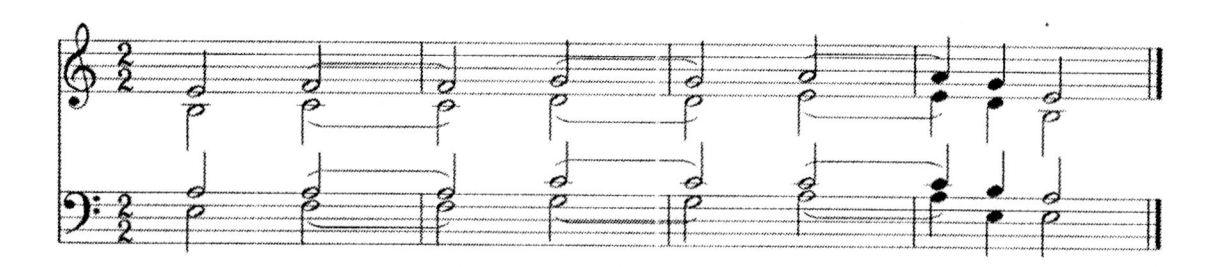

16 **They go to and fro in the | evening;**
    they snarl like dogs and run about the | city.
17 They forage for food,
    and if they are not filled, they | howl.
18 For my part, I will sing of your | strength;
    I will celebrate your | love in the morning;
19 **For you have become my | stronghold,**
    a refuge in the day of my | trouble.
20 To you, O my Strength, will I | sing;
    For you, O God, are my | stronghold and my | merciful God.

Heal Her Sores: Commentary To Psalm 60

HIR"ASHtÁh .ERE3 P:3AMTÁH'   R:PHÁH SH:VÁREYHÁ KHI-MÁtÁh
v.2 You have shaken the earth and split it open;
repair the cracks in it, for it totters.

"Heal the sores thereof," says the 1928 Prayer Book version. You have caused the earth to move (shake, tremble), and you have broken her. Heal her sores (breaks, wounds) for she is tottering.

By the early 1990s the earth was in fact tottering and wounded. The atmosphere was wounded; the ocean was wounded. The land was scarred. Trees were mowed down to build shopping centers and enormous parking lots. Labor-saving devices had created a world where no one had time. Where parents were too busy to care for children. And while the leaders of the West gloated at the fall of communism, their own streets filled with the homeless. The earth was covered with sores, and the leaders had no answers.

v.10 Have you not cast us off, O God?
you no longer go out, O God, with our armies. Another version, "Go forth no longer with our legions" (Feuer, p.756). We can do it ourselves. With science and technology we can put a man on the moon; we can send hardware out of the solar system and messages around the world. Yet we spend hours driving to jobs that give no fulfillment. We can call anyone in the world on the telephone, but we cannot really talk to another person.

God no longer goes out with our armies, our engineers, our social scientists, our teachers, our economists. He no longer goes into our courtrooms or our hospital rooms. God is no longer our king in this brave new world. He is King, but he is not *our* king. We, the subjects, have tried to take control.

HÁVÁh-LLÁNU "EZRÁTH MI33ÁR   W:SHÁW. T:SHU"ATH .ÁDÁM
v.11 Grant us your help against the enemy,
for vain is the help of man. Give us help from trouble (narrowness, straits); and vain is the help (salvation) of man. Another sharp transition. We will never find the answers in science, economics, better laws, the ecology movement, the cause, whatever it may be. The causes and the answers of mankind are utterly vain.

v.12 With God we will do valiant deeds,
and he shall tread our enemies.

<u>Suggestions</u>: Sing refrains to the Tone #a3O3:ROTH (*trumpets*). Always subordinate the cause, no matter how noble, to God. Always put the cause, the great crusade, in second place. There is no cause, no truth, that man cannot distort and corrupt. Even the cause of God. Turn to God in silence, ask for direction.

Psalm 60 (BCP)

Tone: #a3O3:ROTH

1. **O God, you have cast us off and | broken us;**
   you have been | angry;
   /oh, take us / back to you again.
2. \You have shaken the earth and split it \ open;
   repair the cracks in it, for it \ totters.
3. You have made your people know + hardship;
   \you have given us wine that makes us \ stagger.
4. You have set up a banner for those who \ fear you,
   to be a refuge from the power of the + bow.
   [Silence...]
5. **Save us by your right hand and | answer us,**
   /that those who are dear to you may be de/livered.
6. **God spoke from his holy place and | said:**
   "I will exult and parcel out | Shechem;
   /I will divide the valley of / Succoth.
7. \Gilead is mine and Ma\nasseh is mine;
   Ephraim is my \ helmet
   and Judah my + scepter.
8. \Moab is my \ wash-basin,
   on Edom I throw down my sandal to \ claim it,
   and over Philistia will I shout in + triumph."
9. **Who will lead me into the strong | city?**
   /who will bring me into / Edom?
10. **Have you not cast us | off, O God?**
    /you no longer go out, O God, with our / armies.
11. \Grant us your help against the \ enemy,
    for vain is the help of \ man.
12. **With God we will do valiant | deeds,**
    /and he shall tread our enemies under / foot.

From The End Of The Earth: Commentary To Psalm 61

MIQ:3ÉH HÁ.ÁRE3 .ÉLEYKHÁ .EQRÁ.

v.2 From the end of the earth to you I cry.

I started calling this the Oklahoma psalm. In my alienation Oklahoma seemed like the end of the earth. Yet everywhere I have ever lived was the end of the earth. I have moved so many times, discontented wherever I land. When people ask me, "Where are you from?" I answer, "all over the place!"

I envy people who have roots; their "Daddy" and "Granddaddy" were born in that very spot. Sometimes they have a gracious charm that comes from being rooted. They know who they are and where they fit in. They grow old with the people they grew up with. They don't have to explain where they come from. People like that can also be narrow. They cannot imagine a person coming *from all over the place*. Sometimes they can't help looking strangely at such a person. Sometimes they have a way of asking, *What did you say your name was?* or, *What nationality are you?* that makes me acutely uncomfortable.

The word for someone *from all over the place* is stranger. Wherever such a person lands, it feels like the end of the earth. Home is always somewhere else, even after living in one place for years. The Bible talks a lot about strangers. We are told that "the LORD cares for the stranger" (146:8).

The stranger from all over the place knows what others may forget. That we are all strangers. We are all calling to God from the end of the earth, for this earth is not our real home. All the great characters of the Bible were like that, strangers *from all over the place*, called to work at the end of the earth. Abraham. Joseph. Moses. *What did you say your name was? What's the name of that place you come from?*

Jesus was a stranger too. "Foxes have holes and birds of the air have nests, but the son of man has nowhere to lay His head" (Matthew 8:20, NKJ). And nowhere was he more a stranger than in his home town. Did he ever fit in? Did he hang out with the boys and talk about his Daddy and his Granddaddy? No, he was always different. It was always the end of the earth for him. And I think it still is.

Sometimes we play church games: "What if Jesus walked in here now? How would we treat him?" We always assume that we would recognize him. But he will not come with a sign saying, "I am Jesus the Christ." I think he will always be a stranger, Jewish, bearded, saying too many hard sayings. We might hear ourselves asking him, *What did you say your name was?* or, *Where did you say you come from?* The good part is, I think he understands what it's like to be *from all over the place*. I think he understands people like me.

v.4 I will dwell in your house for ever;
I will take refuge under the cover of your wings. [Silence...].

In the place of silence I will take refuge for ever. In the safety of that place, now, wherever I may be, I am at home. Stranger no more.

Psalm 61 (BCP)

Tone: N:GINOTH

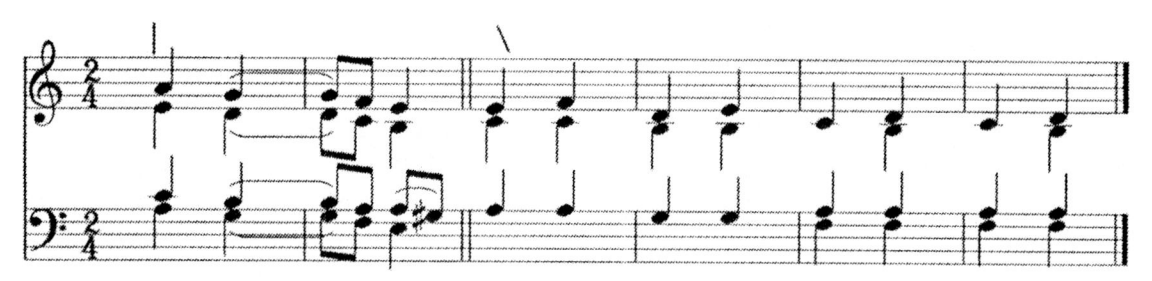

1 **Hear my cry, O | God,**
    and | listen to my | prayer.
2 \I call upon you from the ends of the \ earth
    with heaviness in my \ heart;
    set me upon the rock that is \ higher than I.
3 \For you have been my \ refuge,
    a strong tower against the \ enemy.
4 I will dwell in your house for \ ever;
    I will take refuge under the cover of your \ wings.
            [Silence...]
5 **For you, O God, have heard my | vows;**
    you have granted me the | heritage of those
    who fear your | Name.
6 \Add length of days to the king's \ life;
    let his years extend over many gene\rations.
7 Let him sit enthroned before God for \ ever;
    bid love and faithfulness watch \ over him.
8 **So will I always sing the praise of your | Name,**
    and day by | day I will fulfill my | vows.

My Soul Waits Silently: Commentary To Psalm 62

.AKH .EL-eLOHIM DUMIYYÁH NAPHSHIY   MIM<u>ME</u>NNU Y:SHU"ÁTHIY

v.1 Only for God my soul waits silently;
from him (is) my salvation.

I sat in my office at Christian Hill one morning (that remarkable place where medicine was practiced in harmony with prayer), and I prayed—once again—for my prayer language, the gift of tongues. The evidence (some Christians say) of receiving the Holy Spirit. I had read about it, heard about it and prayed for it, receiving no answer.

I knew how others had received it. To one, it came in letters marching across his forehead in the shaving mirror. To another it came unexpectedly while praying with a friend. Others had received it at charismatic meetings with great excitement.

I prayed and asked God why I had not received this gift. Did he not want me to be spirit-filled? And then I heard—what? Silence! The deepest silence I have ever experienced. My racing thoughts were stilled and there was peace. I have experienced silence before and since, but never have I known so clearly who was communicating with me. Silence. My message from God. "Be content. I have given you what you need. It is enough."

Years before, a different kind of experience in a group therapy workshop. Eight to ten strangers sitting in a room, with no agenda except to experience group process and learn about ourselves. I remember the awkwardness of that session. No one was making connection. One lady curled up on a sofa as if to nap. If anything was said, it must have evoked no response. This seemed to go on for hours, although it was probably just a few minutes.

What I remember most, however, is that when the members did start talking, they turned on me, and attacked me for being "quiet." Somehow I became the focus for the awkwardness of that entire group. I thought about this experience for a long time. I had always been told I was quiet, but now I began to understand what this meant. I understood that quietness is not the same thing as not talking very much. When people said *Why are you so quiet?* what they meant was, *How come you are so inhibited, and so inhibiting to those around you?* They were talking about movement, gesture, rhythm, eyes. They were talking about an awkwardness that went far beyond not saying very much.

Quietness is not the same as silence. A person can be quiet with few words or many. Quietness means closing in, concealment. The nonverbal message might have been *Leave me alone, I'm self-sufficient.* But inwardly I was crying out, *I'm lonely!* Inwardly I rehearsed interesting sentences, but I never found the right time to say them. People could sense, I now know, that inner tension, and they withdrew from me.

A person can also be silent with few words or many. But silence is open; silence can respond to you because there is no internal chatter. In silence I can really listen — even to God. All possibilities are present. Strangely enough, silence takes energy. I cannot be silent when I am ill or tired.

.AKH LÉ.LOHIM DOMMI NAPHSHIY   KI-MIMMENNU TIQWÁTHIY

v.6 Only for God, my soul, wait silently;
for from him (is) my hope.

What is your will for me, Father? What do you want me to do? No words. No agenda. My soul (breath, breathing, life) understands this, for she knows how to commune without words. My soul communes silently and God responds. Alone with God my soul is energized. *They* are no longer important. Conflict and turmoil still surround me, but I have a different perspective. From God and God alone come my hope, my salvation, my safety.

Psalm 62 is about silence in a world of noise and confusion. Three little lessons, two experiences of silence. In vv. 1-5 enemies seek to crush and topple, "like a leaning fence, a toppling wall." The Hebrew is unclear as to whether I am the toppling wall, or the wall is toppling down *on me*. These enemies are dishonest to the core. They delight in lies. They greet me like a long lost friend, "but in their hearts they curse" – [Silence...]. There is no social solution. Go directly to silence.

v.6 Only for God, my soul, wait silently.

My hope will not be found in clever maneuvering, or in anything I might say. My hope, rock, victory, safety, honor—all are in God. There is no point in trying to impress *them*. Credentials won't help. Silence. Go directly to God. My practice of silence must always be directed to God and to God alone. My meditation is not a shortcut to enlightenment nor my access to remarkable powers. "Only for God, my soul, wait silently."

After v. 9, a second silence. The writer goes beyond his personal troubles to discuss human affairs in general. No one is truly reliable, he says. No one can really be trusted in a crisis. Power tactics may work in the short term, but are ultimately doomed to failure. Financial security is also no security; "set not your heart upon it." There are no real answers in the world of thoughts and emotions. My best ideas are already bankrupt. Be silent. Turn from the world of thoughts, wait silently, but only for God.

<u>Suggestions</u>:   Wait silently whenever you encounter *selah* or [Silence...]. Stop everything—words, music, thoughts, anticipations, absent-minded fidgeting—and be silent for five to ten seconds. Then continue. Do this in daily life, as well. In stress or in crisis, stop everything for five to ten seconds and be silent. Listen to God. When you meditate these psalms each day, always begin with prayer. Turn your attention to God. Always conclude with your set time of silence.

Remember that you are not learning a practice of not talking, but of clearing your thoughts, of moving from thoughts to inner silence. Almost at once your inner world fills up with thoughts again; clear it again. It is very easy to do this; it is hard to remember to do it. Now, in formal and informal meditation, practice this teaching. Wait silently for God.

Psalm 62 (BCP)

Twelfth Day: Morning Prayer　　　　　　　　　　　　　　　　Tone: N:GINOTH

1 **For God alone my soul in | silence waits;**
    from | him comes my | salvation.
2 **He alone is my rock and my | salvation,**
    my | stronghold, so that I shall not be
    greatly | shaken.
3 How long will you assail me to crush me,
    all of you together, *
    as if you were a leaning fence, a toppling wall?
4 They seek only to bring me down from my place of honor; *
    lies are their chief delight.
5 They bless with their lips, *
    but in their hearts they curse.
                [Silence...]
6 **For God alone my soul in | silence waits;**
    | truly my hope is in | him.
7 **He alone is my rock and my | salvation,**
    my | stronghold, so that I shall not be | shaken.
8 In God is my safety and my honor; *
    God is my strong rock and my refuge.
9 Put your trust in him always, O people, *
    pour out your hearts before him, for God is our refuge.
                [Silence...]
10 Those of high degree are but a fleeting breath, *
    even those of low estate cannot be trusted.
11 On the scales they are lighter than a breath. *
    all of them together.
12 Put no trust in extortion;
    in robbery take no empty pride. *
    though wealth increase, set not your heart upon it.
13 God has spoken once, twice have I heard it, *
    that power belongs to God.
14 Steadfast love is yours, O Lord, *
    for you repay everyone according to his deeds.

Holy Insomnia: Commentary To Psalm 63

.IM-Z:KHAR<u>T</u>IKHÁ "AL-Y:3U"ÁY   B:.ASHMUROTH .EH:GEh-BÁKH

v.6 When I remember you upon my bed,
and meditate on you in the night watches.

Insomnia time—"the wee hours of the morning." My father suffered terribly from insomnia. He would often be up far into the night puttering about in his book-filled study. He used to complain bitterly of those lonely vigils. His doctors gave him sleeping pills; they did little for him at night, but the next day he would be drowsy, out of sorts. He often spent part of the day in bed, sleeping off those pills from the night before.

The writer of this psalm also suffers insomnia, but he has no sleeping pills. Sometimes he lies in bed moaning, weeping as he thinks of his unhappiness, frustration, problems too many to count, and the looming presence of death. Compare 6. Sometimes he prays as in 119:48, "my eyes are open in the night watches, that I may meditate on your promise."

After an hour or two of prayer he feels much better. Alone with the LORD he poured out his heart in the silence. There were no words in reply but he knows he has been answered. Will he go back to sleep? Or will he sit contentedly, waiting for the dawn? He comes to look forward to these times with God. At least he is alone and undisturbed. He gets up and praises God, talks to God. Sometimes it almost seems the insomnia times are his happiest.

v.5 As (with) marrow and fatness, my soul you satisfy,
and with lips of joy my mouth begins to praise you.

With marrow and fatness, the best, you fill my soul (breath, breathing, life). You more than pacify, you *satisfy*, you bring me to peace, to contentment, to the sense of enough. And my soul clings to you, and your right hand holds me fast, secure in your everlasting protection.

<u>Suggestions</u>: Lift arms in the praise gesture at v.4 ("so will I bless you"), higher at "and lift up my hands." Fold them across the chest in the heart gesture at v. 5 ("my soul is content"), open into the praise gesture at "and my mouth." Practice the same movements with verses 7 and 8.

When you waken at night, for any reason, clear your thoughts. That inner world continues even in sleep, but the thoughts are often jumbled and meaningless. Sometimes I find that those sleeping thoughts are strangely negative, full of fear and anger. Replace those gloomy thoughts with thoughts of praise: "Thank you, Father," or, "Praise you, LORD." Praise for your blessings and your problems as you snuggle back into the sheets.

If sleep still does not come, go to another room, waken completely, and pray these psalms. Stay and pray with him, talk to him, tell him how you hurt. Practice brief moments of silence and listen to his voice. Stay till your eyes grow heavy and your soul is at peace.

Psalm 63 (BCP)

Tone: N:GINOTH

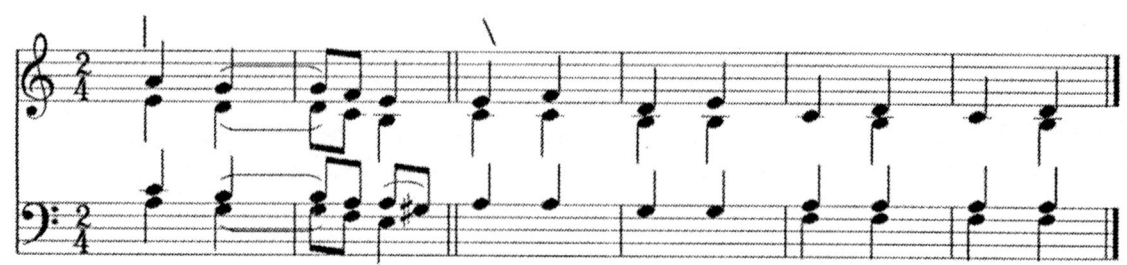

1 **O God, you are my God; eagerly I | seek you;**
   my soul thirsts for you, my flesh | faints for you,
   as in a barren and dry land where there is no | water.

2 \Therefore I have gazed upon you in your \ holy place,
   that I might behold your power and your \ glory.

3 For your loving-kindness is better than \ life itself;
   my lips shall give you \ praise.

4 \So will I bless you as long as I \ live
   and lift up my hands in your \ Name.

5 My soul is content, as with marrow and \ fatness,
   and my mouth praises you with joyful \ lips.

6 **When I remember you upon my | bed,**
   and | meditate on you in the night | watches,

7 \For you have been my \ helper,
   and under the shadow of your wings I will re\joice.

8 My soul \ clings to you;
   your right hand holds me \ fast.

9 **May those who seek my life to destroy it**
   go down into the depths of the | earth;

10 Let them fall upon the edge of the | sword,
   and let them be food for | jackals.

11 \But the king will rejoice in \ God;
   all those who swear by him will be \ glad;
     for the mouth of those who speak lies shall be \ stopped.

And The Heart Is Deep: Commentary To Psalm 64

W:QEREBh .IYSH W:LÉV "ÁMOQ

v.7 and (the) inside of a man and the heart (are) deep.

The Prayer Book translation is looser but meaningful: "The human mind and heart are a mystery."

A troubled young man kills two little girls at the local school; a loner in army fatigues commits a massacre at a fast food restaurant. A disgruntled employee murders fellow workers at the post office. An apparently nice man with a wife and young daughter kidnaps teen-age girls and torments them for days before murdering them. His former baby sitter remembers him as kind and considerate.

When these things happen, it seems, one asks a psychiatrist to explain them. Someone is sure to be interviewing one of us on radio or television. *Why do people do such things? What can be done about it?* My barber is sure to ask me about it on Saturday morning. *Do you think the man is crazy? What makes a person do something like that?* I dread those questions because, to tell the truth, I don't have the slightest idea. I know you don't have to have any known psychiatric illness to do horrible things. I know that anyone can do almost anything under the right circumstances.

Fortunately I don't have to say much, because everyone in the barbershop has a theory. It's drugs. It's the schools. It's permissiveness. It's this or it's that. In the philosophy of science we call this reductionism, the attempt to reduce complex problems to simple explanations. Science has developed by moving away from reductionism. Medicine is not so simple as it used to be. "One germ, one disease" no longer holds.

When it comes to the mind, reductionism lives on. It's all chemical. It's all genetic. It's all how you think. It's all spiritual. This expert blames the environment, that one diet, another the family. Some put their hopes on vitamins, others want deliverance. Some have great faith in psychiatry, while others think it is "of the devil."

Psalm 64 teaches that the inner world of man is a mystery. The inner thoughts of a man, his attitudes, and his reactions—too deep for me to understand. I will get no explanation. That is a great relief to me. I am glad that Scripture is not reductionistic. I don't have to know the answers. Only that God knows; God is in control.

Suggestions: Sing refrains to the Tone "UGÁV (*pipe*).

Practice silence at every opportunity, and observe that inner world. You will notice that one thought leads to another, emotion to emotion, and you find yourself flying from one meaningless goal to another. And you will also notice, *in silence*, that there is more. An opening, a window to One who gives meaning. One who is faithful and trustworthy and righteous. Rejoice in him and put your trust in him.

Psalm 64 (BCP)

Tone: "UGÁV

1 Hear my voice, O God, when I complain; *
 protect my life from fear of the enemy.
2 Hide me from the conspiracy of the wicked, *
 from the mob of evildoers.
3 **They sharpen their tongue like a | sword,**
 and aim their bitter words like | arrows,
4 That they may shoot down the blameless from | ambush;
 they | shoot without warning and are | not afraid.
5 They hold fast to their evil course; *
 they plan how they may hide their snares.
6 They say, "Who will see us?
 who will find out our crimes? *
 we have thought out a perfect plot."
7 **The human mind and heart are a | mystery;**
 but God will loose an | arrow at them,
 and \ suddenly they will be wounded.
8 He will make them trip over their tongues, *
 and all who see them will shake their heads.
9 Everyone will stand in awe and declare God's deeds; *
 they will recognize his works.
10 The righteous will rejoice in the LORD
 and put their trust in him, *
 and all who are true of heart will glory.

Silence Is Your Praise: Commentary To Psalm 65

L:KHÁ DUMIYYÁH TH:HILLÁH   .eLOHIM B:3IYYON

v.1 Silence is your praise, O God in Zion (Feuer, p. 795).

Silence is his praise because it listens to him (compare 62). Not quietness, but energized stillness, like a cat waiting to pounce. Like watching for the exact time to act. Like listening to you, without the slightest idea what I will say next. It is the realization that I pray to a Person; that communion is more than saying words.

I have always longed for silence. I have yearned for it in synagogues and churches. It is in silence, however fleeting, that I really hear. That I see for the first time things long overlooked, and know that they really exist. That I look into the eyes of my cat and know, really know, that he is a conscious individual with feelings. Silence is the heart of prayer, for it is the place of responding. Where I leave the chatter of prayers and come into his presence. And I know he is real. In silence I listen, yearning for instruction. And he teaches me with words compact as atoms.

v.5 O Hope of all the ends of the earth
and of the seas that are far away.

Out of silence he creates: The sea. Vast waters like the primordial deep, like chaos. Where swirling disorder gives rise to apparent structure -- the mountains "girded about with might." And God who is praised in silence is Lord of those waters. He is the resting place of all, even of the ends of the earth.

v.6 You still the roaring of the seas.

Their turbulent and frightening complexity you bring to rest. The roaring of the ocean and of "the peoples," you make still. You calm humanity. You say to the crashing ocean, "Peace, Be still!" (Mark 4:39, NKJ), and to my inner world as well. From the raging of waters without and within you bring peace.

v.9 You visit the earth and water it abundantly. You nourish the world, at every level. Out of silence you prepare my food, you feed me. You fill the rivers, fields and meadows, with a creation that is alive, growing, flourishing, and itself creative. You green the grass, you flock the hills.

Suggestions: Sing to the Tone #ÁLIL (*flute*). Those stanzas whose first line is in boldface type are sung to the last three measures, beginning at the last measure and continuing at the first repeat. Those sections beginning with ordinary type and using the caret marker (^) are sung to the first three measures, up to the second repeat.

For other references to silence, see 37:7, 48:8 and 62:1. Compare also 19, 29, 93. Silence is worship, the highest praise and the greatest reverence. It is the tiny space between thoughts where we begin to listen. It is the source of all spiritual growth. This is the heart of your meditation, nothing more. After each reading of the psalms, be silent for your appointed time. Let the words echo within you. Listen. In daily life, clear your thoughts and be silent whenever you can.

Psalm 65 (BCP)

Twelfth Day: Evening Prayer Tone: #ÁLIL

1 ^You are to be praised, O God, in ^ Zion;
    to you shall vows be performed in Je^rusalem.
2 To you that hear prayer shall all / flesh come,
    because of their trans/gressions.
3 \Our sins are stronger than \ we are,
    but you will blot them \ out.
4 ^Happy are they whom you ^ choose
    and draw to your courts to ^ dwell there!
    they will be satisfied by the beauty of your / house,
    by the holiness of your / temple.
5 \Awesome things will you show us in your \ righteousness,
    O God of our sal\vation,
    O Hope of all the ends of the | earth
    and of the | seas that are | far away.
6 You make fast the mountains by your / power;
    they are girded about with / might.
7 **You still the roaring of the | seas,**
    the | roaring of their | waves,
    and the / clamor
    of the / peoples.
8 \Those who dwell at the ends of the earth will tremble at your marvelous \ signs;
    you make the dawn and the dusk to sing for \ joy.
9 **You visit the earth and water it ab|undantly;**
    you | make it very | plenteous;
    the river of / God is full of / water.
10 \You prepare the \ grain,
    for so you provide for the \ earth.
11 **You drench the furrows and smooth out the | ridges;**
    with heavy | rain you soften the | ground and bless its increase.
12 You crown the year with your / goodness,
    and your paths overflow with / plenty.
13 \May the fields of the wilderness be rich for \ grazing,
    and the hills be clothed with \ joy.
14 ^May the meadows cover themselves with ^ flocks,
    and the valleys cloak themselves with ^ grain;
    let them / shout for joy and / sing.

I Will Lift Up Offerings: Commentary To Psalm 66

v.14 Come and listen, all you who fear God,
and I will tell you what he has done for me.

Sometimes he blesses me with wonders and miracles. I have no doubt that God answers prayer and I want to sing and shout. I want to show anyone who will hear me, "Come and see ... come and listen!"

.ÁVOW. VEYTH:KHÁ V:"OLOTH

v.12 I will enter your house with burnt offerings.

I will enter your temple, that is silence, with "OLOTH (*burnt offerings*) — literally *things lifted up*. I will lift up my life to you. I will lift up the life-blood of animals, symbolically replacing my own. I will lift precious things up to you and let them go. Things that I love; things I enjoy. I will bring them before you and lift them up into your presence, into the spiritual dimension. And I will go into the silence, the place of listening, into your presence.

v.13 I will offer you sacrifices of fat beasts.

I will send up to you things going up, or lifted up (compare 20, 50). Lifted up on an altar; going up in smoke. I will send up good things, fine things. Roast meat, fine wine, incense. Not because you need them, but because you accept them. You allow me to respond to you by lifting things up. You let me transcend myself and my needs by giving you a portion, a little of the best, of the first. You receive these symbolic gifts of myself, my life. And you also let me pray to you in words, calling out with intercessions and supplications. And you listen.

v.18 Blessed be God, who has not turned back
my prayer, nor his love from me.

Platitudes about the answering of prayer leave me cold. Prayer is always answered, I am told, but sometimes the answer is No. This saying is itself the answer to a meaningless question. For prayer is not about asking and wishing. Prayer is responding to God (Prayer Book, p. 856). It is communion, intimacy. And like any intimate relationship it has surprises. Far more important to me than "prayer is always answered" (though undoubtedly true) is that *sometimes* the answer is *experienced*! That sometimes, unpredictably and undeservedly, there is an answering voice in prayer. A silence that is absolutely reassuring. Sometimes, however rarely, there is an answering Presence, and a message so compact and so compelling, that I will live on it for months. This is the miracle of prayer. Blessed be God, who *sometimes* answers my prayers!

Note: Verse 1, "Be joyful in God, all you lands," compare 100:1.

Suggestions: Sing to the movement Turning Drum (see Appendix). Execute the movement with joyful energy. At [Silence...] stop all movement, freeze in position for ten to fifteen seconds. Practice the enjoyment of good things; receive them with gratitude, enjoy them, share them, lift them up to God, let go, be silent.

Psalm 66 (BCP)

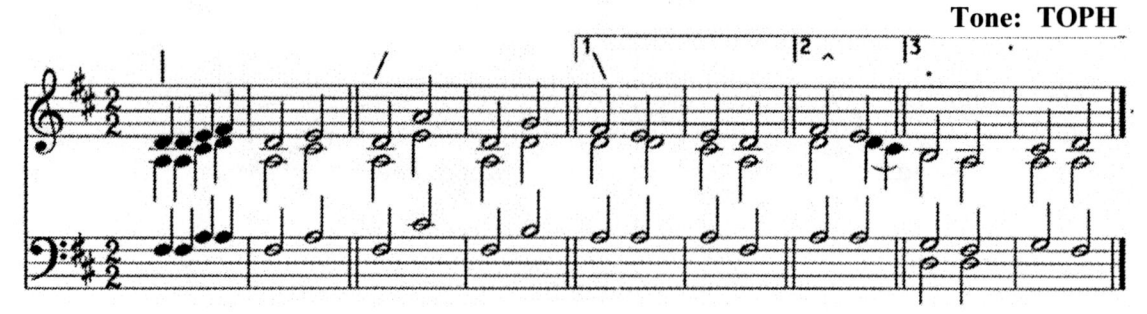

Tone: TOPH

1 /Be joyful in God, all you / lands;
   sing the glory of his / Name;
   sing the glory of his ^ praise.

2 ` ` ` ` **Sày to | Gòd, "How | àwesome are your | dèeds!** `
   becàuse of your great strèngth your ènemies cringe be|fòre you. `

3 /All the earth bows down be/fore you,
   sings to you, sings out your / Name."

              [Silence...]

4 **Còme now and | sèe the | wòrks of | Gòd,** `
   how wònderful he is in his dòing towàrd all | pèople. `
   /He turned the sea into / dry land,
   so that they went through the / water on foot,
   and there we ^ rejoiced in him.

6 /In his might he rules for/ever;
   his eyes keep watch over the / nations;
   let no rebel rise up ^ against him.

              [Silence...]

7 /Bless our God, you / peoples;
   make the voice of his / praise to be heard;

8 \Who holds our souls in \ life,
   and will not allow our \ feet to slip.

9 /For you, O God, have / proved us;
   you have tried us just as / silver is tried.

10 \You brought us into the \ snare;
   you laid heavy burdens on our \ backs.

11 /You let enemies ride over our / heads;
   we went through fire and / water;
   but you brought us out into a place of ^ refreshment.

12 /I will enter your house with burnt / offerings
   and will pay you my / vows,
   \which I promised with my \ lips
   and spoke with my mouth when I was in \ trouble.

13 .I will offer you sacrifices of fat beasts with the smoke of . rams;
   I will give you oxen and . goats.

              [Silence...]

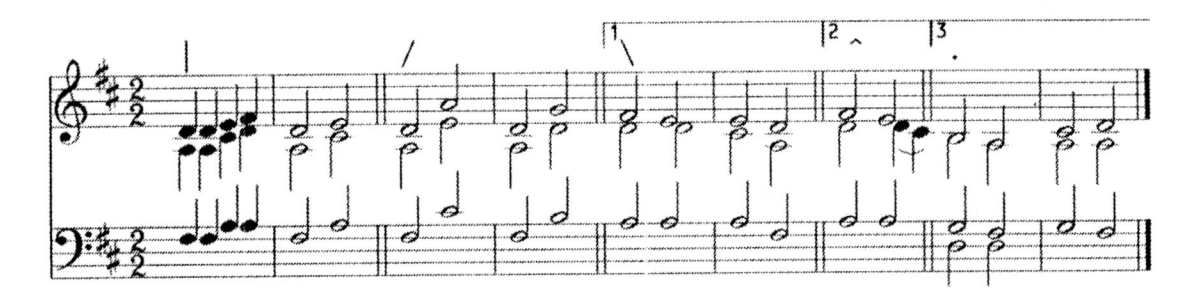

14 **Còme and | lìsten, all | yòu who fear | Gòd, `**
    and I will tèll you what he has | dòne fòr mè.
15 /I called out to him with my / mouth,
    and his praise was on my / tongue.
16 \If I had found evil in my \ heart,
    the Lord would not have \ heard me.
17 .But in truth God has . heard me;
    he has attended to the voice of my . prayer.
18 **Blèssed be | Gòd, who has not re|jècted my | pràyer, `**
    nòr withhèld his | lòve fròm mè.

Harvest Dance: Commentary To Psalm 67

v.1 May God be merciful to us and bless us,
may his face (presence) shine with us [Silence...].

May God bless us so that we can be a blessing (compare 72, 103). Let his face (his presence) shine among us, so that we can be a light to others. Sing this verse and be silent. We begin by saying "Thank you for the harvest," but more than that, "Bless us with your presence. Shine through us."

LÁDA"ATh BÁ.ÁRE3 DAR<u>KE</u>KHÁ   B:KHOL GOYIM Y:SHU"Á<u>THE</u>KHÁ
v.2 To make known in the earth your way,

among all the peoples your salvation. First in the earth, then among all the peoples. The word .ERE3 (*the earth*) occurs four times in this short psalm. Let us make known your way first in the earth, on the ground where we actually live. In our town, our neighborhood, our sidewalk (if we have one), our grass, our trees. It is the spirituality of earth life—life on the ground. It is decent life, lived righteously with actual neighbors, before we invite anyone to the afterlife. And it is green life, the reverent awareness of plants, animals, water, air.

v.4 for you judge the peoples with equity

and guide all nations upon earth [Silence...]. You administer them rightly. You play straight with all peoples and nations. And you guide them on earth, in earth life, real life, on the ground where they actually live. In their ancestral lands, the place where their fathers and mothers are buried, on the dust to which they are dust returning.

.ERE3 NÁTHNÁH Y:VULÁH'   Y:VÁR:<u>KHÉ</u>NU .eLOHIM .eLO<u>HEY</u>NU
v.6 The earth has given her increase;
may God, our own God, bless us.

Her increase. Earth, the mother side of creation, has given her grain; may God continue to bless us with his presence. Bless us with your presence so that we may bless the earth, so that the earth may continue to bless us. It is the never-ending circle that I call the divine economy. Compare 72.

<u>Suggestions</u>: A special form of N:GINOTH (*stringed instruments*) is offered for this psalm. The movement is Swaying Dance: Stand in a large circle, facing the center. Keep the feet grounded, arms in the praise gesture. Sway gently and gracefully from side to side as you sing. As you sway, let the hands swing gracefully from right to left to right. The movement is free and expressive. Omit swaying at the refrains, vv. 3 and 5. At [Silence...] stop all movement, freeze in position for ten to fifteen seconds.

Follow the spiritual path in everyday life, with neighbors, co-workers, friends and strangers. Do not expect dramatic experiences or miracles, but look for fruits of the Spirit—*love, joy, peace, patience...* This will be your evidence of spiritual progress.

Psalm 67 (BCP)

Tone: N:GINOTH *special*

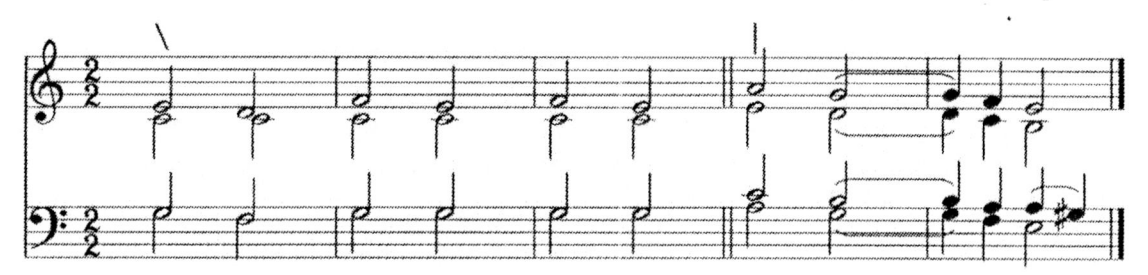

1 \May God be merciful to us and \ bless us,
   show us the light of his countenance and \ come to us.
                [Silence...]
2 \Let your ways be known upon \ earth,
   your saving health among all \ nations.
3 **Let the peoples praise you, O | God;**
   let | all the peoples | praise you.

4 \Let the nations be glad and sing for \ joy,
   for you judge the peoples with \ equity
   and guide all nations upon \ earth.
                [Silence...]
5 **Let the peoples praise you, O | God;**
   let | all the peoples | praise you.

6 \The earth has brought forth her \ increase;
   may God, our own God, give us his \ blessing.

7 \May God give us his \ blessing,
   and may all the ends of the earth stand in \ awe of him.

The Great Procession: Commentary To Psalm 68

YÁQUM .eLOHIM YÁPHU3U .OY:VÁW W:YÁNUSU M:SAN.ÁW MIPPÁNÁW
v.1 Let God arise, let His enemies be scattered;
Let those also who hate Him flee before Him.

The text is colorful but obscure. The great Spurgeon called it "surpassingly excellent and difficult," and added, "its darkness in some stanzas is utterly impenetrable." Yet the sense of energy, exultancy and uplift are unmistakable.

Let God arise. Compare Numbers 10:35: "whenever the ark set out ... Moses said: 'Rise up, O LORD! Let Your enemies be scattered. And let those who hate You flee before You'" (NKJ). Let God rise up among us, in our midst, as easy to discern as a pillar of cloud or a pillar of fire; let the forces of evil be scattered and flee, their deceptive hold on us dissolved; and let the path of surrender become plain to us.

The spiritual path is pictured as a trek through the wilderness, a portable temple carried from place to place through battles, conflicts, dissensions, and endless disappointments. And as a great procession, greater than any procession that ever was, with singers, players and dancers, beautiful girls beating drums, banners and streamers and flashing weapons. Pillar of fire and pillar of cloud and [Silence...]. I see it in brilliant flashes, then I seem to lose it. I see tantalizing glimpses of eternity!

It is the procession from Egypt—slavery, degradation, thought leading to thought and emotion to emotion—to freedom, clarity, coherence, meaning and order; to praise, rejoicing and joy. It is trekking through a wilderness in the actual presence of God. It is a transforming journey of singing, playing, dancing, drumming and [Silence...]. Outward celebration. Inward silence. Inner and outer transformation.

.eLOHIM MOSHIYV Y:#IDIM BAY:THÁH
v.6 God sets the solitary in families. "He gathers (settles) the lonely into a home." He gathers us into fellowship. He takes us from self-centered loneliness to the experience of community. Compare 100, 133. To the sharing of joys and burdens. To the experience of acceptance.

Notes: (*) Translation modified by author. Verse 18, compare Ephesians 4:8.

Suggestions: Note the powerful rhythmic beat, which comes through even in translation. Do not attempt to understand this psalm literally, but experience its rhythm and movement. Form a great circle and carry out the movement Turning Drum with grand, majestic slowness (see Appendix). On [Silence...] stop all movement, freeze in position for ten to fifteen seconds. Stand in place, read softly verses 12-17, 20-24, 29-31.

Participate in the life of your community, in all its services and ceremonies; continue to meditate in silence, day after day.

Psalm 68 (NKJ)

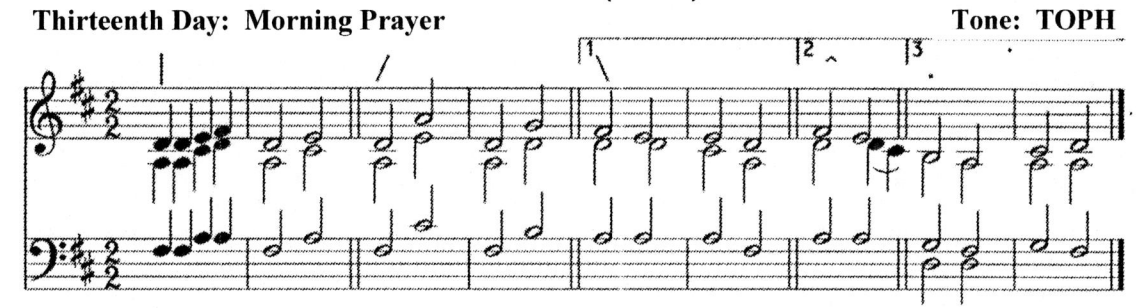

Thirteenth Day: Morning Prayer Tone: TOPH

1 ` ` ` ` **Let | Gòd a|rìse, Let his | ènemies be | scàttered;** `
   Let those àlso who hàte Him flee be|fòre Him. `
2 /As smoke is driven away, so drive them a/way;
   as wax melts before the / fire,
   so let the wicked perish at the ^ presence of God.
3 /But let the righteous be glad; Let them rejoice before / God;
   Yes, let them rejoice ex/ceedingly.
4 \Sing to God, sing praises to His \ name:
   Extol him who rides on the \ clouds,
   by his name . YAH,
   and rejoice be.fore him.
5 **A fàther of the | fàtherless, a de|fènder of | wìdows,** `
   is Gòd in his hòly habi|tàtion. ` (*)
6 /God sets the solitary in / families;
   He brings out those who are bound into pros/perity;
   but the rebellious dwell in a ^ dry land.
7 O Gòd, when You | wènt out be|fòre Your | pèople, `
   Whèn You màrched through the | wìlderness; `
                  [Silence...]
8 /The earth / shook;
   The heavens also dropped rain at the / presence of God;
   \Sinai itself was moved at the \ presence of God,
   the God of \ Israel.
9 **Yòu, O | Gòd, sent a | plèntiful | ràin,** `
   Whereby You confìrmed Your inhèritance, whèn it was / wèary. `
10 /Your congregation / dwelt in it;
   You, O God, provided from Your goodness for the / poor.
11 \The Lord gave the \ word;
   Great was the company of those who pro\claimed it.
                  [Stand]
12 "Kings of armies flee, they flee, *
   and she who remains at home divides the spoil.
13 Though you lie down among the sheepfolds, *
   Yet you will be like the wings of a dove covered with silver,
   And her feathers with yellow gold."

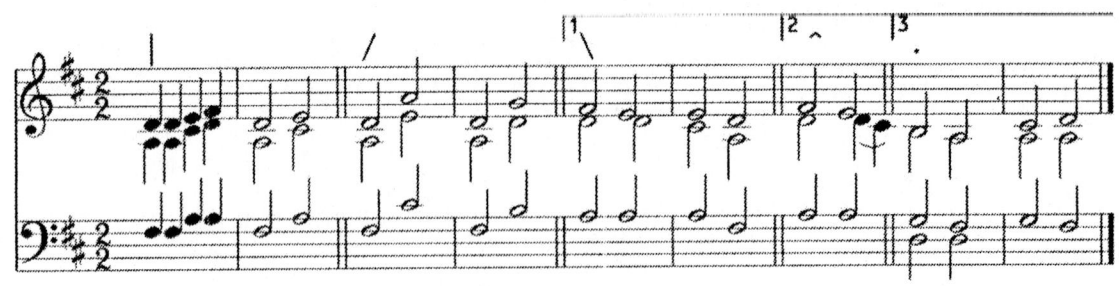

14 When the Almighty scattered kings in it, *
 it was white as snow in Zalmon.

15 A mountain of God is the mountain of Bashan; *
 a mountain of many peaks is the mountain of Bashan.

16 Why do you fume with envy, you mountains of many peaks? *
 This is the mountain which God desires to dwell in; Yes, the LORD will dwell in it forever.

17 The chariots of God are twenty thousand, *
 even thousands of thousands; the Lord is among them, as in Sinai, in the Holy Place.

18 **Yoù have a|scènded on | hìgh, You have led cap|tìvity | càptive:** `
 Yoù have received gìfts among | mèn;
 Èven among the rebèllious, That the LÒRD God might | dwèll there. `

19 **Blèssed be the | Lòrd, Who daily | lòads us with | bènefits,** `
 The Gòd of oùr sal|vàtion!

 [Silence...]
 [Stand]

20 Our God is the God of salvation; *
 and to God the Lord belong escapes from death.

21 But God will wound the head of His enemies, *
 the hairy scalp of the one who still goes on in His trespasses.

22 The Lord said, "I will bring back from Bashan, *
 I will bring them back from the depths of the sea.

23 That your foot may crush them in blood, *
 And the tongues of your dogs may have their portion from your enemies."

24 They have seen Your procession, O God; *
 the procession of my God, my King, into the sanctuary.

25 **Fìrst came the | sìngers, | thèn the | plàyers,** `
 in the mìdst of the gìrls beating | drùms. ` (*)

26 **Blèss | Gòd in the | còngre|gàtions,** `
 The Lòrd, from the fòuntain of | Ìsrael.

27 /There is little Benjamin, their / leader,
 the princes of Judah and their / company,
 \the princes of \ Zebulun
 and the princes of \ Naphtali.

28 Your God has commanded your . strength;
 strengthen, O God, what You have . done for us.

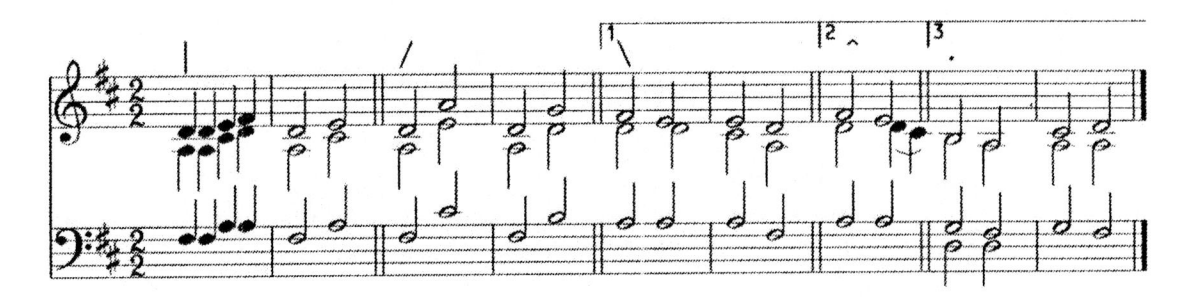

[Stand]

29 Because of Your temple at Jerusalem, *
  Kings will bring presents to You.
30 Rebuke the beasts of the reeds, *
  the herd of bulls with the calves of the peoples,
  Till everyone submits himself with pieces of silver. *
  Scatter the peoples who delight in war.
31 Envoys will come out of Egypt; *
  Ethiopia will quickly stretch out her hands to God.

32 **Sìng to | Gòd, you | kìngdoms of the | èarth;** `
  O sing pràises to the | Lòrd, `
33 /To Him who rides on the heaven of heavens, which were of / old!
  Indeed, He sends out his voice, a / mighty voice.
34 \Ascribe strength to God; his excellence is over \ Israel,
  And his strength is in the \ clouds.
35 /O God, You are more awesome than Your / holy places,
  The God of / Israel!
  \He who gives strength and power to his \ people. (*)

  Blessed be \ God!

187

Drowning: Commentary To Psalm 69

HOSHI"ÉNI .eLOHIM KI VÁ.U MAYiM "AD-NÁPHESh
v.1 Save me, O God, for the waters are come in unto my soul (KJV).

The waters are up to my soul (throat, breath, life). I am drowning. Those pleasant conversations between me and my soul (breath, life) are almost over, for my breath is about to be extinguished. The waters may be marital, social, legal, financial. My troubles are overwhelming; right and wrong are turned upside down. The newspapers have already convicted me, and I cry in outrage:

v.5 Must I then give back what I never stole?

This too will be printed in the paper: STOLE NOTHING, LOUIS SAYS, but the headline will only add to my disgrace. People who never heard of me will assume that I must have stolen *something*.

The community leaders are complaining about me. Everyone has heard about my case. My devotion to God has been "turned to my reproach," ridiculed as a way to stay out of jail. The skid row drunks are singing songs about me, or in modern terms, the late night comedians are making jokes about me. But as for me...

WA.aNIY TH:PHILLÁTHIY-L:KHÁ
v.14 But as for me, this is my prayer to you.

As if an invisible therapist had said, "But what about you, Louis?" or, "How do you feel?" Suddenly I come back to myself. The problem is not with *them* but with me. On one level I am drowning and hope is gone; on another level I can step back and listen. I may not be drowning at all, but drowning myself; thrashing about in panic I have brought myself to the brink of destruction. In vv. 23 to 30 I am going down again. Flailing in self-pity I rage against *them*. Let every bad thing happen to them. Let them be blotted out from the Book of Life. But as for me...

v.31 But as for me, I am afflicted and hurting.

As if that unseen therapist had said, again, "But what about you, Louis? Where are you?" And I said, "I'm really hurting." Transformation of consciousness. Things fall apart and I fall with them; then I step back from the experience. I acknowledge, once again, like the alcoholic, that I am powerless, that I am hurting, that my life has become unmanageable. I give up control, once again. And your salvation (liberation, victory), O God, begins to lift me up.

<u>Suggestions</u>: Sing the refrains as shown. When you find yourself drowning, overwhelmed—stop! The intuitive response is to redouble one's efforts, try harder. The spiritual response is to stop, step back and listen. Recognize that you are helpless and powerless. Turn your attention to God. What often happens then is that you find yourself doing something new and completely different, and the problem somehow becomes less important. Practice this teaching in all desperate times.

Psalm 69 (BCP)

Thirteenth Day: Evening Prayer Tone: HIGÁYON (2)

1 Save me, O God, *
   for the waters have risen up to my neck.
2 I am sinking in deep mire, *
 and there is no firm ground for my feet.
3 I have come into deep waters, *
   and the torrent washes over me.
4 I have grown weary with my crying; my throat is inflamed; *
   my eyes have failed from looking for my God.
5 Those who hate me without a cause are more than the hairs of my head;
   my lying foes who would destroy me are mighty. *
   Must I then give back what I never stole?
6 **O God, you know my | foolishness,**
   and my faults are not | hidden from you.
7 Let not those who hope in you be put to shame through me, Lord GOD of
      hosts; *
   let not those who seek you be disgraced because of me, O God of Israel.
8 Surely, for your sake have I suffered reproach, *
   and shame has covered my face.
9 I have become a stranger to my own kindred, *
   an alien to my mother's children.
10 Zeal for your house has eaten me up; *
   the scorn of those who scorn you has fallen upon me.
11 I humbled myself with fasting, *
   but that was turned to my reproach.
12 I put on sack-cloth also, *
   and became a byword among them.
13 Those who sit at the gate murmur against me, *
   and the drunkards make songs about me.
14 But as for me, this is my prayer to you, *
   at the time you have set, O LORD:
15 "In your great mercy, O God, *
   answer me with your unfailing help.
16 Save me from the mire; do not let me sink; *
   let me be rescued from those who hate me and out of the deep waters.

17 Let not the torrent of waters wash over me, neither let the deep swallow me up; *

  do not let the Pit shut its mouth upon me.

18 Answer me, O LORD, for your love is kind; *

  in your great compassion, turn to me."

19 "Hide not your face from your servant; *

  be swift and answer me, for I am in distress.

20 Draw near to me and redeem me; *

  because of my enemies deliver me.

21 **You know my reproach, my shame, and my dis | honor;**

  my adversaries are all in your | sight."

22 Reproach has broken my heart, and it cannot be healed; *

  I looked for sympathy, but there was none, for comforters, but I could find no one.

23 They gave me gall to eat, *

  and when I was thirsty, they gave me vinegar to drink.

24 Let the table before them be a trap *

  and their sacred feasts a snare.

25 Let their eyes be darkened, that they may not see, *

  and give them continual trembling in their loins.

26 Pour out your indignation upon them, *

  and let the fierceness of your anger overtake them.

27 Let their camp be desolate, *

  and let there be none to dwell in their tents.

28 For they persecute him whom you have stricken *

  and add to the pain of those whom you have pierced.

29 Lay to their charge guilt upon guilt, *

  and let them not receive your vindication.

30 Let them be wiped out of the book of the living *

  and not be written among the righteous.

31 As for me, I am afflicted and in pain; *

  your help, O God, will lift me up on high.

32 **/I will praise the Name of God in / song;**

  I will proclaim his greatness with thanks/giving.

33 This will please the LORD more than an offering of oxen, *

  more than bullocks with horns and hoofs.

34 The afflicted shall see and be glad; *

  you who seek God, your heart shall live.

35 For the LORD listens to the needy, *
   and his prisoners he does not despise.
36 **/Let the heavens and the earth / praise him,**
   the seas and all that moves / in them.
37 For God will save Zion and rebuild the cities of Judah; *
   they shall live there and have it in possession.
38 The children of his servants will inherit it, *
   and those who love his Name will dwell therein.

Aha! Aha! Commentary To Psalm 70

YÁSHUVU "AL-"ÉQEBh BÁSHTÁM HÁ.OMRIM HE.Á# HE.Á#
v.3 Let them fall back on account of their shame,
 (those who) are saying (to me) HE.Á# HE.Á#

HE.Á# HE.Á# — no need even to translate that harsh laugh — it rhymes with Hey, Bach! Hey, Bach! Centuries later we can read it clearly. They laugh and show their teeth, gloating with pretended friendliness as they close in. Victory is at hand for them; they are feeling expansive. In fact their victory is real and final. They show their teeth and laugh, in a form of friendliness. HE.Á# HE.Á# — they laugh, and I laugh too. I do not cry out in rage as this writer cried, for I live in a different age. I must pretend to enjoy those mocking laughs. Be a good sport. Laugh and the world laughs with you.

Meanwhile in my inner thoughts I cry desperately to God. Hurry, God, hurry to help me! Perform some miracle even now, while they laugh and joke. Rescue me from those who actively seek my soul (breath, breathing, life itself). Let them fall back in disgrace, but let those who seek you rejoice and be happy.

WA.aNIY "ÁNIY W:.EVYON
v.5 But as for me, I am poor and needy (God hurry to me).

Compare 69. As if yet again that invisible therapist had said to me, "But what about you? How are you feeling right now?" I have no power over *them* or anyone. I control nothing. But I... But as for me... I am the patient here. In the turbulent flow of my thoughts, a moment of silence. Listening. I know how little I can do, how helpless I am. I acknowledge, once again, that I am powerless. Come to me speedily, O God!

v.6 You are my helper and deliverer. LORD, don't be late!

A subtle but definitive change. Then I was praying in desperate rage; I was self-righteous, blaming, and controlling. I was infuriated with their braying HE.Á# — I wanted God to do something about *them*. Now I pray differently, humbler, surrendering. What is your will here, Father? The situation is lost, LORD, hurry to help me.

Note: Psalm 70 corresponds to 40:14-19.

Suggestions: When all is lost, at the point of desperation, stop whatever you are doing or trying, and — *listen*. Listen to your spouse. Listen to your boss, your fellow workers. What are they trying to tell you? Stop in your desperate moment and practice silence, listening to God. Recognize that you are helpless and powerless; you have no idea what to do. You have none of the answers, *none*. And because you have none of the answers and no idea what to do, because you have started to listen, there is some hope for you.

Psalm 70 (BCP)

Tone: N:GINOTH

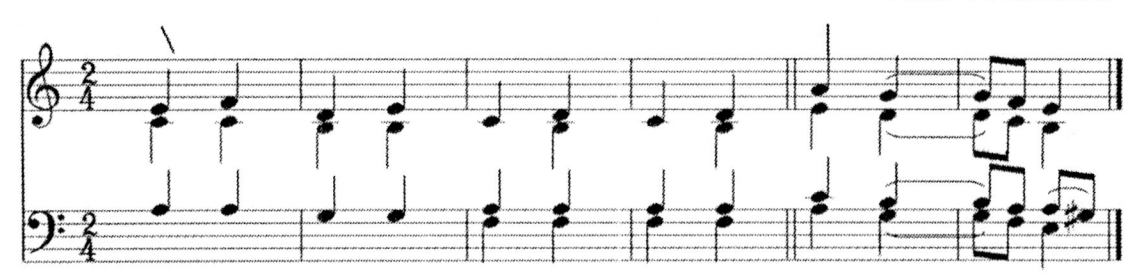

1 \Be pleased, O God, to de\liver me;
    O Lord, make haste to \ help me.
2 **Let those who seek my life be ashamed**
    and altogether dis | mayed;
    let those who take pleasure in my mis | fortune
    draw back and be dis | graced.
3 \Let those who say to me "Aha!" and gloat over me
    turn \ back,
    because they are \ ashamed.
4 \Let all who seek you rejoice and be \ glad in you;
    let those who love your salvation say for \ ever,
    "Great is the \ Lord!"
5 \But as for me, I am poor and \ needy;
    come to me speedily, O \ God.
6 You are my helper and de\liverer;
    O Lord, do not \ tarry.

Do Not Throw Me Away: Commentary To Psalm 71

.AL-TASHLI<u>KH</u>ÉNI L:"ÉTH ZIQNÁH

v.9 Do not cast me off in my old age.

Do not throw me away. Do not discard me in the trash-bin of life as I grow old. I think of my old age and I wonder what will happen to me. The old, who were once called Wisdom Keepers, are now considered a nuisance. They are forgetful, boring, likely to be demented or at least silly. They are forever complaining, they whine and worry, they fill up hospital beds, they cost too much.

Life is in constant motion, playfully changing and changing back. Behind this lively scene, irreversible change, moving in one direction. We call it aging and we try not to think of it. Day by day we grow older, never younger. The cells divide and regenerate, seemingly inexhaustible, till the number of their divisions is exhausted. The end of a human breathing is set from the beginning. The little boy dreams of growing up, and the old man looks back on his youth.

What kind of old man will I be? Will I bore the young with old stories and tiresome warnings? Will I tell the same jokes over and over? I think of old men and old women I admire, still learning at seventy and eighty. They keep growing, trying new things. Retirement means nothing to them; they can hardly wait for work each morning. They look for problems and keep busy serving others.

Admittedly that kind of old age is uncommon. For most of the aging energies decline, opportunities dwindle. Poverty limits creativity. Health may be tenuous. The soul (breath, life) contracts, draws into itself. Loneliness kills by degrees, as surely as cancer. What kind of old man will I be? Mostly, I realize with growing consternation, I will be what I am today, this moment. More obvious, harder to conceal.

v.17 O God, you have taught me since I was young.

W:GAM "AD-ZIQNÁH W:SEYVÁH   .eLOHIM .AL-TA"aZ<u>V</u>ÉNI

v.18 Now also when I am old and gray-headed, O God, forsake me not (KJV). You have brought me a long, long way; a strange, wandering path. You were with me when I searched for you in vain. You were with me in "the Temple" and in church. You brought me and taught me and I was a difficult student. Now bring me on to old age, though I am difficult still. I turn my old age over to you, LORD. I begin my old age now, this moment, with you.

v.20 You will return, you will restore me to life,

and from the depths of the earth (you will return), you will raise me up. Life moves irreversibly to its end; yet there is more. Details unknown. You will come back for me. You strengthen me more and more. You enfold and comfort me.

<u>Suggestions</u>: Continue your spiritual practice year after year. Always keep studying and learning. Let others complain about old age; you keep on learning and praising!

Psalm 71 (BCP)

Fourteenth Day: Morning Prayer   Tone: **N:GINOTH**

1 **In you, O LORD, have I taken | refuge;**
   let me | never be | ashamed.

2 \In your righteousness, deliver me and set me \ free;
   incline your ear to me and \ save me.

3 Be my strong rock, a castle to \ keep me safe;
   you are my crag and my \ stronghold.

4 **Deliver me, my God, from the hand of the | wicked,**
   from the clutches of the | evildoer and the | oppressor.

5 .For you are my hope, O Lord . GOD,
   my confidence since I was . young.

6 I have been sustained by you ever since I was . born;
   from my mother's womb you have been my . strength.
   my praise shall be always of . you.

7 I have become a portent to many;
   but you are my . refuge and my strength.

8 \Let my mouth be full of your \ praise
   and your glory all the day \ long.

9 Do not cast me off in my old \ age;
   forsake me not when my \ strength fails.

10 \For my enemies are talking a\gainst me,
   and those who lie in wait for my life take counsel to\gether.

11 They say, "God has forsaken him;
   go after him and \ seize him;
   because there is none who will \ save."

12 \O God, be not \ far from me;
   come quickly to help me, O my \ God.

13 **Let those who set themselves against me be put to shame and be dis | graced;**
   let those who seek to do me | evil
   be covered with scorn and re | proach.

14 .But I shall always wait in . patience,
   and shall praise you more and . more.

15 My mouth shall recount your mighty acts and saving deeds all day. long;
   though I cannot know the . number of them.

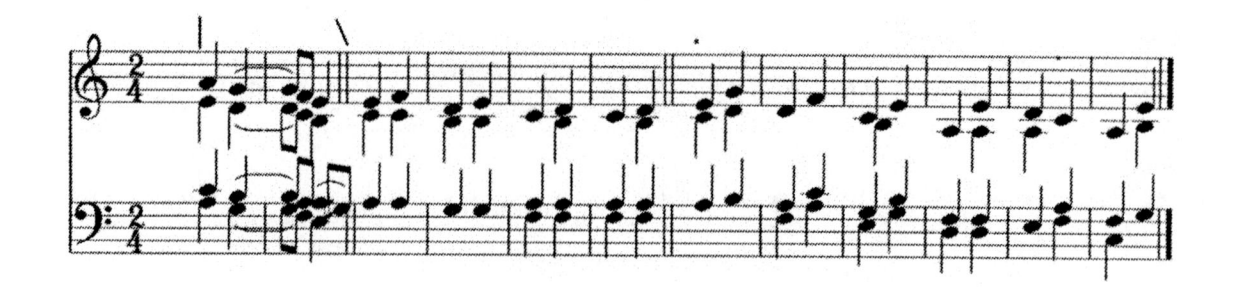

16 I will begin with the mighty works of the . Lord GOD;
   I will begin with your righteousness, yours a.lone.
17 \O God, you have taught me since I was \ young,
   and to this day I tell of your wonderful \ works.
18 And now that I am old and grey-headed, O God, do not for\sake me,
   till I make known your strength to this generation
   and your power to \ all who are to come.
19 .Your righteousness, O God, reaches to the . heavens;
   you have done great things;
   who is . like you, O God?
20 You have showed me great troubles and ad.versities,
   but you will restore my . life
   and bring me up again from the deep . places of the earth.
21 You strengthen me more and more;
   you enfold and . comfort me.
22 .Therefore I will praise you upon the lyre for your faithfulness, O my . God;
   I will sing to you with the harp, O Holy One of . Israel.
23 My lips will sing with joy when I . play to you,
   and so will my . soul, which you have redeemed.
24 My tongue will proclaim your righteousness all day . long,
   for they are ashamed and disgraced
   who sought to do me . harm.

Spiritual Economy: Commentary To Psalm 72

W:YITHPALLÉL BA"aDOW THÁMIYD   KOL-HAYOM Y:VÁR<u>KHEN</u>:HU
v.15 May prayer be made for him always,
and may they bless him all the day long.

Blessing is a circular process. We are blessed so that we can bless others, and in blessing others we are blessed. Spiritual economics is a process of continuing enrichment. Material economics, by contrast, often ends in a spiral of impoverishment. Large numbers for the few; meaningless poverty for the many. Spiritual blessings are invested or lost (Luke 19:11-27). The more you give away the more you increase.

v.1 God, give your judgments to the king (supreme authority),
and your justice to the king's son (lesser authorities, the government).

This economy begins with justice.* The concept of <u>3EDEQ</u> (*justice* or *righteousness*) is not based on fairness—making sure that everyone gets the same amount—but on the protection of those who cannot protect themselves. Among the first duties of a ruler are to defend the needy, rescue the poor, crush the oppressor.

And so the nation begins to prosper. The "righteous flourish," there is "abundance of peace"; in vv. 8-9 the nation becomes the recognized leader of the world. In v. 12, the principles are reviewed lest the leaders forget: "He shall deliver the poor who cries out ... and the oppressed who has no helper."

v.13 He shall have pity on the lowly and the poor;
he shall preserve the souls (lives) of the needy. Imagine living under such a system. Employers would take care of their workers. They would never force a worker to decide between keeping a job and caring for a sick child. The workers in turn would be loyal to the employer and would do everything possible to satisfy the customers. A worker would never say, "That's not my job," and a boss would never exploit or intimidate a worker (Ephesians 6:5-9).

In a covenant relationship based on righteousness, the weakest member is most protected. The mighty corporation has no advantage over an injured customer. The government official would never intimidate a citizen, and the citizen would support the officials with prayer. How rich we would all be.

<u>Notes</u>: v.2 ("that he may rule your people righteously"), see also Isaiah 11:1-5. Verse 17 ("may all the nations bless themselves in him"), see Genesis 12:2-3.

<u>Suggestions</u>: Practice <u>3EDEQ</u> (*justice, righteousness*) in all your affairs. Live, as much as possible, in covenant relationships, not limited to what the law requires. Follow the teaching of Ephesians 6.

---

*Henri Baruk, *TSEDEK. Modern Science reviewed in the light of the Hebraic Civilization.* Swan House, Binghamton, N.Y., 1972.

Psalm 72 (BCP)

Tone: "ÁSOR

1 \Give the King your justice, O \ God,
   and your righteousness to the King's \ Son;
2 **That he may rule your people | righteously**
   and the | poor with | justice;
3 That the mountains may bring prosperity to the / people,
   and the little / hills bring / righteousness.
4 \He shall defend the needy among the \ people;
   he shall rescue the poor and crush the \ oppressor.
5 He shall live as long as the sun and . moon endure,
   from one generation to . another.
6 **He shall come down like rain upon the mown | field,**
   like | showers that water the | earth.
7 In his time shall the righteous / flourish;
   there shall be abundance of / peace till the / moon shall be no more.
8 \He shall rule from sea to \ sea,
   and from the River to the ends of the \ earth.
9 His foes shall bow down . before him,
   and his enemies lick the . dust.
10 **The kings of Tarshish and the isles shall pay | tribute,**
   and the kings of Arabia and | Saba offer | gifts.
11 All kings shall bow down / before him,
   and all the / nations do him / service.
12 \For he shall deliver the poor who cries out in \ distress,
   and the oppressed who has no \ helper.
13 He shall have pity on the lowly and . poor;
   he shall preserve the lives of the . needy.
14 **He shall redeem their lives from oppression and | violence,**
   and dear shall their | blood be in his | sight.
15 \Long may he \ live!
   and may there be given to him gold from \ Arabia;
   may prayer be made for him | always,
   and may they | bless him all the day | long.
16 May there be abundance of grain on the / earth,
   growing / thick even on the / hilltops;
   \may its fruit flourish like \ Lebanon,
   and its grain like grass upon the \ earth.

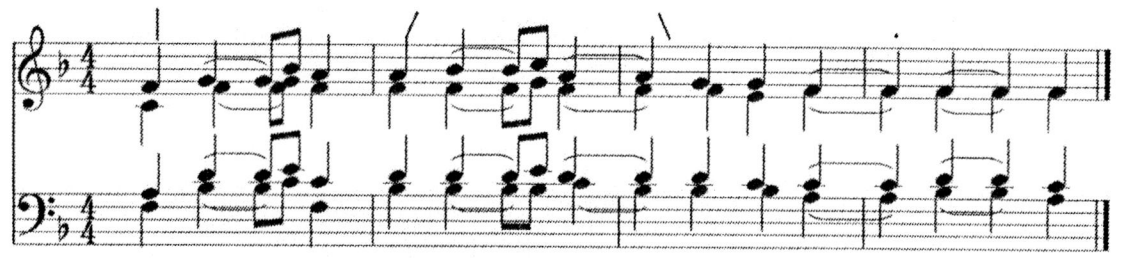

17 May his Name remain for . ever
   and be established as long as the . sun endures;
   may all the nations | bless themselves in him and | call him | blessed.
18 \Blessed be the Lord GOD, the God of \ Israel,
   who alone does wondrous \ deeds!
19 And blessed be his glorious Name for . ever!
   and may all the earth be filled with his glory.
   Amen. . Amen.

Book Three

Therapy Of The Heart: Commentary To Psalm 73

The word LÉV or LÉVÁV (*heart*) occurs six times. The root means hollow (Gesenius, p. 428), hence a hollow organ, a hollow place or space. The hollow or empty place where choices are made. I think of it as attitude — one's basic disposition to life.

A portrait of the inner world, where thought leads to thought, emotion to emotion, and sin to greater sin. My downfall can begin with a single thought. My idle observation that the wicked prosper leads me into a vortex of bitterness. As my turmoil intensifies, I experience confusion. Why do the wicked suffer no pain? Their hearts overflow with wicked thoughts, yet they never seem to suffer like the good. And what is worse, people turn to them and follow them as role models. The more I thought about these matters, the more I saw to upset me. Why do good things happen to bad people?

.AKH- RIYQ ZIK<u>K</u>ITHI L:VÁVIY WÁ.ER#A3 B:NIQQÁYON KAPPÁY
v.13 Surely, in vain have I made clean (purified) my heart,

and continue to wash my hands in innocence. Surely, in vain have I kept a good attitude! Like the man who prayed, "God I thank you that I am not like — this tax-collector" (Luke 18:11, KJV). Comparing myself to the proud I reveal all too clearly that my own goodness is an empty sham. The more I pondered these questions, the harder it was for me to understand.

v.17 Until I come into the sanctuary of God.

Until I come into the place of silence, the place of listening. A temple or a state of mind. I could not understand anything until I began listening to God. There was a point where any thought, any thought, no matter how noble, would only have added to my turmoil. No suggestion, no comfort, not even music would have helped. Until I come into the sanctuary. Until I step completely outside that world of thoughts.

KI YITH#AMMÉ3 L:VÁVIY W:KHILYOTHAY .ESHTONÁN
v.21 When my heart is embittered or "in ferment" like vinegar (Feuer, p. 919), then my inner world is pierced, wounded, in awful distress. Thought leads to thought, and emotion to emotion, and turbulence increases to the point of breakdown. My inner world is imploding. From my bitter preoccupation with *them* — the proud, the wicked — I fall in upon myself. Then, as always, that sharp disjunction:

v.28 But as for me, the closeness of God is good for me. The therapy of the heart is long and difficult. There are so many things I'm sure of that must be unlearned. A psychiatrist cannot do this therapy. Only God can melt hearts. The closeness of God is the only good medicine for them.

<u>Note</u>: (*) Verse 29b is not in the Hebrew text.

<u>Suggestions</u>: Sing refrains. When your heart is in turmoil, do not attempt to find your way out by thinking or reasoning alone. Stop everything and be silent. Turn to God with or without words. For the closeness of God will be good for you.

Psalm 73 (BCP)

Fourteenth Day: Evening Prayer　　　　　　　　　　　　　　　　Tone: HIGÁYON

1 Truly, God is good to Israel, *
　to those who are pure in heart.
2 But as for me, my feet had nearly slipped; *
　I had almost tripped and fallen;
3 Because I envied the proud *
　and saw the prosperity of the wicked:
4 For they suffer no pain, *
　and their bodies are sleek and sound;
5 In the misfortunes of others they have no share; *
　they are not afflicted as others are.
6 Therefore they wear their pride like a necklace *
　and wrap their violence about them like a cloak.
7 Their iniquity comes from gross minds, *
　and their hearts overflow with wicked thoughts.
8 They scoff and speak maliciously; *
　out of their haughtiness they plan oppression.
9 They set their mouths against the heavens, *
　and their evil speech runs through the world.
10 And so the people turn to them *
　and find in them no fault.
11 They say, "How should God know? *
　is there knowledge in the Most High?"
12 So then, these are the wicked; *
　always at ease, they increase their wealth.
13 **In vain have I kept my heart | clean,**
　and washed my hands in | innocence.
14 I have been afflicted all day long, *
　and punished every morning.
15 Had I gone on speaking this way, *
　I should have betrayed the generation of your children.
16 When I tried to understand these things, *
　it was too hard for me;
17 Until I entered the sanctuary of God *
　and discerned the end of the wicked.

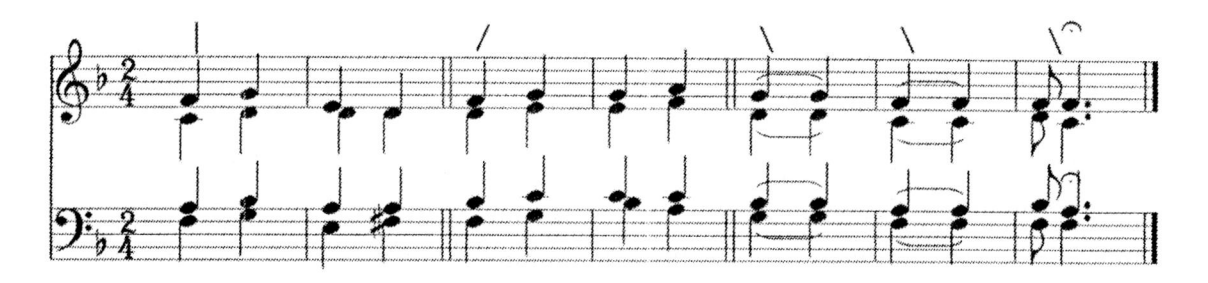

18 Surely, you set them in slippery places; *
   you cast them down in ruin.
19 Oh, how suddenly do they come to destruction, *
   come to an end, and perish from terror.
20 Like a dream when one awakens, O LORD, *
   when you arise you will make their image vanish.
21 **When my mind became em | bittered,**
   I was sorely wounded in my | heart.
22 I was stupid and had no understanding; *
   I was like a brute beast in your presence.
23 **/Yet I am always / with you;**
   you hold me by my right / hand.
24 You will guide me by your counsel, *
   and afterwards receive me with glory.
25 Whom have I in heaven but you? *
   and having you I desire nothing upon earth.
26 **Though my flesh and my heart should waste | away,**
   God is the strength of my heart and my portion for | ever.
27 Truly, those who forsake you will perish; *
   you destroy all who are unfaithful.
28 **/But it is good for me to be near / God;**
   I have made the Lord GOD my / refuge.
29 \I will speak of all your works
   \in the gates
   of the city of \ Zion. (*)

We Do Not See Our Signs: Commentary To Psalm 74

In 587 B.C., Jerusalem falls and the temple is destroyed. The first of the great national catastrophes of Judaism. It is the end of a world. Compare 79, 137.

v.3b The enemy has damaged everything in the sanctuary.
v.4a Your enemies roar in the midst of Your meeting place.

In the place where no one was to enter, the place of silence, they came swinging axes and hammers, roaring and making noise. And the holy place, the place of silence, was no more. The Hebrews said that God lived on that hill, in that building; yet they knew that God is not confined in space or time. It was their way of describing the center, the place of listening to God. Without that center, they believed, there really was no center. Life was fragmented and meaningless.

SÁMU .OTHOTHÁM .OTHOTH
v.4 They set up their banners for signs.

They—the conquerors, the destroyers, whoever they are—have set up their signs (symbols, values) as the new signs and symbols. Alien values determine meaning. The agenda of life is now defined by an alien jargon. Words are created to deceive, to gain adherents. Whatever does not fit this jargon is foolishness, not worth discussing. The intellect cannot tell what has been lost, for words are constantly changing. Words have become chameleons, meaning what others think we want to hear.

.OTHOTHEYNU LO.-RÁ.INU
v.9 We do not see our signs;
there is no longer any prophet;
nor is there any who knows how long.

Our own signs (values) are lost. The codes that nurtured us cannot be decoded. An aging generation tries to tell its children, but the children cannot hear, for meaning itself has disappeared. It is not fashion that has changed—the length of hair or dresses—but the core values of life. For whom do we live? Without that, all is relative. And the prophet, who speaks out of absolute value, speaks no more. We have experts to tell us the latest views, but no one can speak for God (though many use his Name). We grope for answers in politics or in court. We cast votes to determine what is right.

The old ways will never return. We may try to bring them back with symbols, but we deceive ourselves. The meaning of symbols changes as we speak. Thought leads to thought and emotion to emotion; all too easily we follow symbols to destruction.

Suggestions: In a world of axes and hammers, where nothing stays the same, put not your faith in symbols. Turn back, again and again, to your center, to silence; listen to God. Not to a symbol of silence or the thought of silence, but silence itself—the temple that endures.

Psalm 74 (NKJ)

Tone: "UGÁV

1 O God, why have You cast us off forever? *
   Why does your anger smoke against the sheep of your pasture?
2 **Remember Your congregation, which you have purchased of | old,**
   The tribe of your inheritance, which You have re|deemed —
   This Mount \ Zion where You have dwelt.
3 Lift up Your feet to the perpetual desolations. *
   The enemy has damaged everything in the sanctuary.
4 Your enemies roar in the midst of Your meeting place; *
   They set up their banners for | signs.
5 They seem like men who lift up | axes
   a\mong the thick trees.
6 And now they break down its carved work, all at once, *
   With axes and hammers.
7 They have set fire to Your sanctuary; *
   They have defiled the dwelling place of Your name to the ground.
8 They said in their hearts,
   "Let us destroy them altogether." *
   They have burned up all the meeting places of God in the land.
9 **We do not see our | signs;**
   There is no longer any | prophet;
   Nor is there any among us who \ knows how long.
10 O God, how long will the adversary reproach? *
    Will the enemy blaspheme Your name forever?
11 Why do you withdraw Your hand, even Your right hand? *
    Take it out of Your bosom and destroy them.
12 For God is my King from of old, *
    Working salvation in the midst of the earth.
13 You divided the sea by Your strength; *
    You broke the heads of the sea serpents in the waters.
14 You broke the heads of Leviathan in pieces, *
    And gave him as food to the people inhabiting the wilderness.
15 You broke open the fountain and the flood; *
    You dried up mighty rivers.
16 The day is Yours, the night also is Yours; *
    You have prepared the light and the sun.

17 You have set all the borders of the earth; *
    You have made summer and winter.
18 **Remember this, that the enemy has re | proached, O LORD,**
    And that a foolish people has blasphemed Your | name.
19 Oh, do not deliver the life of Your turtledove to the wild | beast!
    Do not | forget the life of Your | poor forever.
20 Have respect to the covenant; *
    For the dark places of the earth are full of the habitations of cruelty.
21 Oh, do not let the oppressed return ashamed! *
    Let the poor and needy praise Your name.
22 Arise, O God, plead Your own cause; *
    Remember how the foolish man reproaches You | daily.
23 Do not forget the voice of Your | enemies;
    The tumult of those who rise up a | gainst You
    in | creases con | tinually.

Boast No More: Commentary To Psalm 75

.ÁMARTI LAHOL:LIM .AL-TÁHOLLU W:LÁR:SHÁ"IM .AL-TÁRIMU QÁREN
v.4 I have said to the boasters, "Do not boast,"
and to the wicked, "Do not lift up your horns." For the word HOL:LIM Feuer* renders "madmen" and KJV "fools." The root (same as for praise) refers to brilliance, hence to glorify oneself or others, celebrate, make a show; and by further extension to be foolish or mad (Gesenius, p. 226). How interesting that the same excitement can turn to praise or madness.

Put two male animals in the same territory and they will fight for dominance—a fight to death or flight. Tossing horns or baring teeth, one wins, one flees. Listen to men conversing: *My car* (boat, house, income, wife, child—whatever) *is better than yours.* And the other man answers, in effect, *Ha! my* (whatever) *is greater than that!* Sometimes it's crude—*I can prove I'm a man!*—other times sophisticated—*But have you read?* (as I have)... *Have you ever met?* (as I have)... Some men compete over sports cars, others over numbers of publications.

The competitiveness of women may be more subtle. *Oh, it was nothing,* they may say, or, *I overcooked the spinach,* waiting for the other to insist that their (whatever) is really the greatest. Women, especially in the South, do not toss their horns so high as men, but they still boast and compete.

"All evildoers are full of boasting" (94:4). Those who lift up their horns over others. Boasting and gloating—putting down other and lifting up self—is spiritual madness. Although rarely brought to a psychiatrist, it is true insanity. It is the most common form of insanity, for whoever compares him- or herself to another, has it.

The more we try to subdue this insanity, the more virulent it becomes. Open boasting is easy to recognize. I gloated maniacally when I was winning at Monopoly. I owned Park Place and Boardwalk. I couldn't stop laughing as I scooped up all the money. Then I saw how my family looked at me: Revenge comes in the next game! But if I think to myself, *I'm not like those people,* or, *I'm more spiritual than that*—who is going to set me straight? If I start thinking, *Thank God I'm not like that Pharisee* (Luke 18: 9-14)—who will be able to correct me? So the more spiritual I try to be, the more insane I become. The only antidote is a sense of humor. If I can still laugh at myself, there may be hope.

v.7 For it is God who judges.
This (one) he puts down and this (one) he lifts up.

Suggestions: Sing the refrains. Avoid boasting, but do not make a show of humility. Do not seek to be first *or last*. Practice laughing at yourself in all situations. If someone pays you a compliment, accept it graciously. You are insane: accept it with grace. How can you do these things? By continuing in meditation. By listening.

---

*Rabbi Avrohom Chaim Feuer: *Tehillim (Psalms)/ A New Translation with a Commentary Anthologized from Talmudic, Midrashic and Rabbinic Sources.* Mesorah Publications, Ltd., Brooklyn, NY, 1977, p. 942.

Psalm 75 (BCP)

Fifteenth Day: Morning Prayer Tone: "UGÁV

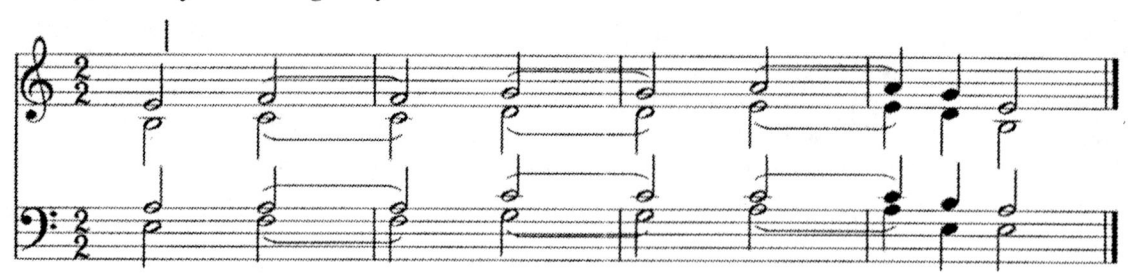

1 We give you thanks, O God, we give you thanks, *
 calling upon your Name and declaring all your wonderful deeds.
2 "I will appoint a time," says God; *
 "I will judge with equity.
3 Though the earth and all its inhabitants are quaking, *
 I will make its pillars fast.
 [Silence...]
4 **I will say to the boasters, 'Boast no | more,'**
 and to the wicked, 'Do not toss your | horns;
5 Do not toss your horns so | high,
 nor | speak with a proud | neck.'"
6 For judgment is neither from the east nor from the west, *
 nor yet from the wilderness or the mountains.
7 It is God who judges; *
 he puts down one and lifts up another.
8 For in the LORD's hand there is a cup,
 full of spiced and foaming wine, which he pours out, *
 and all the wicked of the earth shall drink and drain the dregs.
9 **But I will rejoice for | ever;**
 I will sing praises to the God of | Jacob.
10 He shall break off all the horns of the | wicked;
 but the horns of the | righteous shall be ex | alted.

After The Final Battle: Commentary To Psalm 76

"And it will come to pass at the same time, when Gog comes against the Land of Israel," says the LORD God, "that My fury will show in My face .... I will call for a sword against Gog ... and I will bring him to judgment" (Ezekiel 38:18-22, NKJ).

SHÁMMÁH SHIBBAR RISHPHEY-QÁSHETh MÁGÉN W:#EREBh UMIL#ÁMÁH
v.3 There he broke the flashing arrows,

the shield, the sword, and the weapons of battle. A last cataclysmic battle. No one was sure how it ended. Equipment was scattered for miles, and the troops by their thousands lay as if asleep. It was the end for our combative nature, our competitive madness and rages. We did not finish this battle by military genius. It was you who broke the arrows, the shield and the sword.

KI-#aMATH .ÁDÁM TODEKHÁ SH:.ÉRITH #ÉMOTH TA#GOR
v.10 Surely the wrath of man shall praise thee:

the remainder of wrath shalt thou restrain (KJV). "The fierceness of man shall turn to thy praise" (the 1928 Prayer Book, p. 433). A radical transformation, for the wrath and rages of mankind will change, in some unexplained way, to affirmation. To praising and thanking God. Anger will not disappear, but its destructive power will be drastically reduced.

What little remains will be controlled and channeled. "With the remainder of wrath You shall gird Yourself" (NKJ). You will turn it to some productive use. Exactly how this will happen I do not know. But not, it seems, by repression or self-control. Not by denial (*I never get angry*) and not by projection (*They are the angry ones, not me*) but by conversion. By turning it completely around into something new. Out of the most deadly emotion a force for good.

When I look at the world around me, I know how terribly we need this. When I read the newspaper it seems that everyone is angry about something. I read the Letters to the Editor with fascination; everyone seems to have grievances, bitterness, slogans, and rallying cries. We move in an atmosphere where anger is more plentiful than oxygen. Great leaders bait each other with false accusations and stir their people to hatred; adolescent boys murder each other over real or fancied disrespect. When, I ask, will it begin to turn around? When will we turn all this anger into something constructive?

Scripture alludes to it often — the conversion of the world. Some wait for it, dreaming of the day. Some would predict the day and hour. Yet in Christ it has already begun. In tiny seeds, tiny beginnings, in one human breathing at a time, it is growing. Let it now be growing in me. Let my wrath turn to thank you, LORD. And bind what is left. Take it from me, turn it around, make it a force for building. And use what is left.

Suggestions: Contribute to the conversion of the world, the breaking of those flashing arrows. Practice moments of silence and let go of anger; at home, in the workplace, when you listen to the news.

Psalm 76 (BCP)

Tone: #a303:ROTH

1 **In Judah is God | known;**
   his Name is great in | Israel.
2 / At Salem is his / tabernacle;
   And his dwelling in | Zion.
3 There he broke the flashing | arrows,
   / the shield, the sword, and the weapons of / battle.
                [Silence...]
4 **How glorious you | are!**
   / more splendid than the everlasting / mountains!
5 +The strong of heart have been de+spoiled;
   they sink into / sleep;
   none of the warriors can lift a \ hand.
6 **At your rebuke, O God of | Jacob,**
   / both horse and rider lie / stunned.
7 **What terror you in | spire!**
   / who can stand before you when you are / angry?
8 +From heaven you pronounced + judgment;
   the earth was afraid and was / still;
9 When God rose up to \ judgment
   and to save all the oppressed of the \ earth.
                [Silence...]
10 +Truly, wrathful Edom will give you + thanks,
   and the remnant of Hamath will keep your / feasts.
11 Make a vow to the LORD your God and \ keep it;
   +Let all around him bring gifts to him who is worthy to be + feared.
12 He breaks the spirit of / princes,
   and strikes terror in the kings of the \ earth.

Faith Crisis: Commentary To Psalm 77

Another night of insomnia, and it seems as if the writer is losing faith. All night he tosses and turns, praying but receiving no answer. In v. 7 he begins to wonder, "Will the LORD cast me off for ever?" In v. 8, "Has his loving-kindness come to an end for ever?" In v. 9, "Has God forgotten to be gracious?" Finally, after a deep silence, "the right hand of the Most High has lost its power." I have placed my trust in a delusion.

Is faith delusion? Is delusion faith? What is the difference? A delusion, in psychiatry, is a fixed, false belief that cannot be corrected by external evidence. Talking to a deluded patient is a humbling experience. No logic, no evidence, prevails against the false idea. You may be courteous and gracious, but to no avail. Not for a moment does the deluded one question or doubt. If the communists are after me, or if there is a great conspiracy against me, well, so it is then. It would never occur to me to wonder, *Why me?* or, *Could there be some mistake?*

Talk to me ten or twenty years later, you will hear the same idea, the same words, the same names, even the same inflections of the voice. The world may change, but the deluded one does not. The persecutors are the same as twenty years ago, figures from the headlines of yesteryear. Delusion is remarkably constant, yes, but it is not faith.

.EZKOR MA"AL:LEY YÁH'   KI-.EZK:RÁH MIQQEDEM PIL.EKHÁ
v.11 I will recall the works of the LORD,
when I begin to remember, from of old, your wonder(s).

Faith is reliable by intention, not compulsion. I have seen the evidence and I have chosen to believe. Still, I wonder. Sometimes when I'm not seeing the evidence, I question. *Is God real? Do I really believe? Is it all a myth?* Faith is the evidence of things not seen for the moment. Faith is the constancy that keeps me on a path not always obvious. I continue on the path because I choose to continue, not because I am driven to do so. In a strange way, we may say that without some doubt there really is no faith. I question, and then I remember; I call to mind; I meditate. I remember what God has shown me and taught me, and I choose to continue in belief.

Out of that choice comes deeper understanding. Out of questioning, deeper commitment. I am overwhelmed with the greatness of God. I grow in faith, to deeper faith. As years go by, my faith is stronger, tested by experience. And I still have questions.

<u>Suggestions</u>: Memorize a verse or line whenever you meditate. Take up this verse or line again and again during your silent time; let it go, and return to silence. Return to your chosen verse or line again and again throughout the day; remember it, let it go and be silent. This will be a great help to you in meditation. Practice taking a deep breath through the nose and chanting your verse or line slowly, softly, on this same breath, for ten to fifteen seconds. Continue this practice for two to three minutes each time you meditate. Pray this psalm at night whenever you cannot sleep.

Psalm 77 (BCP)

Tone: N:GINOTH

1 I will cry aloud to God; *
 I will cry aloud, and he will hear me.
2 In the day of my trouble I sought the LORD; *
 my hands were stretched out by night and did not tire;
 I refused to be comforted.
3 **I think of God, I am | restless,**
 I | ponder, and my spirit | faints.
  [Silence...]
4 You will not let my eyelids close; *
 I am troubled and I cannot speak.
5 **I consider the days of | old;**
 I re|member the years long | past;
6 **I commune with my heart in the | night;**
 I | ponder and search my | mind.
7 Will the LORD cast me off for ever? *
 will he no more show his favor?
8 Has his loving-kindness come to an end for ever? *
 has his promise failed for evermore?
9 Has God forgotten to be gracious? *
 has he, in his anger, withheld his compassion?
  [Silence...]
10 And I said, "My grief is this: *
 the right hand of the Most High has lost its power."
11 **I will remember the works of the | LORD,**
 and call to | mind your wonders of | old time.
12 **I will meditate on all your | acts**
 and | ponder your mighty | deeds.
13 Your way, O God, is holy; *
 who is so great a god as our God?
14 You are the God who works wonders *
 and have declared your power among the peoples.
15 By your strength you have redeemed your people, *
 the children of Jacob and Joseph.
  [Silence...]

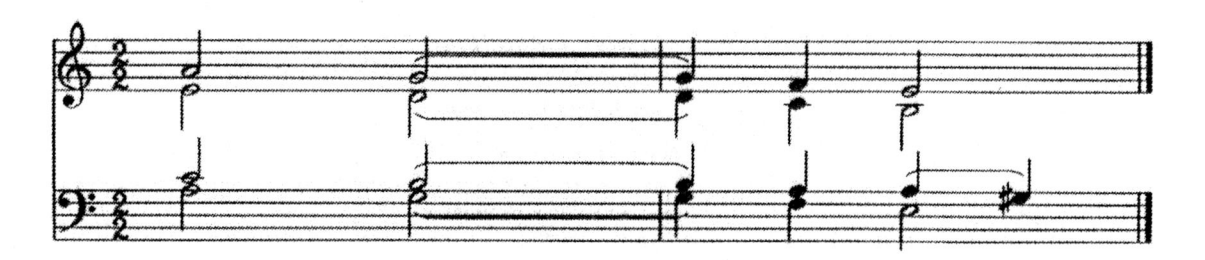

16 The waters saw you, O God; the waters saw you and trembled; *
    the very depths were shaken.
17 The clouds poured out water; the skies thundered; *
    your arrows flashed to and fro;
18 The sound of your thunder was in the whirlwind;
    your lightnings lit up the world; *
    the earth trembled and shook.
19 Your way was in the sea,
    and your paths in the great waters, *
    yet your footsteps were not seen.
20 You led your people like a flock *
    by the hand of Moses and Aaron.

They Forgot: Commentary To Psalm 78

This is one of a series. Stories from Hebrew history are re-lived to teach about faith. Compare 89, 105, 106.

v.7 so that they might put their trust in God,
and not forget the deeds of God. So that we might develop our faith. Not a feeling, but enlightened constancy. We develop faith by experiencing God's love, and by telling and retelling these experiences. Remembering these things, which have actually happened, we come to trust.

It is the same in any important relationship. My wife and I retell stories of our life together. As we recall this or that incident we re-live the sharing of the incident; we remember how we have struggled and enjoyed together; how important our relationship is; how we have always been able to count on each other. *Do you remember the time when... ?*

Some of the times were funny, some painful. We have talked about some episodes hundreds of times. When we meet new people we may tell them some of our stories. They are not about earth-shaking events, but they tell about us, our history. They remind us that our relationship is trustworthy even when it doesn't feel so. They remind us how much we have invested in each other.

In the same way God's people tell stories about their relationship with him. Not merely because they are interesting, but to help them remember. To build the relationship. Here in these highlights from Hebrew history, two verses are placed side by side to illustrate a contrast: God is reliable and trustworthy. We are not.

v.11 They forgot what he had done,
and the wonders he had shown them.

v.12 He worked marvels in the sight of their forefathers. We forget. God remembers. We forget. God takes care of us anyway. We are grateful, but quickly forget. We chase after instant relief.

LO.-ZÁRU MITA.aWÁTHÁM "OD .ÁKHLÁM B:PHIHEM
v.30 But they did not stop their craving,
though the food was still in their mouths.

We become a nation of addicts. We have everything, but nothing is enough. God is furious but he saves us once again. Eventually, let us hope, we begin to remember. We develop internal stability. We begin to sense his constancy as we develop our own. Each in our own way, telling our stories.

<u>Suggestions</u>: Form a great circle and do the psalm as walking meditation, much as you did Psalm 26. Let each ` represent a step, and note the extra steps in v.22. Stand in place for the sung refrains, and for vv. 40-51 and 56-72. Memorize a verse or a line each day as you meditate. Recall your verse or line whenever you can throughout the day, and be silent.

Psalm 78 (BCP)

Fifteenth Day: Evening Prayer   Tone: **KINNOR (1)**

[Walk]

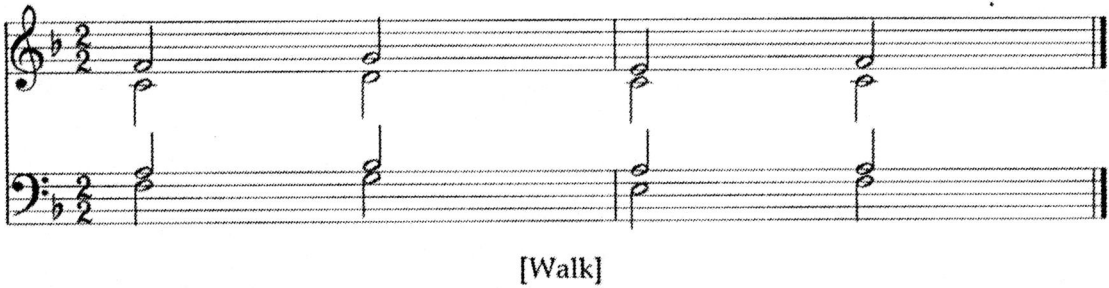

1 Hèar my tèaching, O my pèople; `
  incline your èars to the wòrds of my moùth. `
2 I will òpen my moùth in a pàrable; `
  I will declàre the mysteries of ancient tìmes. `
3 Thàt which we have hèard and knòwn, `
  and whàt our forefàthers have tòld us, `
  wè will not hìde from their chìldren. `
4 We will recòunt to generàtions to còme `
  the praiseworthy deeds and the power of the | LORD,
  and the wonderful works he has | done.
5 He gàve his decreès to Jàcob `
  and estàblished a làw for Ìsrael, `
  which he commànded them to tèach their chìldren. `
6 That the generàtions to còme might knòw, `
  and the chìldren yèt unbòrn; `
  that they in their tùrn might tèll it to their chìldren; `
7 So that thèy might put their trùst in Gòd, `
  and not forgèt the deèds of Gòd, `
  but keèp his commàndments. ``
8 And nòt be lìke their forefàthers, `
  a stùbborn and rebèllious generàtion, `
  a generàtion whose heàrt was not stèadfast, `
  and whose spìrit was not fàithful to Gòd. `
9 The people of Èphraim, àrmed with the bòw, `
  turned bàck in the dày of bàttle; `
10 They did not keèp the còvenant of Gòd, `
  and refùsed to wàlk in his làw; `
11 **They forgot what he had | done,**
  and the wonders he had | shown them.
12 He worked màrvels in the sìght of their fòrefathers, `
  in the land of Ègypt, in the field of Zòan.
13 **He split open the sea and let them pass | through;**
  he made the waters stand up like | walls.

14 He lèd them with a clòud by dày, `
 and all the night thròugh with a glòw of fire. `
15 **He split the hard rocks in the | wilderness**
 and gave them drink as from the great | deep.
16 He brought strèams òut of the clìff, `
 and the wàters gushed òut like rìvers. `
17 But they wènt on sìnning agàinst him, `
 rebèlling in the dèsert agàinst the Most Hìgh. ``
18 They tèsted Gòd in their heàrts, `
 demànding fòod for their cràving. `
19 They ràiled against Gòd and saìd, `
 "Can Gòd set a tàble in the wìlderness? `
20 Trùe, he struck the ròck, the waters gushed òut, `
  and the gùllies òverflòwed; `
 but ìs he àble to give brèad `
 òr to provide mèat for his pèople?" `
21 When the LORD hèard this, hè was full of wràth; `
 a fire was kìndled against Jàcob, `
 and his ànger moùnted against Ìsrael. `
22 For they hàd no faìth in Gòd, `
 nòr did they pùt their trùst `` in his sàving pòwer. `
23 So he commànded the cloùds abòve `
 and òpened the doòrs of hèaven. `
24 **He rained down manna upon them to | eat**
 and gave them grain from | heaven.
25 So mòrtals àte the bread of àngels; `
 he provìded for them fòod enòugh. `
26 He caused the east wìnd to blòw in the hèavens `
 and led òut the south wìnd by his mìght. `
27 **He rained down flesh upon them like | dust**
 and winged birds like the sand of the | sea.
28 He let it fàll in the mìdst of their càmp `
 and roùnd aboùt their dwèllings. `
29 So they àte and were wèll filled, `
 for he gàve them whàt they cràved. `
30 But thèy did not stòp their cràving, `
 though the fòod was stìll in their mòuths. `

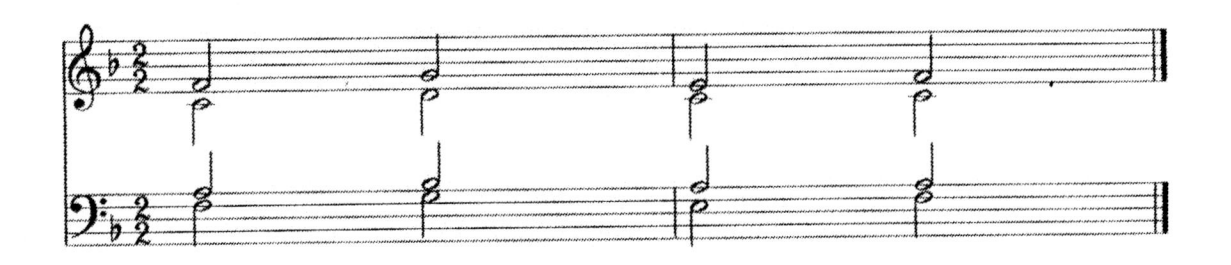

31 So God's ànger mòunted agàinst them; `
    he slèw their stròngest mèn `
    and laid lòw the yòuth of Ìsrael. `

32 In spite of all thìs, they wènt on sìnning `
    and had no fàith in his wònderful wòrks. `

33 So he brought their dàys to an ènd like a brèath `
    and their yèars in sùdden tèrror. `

34 Whenèver he slèw them, they would sèek him, `
    and repènt, and diligently sèarch for Gòd. `

35 **They would remember that God was their | rock,**
    and the Most High God their | redeemer.

36 But they flàttered hìm with their mòuths `
    and lìed to hìm with their tòngues. `

37 Their hèart was not stèadfast towàrd him, `
    and thèy were not fàithful to his còvenant. `

38 But he was so mèrciful that he forgàve their sìns
    and did nòt destròy them; `
    many tìmes he held bàck his ànger `
    and did nòt permit his wràth to be roùsed. `

              [Stand]

39 **For he remembered that they were but | flesh,**
    a breath that goes forth and does not re | turn.

              Part II

40 How often the people disobeyed him in the wilderness *
    and offended him in the desert!

41 Again and again they tempted God *
    and provoked the Holy One of Israel.

42 **They did not remember his | power**
    in the day when he ransomed them from the | enemy;

43 How he wrought his signs in Egypt *
    and his omens in the field of Zoan.

44 He turned their rivers into blood, *
    so that they could not drink of their streams.

45 **He sent swarms of flies among them, which ate them | up,**
    and frogs which de | stroyed them.

46 He gave their crops to the caterpillar, *
   the fruit of their toil to the locust.
47 He killed their vines with hail *
   and their sycamores with frost.
48 He delivered their cattle to hailstones *
   and their livestock to hot thunderbolts.
49 **He poured out upon them his blazing anger:**
   fury, indignation, and dis | tress,
   a troop of destroying | angels.
50 He gave full rein to his anger;
   he did not spare them from death; *
   but delivered their lives to the plague.
51 **He struck down all the first born of | Egypt,**
   the flower of manhood in the dwellings of | Ham.
              [Walk]
52 He lèd out his pèople like shèep `
   and guìded them in the wìlderness like a flòck. `
53 He led them to sàfety, and thèy were not afraìd `
   but the sèa overwhèlmed their ènemies. `
54 He bròught them to his hòly lànd, `
   the moùntain his rìght hand had wòn. `
55 He dròve out the Cànaanites befòre them `
   and appòrtioned an inhèritance to thèm by lòt; ``
   he made the tribes of Ìsrael to dwèll in their tènts. `
              [Stand]
56 But they tested the Most High God, and defied him, *
   and did not keep his commandments.
57 They turned away and were disloyal like their fathers; *
   they were undependable like a warped bow.
58 They grieved him with their hill-altars *
   and provoked his displeasure with their idols.
59 When God heard this, he was angry *
   and utterly rejected Israel.
60 He forsook the shrine at Shiloh, *
   the tabernacle where he had lived among his people.
61 He delivered the ark into captivity; *
   his glory into the adversary's hand.

62 He gave his people to the sword *
   and was angered against his inheritance.
63 The fire consumed their young men; *
   there were no wedding songs for their maidens.
64 Their priests fell by the sword, *
   and their widows made no lamentation.
65 Then the LORD woke as though from sleep, *
   like a warrior refreshed with wine.
66 **He struck his enemies on the | backside**
   and put them to perpetual | shame.
67 He rejected the tent of Joseph *
   and did not choose the tribe of Ephraim;
68 **He chose instead the tribe of | Judah**
   and Mount Zion, which he | loved.
69 He built his sanctuary like the heights of heaven, *
   like the earth which he founded for ever.
70 **He chose David his | servant,**
   and took him away from the | sheepfolds.
71 He brought him from following the ewes, *
   to be a shepherd over Jacob his people
   and over Israel his inheritance.
72 So he shepherded them with a faithful and true heart *
   and guided them with the skillfulness of his hands.

Is Nothing Sacred? Commentary To Psalm 79

.eLOHIM BÁ.U GOYIM B:NA#aLÁTHEKHÁ

v.1 O God, the heathen have come into your inheritance. "The peoples" have crossed a boundary, into a place that was not to be entered, the place of silence. It may have seemed like a small thing to them; to us it was the beginning of the end. Crossing that boundary into holy ground was the beginning of our unraveling.

tIMM:.UW .ETH-HEYKHAL QODSHEKHÁ

v.1b they have profaned (defiled, polluted, made unclean) your holy temple. Soon there are no more boundaries at all. The unthinkable happens. Blood runs in the streets like water. Blood runs in the streets now every day, somewhere in the world. We may read about it or we may not. We get used to it. But in the temple? Yes, always in someone's temple, the place that is sacred to someone; in home or family, blood is running. It runs, then it dries, it is scrubbed away. Is nothing sacred?

No, nothing is sacred unless we keep it so. Unless we maintain our boundaries. Unless we are strong enough to protect them. Unless the world leaves us alone to reverence them. They will not leave us to our holy things, as we will not leave them to theirs. Nothing is sacred unless we keep it so, by choice, by vigilance, by luck, by being too small to be a threat, by being too strong to attack. Nothing is sacred, really, until everything is sacred.

In a world of insidious weapons and porous defenses, nothing will ever be holy for long, until we all make holiness together. Until we learn to respect the boundaries of others, their culture, their sacred traditions, their differences. Until the world becomes Jerusalem—holy community. We cry for pity and revenge, and it is natural to do so. And yet, in Hebrew thought, we must also learn. Something must be learned from this disaster, and not just to get even. We must learn something vital about ourselves. The first three words of the psalm begin with the first three letters of the alphabet; the last word begins with the last. What are we to learn?

WA.aNA#NU "AM:KHÁ W:3O.N MAR"ITHEKHÁ NODEH L:KHÁ L:"OLÁM

v.13 But we (but as for us, we) are your people;
we will thank you (praise you) for eternity.

We are your people; we belong to you. We did not create the world or the peoples. We are the sheep. You teach us your ways as you have taught all peoples, giving to each their place, their boundaries, their sacred traditions, their ways of seeking you and finding you. To each of us, your peoples, you have given a form of your *Torah*, an alphabet, steps, boundaries, life-giving laws.

<u>Suggestions</u>: Compare 48 and 74. Study the Book of Lamentations. Practice the respecting of boundaries in everyday life. Respect the customs and traditions of others, no matter how trivial they may seem. Respect and honor differences.

Psalm 79 (BCP)

Sixteenth Day: Morning Prayer   Tone: SHO.ÁH

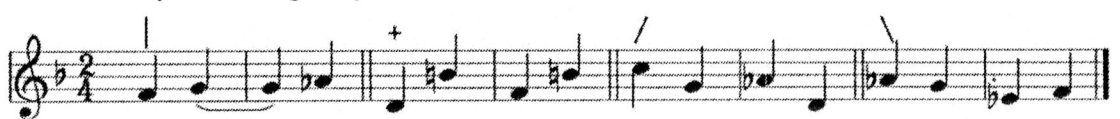

1 **O God, the heathen have come into your | inheritance;**
     they have profaned your holy | temple;
     +they have made Jerusalem a heap of + rubble.
2 They have given the bodies of your servants as food for
     the + birds of the air,
     /and the flesh of your faithful ones to the / beasts of the field.
3 They have shed their blood like water on every side of / Jerusalem,
     \and there was no one to \ bury them.

4 **We have become a reproach to our | neighbors,**
     an object of scorn and derision to those a | round us.
5 +How long will you be angry, O + LORD?
     will your fury blaze like fire for + ever?
6 /Pour out your wrath upon the heathen who have not / known you
     and upon the kingdoms that have not called upon your / Name.

7 **For they have devoured | Jacob**
     and made his dwelling a | ruin.
8 +Remember not our past sins;
     let your compassion be swift to + meet us;
     for we have been brought very + low.
9 /Help us, O God our Savior, for the glory of your / Name;
     deliver us and forgive us our sins, for your / Name's sake.
10 **Why should the heathen say, "Where is their | God?"**
     Let it be known among the heathen and in our sight
     that you avenge the shedding of your servants' | blood.
11 +Let the sorrowful sighing of the prisoners come be+fore you,
     and by your great might spare those who are condemned to + die.
12 /May the revilings with which they reviled you, O / LORD,
     return seven-fold into their / bosoms.
13 \For we are your people and the sheep of your \ pasture;
     we will give you thanks for \ ever
     and show forth your praise from age to \ age.

Restore Us: Commentary To Psalm 80

They asked Him, saying, "Lord, will You at this time restore the kingdom to Israel?" And He said to them, "It is not for you to know" (Acts 1:6-7, NKJ).

After devastation, restoration. There will certainly be healing, but not as we imagined it or planned it.

.eLOHIM HaSHIVÉNU   W:HÁ.ÉR PÁNEYKHÁ W:NIWÁSHÉ"Áh
v.3 O God, restore us (turn us back);
and let your face shine, and we shall be saved. The word HaSHIVÉNU (*restore us*) derives from SHUV (*to turn, return,* or *turn back*), by extension meaning to repent. Turning back (to roots, to core values, to what we were meant to be) is a step of the journey. Turning back to the place where we started, before we lost the way. "Repent," Jesus said, "for the kingdom of heaven is at hand" (Matthew 4:17, NKJ). Repentance (returning) is the first step of healing.

Restoration (causing to turn back) may be the most common theme of prayers. Let things be like they used to be, O God! Turn back the clock! Yet things are seldom restored as we hoped or pictured. Things will be good, but never quite the same. There is a painful law of irreversibility. The universe flows in one direction, and what has happened will never unhappen. Some decisions can never be undone.

I like to read stories about time travel. Writers have struggled with the paradoxes of the time machine. The basic idea is that if I went back to visit my earlier self, I would change it irreparably; and the self I am now could never have come to be. And I could never have decided to change what never was. So the trip to the past never happened precisely because it happened. What I dream about, really, is not time travel, but the ability to have it both ways—to be who I am, the product of all my choices; and to be able to try again, with different choices.

v.18 Restore us then, O LORD God of hosts;
and let your face shine and we shall be saved.

Restore me then, O LORD, God of all forces. Restore not things that were or times that have gone, but me. Restore me to wholeness, LORD. Restore me to the right path. Turn me and teach me to repent and bring me back to you. Thank you, LORD, for all that is past and for all that is changing. All that was good in my life has come from you. Help me turn back to you, source of my life. Restore me, then, LORD God of hosts, and let your face shine upon me, and I will be saved.

Note: Verse 14c is in the Hebrew text but not in the Prayer Book.

Suggestions: Sing refrains. Practice repentance continually, the practice of turning back, from your own way, your own thoughts, to God and his way. Seek to be restored to harmony, to relationship with God, to inner peace; ask not for things to be put back or change to be undone. Personal restoration begins in those moments of silence. For an instant I can see all things new!

Psalm 80 (BCP)

Tone: "ÁSOR

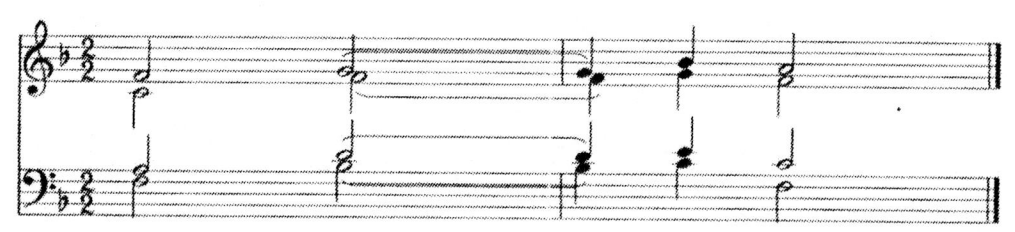

1 Hear, O Shepherd of Israel, leading Joseph like a flock; *
    shine forth you that are enthroned upon the KRUVIM.
2 In the presence of Ephraim, Benjamin and Manasseh. *
    stir up your strength, and come to help us.
3 **Restore us, O God of | hosts;**
    show the light of your countenance, and | we shall be | saved.
4 O LORD God of hosts, *
    how long will you be angered despite the prayers of your people?
5 You have fed them with the bread of tears; *
    you have given them bowls of tears to drink.
6 You have made us the derision of our neighbors, *
    and our enemies laugh us to scorn.
7 **Restore us, O God of | hosts;**
    show the light of your countenance, and | we shall be | saved.
8 You have brought a vine out of Egypt; *
    you cast out the nations and planted it.
9 You prepared the ground for it; *
    it took root and filled the land.
10 The mountains were covered by its shadow *
    and the towering cedar trees by its boughs.
11 You stretched out its tendrils to the Sea *
    and its branches to the River.
12 Why have you broken down its wall, *
    so that all who pass by pluck off its grapes?
13 The wild boar of the forest has ravaged it, *
    and the beasts of the field have grazed upon it.
14 Turn now, O God of hosts, look down from heaven; behold and tend this vine; *
    preserve what your right hand has planted,
    and the son you have made so strong for yourself. (*)
15 They burn it with fire like rubbish; *
    at the rebuke of your countenance let them perish.
16 Let your hand be upon the man of your right hand, *
    the son of man you have made so strong for yourself.
17 And so will we never turn away from you; *
    give us life that we may call upon your Name.
18 **Restore us, O LORD God of | hosts;**
    show the light of your countenance, and | we shall be | saved.

A Voice I Never Knew: Commentary To Psalm 81

We were having a beautiful ceremony, singing and playing; shouting and blowing the ram's-horn. It was the New Moon feast, and we were celebrating with great style. That is how we worship in our little community. Then it became very quiet.

S:PHATH LO.-YÁ<u>DA</u>"TI .ESHMÁ"   HASI<u>RO</u>THI MISS<u>É</u>VEL SHIKHMOW
v.6 I heard an unfamiliar voice saying,
"I eased his shoulder from the burden."

A voice (or language) I never knew, I begin to hear. A voice that whispers to me in a compelling way. "You have called on me in trouble, and I begin to deliver you. I begin to answer you from the secret place ... I begin to test you." [Silence...]. The writer is not hearing voices, but listening to the silence. The voices of psychiatric patients are intrusive and tormenting. But "the voice I never knew" is the gentlest of all voices. It never intrudes; it never speaks until I am ready to listen.

Like any form of communication, prayer has two aspects. Expressive prayer is outward—the singing, playing, shouting, horn-blowing. Expressive prayer is what we do in prayer. Receptive prayer is listening, trying to understand. Receptive prayer is what we hear in prayer—the voice I hever knew. Listening to a voice that is always surprising, always unexpected.

Psalm 81 speaks to me of a balance in prayer. Expressive prayer balanced with receptive. If God has commanded us to sing and play in our worship, he also wants us to listen. The expressive part comes easy to us. We love to hear ourselves praying and we enjoy what we call a beautiful service. The listening is more difficult. When we pray and sing we know the words. But when we listen, really listen, we have no idea what we will hear. When we listen, we give up control.

And so God says,

v.13 If only my people would listen to me.

Sometimes I think of prayer as a wonderful, mystical telephone. You could pick up this telephone and actually call up God. If you did, you would never hear a busy signal or find yourself talking to an answering machine. And all too often we see ourselves picking up the telephone and reading to God; reciting long prayers, wailing, begging, manipulating, going through long intercessory prayer lists. We are not told that we can actually communicate, not with some mythical personage, but with the real God. And that means listening.

<u>Suggestions</u>: I am the LORD your God, compare Exodus 20:2. Oh, that my people would listen to me, compare Deuteronomy 6:4 (Listen, O Israel), and the account of the Transfiguration (Matthew 17:5, NIV) where God says, "This is my Son, whom I love ... Listen to him!" God is always exhorting his people to listen, but all too often the word *listen* replaces the listening. In your meditation, listen and keep listening.

Psalm 81 (BCP)

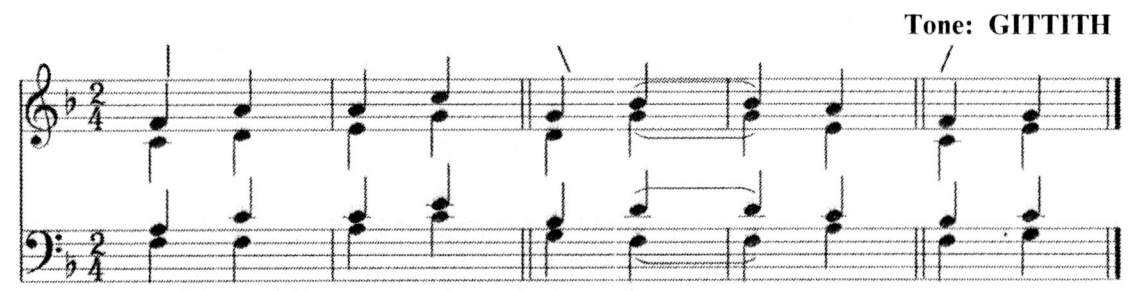

Tone: GITTITH

1 **Sing with joy to God our | strength**
    and raise a loud shout to the God of | Jacob.
2 \Raise a song and sound the \ timbrel,
    the merry harp, and the \ lyre.
3 /Blow the ram's-horn at the / new moon,
    /and at the full moon, the day of our / feast.
4 **For this is a statute for | Israel,**
    a law of the God of | Jacob.
5 \He laid it as a solemn charge upon \ Joseph,
    when he came out of the land of \ Egypt.
6 I heard an unfamiliar voice saying, *
    "I eased his shoulder from the burden;
    his hands were set free from bearing the load."
7 You called on me in trouble, and I saved you; *
    I answered you from the secret place of thunder
    and tested you at the waters of Meribah.
              [Silence...]
8 **Hear, O my people, and I will ad|monish you:**
    O Israel, if you would but | listen to me!
9 There shall be no strange god among you; *
    you shall not worship a foreign god.
10 I am the LORD your God,
    who brought you out of the land of Egypt and said, *
    "Open your mouth wide, and I will fill it."
11 **And yet my people did not hear my | voice,**
    and Israel would not o|bey me.
12 So I gave them over to the stubbornness of their hearts, *
    to follow their own devices.
13 **Oh, that my people would | listen to me!**
    that Israel would walk in my | ways!
14 I should soon subdue their enemies *
    and turn my hand against their foes.
15 Those who hate the LORD would cringe before him, *
    and their punishment would last for ever.
16 But Israel would I feed with the finest wheat *
    and satisfy him with honey from the rock.

In The Council Of Power: Commentary To Psalm 82

So Jehoshaphat dwelt at Jerusalem; and he went out again among the people ... and brought them back to the LORD God of their fathers. Then he set judges in the land ... and said to the judges, "Take heed to what you are doing, for you do not judge for man but for the LORD, who is with you in the judgment" (2 Chron 19:4-6, NKJ).

.eLOHIM NI33ÁV BA"aDATH-.ÉL   B:QEREBh .eLOHIM YISHPOt
v.1 God stands up in the council of power,
in the midst of the powerful he judges. That is, he administers, makes decisions. My interpretation follows Feuer (p. 1039). The words .eLOHIM and .ÉL refer here to god-like power, rather than to supernatural beings. Here it seems they are applied to judges, those who make god-like decisions. It applies to all of us who make decisions that affect others. God-like power is given to us, a power we cannot handle, for we do not know, neither do we understand. God is in our midst, asking this question:

v.2 How long will you judge unjustly,
and lift the face of the wicked? [Silence...].
Real justice sounds easy enough: "Judge for the weak (or sick) and the orphan; obtain righteousness for the humble and needy; rescue the weak (or sick) and the poor; deliver them from the power of the wicked." Compare 72. Here is how I want you to administer: First look after those who cannot protect themselves. Only then take care of the wealthy, the influential, those who contribute money to the party, celebrities. But the "important people" know how to intimidate. They are the ones who give money and the ones who vote. How can I do good for the poor if I cannot get re-elected? Real justice sounds easy, but we cannot achieve it.

.aNIY-.ÁMARTI .eLOHIM .ATTEM UV:NEY "ELYON KULL:KHEM
v.6 I have said (to you), "You are godlike beings,
and children of the Most High, all of you." God-like power and responsibility have been given to you. You do not have the wisdom for this job, for the decisions you make will have effects long after you are gone. For you will administer for a little time, and you will die like any child of earth.

v.8 Rise up, O God, administer the earth. Compare 10. Rise up in us, O God; judge, decide, administer through us. Show us how to do justice and righteousness—today, in this case, this decision, this situation.

Suggestions: Sing the refrains. When you study the psalms in groups, sit in a circle. Let each member read a verse in turn, but sing the refrains in unison.

When you have to make decisions that will affect others, pray for God to direct you. Ask for his will in this situation, this decision. If you are willing to do whatever God wills, then you are ready to decide.

Psalm 82 (BCP)

Sixteenth Day: Evening Prayer Tone: **SH:MINITH**

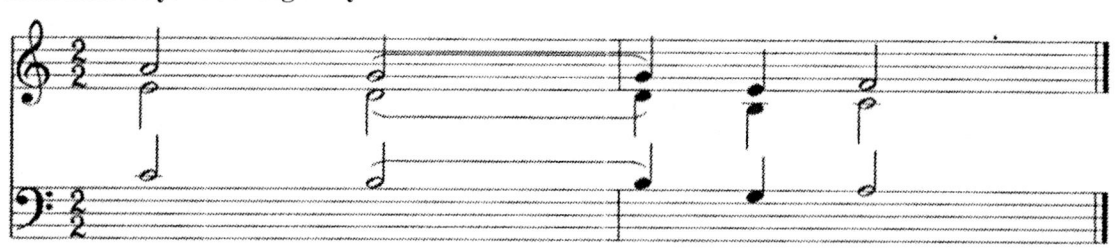

1 God takes his stand in the council of heaven; *
   he gives judgment in the midst of the gods:
2 **"How long will you judge un | justly,**
   and show | favor to the | wicked?
                         [Silence...]
3 Save the weak and the orphan; *
   defend the humble and needy;
4 **Rescue the weak and the | poor;**
   de | liver them from the power of the | wicked.
5 They do not know, neither do they understand;
   they go about in darkness; *
   all the foundations of the earth are shaken.
6 Now I say to you, 'You are gods, *
   and all of you children of the Most High;
7 Nevertheless, you shall die like mortals, *
   and fall like any prince.'"
8 Arise, O God, and rule the earth, *
   for you shall take all nations for your own.

Your Enemies Begin To Howl: Commentary To Psalm 83

It happened after this that the people of Moab with the people of Ammon, and others with them besides the Ammonites, came to battle against Jehoshaphat. Then some came and told Jehoshaphat, saying, "A great multitude is coming against you" (2 Chron 20:1-2, NKJ).

We are never told why this alliance came against us. Just when things are going well, old enemies reappear. An evil coalition has gathered to surround us. The story points to something deeper. The people of God, more often than not, are a surrounded people. Wanting to share good news, surrounded by enemies!

v.2 For behold your enemies begin to howl,
and your haters have lifted up the head.
I hear that howling sound afar off, like a dull humming or buzzing on the horizon, growing louder till it is all around me. Like buzzing bees, like wolves, like the dog who howls and runs about the city, as in Psalm 59. Like the buzz of rumor and accusation. Like the howl of every mob that has ever gathered. From every direction, for every good reason, for every false reason, even in the name of God. "For God," as often as not, they come against God!

v.4 Come, let us wipe them out from being a nation. It is often like this with God's people. Like a foreign body in the flesh, they stir up rejection. Something within us rebels against all they stand for, aliens living among us with alien values. So we gather together and surround them. Yes, all too often it is we, God's people, who surround, even as we have been surrounded.

A sad tale, hard to understand. Giving our allegiance to God we are foreign to the world. Living in the world our allegiance insidiously changes. Pride comes in like a virus. And the sharers of Good News turn into thought police. Our allegiance has changed: to a culture, customs, an exact way to be saved or spirit-filled. A certain exact way to think, specific words. Certain beliefs about *them*, whoever they are.

Let us pray, then, from the Good Friday liturgy, "for all who have not received the Gospel of Christ ... for those who are enemies of the cross of Christ and persecutors of his disciples," and, "for those who in the name of Christ have persecuted others" (Prayer Book, p. 279).

v.18 Let them know that you, whose Name is YHWH —
you alone are the Most High over all the earth.

<u>Suggestions</u>: Alternate reading and singing as shown. Compare Judges 4 and 8. The Name YHWH may be rendered "the LORD" or "I am" or *Adonai*.

Look for that tendency to religious persecution, but only in yourself. What group, religion or denomination do you find most upsetting? What group in your own religion is most upsetting to you? Ask yourself what you can learn from this group. What do they force you to look at in yourself?

Psalm 83 (BCP)

Tone: N:GINOTH

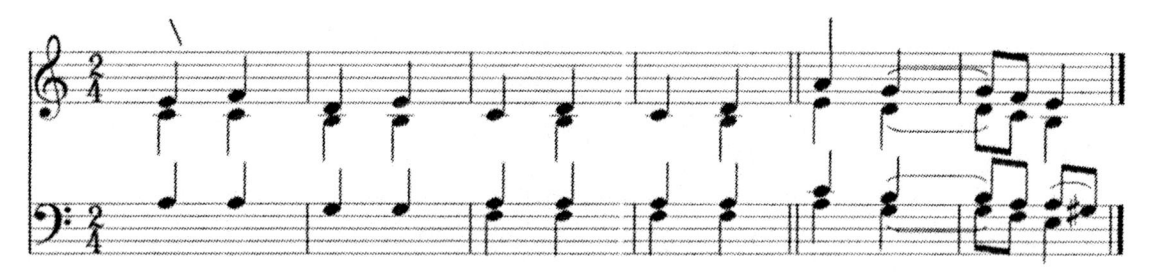

1 O God, do not be silent; *
  do not keep still nor hold your peace, O God;
2 \For your enemies are in \ tumult,
  and those who hate you have lifted up their \ heads.
3 They take secret counsel against your \ people
  and plot against those whom you pro\tect.
4 They have said, "Come, let us wipe them out from among the nations; *
  let the name of Israel be remembered no more."
5 They have conspired together; *
  they have made an alliance against you:
6 The tents of Edom and the Ishmaelites; *
  the Moabites and the Hagarenes;
7 Gebal, and Ammon, and Amalek; *
  the Philistines and those who dwell in Tyre.
8 The Assyrians also have joined them, *
  and have come to help the people of Lot. [Silence...]
9 Do to them as you did to Midian, *
  to Sisera, and to Jabin at the river of Kishon:
10 They were destroyed at Endor; *
  they became like dung upon the ground.
11 Make their leaders like Oreb and Zeeb, *
  and all their commanders like Zebah and Zalmunna,
12 Who said, "Let us take for ourselves *
  the fields of God as our possession."
13 \O my God, make them like whirling \ dust
  and like chaff before the \ wind;
14 Like fire that burns down a \ forest,
  like the flame that sets \ mountains ablaze.
15 Drive them with your tempest *
  and terrify them with your storm;
16 Cover their faces with shame, O LORD, *
  that they may seek your Name.
17 **Let them be disgraced and terrified for | ever;**
  let them be | put to confusion and | perish.
18 \Let them know that you, whose Name is \ YHWH—
  you alone are the Most High over all the \ earth.

Highways In Their Hearts: Commentary To Psalm 84

NIKHS:PHÁH W:GAM-KÁL:THÁH NAPHSHIY   L:#A3ROTH YHWH
v.1 My soul longeth, yea even fainteth for the courts of the LORD (KJV).

My soul (my inner self, breath, breathing, life) grew pale, pining and languishing for the courtyards of the LORD, the place where God lives. I felt it all those years: that restlessness, that longing without a name. It was you — my soul, my breathing — longing for God. You were pining and languishing within me, drawing me on a search I could not explain. Drawing me I knew not where. I should have been happy. I was raised in a godly home; my parents loved me. I heard about God in my childhood, in lovely Reform synagogues that were always called "the Temple"; I heard beautiful prayers and Scriptures. But my soul would not rest.

Until one day, for no reasonable reason at all, I found myself in a little Episcopal church, seeking and praying to know you, LORD. And you told me I could find you in church or in synagogue, but I must decide, commit myself. There would be no more playing and flirting with you, but a lifelong walk.

v.2 Also the bird has found a home,
and the swallow a nest for herself.

Once it was a building, where a bird could rest and nest. Now it is silence, here or anywhere, wherever I seek you in spirit and truth (John 4:23), that is surrender and constancy. Where I give up knowing better and make a commitment. And the little bird is my soul (breath, life), fluttering and settling down to rest.

.ASHREY .ÁDÁM "OZ-LO VÁKH   M:SILLOTH BIL:VÁVÁM
v.4 Happy are the people whose strength is in you —
highways in their hearts!

I love that strange expression. I did not choose this path, the path chose me, runs through me, out of me, beyond me. There in my heart (my inner space, my attitude) it runs, to parts unknown. The metaphors become confusing. Your house, where even a bird could nest, has turned to highways, taking me — who knows where? To a place called the Valley of Weeping. And to springs of water, and to climbing from strength to strength. It is the highway of surrender.

.ASHREY .ÁDÁM BOtÉa# BÁKH
v.12 O how very happy is the man who trusts in you.

<u>Suggestions</u>: Continue to practice your meditation, morning and evening. Practice faithfully, keeping a regular time and place. Let this be your temple. Always begin with prayer and end with silence. Do not consciously think about the verses you have read or try to analyze them. Clear your thoughts and be silent, so that God can speak to you.

Psalm 84 (BCP)

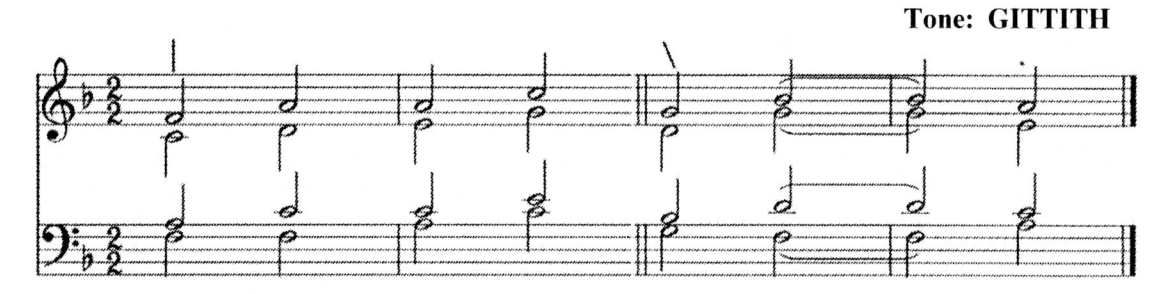

Tone: **GITTITH**

1 How dear to me is your dwelling, O LORD of hosts! *
   My soul has a desire and longing for the courts of the LORD;
   my heart and my flesh rejoice in the living God.
2 The sparrow has found her a house
   and the swallow a nest where she may lay her young; *
   by the side of your altars, O LORD of | hosts,
   my King and my | God.
3 \Happy are they who dwell in your \ house!
   they will always be \ praising you.
              [Silence...]
4 Happy are the people whose strength is in you! *
   whose hearts are set on the pilgrims' way.
5 Those who go through the desolate valley will find it a place of springs, *
   for the early rains have covered it with pools of water.
6 They will climb from height to height, *
   and the God of gods will reveal himself in Zion.
7 **LORD God of hosts, hear my | prayer;**
   hearken, O God of | Jacob.
              [Silence...]
8 Behold our defender, O God; *
   and look upon the face of your Anointed.
9 For one day in your courts is better than a thousand in my own room, *
   and to stand at the threshold of the house of my God
   than to dwell in the tents of the wicked.
10 For the LORD God is both sun and shield; *
   he will give grace and glory.
11 No good thing will the LORD withhold *
   from those who walk with integrity.
12 **O LORD of | hosts,**
   happy are they who put their | trust in you!

Restore Us Then: Commentary To Psalm 85

v.10 Mercy and truth have met together;
righteousness and peace have kissed each other.

In fact, mercy and truth are often at odds. Righteousness and peace are rarely seen kissing. The public insists upon both; in private I must often choose. I try to reconcile mercy and truth the best I can. Sometimes I can't seem to reconcile them at all. My patient has rights, my patient's spouse has rights, the victim my patient might injure two years from now has rights, the insurance company has rights, and I like to think that I have rights. So I juggle and struggle and try to make sense of the puzzle. I work out compromises that leave me with a gnawing ache. I keep thinking that someone older or wiser could figure it out. Righteousness and peace would be kissing in his office, while I go home weary and agitated.

Ethical questions are addressed by all sorts of experts now: lawyers, doctors, clergy, activists of all kinds. Everyone knows the right answers in the abstract, but in actual situations all choices are partial. Mercy and truth are barely speaking. Righteousness and peace have lawyers. If I consult an expert on ethics I will learn only this: there are many choices, all painful.

Sometimes I have a wistful sense that ethical questions are not so complex after all. The answers are obvious, until I share them with someone. Then it seems the discussion comes down to one question: *who decides?* The principles may be simple enough, but who can be trusted to apply them? At the moment of decision, I will act out of personal self-interest, regardless of principle. That is why we pray:

SHUVÉNU .eLOHEY YISH"ÉNU

v.4 Restore (return) us then, O God of our salvation. In our fallen condition none of us can be trusted. Restore us then, to what we were meant to be. Make us whole, so that mercy and truth will hold hands again. So that righteousness and peace will kiss again. Righteousness will no longer be moralistic posturing, but real righteousness, the right ordering of things. And peace will be real peace — *shalom* — wholeness, completeness, health.

v.8 I will listen to what the LORD God is saying,

for he is speaking peace to his faithful people. I will listen. Restoration will come, the kissing of righteousness and peace, not by intellectual brilliance or creativity but by surrender. By listening, giving up control to a Higher Power. By the realization that I have no answers, that there exist no real solutions. The problems are hopeless and my efforts are making them worse. And with this realization, hopefully, I can finally stop talking and listen. I can take direction.

<u>Suggestions</u>: Sing refrains. Remember that real-life ethical problems have no solutions. They are problems because one ethical value, one absolute good, is pitted against another. Practice moments of silence and ask God for direction.

Psalm 85 (BCP)

Tone: ʿÁSOR

1 You have been gracious to your land, O LORD, *
   you have restored the good fortune of Jacob.
2 You have forgiven the iniquity of your people *
   and blotted out all their sins.
                    [Silence...]
3 You have withdrawn all your fury *
   and turned yourself from your wrathful indignation.
4 **Restore us then, O God our | Savior;**
   let your | anger de | part from us.
5 Will you be displeased with us for ever? *
   will you prolong your anger from age to age?
6 Will you not give us life again, *
   that your people may rejoice in you?
7 **Show us your mercy, O | LORD,**
   and | grant us your sal | vation.
8 I will listen to what the LORD God is saying, *
   for he is speaking peace to his faithful people
   and to those who turn their hearts to him.
9 Truly, his salvation is very near to those who fear him, *
   that his glory may dwell in our land.
10 Mercy and truth have met together; *
   righteousness and peace have kissed each other.
11 Truth shall spring up from the earth, *
   and righteousness shall look down from heaven.
12 The LORD will indeed grant prosperity, *
   and our land will yield its increase.
13 Righteousness shall go before him, *
   and peace shall be a pathway for his feet.

Make Joyful The Breathing: Commentary To Psalm 86

SAM<u>MÉ</u>a# <u>NE</u>PHESh "AV<u>DE</u>KHÁ KI-.ÉLEYKHÁ .aDONÁY NAPHSHIY .ESSÁ.
v.4 Rejoice the soul of thy servant;
for unto thee, O LORD, do I lift up my soul (KJV).

Again let us translate the word NEPHESh as breath or breathing. I am not a ghostly soul inhabiting a body; rather "I," the real me, *is* a living soul, that is, a human breathing. Compare Psalm 3. A tide of breath flowing in and out, self-organizing and self-regulating. "I" does not own the breathing or control it. Rather, that mysterious self-regulating breathing is what "I" really is.

That "I" is other to me. Because what *I* think of as I is the talk, the internal chatter. "I" thinks of the breathing as "my breathing" and "my body." "I" feels driven to control and improve that breathing organism, of which it is actually but a fragile creation. As though the threads were to say "I must do something about my loom," or the music notes were to say, "I really must improve my piano." And that, as Gerald May explains so well, is crazy!*

Walking the psalms I grow more familiar with my inner world. My old understanding of who I am was so inadequate. If anything, I am a dialogue, conversations between thoughts and a breathing, neither complete without the other. And both together incomplete without Other, that is, God. *Will the real me please stand up?* No answer. *Who am I? Why am I here? Where is happiness?* From within the dialogue, no answer. The answer comes, always, from Other.

So I say to God (someone or something says to God), "Make joyful the breathing of your servant." Make my breathing happy breathing. For to you, O LORD, I begin to lift my breathing up. Meaning, at one level, that I take in a deep, quick breath, filling my lungs as quick and as full as possible; as I do so, I awake to full alertness. And as I awaken I lift my eyes and I turn my attention to you, my eternal Other, my LORD.

We have been told that happiness does not depend on circumstances, until we are tired of hearing it. We have been told that happiness lies within ourselves, but we cannot find it. We despair of ever finding it, so we settle for weekends, we settle for moments of relief.

Happiness arises always in a context, in relationship to a task or an other. Intimacy. I and my breathing. I and my inner self. Intimacy with you, my wife. Listening without an agenda, willing to be surprised. Most of all, intimacy with you, my God. "Lean your ear to me ... answer me ... preserve my breathing ... save your servant who trusts in you ... have mercy on me, LORD, for to you I cry all the day long."

v.11 Teach me your ways, O LORD, and I will begin to walk in your faithfulness. Unify my heart (attitude) with you. I am giving up control, learning to surrender. So that now I can say, "Make my breathing happy, for to you, O LORD, I have lifted my breathing up. For you, O LORD, are good and forgiving, full of love (or mercy) for all who cry to you."

What keeps me from being happy is not a lack of blessings, but a lack of willingness. I listen to my patients and myself and I hear the same thing. "I will not be happy until... I will never be happy unless... " Still in control.

I ask my patients to work on small goals. Don't try to swallow the whole elephant. Take little steps. How would you like to feel better within this hour? They do it reluctantly, trying to please me. Sometimes they won't do it at all. "My problems are too big for that," or, "I don't want to get better an hour at a time. That won't help me."

I thought I would never be happy until I married. Now I dream of being closer, more intimate. I will never be happy until I publish a book. Or become "famous." Sometimes I think I will never be happy in psychiatry. I will be happy when I can stay home all day and write, in a secluded house in the woods. I will be famous yet totally private. Everyone will love me, but no one will ever call me with a problem. I will give lectures all over the country yet I will always be home.

And if God says to me, "I want to bless you with happiness right now," will I accept it? Will I say, "Well, what's the deal? Do I still get to be famous?" Or will I say, "Make joyful the breathing of your servant," and take a deep, joyful breath and lift up my eyes, my attitude, and say, "for to you, O LORD, I lift up my breathing"?

She was chronically depressed, she struggled with it all her life. Remission came in old age, the struggle eased. A kind of contentment came in her final years. She had finally realized, she said, that we are not meant to be happy. I think of this wise old lady often since I heard her story. Happiness can never be achieved, it may be received.

I cannot make myself happy. I cannot improve myself, though I have consciously tried at least since the age of five. I will never grow up. I will never achieve fulfillment. All I can do is give up, and turn to you. Make glad the soul (breath, breathing, life itself) of your servant ... for you, O LORD, are good and forgiving.

<u>Suggestions</u>: Sing the refrains. Choose happiness moment by moment as you go through the day. Take a deep breath through the nose, lift your eyes slightly toward heaven, turn your attention to God. Clear your thoughts and be silent, however briefly. Practice this informal meditation whenever you can.

---

*Gerald May: *Simply Sane. The Spirituality of Mental Health*, Crossroad, New York, 1977. This little book has affected me profoundly. Everything written in these commentaries, in one way or another, has been influenced by his lucid spirituality. Compare 37, 101.

Psalm 86 (BCP)

Seventeenth Day: Morning Prayer   **Tone: KINNOR (1)**

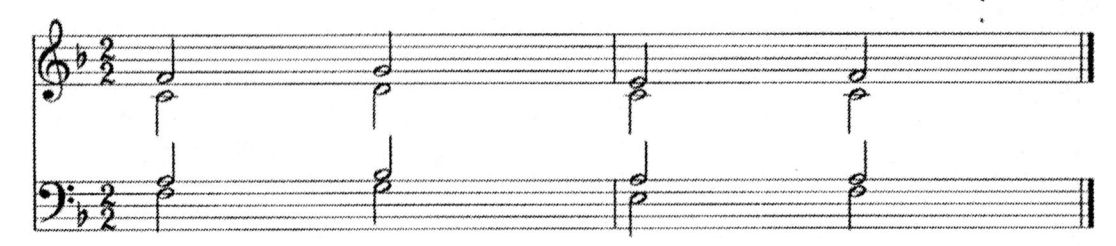

1 Bow down your ear, O LORD, and answer me, *
   for I am poor and in misery.
2 Keep watch over my life, for I am faithful; *
   save your servant who puts his trust in you.
3 Be merciful to me, O LORD, for you are my God; *
   I call upon you all the day long.
4 Gladden the soul of your servant, *
   for to you, O LORD, I lift up my soul.
5 **For you, O LORD, are good and | forgiving,**
   and great is your love toward all who | call upon you.
6 Give ear, O LORD to my prayer, *
   and attend to the voice of my supplications.
7 In the time of my trouble I will call upon you, *
   for you will answer me.
8 Among the gods there is none like you, O LORD, *
   nor anything like your works.
9 All nations you have made will come and worship you, O LORD, *
   and glorify your Name.
10 **For you are great; you do wondrous | things;**
   and you alone are | God.
11 Teach me your way, O LORD,
   and I will walk in your truth; *
   knit my heart to you that I may fear your Name.
12 I will thank you, O LORD my God, with all my heart, *
   and glorify your Name for evermore.
13 For great is your love toward me; *
   you have delivered me from the nethermost Pit.
14 The arrogant rise up against me, O God, and a band of violent men seeks my life; *
   they have not set you before their eyes.
15 **But you, O LORD, are gracious and full of com | passion,**
   slow to anger, and full of kindness and | truth.
16 Turn to me and have mercy upon me; *
   give your strength to your servant; and save the child of your handmaid.
17 Show me a sign of your favor,
   so that those who hate me may see it and be ashamed; *
   because you, O LORD, have helped me and comforted me.

A Dance Of Inclusion: Commentary To Psalm 87

An article in *U.S. News and World Report,* November 1990, was entitled "The Roots of Language: How Modern Speech Evolved From a Single, Ancient Source." I was amazed! Certain audacious researchers were suggesting a common ancestor to all known languages. It was the dialect of a small band of hunter-gatherers somewhere in Africa. Genetics offered supporting evidence. The genetic material of all living humans could be traced to a handful of individuals. Restless and driven as ourselves, they spread out and peopled the globe.

Once we knew everyone by name. Everyone in the world was there; we ate together, slept together, spoke the common tongue. As the years went by and the children moved away, it was harder to keep in touch. Just as now, it was hard to keep track of the grandchildren, the cousins and their cousins.

Who knew where we were or what we were learning, as we spread over the earth, branching again and again from the original stock? Had we later encountered our distant cousins, we would have found them hard to understand. As time went on we became different. Different hair, skin, clothing, cultures. Who would have thought we were kin? Yet Scripture has always said so. "Now the whole earth had one language and one speech" (Genesis 11: 1, NKJ). And, "Have we not all one Father?" (Malachi 2:10, NKJ).

Psalm 87 says to me that we are all family in a spiritual sense. Everyone was born there, not in a village in Africa, but on Zion, his holy mountain. What does this mean? Perhaps that all revelation, all spiritual growth, begins in the same place. In silence, surrender, yearning. In giving up the answers we have heard since childhood, and turning helplessly to God. It is an opening open for everyone, everyone is included in that call, yet hardly anyone goes in.

.IYSH W:.IYSH
v.4 A man and a man (every man and every man).

Each of us is included. Once we seek God and his will, we are spiritual cousins. Everyone. We cannot choose who will be in the family. We may not test them on the Nicene Creed nor ask if they are spirit-filled. They have already been invited. The Babylonians, the Egyptians, the Germans, the Jews, the Palestinians. Those who already know they are cousins, and those who never heard of this family. God knows each of them by name.

Jesus said, "And other sheep have I which are not of this fold; them also must I bring, and they will hear My voice; and there will be one flock and one shepherd" (John 10:16 NKJ). "These also were born there," and we cannot choose who they are. I believe God finds this tremendously amusing. The psalm is lyrical with a dance-like rhythm.

<u>Suggestions</u>: Sing to the movement Twirling Dance (see Appendix). At [Silence...] stop all movement, freeze in position for ten to fifteen seconds. Share your faith freely with others, but give no religious tests. If anyone asks to be included in your group, anyone at all, let that person be included.

Psalm 87 (BCP)

Tone: MÁ#OL

1 \On the holy mountain stands the city he has \ founded;
   the LORD loves the gates of \ Zion
   more than all the dwellings of \ Jacob.
2 **Glorious things are | spoken | of you,**
   O city of our | God.
                              [Silence...]
3 \I count Egypt and Babylon among those who \ know me;
   behold Philistia, Tyre, and Ethi\opia:
   in Zion were they \ born.
4 \Of Zion it shall be \ said,
   "Everyone was \ born in her,
   and the Most High himself shall sus\tain her."
5 **The LORD will recall as he | enrolls the | peoples,**
   "These also were | born there."
                              [Silence...]
6 **The singers and the | dancers will | say,**
   "All my fresh springs are in | you."

In The Tomb: Commentary To Psalm 88

We hear so much about crucifixion and resurrection, but seldom do we hear about the tomb. What was it like for him after the horror was over, and there was—nothing? We think we can imagine the trial, the scourging, the stations. But we cannot imagine the tomb. We cannot imagine what it is like to be dead, to be without consciousness. It is one of the limits of the human mind. We can imagine ourselves losing almost everything; but to have lost even self, we cannot picture.

We never wanted him to go to Jerusalem at all; we never wanted him to suffer the betrayal; we could not believe he would go through the agony; we kept hoping he would come down from that cross. We would like to believe he was pretending. We would like to imagine that he, the real Jesus, was somewhere else, watching the scene in mystical detachment. Some of the gnostic gospels suggest exactly that: his suffering was only a charade.

But the Apostles' Creed tells us that he really died. He was buried and descended to the dead. He went through the experience of the tomb—the darkness, the emptiness, the nothingness. He went down into the shadow world where there is no hope. To the land where all is forgotten. The place I cannot imagine, because when I am there, there will no longer be any me.

HIR#AQTÁ M:YUDDÁ"AY MIMMENNI
v.9 You have put far from me those of my acquaintance.

It is not death we fear so much as abandonment. Dying alone in a room where no one visits. Dying alone with no one to touch my hand. It begins, perhaps, with a diagnosis. When the friends run away. The tomb experience is this: you have made far from me all who would know me, as in Psalm 22.

It is loneliness, utter and complete. It is like what Scott Peck calls emptiness. The place we avoid at all cost. It is SH.OL (*Sheol*, the Pit)—the world of pale shadows unable to love. It is the loneliest, emptiest nowhere that ever could be.

HIR#AQTÁ MIMMENNI .OHÉV WÁRÉa"
v.19 You have put far from me lover and friend.

Scripture doesn't offer a definitive map of death. It never precisely says that I will go to a place called heaven or that my soul will go to heaven. It gives me a number of pictures and a lasting hope. One of the pictures is this one—the picture of the tomb. It is the darkest and saddest moment in the psalms. God wants me to think about this moment.

<u>Suggestions</u>: Kneel. Read slowly without music. Observe the silences at greater length than usual. Read the refrains in a whisper. In group study, let each member read a verse in turn, but read the refrains softly in unison.

Read Psalm 88 in your darkest moments, when all is lost.

Psalm 88 (BCP)

1 O LORD, my God, my Savior, *
   by day and night I cry to you
2 Let my prayer enter into your presence; *
   incline your ear to my lamentation.
3 For I am full of trouble; *
   my life is at the brink of the grave
   I am counted among those who go down to the Pit; *
   I have become like one who has no strength.
5 Lost among the dead, *
   like the slain who lie in the grave,
6 Whom you remember no more, *
   for they are cut off from your hand.
7 You have laid me in the depths of the Pit, *
   in dark places, and in the abyss.
8 Your anger weighs upon me heavily, *
   and all your great waves overwhelm me.
   [Silence...]
9 **You have put my friends far from me; you have made me to be abhorred by them;** *
   I am in prison and cannot get free.
10 My sight has failed me because of trouble; *
   LORD, I have called upon you daily; I have stretched out my hands to you.
11 Do you work wonders for the dead? *
   will those who have died stand up and give you thanks?
   [Silence...]
12 Will your loving-kindness be declared in the grave? *
   your faithfulness in the land of destruction?
13 Will your wonders be known in the dark? *
   or your righteousness in the country where all is forgotten?
14 But as for me, O LORD, I cry to you for help; *
   in the morning my prayer comes before you.
15 LORD, why have you rejected me? *
   why have you hidden your face from me?
16 Ever since my youth I have been wretched and at the point of death. *
   I have borne your terrors with a troubled mind.
17 Your blazing anger has swept over me; *
   your terrors have destroyed me.
18 They surround me all day long like a flood; *
   they encompass me on every side.
19 **My friend and my neighbor you have put away from me,** *
   and darkness is my only companion.

Where Are Your Lovingkindnesses? Commentary To Psalm 89

And your house and your kingdom shall be established forever before you. Your throne shall be established forever (2 Samuel 7:16, NKJ).

v.1 Your love, O LORD, for ever will I sing. At one level this is an extended commentary on that promise in 2 Samuel—an eternal covenant with a royal house. A covenant that has apparently been broken. The singer begins with "Your love (your acts of fierce devotion), O LORD, for ever will I sing," but soon we are hearing, "You have broken your covenant with your servant." The great procession starts with a bang, as in 68, and ends with questions.

At a personal level, my spiritual journey is like this. It begins with great excitement. Baptism at Easter Vigil, candles blazing in a darkened church. There is a story to tell, books to read, new understandings almost daily. There is a new serenity, new certainty. Miracles happen. I want to tell everyone. I wear a big silver cross. "Your love, O LORD, forever will I sing!" I have so many questions. I want to hear famous preachers. I love to discuss miracles and healings. I long to talk about angels, apparitions, and the levitations of Saint Teresa of Àvila.

Later come the long days of daily life. Christians who reject other Christians. Preachers who disappoint and Great Evangelists who disillusion. The miracles come more slowly. The words from God are few and far between. Circumstances continue as always, good and bad. Good things happen when I least expect them. Other good things are taken away. I ask "Why?" and receive no answer. I ask for some things that don't come. Reasonable things that I *ought* to have, things I deserve. "Why not?" I cry, and the silence of God is deafening.

With time I become more thoughtful, balanced, more stable, yet I don't know all the answers. I find myself questioning more. I accept my limitations. I accept the limitations of Jews, of rabbis, of Christians, of the church, of preachers. I accept that I will never be accepted, not completely. I realize that your church is not a club. To serve you is not always to be loved, even by your people. I will never be completely grown up. I will never understand it all. And I still complain to you:

v.49 Where are your former lovingkindnesses (acts of fierce, protective love), O LORD? I ask this question plaintively, and I urge God to remember (vv. 47, 50), but it is I who forget all too quickly. LORD help me remember!

Suggestions: Sing vv. 1-18 to the movement Turning Drum (see Appendix). Be seated, sing refrains only vv. 19-52. Verse 46 ("How long will you hide yourself?") may be sung slowly, like 13:1-2 or 27:18.

Practice remembering. Remember how God has been with you and remember his acts of love year after year. Memorize a verse or line whenever you meditate. Remember it, let it go, and be silent, again and again throughout the day. This will be a powerful help in meditation. More powerful yet, remember your verse or line slowly. Recall it with exquisite slowness, word by word, let it go and be silent.

Psalm 89 (BCP)

Seventeenth Day: Evening Prayer Tone: TOPH

1 ` ` ` ` **Your | lòve, O | LÒRD, for | èver will I | sìng; `**
   from àge to àge my mòuth will proclàim your | fàithfùlnèss.
2 /For I am persuaded that your love is established for / ever;
   you have set your faithfulness firmly in the / heavens.
3 \"I have made a covenant with my \ chosen one;
   I have sworn an oath to David my \ servant:
4 \ 'I will establish your line for \ ever,
   and preserve your throne for all gene\rations.'"
              [Silence...]
5 The heavens bear witness to your . wonders, O LORD,
   and to your faithfulness in the assembly of the . holy ones;
6 **For | whò in the | skìes can be com|pàred to the | LÒRD? `**
   whò is like the LÒRD among the | gòds?
7 /God is much to be feared in the council of the / holy ones,
   great and terrible to all those round a/bout him.
8 \Who is like you, LORD God of \ hosts?
   O mighty LORD, your faithfulness is all a\round you.
9 \You rule the raging of the \ sea
   and still the surging of its \ waves.
10 You have crushed Rahab of the deep with a . deadly wound;
   you have scattered your enemies with your . mighty arm.
11 **Yòurs are the | hèavens; the earth | àlso is | yòurs; `**
   you làid the foundàtions of the wòrld and àll that is | ìn ìt.
12 /You have made the north and the / south;
   Tabor and Hermon rejoice in your / Name.
13 \You have a mighty \ arm;
   strong is your hand and high is your \ right hand.
14 Righteousness and justice are the foundations of your . throne;
   love and truth go before your . face.
15 **Hàppy are the | pèople who | knòw the festal | shòut! `**
   they wàlk, O LÒRD, in the lìght of your | prèsence.
16 /They rejoice daily in your / Name;
   they are jubilant in your / righteousness.
17 \For you are the glory of their \ strength,
   and by your favor our might is ex\alted.

18 Truly, the LORD is our . ruler;
   the Holy One of Israel is our . King.

Part II

19 You spoke once in a vision and said to your faithful people: *
   "I have set the crown upon a warrior
   and have exalted one chosen out of the people.

20 **\I have found David my \ servant;**
   with my holy oil have I a\nointed him.

21 My hand will hold him fast *
   and my arm will make him strong.

22 No enemy shall deceive him, *
   nor any wicked man bring him down.

23 I will crush his foes before him *
   and strike down those who hate him.

24 My faithfulness and love shall be with him, *
   and he shall be victorious through my Name.

25 I shall make his dominion extend *
   from the Great Sea to the River.

26 He will say to me, 'You are my Father, *
   my God, and the rock of my salvation.'

27 I will make him my firstborn *
   and higher than the kings of the earth.

28 I will keep my love for him for ever *
   and my covenant will stand firm for him.

29 I will establish his line for ever *
   and his throne as the days of heaven."

30 "If his children forsake my law *
   and do not walk according to my judgments;

31 If they break my statutes *
   and do not keep my commandments;

32 I will punish their transgressions with a rod *
   and their iniquities with the lash;

33 But I will not take my love from him, *
   nor let my faithfulness prove false.

34 I will not break my covenant, *
   nor change what has gone out of my lips.

35 **\Once for all I have sworn by my \ holiness:**
   'I will not lie to \ David.

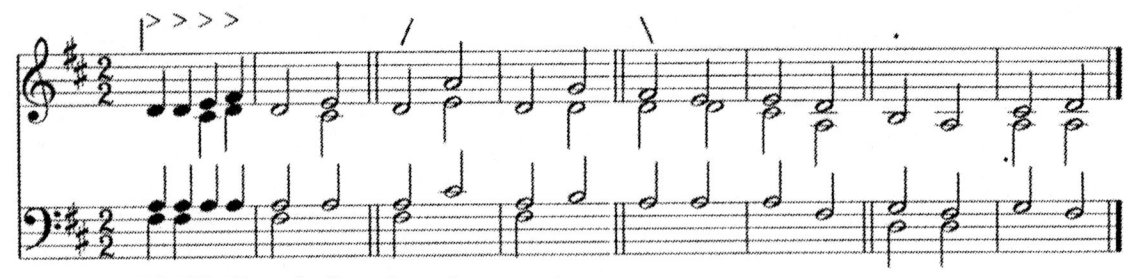

36 His line shall endure for ever *
  and his throne as the sun before me;
37 It shall stand fast for evermore like the moon, *
  the abiding witness in the sky.'"
                    [Silence...]
38 But you have cast off and rejected your anointed; *
  you have become enraged at him.
39 \You have broken your covenant with your \ servant,
  defiled his crown, and hurled it to the \ ground.
40 You have breached all his walls *
  and laid his strongholds in ruins.
41 All who pass by despoil him; *
  he has become the scorn of his neighbors.
42 You have exalted the right hand of his foes *
  and made all his enemies rejoice.
43 You have turned back the edge of his sword *
  and have not sustained him in battle.
44 \You have put an end to his \ splendor
  and cast his throne to the \ ground.
45 You have cut short the days of his youth *
  and have covered him with shame.
                    [Silence...]
46 How long will you hide yourself, O LORD?
  will you hide yourself for ever? *
  how long will your anger burn like fire?
47 \Remember, LORD, how short \ life is,
  how frail you have made all \ flesh.
48 Who can live and not see death? *
  who can save himself from the power of the grave?
                    [Silence...]
49 Where, Lord, are your loving-kindnesses of old, *
  which you promised David in your faithfulness?
50 \Remember, Lord, how your servant is \ mocked,
  how I carry in my bosom the taunts of many \ peoples,
51 The taunts your enemies have hurled, O LORD, *
  which they hurled at the heels of your anointed.
52 Blessed be the LORD for evermore! *
  Amen, I say, Amen.

Book Four

A Song Of Time: Commentary To Psalm 90

Notice the many references to time: from generation to generation ... before the mountains were born ... from eternity to eternity ... a thousand years ... yesterday ... in the morning ... in the evening ... all our days ... seventy years ... eighty. Notice that the life-span of a human breathing has changed but little since these verses were written.

    LIMNOTH YÁMEYNU KÉN HODA" W:NÁVIY. L:VAV #ÁKHMÁH
v.12 So teach us to number our days
that we may apply our hearts to wisdom.

Forgetting how short my life is, I run around worrying what this one thinks of me and if that one approves of me. I work myself up trying to prevent what cannot be and to bring about what happens of itself. I come home exhausted and ask myself where the day went. I worried and fretted, protected my image, looked for praise, waited for lunch, was irritated at this one and talked about that one. I hoped I would not have too many problems. I forgot to number my days.

I kept forgetting that each breath could be my last, each encounter my last. I kept forgetting to be here now, with you; I was waiting for the praise, the recognition. I was preparing my acceptance speech for some nameless prize. I was preparing my defense for some unnamed court of law. I was thinking about sex. I was trying to come up with a joke.

LORD, you live in eternity, the invisible realm. Time means nothing to you. And I am a creature of time, dying with every breath. This moment is all I have. And so I say to the LORD, make this intimately known to me, this numbering of my days, so that I may acquire a heart of wisdom. Set me free from that net of foolish concerns, to enjoy this moment. Satisfy me in the morning. Compare 17, 103. In the moments that remain, let me enjoy what is. Let me awaken with a sigh of "Enough!"

    UMA"aSÉH YÁ<u>DEY</u>NU KON:NÁH "Á<u>LEY</u>NU UMA"aSÉH YÁDEYNU KON:<u>NÉ</u>HU
v.17 and the work of our hands establish upon us,
and the work of our hands, establish it.

Let it not have been meaningless. Establish the little work of my hands, give it meaning. Something I did in those few moments, something I said, someone I touched — O LORD, let it be fruitful.

<u>Suggestions</u>: Practice the enjoyment of time, moment by moment. You cannot save time, use it, or lose it, for it does not belong to you. Clear your thoughts as often as you can, and be where you are, silent and fully present. Sometimes the easiest way to do this is to look at the clock. What is the exact time, now?

Psalm 90 (BCP)

Eighteenth Day: Morning Prayer   Tone: HIGÁYON

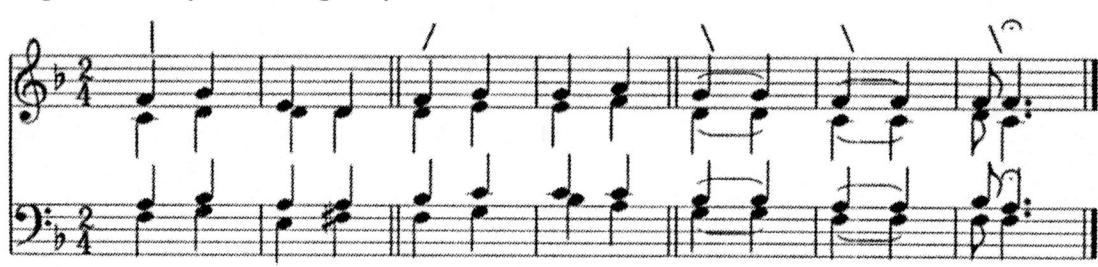

1 Lord, you have been our refuge *
   from one generation to another.
2 Before the mountains were brought forth, or the land and the earth were born, *
   from age to age you are God.
3 You turn us back to the dust and say, *
   "Go back, O child of earth."
4 For a thousand years in your sight are like yesterday when it is past *
   and like a watch in the night.
5 You sweep us away like a dream; *
   we fade away suddenly like the grass.
6 In the morning it is green and flourishes; *
   in the evening it is dried up and withered.
7 **For we consume away in your dis | pleasure;**
   we are afraid because of your wrathful indig | nation.
8 Our iniquities you have set before you, *
   and our secret sins in the light of your countenance.
9 When you are angry all our days are gone; *
   we bring our years to an end like a sigh.
10 The span of our life is seventy years, perhaps in strength even eighty; *
   yet the sum of them is but labor and sorrow,
   for they pass away quickly and we are gone.
11 **Who regards the power of your | wrath?**
   who rightly fears your indig | nation?
12 So teach us to number our days *
   that we may apply our hearts to wisdom.
13 Return, O LORD, how long will you tarry? *
   be gracious to your servants.
14 /Satisfy us by your loving-kindness in the / morning;
   so shall we rejoice and be glad all the days of our / life.
15 Make us glad by the measure of the days that you afflicted us *
   and the years in which we suffered adversity.
16 **/Show your servants your / works**
   and your splendor to their / children.
17 \May the graciousness of the LORD our God be upon us;
   \prosper the work of our hands;
   prosper our \ handiwork.

Song Of The Demons: Commentary To Psalm 91

LO.-TH:.UNNEH .ÉLEYKHÁ RÁ"ÁH
v.10 There shall no evil happen to you.

Psalm 91 is known in Hebrew as SHIR SHEL P:GÁ"IM or Song of the Demons, traditional protection against the forces of evil. Some Christians invest it with magical efficacy. They invoke it in every imaginable crisis—even armed robbery! There are Christians who consider it their favorite Scripture; I have heard many stories of its powers.

But it does not always match our experience. Evil does happen to good people, every day. How shall we take it, then? We might consider the psalm as being metaphorical. Or assume that it speaks of spiritual, not physical dangers. It can keep away demons, but not burglars. Perhaps it is only poetry, not to be taken literally. Of course, we can blame the victims: they did not remember to quote Psalm 91, or they did so ineffectively. They were lacking in faith. Or, we might decide that Psalm 91 represents a different level of reality—a miraculous reality—that is only accessible, and then only in part, to those who commit to it.

Thinking along these lines I realized that Scripture itself is an encoded other reality. When I was a casual reader it was merely ancient literature, hard to understand. But when I decided that it was the Word of God; when I began to ask the Holy Spirit to interpret it for me; then the code was broken, and the words began to light up with personalized meaning. In this same way, there is something awesome about Psalm 91, something we do not fully understand. Perhaps it is our coded entry to the miraculous protection of God.

Before we go too far in this direction, let us consider something else. We are fortunate to have Jesus' own commentary to this psalm. In Matthew 4:5-7 (NKJ), Jesus is tempted by Satan, who tells him, quoting vv.11-12, "If You are the Son of God, throw Yourself down. For it is written:

'He shall give His angels charge concerning you,' and,

'In their hands they shall bear you up,
Lest you dash your foot against a stone.'"

Jesus said to him, "It is written again, 'You shall not tempt the LORD your God.'"

Let us turn back now to the beginning of the psalm.

YOSHÉV B:SÉTHER "ELYON   B:3ÉL SHADDAY YITHLONÁN
v.1 Who is sitting in the secret place of the Most High,
abides in the shadow of the Almighty.

In the secret or hidden place, he dwells. In the protective shadow of *Shaddai*, the Most Powerful, he makes his home. In the secret or hidden place of the heart, that inner place where I set my approach to life. In the secret or hidden place of the temple; in silence, the place of listening, the place where God is found. This is not a psalm about magic, but about trust. He who sits in that secret or hidden place does not call upon

God's protection, manipulate it, or use it, but lives within it. He trusts God completely. There is no need to invoke his protection with magical phrases or prayers.

Such a man could say to God, honestly, "You are my refuge and my stronghold." Such a person has turned his personal welfare over to God in a complete way, so that, really, no evil could happen to him or her. Whatever happened to this individual is simply what was meant to be. Jesus could have hurled himself from the pinnacle of the temple shouting verses from Psalm 91; he chose instead to let the Father take care of him.

There is a kind of prayer that I have learned to call pray-wishing. I used to do this a lot when I was on call for the hospital. *Please, God, don't let the phone ring. Please let it be an easy night. Please, let me not have to go back in to the emergency room tonight. Please let this turn out all right.* I gradually came to realize that the more I pray-wished, the worse I felt. The more I worried and fretted and tried to manipulate God to go easy on me, the more anxious and miserable I became. How much better I felt when I finally learned to say *Your will be done* and *Yes, LORD, thank you for this assignment.* I cannot control the telephone or God. I can learn to trust God.

Shall we give up praying, then? Of course not! But we pray always to One who can say no. We do not know the outcome. Faith, not magic. That is why, when prayer is answered, we come into some danger. Why? Because we begin to expect our prayers to be answered: if we pray in the same way, the same words, the same order, we will have the same result. At that moment we have slipped over the line from miracle to magic. From that moment prayer deteriorates into pray-wishing. The sense of security begins draining away. I become more anxious even as I pray harder.

Yes, I believe that some people have miraculously survived armed robbery by shouting a verse from Psalm 91. I can't explain it, but I accept it. And I believe that some people have warded off the Powers of Darkness by earnestly praying Psalm 91. I can't explain that either. But for me, it is more important to turn my safety over to God himself, to learn to trust him as my refuge and stronghold. Compare 27, 46.

<u>Suggestions</u>: Sing the refrains. Practice the teaching of the secret place in every trouble or danger. Clear your thoughts and be silent. Pray for direction and not magic. Father, what do you want me to do?

Psalm 91 (BCP)

Tone: KINNOR (1)

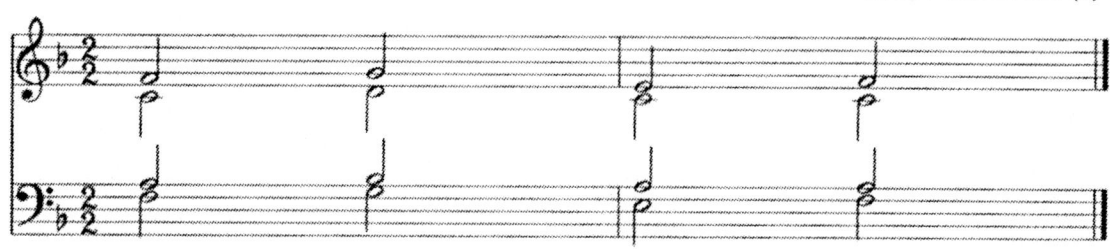

1 He who dwells in the shelter of the Most High, *
   abides under the shadow of the Almighty.
2 **He shall say to the LORD,**
   "You are my refuge and my | stronghold,
   my God in whom I put my | trust."
3 He shall deliver you from the snare of the hunter *
   and from the deadly pestilence.
4 He shall cover you with his pinions,
   and you shall find refuge under his wings; *
   his faithfulness shall be a shield and buckler.
5 You shall not be afraid of any terror by night, *
   nor of the arrow that flies by day;
6 Of the plague that stalks in the darkness, *
   nor of the sickness that lays waste at mid-day.
7 A thousand shall fall at your side
   and ten thousand at your right hand, *
   but it shall not come near you.
8 Your eyes have only to behold *
   to see the reward of the wicked.
9 **Because you have made the LORD your | refuge,**
   and the Most High your habi | tation,
10 There shall no evil happen to you, *
    neither shall any plague come near your dwelling.
11 For he shall give his angels charge over you, *
    to keep you in all your ways.
12 They shall bear you in their hands, *
    lest you dash your foot against a stone.
13 You shall tread upon the lion and adder; *
    you shall trample the young lion and the serpent under your feet.
14 Because he is bound to me in love,
    therefore will I deliver him; *
    I will protect him, because he knows my Name.
15 He shall call upon me, and I will answer him; *
    I am with him in trouble;
    I will rescue him and bring him to honor.
16 With long life will I satisfy him, *
    and show him my salvation.

It Is Good: Commentary To Psalm 92

    tOV L:HODOTH LAYHWH UL:ZAMMÉR L:SHIMKHÁ "ELYON
v.1 It is a good thing to give thanks to the LORD.

 The word tOV means good. Also pleasant, agreeable, fragrant; or prosperous, happy, merry (Gesenius, p. 319). The way God sees creation (Genesis 1:4). Original blessing, to use Matthew Fox's expression. It is good! Or, a good thing. All flows from this: It is good to give thanks, to sing praises.

    L:HAGGIYD BABBOQER #ASDEKHÁ WE.eMUNÁTH:KHÁ BALLEYLOTH
v.2 To tell of (show) your loving-kindness early in the morning,
and of your faithfulness in the night season;
v.3 On the psaltery and on the lyre.

 It is a good thing for me to tell of you, not to talk religion, but to show you, make you manifest. To tell of your love and your faithfulness. It is good that I tell of you day and night, at work and at home. To sing your praise with different instruments—with different faculties, abilities, talents and moods. It is good when my whole life tells of you.

 v.4 For you have made me glad (happy) ...
 I begin to shout for joy!

 For you have already made me happy (perfective form) if I will only accept that, as in Psalm 86. No longer happy when, or happy if, but happy now, in the moment. Not situational. Not based upon the grades I get in school or at work. I went through life trying and complaining. Trying to improve myself and everyone else and getting nowhere. But when I began to thank you and praise you and tell of you, I began to feel better at once.

 Things in the world seem to be falling apart. The wicked are growing like weeds and the evildoers appear to be flourishing. The streets of America are not safe; the leaders do not know how to respond. But appearances can be deceiving. Dullards and fools cannot understand what is happening. The underlying reality, overlooked by almost everyone, is good.

    L:HAGGIYD KI-YÁSHÁR YHWH
v.14 To tell (or show) that the LORD is upright.

 It is for this that the righteous flourish and spread out, still vigorous in old age, still putting forth green leaves and bearing fruit. It is good!

Suggestions: Stand, sing to the Tone #ÁLIL (*flute*). Those stanzas whose first line is in boldface type are sung to the last three measures, beginning at the last measure and continuing at the first repeat. Those sections beginning with ordinary type and the caret marker (^) are sung to the first three measures, up to the second repeat.

Psalm 92 (BCP)

Tone: #ÁLIL

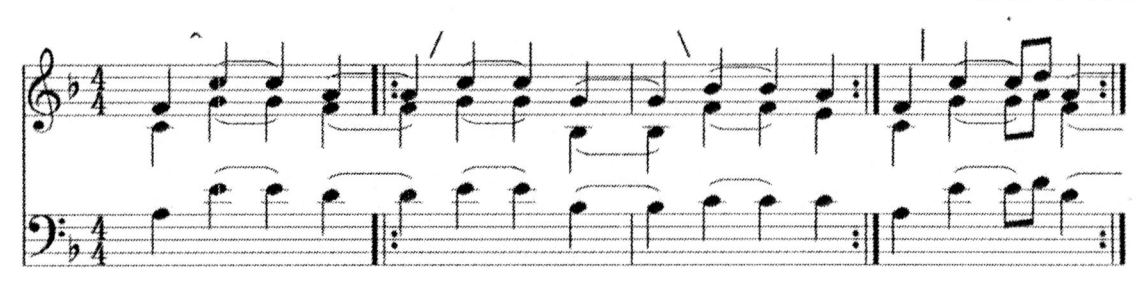

1 ^It is a good thing to give thanks to the ^ LORD
    and to sing praises to your Name, O Most ^ High;
2 **To tell of your loving-kindness early in the | morning**
    and of your | faithfulness in the night | season;
3 /On the psaltery, and on the / lyre,
    and to the melody of the / harp.
4 \For you have made me glad by your \ acts, O LORD;
    and I shout for joy because of the works of your \ hands.
5 **LORD, how great are your | works!**
    your | thoughts are very | deep.
6 /The dullard does not know,
    nor does the fool / understand,
    that though the wicked grow like weeds,
    and all the workers of iniquity / flourish,
7 \They flourish only to be destroyed for \ ever;
    but you, O LORD, are exalted for \ evermore.
8 ^For lo, your enemies, O LORD,
    lo, your enemies shall ^ perish,
    and all the workers of iniquity shall be ^ scattered.
9 /But my horn you have exalted like the horns of wild / bulls;
    I am anointed with fresh / oil.
10 \My eyes also gloat over my \ enemies,
    and my ears rejoice to hear the doom of the wicked who rise up a\gainst me.
11 **The righteous shall flourish like a | palm tree,**
    and shall spread a | broad like a cedar of | Lebanon.
12 /Those who are planted in the house of the / LORD
    shall flourish in the courts of our / God;
13 \They shall still bear fruit in old \ age;
    they shall be green and \ succulent;
14 **That they may show how upright the | LORD is,**
    my | Rock in whom there is no | fault.

Hurricane Psalm: Commentary To Psalm 93

MIQQOLOTH <u>MA</u>YiM RABBIM .ADDIRIM MISHB:REY-YÁM
v.5 Mightier than the sound of many waters,

mightier than the breakers of the sea. When the Hebrew poets want to convey awesome power, they speak of water. The raging of the ocean and the crashing of its waves; the storms, the primordial depths. The earth itself was founded on turbulent waters. The Hebrews were not a sea-faring people but they knew of the sea. They were awed by its crashing waves and breakers. Nothing seemed more hopeless than to go down in those depths (Jonah 2:2-9) or to have the waters "up to my throat" (69:1).

I was a young and foolish medical student in Charleston, South Carolina, when I encountered my first hurricanes. For hours the sky would darken and the winds would roar through the city; how well I remember hundreds of palmetto trees bending before the fierce winds, all in the same direction. Then there was silence, a brief calm, and the winds would return, driving the helpless palmettos in the opposite direction.

We considered it great fun to go out in the hurricane, to walk and wade through the old streets of Charleston. An old sea captain sat on his porch on Water Street serving drinks to any who would stop and chat. An enormous jelly-fish floated past us on Church Street. The winds grew fiercer. Power lines were down. As we approached the Battery, the historic tip of the peninsula, we saw waves, unimaginably high, crashing over the sea-wall; and the sea-gulls beating their wings in vain, unable to fly against that wind. I remember clinging to a tree and watching in awe. And I remember dimly realizing, even in my adolescent fog, that I was in mortal danger. Now as I remember that day it is even more frightening. How many have died in hurricanes since I foolishly played in that storm!

This is the power, the power of the crashing waves, that our writer uses to evoke the power of God. Unimaginable, terrifying and awesome, too great for me to bear, is the power of those pounding waves. Yet the power that upholds the world is infinitely greater. It is holy and incorruptible. It is power I can only imagine, concealed and invisible everywhere, veiled in mysterious "apparel." It is eternal power, faithful and trustworthy. It is the power that watched over me in the hurricane.

The storms of the sea may be deadly, the storms within deadlier still. The inner rages of a human breathing have caused more misery than all the hurricanes of all time. Thought leads to thought and emotion to emotion; one human breathing provokes another, and soon, in days or years, the world is on fire. Here too, the LORD is King, girded in that mysterious apparel, mightier than those pounding waves and breakers. Mightier than the rages of my inner world is God who dwells on high.

<u>Suggestions</u>: Sing majestically to the movement Standing Drum (see Appendix).

Do not go out in hurricanes and do not trifle with thoughts and emotions. Remember that a thought, yes, a thought, can end in murder. Practice moments of silence whenever you can, and lift your emotions to God. Ask God to take control of those turbulent waves and breakers.

Psalm 93 (BCP)

Eighteenth Day: Evening Prayer Tone: #a303:ROTH

1 \`\`\`\` **The LȮRD is Kìng;**
   he has pùt on splèndid | appàrel; \`
   The LȮRD has put òn his | appàrel \`
   /and gìrded himsèlf with / strèngth. \`
2 /He has màde the whole wòrld so sùre
   that it cànnot be / mòved. —
3 Èver since the wòrld begàn, your thròne has
   been | estàblished; \`
   /you àre \` from / everlàsting. —
4 The wàters have lìfted up, O | LȮRD, \`
   the wàters have lìfted up their | vòice; \`
   /the wàters have lìfted ùp their pòunding / wàves. \`\`\`
5 **Mìghtier thàn the sòund of màny | wàters,** \`\`\`
   mìghtier thàn the brèakers òf the | sèa, \`\`\`
   /mìghtier is the LȮRD who dwèlls on / hìgh. —
6 **Your tèstimonies àre very sùre,** \`
   and hòliness adòrns your | hòuse, O LȮRD, \`
   /for èver \` and for / èvermore.

In The Multitude Of My Thoughts: Commentary To Psalm 94

v.17 Unless the LORD had been my help,
my soul had almost dwelt in silence (KJV).

In a world gone mad, the wicked seem to be taking over everywhere, even in the courts of law; no one seems to care what is right. Then, on the edge of disillusionment, a moment of truth: Unless the LORD were my help, my soul would already be lying in the world of nothingness. There would be no more inner talk between "me" and "my soul" (breath, breathing, life).

v.18 As often as I said, "My foot has slipped,"
your love, O LORD, upheld me.

If (ever) I have said (perfective verb), my foot has slipped. The Hebrew verb means to be shaken, totter; to be overthrown or toppled. If ever I have said, *Uh-oh, I'm losing it* or *I'm about to go under*; that is when your fierce protective love continued (*and continues*) to support me (imperfective form). When I have decided, in my haste, that all is lost, your love is there, sustaining me.

B:ROV SAR"APPAY B:QIRBIY   TAN#U<u>ME</u>YKHÁ Y:SHA"SH"UW NAPHSHIY
v.19 In the multitude (or multiplying) of my thoughts within me,
your consolations delight (stroke, caress) my soul (breathing, life).

Note that there is no "mind" in the Hebrew. The word SAR"APPAY (*my thoughts*) is from a root that means to branch (Gesenius, p. 592). My thoughts branch and multiply inside me, leading only to more thoughts. *How about -- this? But what if -- that? I could try this -- but what about that?* My thinking branches and branches again, becoming ungovernable. Even *I*, who claims to be in charge here, is but another restless thought. Compare 86.

In that sorry state of agitation, your consolations continue to delight (caress, stroke) my soul (inner self, breath, life). You do not argue with my thoughts, but you stroke and caress me (the real me, my breath, my life) and calm my breathing.

An intimate moment with God; a moment of clarity. I thought that all was lost, but your love was there, sustaining me. I realize that you have been there all the time, stroking and caressing me. Outwardly nothing has changed. The wicked still reign. But "The LORD has become my stronghold."

<u>Suggestions</u>: When you find your thoughts branching and multiplying, and you feel the first twinges of panic, remember Psalm 94. Inhale sharply through the nose and exhale slowly and smoothly. Lift your attention from those branching thoughts to God. Step out of them completely. Be silent. Listen. Ask God to comfort your soul (breath, breathing, life itself). You cannot change an unjust world or the arrogance of the wicked. You have a right to feel overwhelmed. God knows your human thoughts, yet he does not argue with them or try to change them. And he knows how to cheer your soul. He knows how to comfort you.

Psalm 94 (BCP)

Tone: HIGÁYON

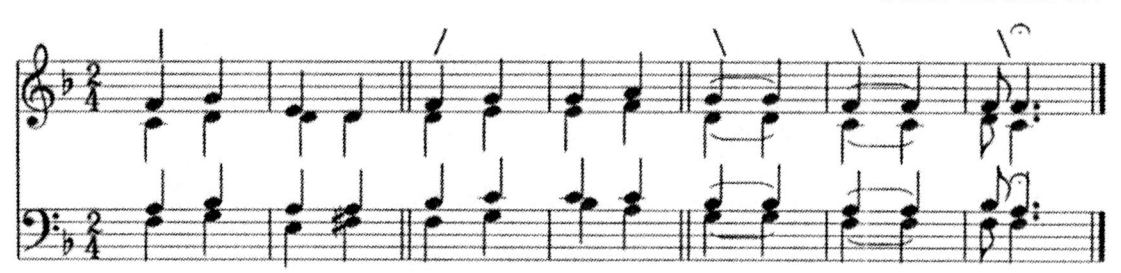

1 O LORD God of vengeance, *
    O God of vengeance, show yourself.
2 Rise up, O Judge of the world; *
    give the arrogant their just deserts.
3 How long shall the wicked, O LORD, *
    how long shall the wicked triumph?
4 They bluster in their insolence; *
    all evildoers are full of boasting.
5 **They crush your people, O | LORD,**
    and afflict your chosen | nation.
6 They murder the widow and the stranger *
    and put the orphans to death.
7 Yet they say, "The LORD does not see, *
    the God of Jacob takes no notice."
8 Consider well, you dullards among the people; *
    when will you fools understand?
9 He that planted the ear, does he not hear? *
    he that formed the eye, does he not see?
10 He who admonishes the nations, will he not punish? *
    he who teaches all the world, has he no knowledge?
11 The LORD knows our human thoughts; *
    how like a puff of wind they are.
12 Happy are they whom you instruct, O LORD! *
    whom you teach out of your law;
13 To give them rest in evil days, *
    until a pit is dug for the wicked.
14 **/For the LORD will not abandon his / people,**
    nor will he forsake his / own.
15 For judgment will again be just, *
    and all the true of heart will follow it.
16 Who rose up for me against the wicked? *
    who took my part against the evildoers?
17 **If the LORD had not come to my | help,**
    I should soon have dwelt in the land of | silence.

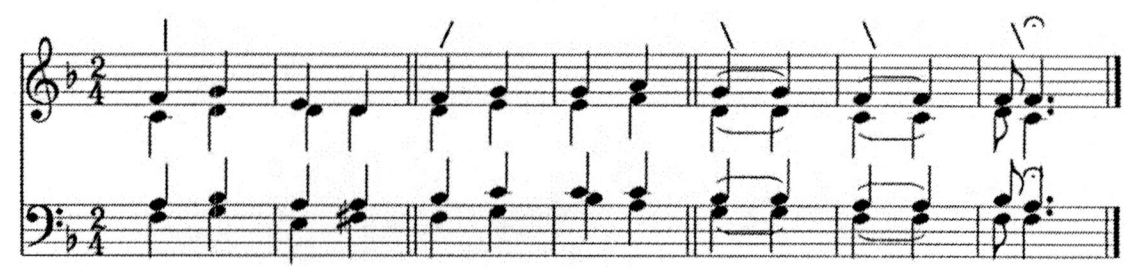

18 As often as I said, "My foot has slipped," *
    your love, O LORD, upheld me.
19 /When many cares fill my / mind,
    your consolations cheer my / soul.
20 Can a corrupt tribunal have any part with you, *
    one which frames evil into law?
21 They conspire against the life of the just *
    and condemn the innocent to death.
22 /But the LORD has become my / stronghold,
    and my God the rock of my / trust.
23 \He will turn their wickedness back upon them
    \and destroy them in their own malice;
    the LORD our God will de\stroy them.

Do Not Harden Your Hearts: Commentary To Psalm 95

The psalm falls into contrasting sections, what Spurgeon* calls the Invitation and the Warning. First, a magnificent invitation to worship, the *Venite*. Come, let us sing ... shout ... come before his presence ... For the LORD is a great God and great King. As in 81, the outward or expressive phase of worship. It is beautiful and glorious—the singing, shouting, coming into the temple courts, chanting of psalms—and it is the easier part. I respond to this invitation with delight. I enjoy the singing and shouting. I begin to feel good. I am celebrating the grandeur of God, his kingship and majesty, his reign over caverns and hills and sea, and I begin to feel good about myself. Yes, I really am special and chosen, to know such a God, and to realize his greatness.

v.6 Come, let us bow down and bend the knee.

Moving now from religious enthusiasm to surrender, I recall that bowing and kneeling are symbolic of breaking down, surrender and powerlessness. Bowing is the gesture of submission, humbling myself before higher authority. Bowing in prayer is the ancient Jewish expression of reverence (compare 5), not to some capricious king or president, but to One who is all-knowing, guiding, protecting, saving and healing. Kneeling takes me down off my feet, to the state of helplessness, without defense (compare 103). Yet these actions can be mere gestures. It is easy to bow from the waist, to humble myself symbolically; it is incredibly difficult to achieve humility. Likewise it may be easy to kneel, at least for a short time, to portray the defenseless state; almost impossible to live without defensiveness.

This is not so much fun as the singing and shouting. This is more demanding, testing and transforming me. It is the slow, dry passage from religion to spirituality, to living in the will of the Father. And so I move on to the concluding section, the Warning (vv. 8-11). Now the tone grows somber. God himself is speaking to me here, and his words cut deeply. Outwardly religious, I carry within me a fatal spiritual illness, a virus of the heart.

Now symptoms of the soul (breath, breathing, life) are easily treated in psychiatry, at least in theory. Symptoms of the biological self often respond to medications, rest, exercise and self-study. The patients may be asked to carry out therapeutic tasks such as writing letters to those they have wronged, telling their spouses how they really feel, redirecting their thoughts from complaining to gratitude, forgiving those who have hurt them, or giving up old resentments. If they actually do these tasks, their symptoms will often improve.

Symptoms of the heart are more difficult. Symptoms of the heart are curable, yes, but not treatable. For there is really but one important symptom of the heart, and that is hardness. The stubborn attitude that is manifest as refusal, denial, or defensiveness. *You can't make me. I don't care. What good will that do? No one can help me.* Or, as one patient told me, "I'm a brick wall. You will never change me!"

No therapy can treat these symptoms, for they are symptoms of choice. We may at times abuse our power with patients, but we cannot change their attitudes. We cannot make them say yes to health. Not even prayer can do that. Families and friends may find that hard to accept. Patients themselves may challenge us to break open their hearts. Yet it seems God will not abrogate free choice. And so, at the conclusion of this beautiful praise-hymn, we hear God pleading to his people,

.AL-TAQSHUW L:VAV:KHEM

v.8 Do not harden your hearts.

Your ancestors were across the Red Sea in one day, but it took them forty years to break free from slavery (compare 114). Why? Because of their stubborn attitudes! Don't be like that, God is pleading, and I hear him but I "cannot" respond. I am as stubborn as my ancestors. I want to be free, O God, but you can't make me—and he doesn't. How ironic, and no accident, that in the midst of "Come, let us sing to the LORD," at the climax of my worship experience, I hear that faint pleading voice: "Do not harden your hearts." God pleads to me as I plead to my patients. And I answer as my patients answer, "Yes, LORD, I'll do anything you say. Anything but *that*."

It is the nature of a human breathing to resist, to cling to ignorance. So it was that Jesus taught of the sower (Matthew 13:3-9 and 18-23). Of all that was sown, three quarters perished. The sower was good and the seed was good, but the soil was unreceptive. Then as now it was easy to hear without depth and agree without conviction. Then as now, it was hard to surrender, to hear without passing judgment, to listen with a teachable spirit. Then as now it was easier to say, *Lord, Lord*, or, *Jesus saves*, or, *Come, let us sing*, than to listen to the still, small voice of God. That is why God says of them and us, "This people are wayward in their hearts; they do not know my ways."

<u>Suggestions</u>: Stand. Sing to the Tone HIGÁYON (*meditation*), but omit hand movements. The music is the same as for Psalm 94. Bow deeply from the waist on v. 6 ("Come, let us bow down") and then immediately kneel from "bend the knee" to the end of the psalm.

When the discussion is going badly, when no one seems to get the point but you, when the family is upset with you, and the fellow-workers are not getting along with you, listen! Do not harden your heart, but listen. What are they trying to tell you? What is God trying to tell you?

Worship God with singing and shouting, dancing and drums; worship him also with silence, listening, willingness. You have come a long way and learned much, but you still do not know his ways. You have so much to learn.

---

*C.H. Spurgeon: *The Treasury of David*, containing an original exposition of the Book of Psalms; a collection of illustrative extracts from the whole range of literature; a series of homiletical hints upon almost every verse; and lists of writers upon each psalm. In Three Volumes. Hendrickson Publishers, Peabody, MA., Vol. II, p. 164.

Psalm 95 (BCP)

Nineteenth Day: Morning Prayer

1 /Come, let us sing to the / LORD;
   let us shout for joy to the Rock of our sal/vation.
2 /Let us come before his presence with thanks/giving
   and raise a loud shout to him with / psalms.
3 **For the LORD is a great | God,**
   and a great King above all | gods.
4 /In his hand are the caverns of the / earth,
   and the heights of the hills are his / also.
5 **The sea is his, for he | made it,**
   and his hands have molded the | dry land.
6 /Come, let us bow down, and bend the / knee,
   and kneel before the LORD our / Maker.
7 \For he is our God,
   \and we are the people of his pasture and the sheep of his hand.
   Oh, that today you would hearken to his \ voice!
8 **Harden not your hearts,**
   as your forbears did in the | wilderness,
   at Meribah, and on that day at Massah, when they | tempted me.
9 /They put me to the / test,
   though they had seen my / works.
10 \Forty years long I detested that generation and said,
   \"This people are wayward in their hearts;
   they do not know my \ ways."
11 **So I swore in my | wrath,**
   "They shall not enter into my | rest."

A Song Of Good News: Commentary To Psalm 96

SHIRU LAYHWH SHIR #ÁDÁSH

v.1 Sing to the LORD a new song (Compare 33, 40, 98). *New song*. Not necessarily a novel song, a song with unheard of new notes, but a renewed song. A fresh song, newly experienced. Understood now, as if for the very first time. I have heard these words hundreds of times, but today, for the very first time, I really heard them. Today for the very first time, they were sung *for me!*

It is written, "there is nothing new under the sun" (Ecclesiastes 1:9), yet experience tells me otherwise. All things can be made new when you look at me and really see me; when I know I have touched you by something I said; when a face like any other face becomes a person to me, someone with a name, a history, dreams. When I realize that someone really understands me, and accepts me just as I am. When I experience the presence of God in a moment of silence, or in church. When I kneel at the altar rail and I look up and see a baby wide-eyed with wonder and delight. All things are new when I am really present, here and now.

Sing to the LORD a new song, an intimate song, this moment, here and now. Lift up the song from this page and sing it to him. Now. He is listening. He is here among us. Sing a new song of the LORD, to me, right now. Not an unusual song, but a renewed song, a fresh song. A song from your heart to my loneliness. Look into my eyes, and sing to me. Tell me the details. Tell me what God has done for you, and let me tell you what he has done for me.

Don't ask me, *Have you read?* or *Have you heard?* Don't hand me a tape or a book, just stay with me. Be with me, look at me, listen to me, sing me your song. Be to me a letter from God, postmarked today. That is a new song, a fresh song.

v.3 Proclaim the good news of his salvation from day to day.

The word BASS:RUW (*bear glad tidings*) is from a root meaning "to be joyful, cheerful, especially in receiving glad tidings" (Gesenius[*]). The primary meaning of the root (he adds) is "beauty ... since a face is made more beautiful by joy and cheerfulness." The Good News is that God became flesh and lived among us, like one of us. And lives among us yet, here in our midst. I cannot find this news in my newspaper. Pastor Wonderful cannot do this on the radio. Only you can sing this song for me.

Psalm 96 is built of three-fold repetitions. I have tried to show this unusual pattern, which is concealed by the verse numbers.

<u>Suggestions</u>: Stand. Sing with variations by moving freely between the upper and lower notes. Move easily from one variation to another, beginning with some form of the first three measures, and ending the psalm with some form of the last two measures. Bow deeply from the waist on "Worship" (v.9).

---

[*]H.W.F. Gesenius: *Gesenius' Hebrew-Chaldee Lexicon to the Old Testament Scriptures* (Translated by Samuel Prideaux Tregelles), Baker Book House, Grand Rapids, MI, 1979, p. 146.

Psalm 96 (BCP)

Tone: **#a3O3:ROTH** *variations*

1 **Sing to the LORD a new + song;**
   sing to the LORD, all the whole / earth.
2 Sing to the LORD and bless his \ Name;
   Proclaim the good news of his salvation from + day to day.
3 Declare his glory among the / nations
   and his wonders among all \ peoples.
4 **For great is the LORD and greatly to be + praised;**
   he is more to be feared than all / gods.
5 As for all the gods of the nations, they are but \ idols;
   But it is the LORD who made the + heavens.
6 Oh, the majesty and magnificence of his / presence!
   Oh, the power and the splendor of his \ sanctuary!
7 **Ascribe to the LORD, you families of the + peoples;**
   ascribe to the LORD honor and / power.
8 Ascribe to the LORD the honor due his \ Name;
   Bring offerings and come into his + courts.
9 Worship the LORD in the beauty of / holiness;
   let the whole earth tremble be\fore him.
10 **Tell it out among the nations, "The LORD is + King!**
   he has made the world so firm that it cannot be / moved;
   he will judge the peoples with \ equity."
11 **Let the heavens rejoice, and let the earth be + glad;**
   let the sea thunder and all that is / in it;
   let the field be joyful and all that is \ therein.
12 **Then shall all the trees of the wood shout for + joy**
   before the LORD when he / comes,
   when he comes to judge the \ earth.

13 **He will judge the world with | righteousness**
   /and the peoples with his / truth.

Seeds Of Light: Commentary To Psalm 97

v.1 The LORD is King, let the earth rejoice,

let the many islands be happy.

Like 93, 96, 98 and others this has been called a kingship or enthronement psalm. Scholars give us fanciful pictures of enthronement ceremonies, grand processions in which God would have been enthroned as king. I like to think of these as energy psalms. Notice the transformations of energy—the fire, lightning, mountains melting like wax, light—all reflecting God's unspeakable power. It is this energy and power that are spoken of as kingship.

The image of a king has faded for us. Kings today might be thought of as museum kings, royal figures who perform ceremonial functions; we read of their wealth and their troubles in the news, and find little to inspire us. Kings and queens and princesses today are people like us, searching for meaning in a world of moral confusion. Sometimes we think of kings as fairy-tale kings, mythic figures of majesty and wisdom, with golden crowns and beautiful daughters. We dream of kings like that, but we will not entrust such power to anyone.

The real meaning of king is ultimate authority. But as we move away from biblical values, we are increasingly uncertain of authority. Those who claim authority show little leadership. Impotent leaders exhort followers who despise them; or stay in power by force and terror. Some of us would like to base authority on elections; yet the elections are all too often fraudulent, won by deceptive commercials and slogans.

From great nations to little families, authority is suspect and fleeting. The subjects put little faith in the authorities and those in authority show little respect for their subjects. Parents abuse their children, and children have no respect for parents. Bosses intimidate those who work for them, and the workers steal from those who hire them. The search for authority goes on but is hopeless. Real authority cannot be invented.

Real authority comes from God, and it is based on righteousness and justice. When God takes over as ultimate Authority, the entire earth will be joyful, and the islands, the farthest outposts of humanity, will be happy. For he will transform the world as we know it. Everything will be changed, even the physical structure of the mountains. There will be a radical transformation of government, for the wicked will not be treated as the good. All will be treated according to their personal actions.

v.11 Light is sown (like seed) for the righteous,

and happiness for those who are true of heart. In a world of apparent darkness, seeds of light have been sown. Sparks of divine light are germinating all around us, hidden but growing. When God takes over as King there will be a blaze of light and happiness. Therefore the righteous can rejoice, aware of those seeds all around them, in every thing and person.

Suggestions: Stand. Sing cheerfully to the Tone #a3O3:ROTH (*trumpets*). Bow deeply from the waist on "Bow" (v.7b). Clear your mind of thoughts, again and again, and look for those seeds of light in every person you encounter.

Psalm 97 (BCP)

Tone: #a3O3:ROTH

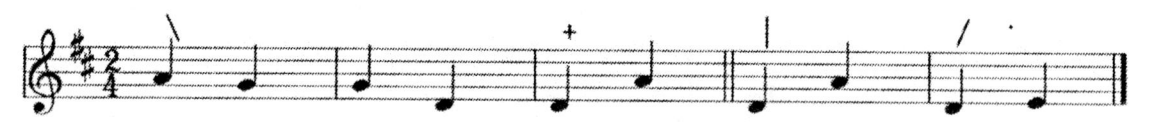

1 \The Lord is King;
   let the earth re\joice;
   let the multitude of the isles be \ glad.
2 Clouds and darkness are round a+bout him;
   \righteousness and justice are the foundations of his \ throne.
3 A fire goes be\fore him
   and burns up his enemies on every + side.
4 **His lightnings light up the | world;**
   /the earth sees it and is a/fraid.
5 /The mountains melt like wax at the presence of the Lord,
   at the presence of the Lord of the whole / earth.
6 **The heavens declare his | righteousness,**
   /and all the peoples see his / glory.
7 \Confounded be all who worship carved \ images
   and delight in false \ gods!
   Bow down before him, all you + gods.
8 /Zion hears and is glad, and the cities of Judah rejoice,
   because of your judgments, O / Lord.
9 \For you are the \ Lord,
   most high over all the \ earth;
   you are exalted far above all + gods.
10 \The Lord loves those who hate \ evil;
   he preserves the lives of his \ saints
   and delivers them from the hand of the + wicked.
11 **Light has sprung up for the | righteous,**
   /and joyful gladness for those who are true/hearted.
12 **Rejoice in the Lord, you | righteous,**
   /and give thanks to his holy / Name.

Like The Very First Time: Commentary To Psalm 98

SHIYRU LAYHWH SHIR #ÁDÁSH   KI-NIPHLÁ.OTH "ÁSÁH

v.1 Sing to the LORD a new song,
for he has done marvelous things.

Sing, once again, a new song, as in 33, 40, 96. Yet how strange to be singing "sing a new song" as I sing this old song. This song was old two thousand years ago, every letter counted and fixed. Sing a new song *in* the old song, sing it new. Change not a word, not a letter, but sing it new, like the very first time. Sing it like your very first kiss. Sing it like the night we first met. Hear it for the very first time.

PI3#UW W:RAN:NUW W:ZAMMÉRU   ZAMM:RUW LAYHWH B:KHINNOR

v.5 Break out (burst forth) and rejoice and sing!
v.6 Sing to the LORD with the harp.

Break out of ritual trance and religious ways of talking. Break out of churchly formality. Lift the bowed head. Break forth in real singing. Sing with new instruments, new feelings, new attitudes, new insight. Hear yourself sing. Be surprised. Say something new today in prayer. Say something old in a new way before this day is over. The rivers are clapping their watery hands; the mountains are shouting for joy!

Break out of old ways of thinking and perceiving. I go through life in trance, seeing concepts—that is a dog; this is a pompous old man; this is my wife. And because I see in concepts I see nothing at all. I see what my brain has stored since childhood—cartoon figures of a dog, a pompous old man, a wife. I do not see *this dog* at all.

Break out of old thoughts of God. The marvelous things are real, but we tire of hearing. We have heard the words too many times. We have quoted them and read them responsively. We have heard about God till we can no longer hear. We have read about God till our eyes glaze over. How can we see again?

This is the deeper meaning to new song—the challenge of spiritual awakening. It is the challenge of wakening from trance, from living automatically. The psychiatrist Arthur Deikman[*] calls it de-automatization—learning to see things new, moment by moment. As the artist learns to see—really see—the apple on that folded cloth. Not a remembered apple, but a real apple, *this apple*. As if for the very first time.

<u>Suggestions</u>: Stand. Sing cheerfully to the Tone #a3O3:ROTH(*trumpets*). Practice seeing things new. As you go through the day, stop and look at things from different angles. Look at people you know and really see them, as an artist would see them. Look at someone you love, as if for the very first time.

---

[*]Arthur J. Deikman: Deautomatization and the Mystic Experience. *Psychiatry* 29:324-338, 1966.

Psalm 98 (BCP)

Nineteenth Day: Evening Prayer Tone: #3O3:ROTH

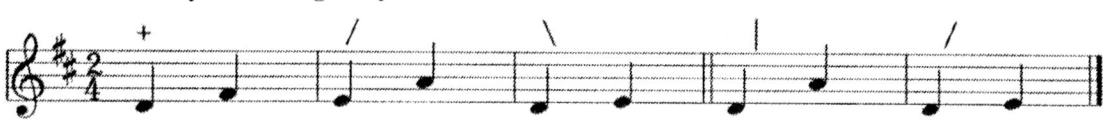

1 +Sing to the LORD a new + song,
   for he has done marvelous / things.
2 With his right hand and his holy arm
   has he won for himself the \ victory.
3 +The LORD has made known his + victory;
   his righteousness has he openly / shown
   in the sight of the \ nations.
4 He remembers his mercy and faithfulness to the house of \ Israel,
   +And all the ends of the earth have + seen
   the victory of our / God.
5 Shout with joy to the LORD, all you \ lands.
   +Lift up your voice rejoice and + sing.
6 Sing to the LORD with the / harp,
   with the harp and the voice of \ song.
7 With trumpets and the sound of the \ horn.
   +Shout with joy before the King, the + LORD.
8 Let the sea make a noise and all that is / in it,
   the lands and those who dwell there\ in.
9 +Let the rivers clap their + hands,
   and let the hills ring out with joy before the / LORD,
   when he comes to judge the \ earth.
10 **In righteousness shall he judge the | world**
   /and the peoples with / equity.

Enthroned Upon Wings: Commentary To Psalm 99

And you shall make two KRUVIM of gold ... at the two ends of the mercy seat ... and the KRUVIM shall stretch out their wings above, covering the mercy seat with their wings (Exodus 25:18-20 adapted from NKJ).

YOSHÉV KRUVIM TÁNUt HÁ.ÁRE3

v.1 He is seated between KRUVIM
let the earth begin to shake.

Seated on the heavy gold slab that was the cover of the ark were these awesome creatures, aliens from an alien world. I picture them, wings rustling ever so slightly as they wait for God's command. When he calls they will spring into flight, whisking him out of our presence, to the far corners of the universe. Perhaps this is their meaning. God comes to us loving and gracious, but he can also fly away. God will not be bound.

Compare also 18:11, "He mounted on KRUVIM and flew; he swooped on the wings of the wind," and 80:1, "(You that are) enthroned upon KRUVIM—shine forth!" It is the borderland of reality as we know it. It is beyond what Morton Kelsey calls "the box," the constricted materialism that we consider real. Strange encounters shatter abstract ideas. All theology is false. God will not be bound.

It is easy to picture God as white-bearded grandfather or sentimental Jesus. Blond, blue-eyed Jesus looking up as if in trance. Or Jesus with black, curly hair, eyes twinkling, as I used to picture him. I remember that day in church he turned to me, during communion, and gave me a thick chunk of bread. I loved that intimate moment, but I could not stay there. Images of God are openings to further surrender. I needed to encounter him there on that grassy hillside, giving bread. And I need to see him also in cosmic action—swooping on wings of creatures I cannot imagine.

v.5 He is holy! He is set apart, untouchable, unreachable. He lives in heaven, but he will never be found on any star or planet. No theologian will ever understand him completely. No preacher will ever truly explain him. And no one will ever escape from his presence. He is holy in a way that nothing on earth can be holy. No word, no idea, no picture can ever contain him. No ark encased in gold can ever hold him.

Notes: v.1, compare Exodus 25:22, and v.7 ("pillar of smoke"), Exodus 33:9.

Suggestions: Stand. Sing to the Tone SHÁRIM (*singers*), and refrains to the movement Standing Drum (see Appendix). Bow deeply from the waist on verses 5 and 9, at the words "And worship."

Let go of your images of God, pictures and word-pictures from childhood, icons from a life of searching, scholarly conceits about Jesus, the shroud of Turin. Seek his presence, now. Pray to know him and allow him to surprise you. No golden ark is needed, no winged creatures, no temple built of stones. Only silence, the listening and the willingness.

Psalm 99 (LNG)

Tone: SHÁRIM

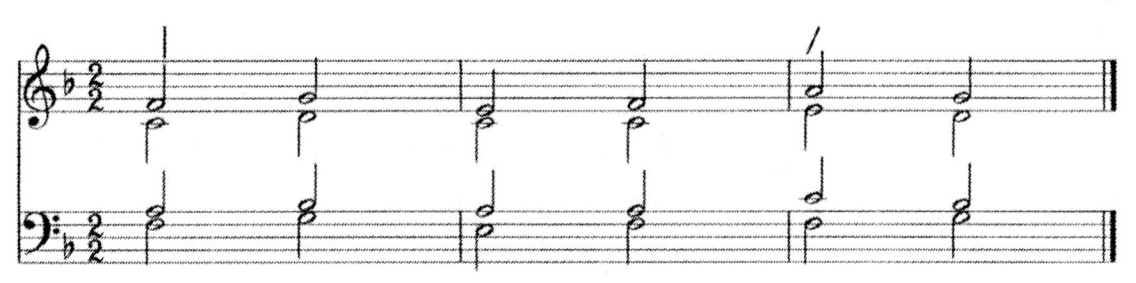

1 The LORD is King, let the peoples | tremble!
　　Seated between KRUVIM — let the earth be | shaken!
2 /The LORD in Zion is / great and high,
　　Hè is abòve all the | pèoples. `
3 Let them pràise your Nàme great and | àwesome —
　　/Hè is / hòly!

4 O Strength of the King, lover of | justice,
　　You have established what is | right;
　　/Justice and righteousness in / Jacob you have made!

5 **Exàlt the LÒRD our | Gòd, `**
　　And wòrship àt his | fòotstool; —
　　/Hè is / hòly!

6 Moses and Aaron were of his | priests,
　　And Samuel of those who | called on his Name,
　　/calling on the LORD and he / answered them!
7 In a pillar of smoke he | spoke to them;
　　they faithfully guarded his testimonies, and the decree that he | gave them.
8 O LORD our God, you have | answered them;
　　a forgiving God you have | been to them,
　　/yet punishing their / deeds.

9 **Exàlt the LÒRD our | Gòd `**
　　And wòrship at his hòly | hìll; —
　　/For the LÒRD our Gòd is / hòly!

Shout For Joy: Commentary To Psalm 100

HÁRIY"U LAYHWH KOL-HÁ.ÁRE3   "IVDUW .ETH-YHWH B:SIM#ÁH
v.1 Shout for joy to the LORD, all the earth;
serve the LORD with gladness.

The verb HÉRIa" means to cry out with a loud voice, as a war cry or shout for joy (Gesenius, p. 762). Or sounding trumpets, as for an alarm. Whatever else it may mean, this is a noisy psalm. More like Yee-hah! than *Jubilay-tee* or *Jubilah-tay*.

Imagine jumping up in church, spontaneously, shouting "Praise God! Yee-hah!" and then laughing in amazement. Such a manner of worship is as alien to most Americans as the worship of idols. Some churches may come close on occasion. Renewal music with guitars is nowhere near it. I can picture it, but not in any church I have actually attended.

Because it is totally without self-consciousness. To worship like this is to be so absorbed in God that the pastor is forgotten, the choir is forgotten, everyone else in the church is forgotten, and you can laugh until you cry. It is the kind of worship where you serve him with gladness, and actually come into his presence. You know intimately that he is God. Compare Psalm 1. It is personal and overwhelming. Yee-hah!

What would it take to pray like that? I think it would take a church where you would never feel judged. You would be appreciated precisely for yourself. It would be safe to laugh yourself silly and safe to cry. It would be safe to jump up in the air and shout "Yee-hah!" because it would also be safe to sit quietly and say nothing. And if you did, no one would question you. What is this picture? Community.* Where persons are valued for being exactly what they are. Compare 122, 133.

BO.U SH:"ÁRÁW B:THODÁH
v.3 Come in(to) his gates with thanksgiving. Come in. You are welcome here. You belong here. This is your church! No one will ask you to prove you belong in this house. No one will ask you to stand up or sit down or do anything at all. We are just glad you have come home.

Suggestions: Sing to the movement Marching Dance (see Appendix). Professor Clynes has shown that joy, like every emotion, has its characteristic form—a light, skipping or lilting shape. Experiment with the movement until you find the precise step (light and skipping) that feels joyful.

Join or form a community, if you possibly can. Look for a group that is committed to staying together, where no one will try to fix you or convert you, where differences are appreciated. Where you can be yourself, without pretense.

---

*M. Scott Peck, M.D. *The Different Drum. Community Making and Peace*. Simon and Schuster, New York, 1987.

Psalm 100 (BCP)

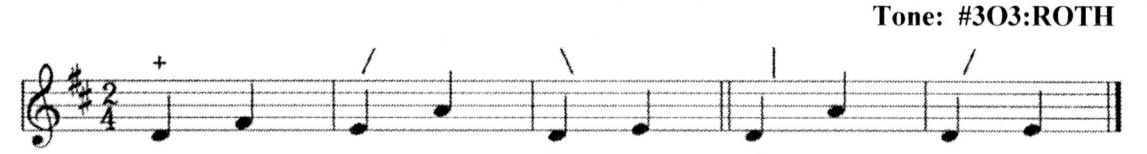

Tone: #3O3:ROTH

1 ` ` ` ` ` +Be jòyful in the LÒRD, all you + lànds; `
    sèrve the LÒRD with / glàdness `
    and còme before his prèsence with a \ sòng.`

2 +Knòw this: the LÒRD himself is + Gòd; `
    he himsèlf has made ùs, and we are / hìs; `
    wè are his pèople and the shèep of his \ pàsture. --

3 +Ènter his gàtes with thanks+gìving; `
    gò into his còurts with / pràise; `
    give thànks to him and càll upon his \ Nàme.`

4 **For the LÒRD is gòod;**
    his mèrcy is ever | làsting; —
    /and his fàithfulness endùres from age to / àge. `

Walking Simply, Again: Commentary To Psalm 101

ASKIYLÁh B:DEREKh TÁMIM   MÁTHAY TÁVOW. .ÉLÁY

v.2a   Let me study the way of integrity;
when will you come to me?

Let me study (consider, discern) the way of wholeness. Compare 15, 26, 119. It is the way of TÁMIM (*completeness*), which could be called innocent simplicity. It is the way of walking simply, all that I am, without trying to look better than I am, without hidden agendas. It is the spiritual way and it is hard. Let me but walk one step and I look for results. When will you come to me?

I walk one step in innocence and I am free, and I catch myself. Look at me! For a moment I was there, just breathing; then, "How am I doing?" (May*). It is hard to stay innocent, and it gets harder, not easier. That self-absorption grows ever more subtle, creative and tenacious. Yesterday, for a moment, I could just be; today maybe not.

When will you come to me, LORD? I will walk in innocence, LORD. I will walk in purity, avoiding all forms of evil. Let the devious heart turn away from me. Let the proud stay away from me. I'm getting so spiritual, LORD; when will you come to me?

v.2b   Let me walk with a heart of integrity
in the midst of my house.

I will begin to walk, that is, to live, with a heart of wholeness, innocent simplicity. In the innermost part of my house, where no one can see me, I will begin to simplify. I will begin to crucify, placing my self on the cross. I will let go of my importance, feelings, image, my need to be consulted on big decisions. I will try to be complete, that is whole, all that I am, good, bad and ugly. I will put away false fronts.

And I will fail. I have already failed. When will you come to me? I cannot save myself, LORD. I cannot be innocently simple for more than a few seconds. I cannot just breathe and follow you without hidden agendas. I cannot just do your will without looking for results. I cannot just belong to your people, without looking for attention. I cannot stop looking in the mirror.

I cannot be perfect as you are perfect because I keep twisting that word to mean something else—better, or the best, or beyond criticism. It is impossible for me, and yet, I keep walking. You call me onward and I follow, one step at a time. Let me study the way of integrity. Let me walk.

Suggestions: Sing to the Tone MÁ#OL (*dance*) and the movement Twirling Dance (see Appendix). Execute the movement slowly, reflectively. The second Order (\) verses may be rendered as metrical walking meditation, like 26. As you advance on the spiritual path, be ever vigilant. It becomes easier to deceive yourself, not harder. And it becomes harder to be silent, just to be there without thoughts, not easier.

---

*Gerald May: *Simply Sane. The Spirituality of Mental Health*. Crossroad, New York, 1977, p.7. Compare 37, 86.

Psalm 101 (LNG)

Tone: MÁ#OL

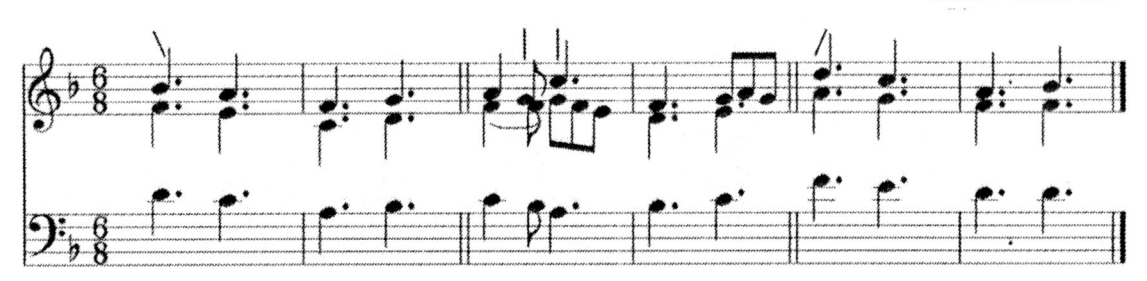

1 \Lèt me sing of mèrcy and \ jùstice; `
   lèt me sing \ pràise to you, LÒRD. `
2 **Let me study the | way of in|tegrity;**
   When will you | come to me?
   Let me walk with a | heart of in|tegrity
   in the midst of my | house.
3 \Lèt me not sèt before my èyes any \ vìle thing. ``
   Ì hate per\vèrsity; ``
   mày it not \ clìng to me. ``
4 /May the devious heart turn a/way from me;
   let me not know / evil.
5 \Thòse who slànder their frìends in \ sècret ``
   lèt me bring to \ sìlence.
   /Those with lofty looks and a / proud heart
   I cannot / bear.
6 \My èyes are on the fàithful of the \ lànd `
   to \ dwèll with mè.
   Those who walk in the | way of in|tegrity,
   let them | serve me.
7 **May there dwell in the | midst of my | house**
   no worker of de|ception.
   \Lèt not thòse who tell lìes be es\tàblished ``
   befòre my \ èyes.
8 /Every morning let me bring to / silence
   all the wicked in the / land.
   \To cut òff from the cìty of the \ LÒRD `
   àll who do \ èvil.

My Days Drift Away Like Smoke: Commentary To Psalm 102

Psalm 102 is titled "A Prayer of the afflicted, when he is overwhelmed and pours out his complaint before the LORD" (NKJ). The first part (vv. 1-11) is like a portrait of the illness called Major Depression. I am wasting away, unable to sleep or eat. I cry uncontrollably. Food is tasteless. Nothing gives pleasure. I feel rejected even by God. I try to pray, but I feel that God has "lifted me up and cast me away."

> v.8 My enemies revile me all day long,
> and those who scoff at me have taken an oath against me.

Everywhere I go they make fun of me, but worse, they are planning my demise. I will soon be on the trash heap of life. I "know" this, because anything negative is a certainty for me. What is one to learn from this dreary lament? Perhaps to empathize with someone profoundly depressed. Perhaps to accept one's own dark valleys. Seekers have walked this gloomy path before me.

Major Depression often begins with a loss or life change; surprisingly it can also start with a "high." For a very short time I'm on the mountain top, doing unusually well. I hear it from Christian patients: *I had just become spirit-filled when... I was full of the Holy Spirit. I was going from one evangelistic meeting to another when... I had never felt so good in my whole life when...* The mountain top and then the crash. One moment almost perfect, soaring; the next on the trash heap of life.

A Christian with a certain genetic predisposition is flying too high, trying too hard to be perfect, getting no rest. Then he or she stumbles, trips, things fall apart. Working out the fine points of heaven but neglecting the home. Then, the crash. The high-flying saint is grounded and cannot get up again. Our saint has more than the blues. An illness, a derangement that may have begun in thoughts, but ends in brain chemistry. The saints cannot "snap out of it," try though they might. Exhortations to have more faith only add to the sense of failure. Chemistry must be changed before they can hear you.

The black vortex goes on endlessly without exit. Dark thoughts of self overshadow all. Life is reduced to what Matilda Nordtvedt* calls a "tunnel" of repetitive thoughts. One explanation. One solution. If only I could get some sleep. If only I had never smoked that cigarette. Maybe suicide. Yes, that must be it. From within the tunnel there is no way out. Like a Moebius strip** it curves round on itself without end.

> v.12 But you, O LORD, endure for ever,
> and your Name from age to age.

Total change of perspective, turning point! The LORD is outside of time, in eternity. We leap from depression to a place outside of self. Indeed, from v.12 to v.22 there is scarcely another mention of our saint and his (or her) problems. In vv.23-24, a desperate prayer for help. And in vv. 25-28, again, that cosmic perspective.

Her depression was profound and persistent. Her husband used to console the psychiatrist, cure not expected. Week after week she came, hopeless, with suicide plan. Slowly she began to improve by imperceptible shades. Months dragged by and she smiled on rare occasions. After a year she felt good. After two years, better. Her psychiatrist asked what had helped. Her answer surprised him. "You always seemed to have hope." He could never have reached her with argument or Scripture. He never told her to have faith. He just stayed there week after week and believed she would get well. And she saw in him something—who really knows what?—outside of her darkness.

There is no easy self-help for Major Depression, but one thing seems clear. The answer is never found within the tunnel. Analyzing yourself and brooding about your failures will never lead you out. Thinking about suicide will never bring you home from depression. The answers must come from outside of self. Talk to me. Look at me! Look into my eyes and see if you can get me to laugh. Come for a walk with me. Do something, however small. Get out of bed. Brush your teeth. Make a decision to live without knowing if things will get better. Abandon suicide as an option. Help someone more depressed than you, even though you "know" you can help no one. Take this medicine, even though you "know" it can't help.

Psalm 102 speaks to my work. Treating the profoundly depressed takes infinite patience, infinite reserves of hope. It takes more than I have, something beyond me. "LORD, what do you want me to do for her today? What can I say to him?" Something outside their tunnel. Something of life. Something to remind them who they really are. Something to awaken a smile. Whatever it takes.

v.13 You will arise and have compassion on Zion ...
v.14 For your servants love her very rubble.

The image suggests a late origin for the psalm, that it was written after the fall of Jerusalem and exile. Compare 74, 79, 137. The references can also be taken in a spiritual sense. For if we take temple to mean the place of silence, listening; then Zion, the holy mountain, is the way up to that silence. Think of it as aspiration, seeking, the innate yearning to find one's higher self. When Zion is in rubble, that upward search is blocked. There is no more yearning for enlightenment. It is the dark night, when spiritual things seem pointless and prayer is impossible.

Suggestions: Continue your practice of liturgy, psalms, and silent meditation, always; no matter how bad you may feel, no matter how pointless your practice may seem. If you can do nothing but sit in your chair and say the Lord's Prayer, do that. If you can read (sing, walk) the psalms of the day, do that. If all you can do is moan and sigh without words, do that. In due time Zion will be restored. Your aspiration, seeking and hope will surely return.

---

*Matilda Nordtvedt: *Living Beyond Depression*. Bethany House, Minneapolis, 1978.
**The Moebius strip, beloved of science fiction writers, is made like this: take a narrow strip of paper or ribbon and bring the ends together to form a ring. Twist it so that the bottom of the right end meets the top of the left end. Paste or tape it together. It now has but one side, one edge, and one surface, that goes round and round forever.

Psalm 102 (BCP)

Twentieth Day: Morning Prayer Tone: N:GINOTH

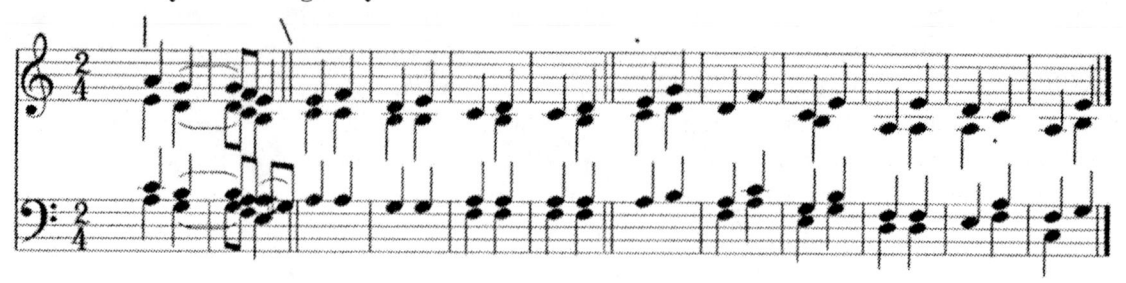

1 **LORD, hear my prayer, and let my cry come be|fore you;**
   hide not your | face from me in the day of my | trouble.
2 \Incline your \ ear to me;
   when I call, make haste to \ answer me.
3 For my days drift away like \ smoke,
   and my bones are hot as burning \ coals.
4 \My heart is smitten like grass and \ withered,
   so that I forget to \ eat my bread.
5 Because of the voice of my \ groaning
   I am but skin and \ bones.
6 \I have become like a vulture in the \ wilderness,
   like an owl among the \ ruins.
7 I lie awake and \ groan;
   I am like a sparrow, lonely on a \ house-top.
8 **My enemies revile me all day | long,**
   and those who | scoff at me have taken an | oath against me.
9 \For I have eaten ashes for \ bread
   and mingled my drink with \ weeping.
10 Because of your indignation and \ wrath
   you have lifted me up and thrown me a\way.
11 \My days pass away like a \ shadow,
   and I wither like the \ grass.
12 But you, O LORD, endure for \ ever,
   and your Name from age to \ age.
13 **You will arise and have compassion on | Zion,**
   for it is time to have | mercy upon her;
   indeed, the appointed | time has come.
14 \For your servants love her very \ rubble,
   and are moved to pity even for her \ dust.
15 The nations shall fear your \ Name, O LORD,
   and all the kings of the earth your \ glory.
16 \For the LORD will build up \ Zion,
   and his glory will ap\pear.
17 He will look with favor on the prayer of the \ homeless;
   he will not despise their \ plea.

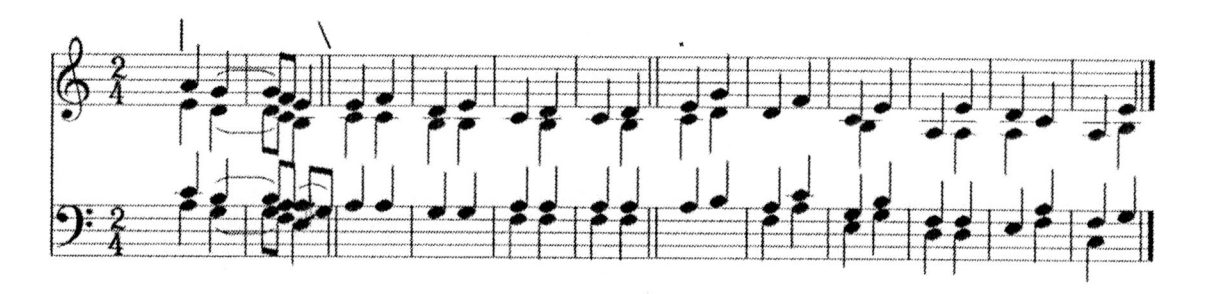

18 .Let this be written for a future gene.ration,
 so that a people yet unborn may . praise the LORD.
19 For the LORD looked down from his holy place on . high;
 from the heavens he beheld the . earth.
20 That he might hear the groan of the . captive
 and set free those condemned to . die;
21 .That they may declare in Zion the . Name of the LORD,
 and his praise in Je.rusalem;
22 When the peoples are gathered to.gether,
 and the kingdoms also, to . serve the LORD.
23 He has brought down my strength before my . time;
 he has shortened the number of my . days;
24 **And I said, "O my God,**
 do not take me away in the midst of my | days;
 your | years endure throughout all gene|rations.
25 \In the beginning, O LORD, you laid the foundations of the \ earth,
 and the heavens are the work of your \ hands.
26 They shall perish, but you will en\dure;
 \they all shall wear out like a \ garment;
 as clothing you will \ change them,
 and they shall be \ changed;
27 \But you are always the \ same,
 and your years will never \ end.
28 The children of your servants shall \ continue,
 and their offspring shall stand fast in your \ sight."

All That Is Within Me: Commentary To Psalm 103

BÁR:KHIY NAPHSHIY .ETH-YHWH   W:KHOL-QRÁVAY .ETH-SHÉM QODSHOW
v.1 Bless the LORD, O my soul,
and all that is within me, bless his holy Name.

BARÉKH (*to bless*), from a root that means knee. Blessing relates somehow to kneeling, that gesture of humility. It is in breaking down (surrender) that I am enriched, or blessed. If blessing is a gift I receive by surrendering, it is also something I give. In that process of willing surrender, I bless others, even as I am blessed. Somehow I can even bless the LORD who blesses me. It is what I call the divine economy—the one who is blessed blesses others. Compare 72 and Genesis 12:1-3.

Bless the LORD, O my soul, (my real self, my inner other, my breath, my life), and my inward parts, the nameless internal parts of me. Whatever is in me—"the good, the bad, and the ugly." Whatever it is that I would say of it, "That's just the way I am." Bless the LORD, all of me! For it is in that willing surrender that I become whole. And it is only in wholeness, completeness, that I can really bless. It is the paradoxical economy of healing. Bless, O my soul (my breath, breathing, life itself). Start now, with my very next breath. Bless, O my breath, the LORD!

v.2 And forget not all his benefits. As I bless, I am blessed, more and more, more whole, more integrated. For I have said, all that is within me, all. Surrendering even the right to select, I will bring all of me before him. I am not going to be, as Bonhoeffer said, "more spiritual than God," for it is all precious to him.* All that is within me I surrender to him, all that is within me he returns to me, puts me together.

Forget not all his benefits, the many ways in which God has blessed you, protected you; the ways in which God has been present to you in difficult situations. It is all too easy to forget these things. We live, for the most part, not in the moment, but in the emotion of the moment, in whatever cycle of thoughts we are thinking at the moment. The experiences of God are so foreign to these familiar ways of being, so completely outside our universe of thoughts, that we find it hard to hold onto them. Like those who walk in their sleep, we are constantly forgetting.

HASSOLÉa# L:KHOL-"aWONÉKHI   HÁROPHÉ. L:KHOL TA#aLU.ÁY:KHI
v.3 Who is forgiving all your sins (depravities, deliberate transgressions),
and healing all your illnesses.
Correcting all deviations from your path, and healing all internal splits and fractures. All the internal divorces and divisions, he is healing. Me against God. Me against my parents. Me against the rules. Tissue against tissue and cell against cell. All these he is knitting together. No one is blamed or condemned. Sin and sickness are repaired simultaneously.

v.4 Who is redeeming your life from the grave,
who is crowning you with mercy and loving-kindness. Redeeming your life—still talking to her, my soul, breath, breathing, life itself—from the Pit, from destruction. Compare 30.

HAMMASBIa" BAttOV "EDYÉKH   TITH#ADDÉSH KA<u>NE</u>SHER N:"U<u>RÁ</u>Y:KHI
v.5 Who is satisfying your mouth with good things,
(and) your youth is renewed like an eagle.

Not merely filling but satisfying, bringing me to that moment of enlightenment, when I can put down the spoon and sigh, "It is enough." The abundant life, where little or much is enough. Then, literally, "Your youth renews herself like an eagle"; your youth is soaring effortlessly on thermals, those columns of warm air that rise invisibly from the earth. It is life in the Spirit.

The healing of God is integration. Things that cannot live together come together. Physicians can only dream of such healing, in which nothing is destroyed, nothing killed, nothing suppressed. Where the alien cell is not cut out but reconciled. The body forgives and the cell goes back to work. Where "voices" are not drugged but heard. Where the patient is never blamed for the illness. Where no one would ever tell a patient that her illness is the result of sin.

Where the resources of cells and of nations would be so ingeniously redistributed that there would be enough, and enough to do, for everyone. Where the most intractable conflicts would become answers, like long lost pieces of a puzzle. Where the quarreling forces of my personality and of my world would work together.

BÁR:KHUW YHWH KOL-MA"aSÁW
v.22 Bless the LORD, all you works of his.

All his works, including me, including all that is within me. Healing *is* holistic, it is making things whole. True healing brings all together. Me as a whole, all parts in balance, part of a world. I cannot change myself or anything. It is in giving up trying to cure, that the doctor may become a healer.

<u>Suggestions</u>: Pray always with your whole self, all that is within you, and not with some carefully selected image or facet of yourself. With God, in the privacy of your prayer room, you may be selfish, complaining, childish, resentful, unhappy, or confused. And you will also be your better self, you at your very best. Sometimes in the very act of prayer you will experience the movement from one to the other.

Bless the LORD with your whole self, all that is within you, at all times and in all situations. Bring all that is within you into that developing relationship with God. Deepen that relationship in meditation, morning and evening, and in moments of silence as you go through the day. Allow God to heal you, knit you together, forgive you and redeem you from the grave. As you progress in the way of silence, God may call upon you to heal others. When you do, pray for each person by name, lift up the name to God. Pray not only for the cure of diseases, but for the healing of persons.

---

*Dietrich Bonhoeffer: *Meditating on the Word*, Ed. and Trans. by David McI. Gracie, Cowley, Cambridge MA, 1986, p.110.

Psalm 103 (BCP)

Tone: "ÁSOR

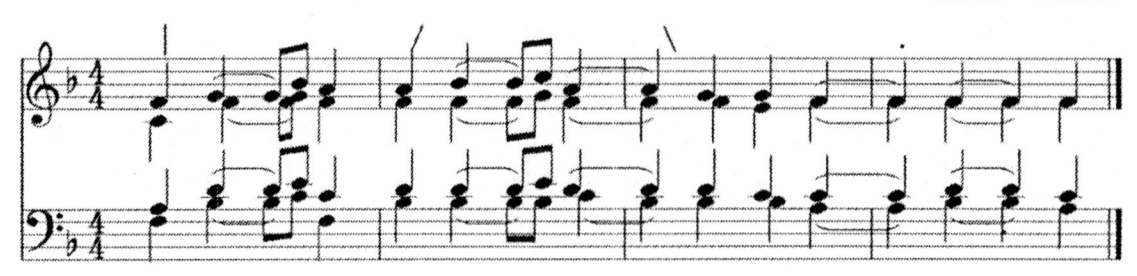

1 **Bless the LORD, O my | soul,**
   and all that is within me, | bless his holy | Name.
2 Bless the LORD, O my / soul,
   and forget not / all his / benefits.
3 \He forgives all your \ sins
   and heals all your in\firmities;
4 He redeems your life from the . grave
   and crowns you with mercy and loving.kindness.
5 He satisfies you with good . things,
   and your youth is renewed like an . eagle's.
6 **The LORD executes | righteousness**
   and judgment for | all who are op|pressed.
7 He made his ways known to / Moses
   and his / works to the children of / Israel.
8 \The LORD is full of compassion and \ mercy,
   slow to anger and of great \ kindness.
9 He will not always ac.cuse us,
   nor will he keep his anger for . ever.
10 He has not dealt with us according to our . sins,
   nor rewarded us according to our . wickedness.
11 **For as the heavens are high above the | earth,**
   so is his mercy great upon | those who | fear him.
12 As far as the east is from the / west,
   so / far has he removed our / sins from us.
13 \As a father cares for his \ children,
   so does the LORD care for those who \ fear him.
14 For he himself knows whereof we are . made;
   he remembers that we are but . dust.
15 \Our days are like the \ grass;
   we flourish like a flower of the \ field;
16 When the wind goes over it, it is . gone,
   and its place shall know it no . more.
17 **But the merciful goodness of the LORD endures for ever on**
   those who | fear him,
   and his righteousness on | children's | children;

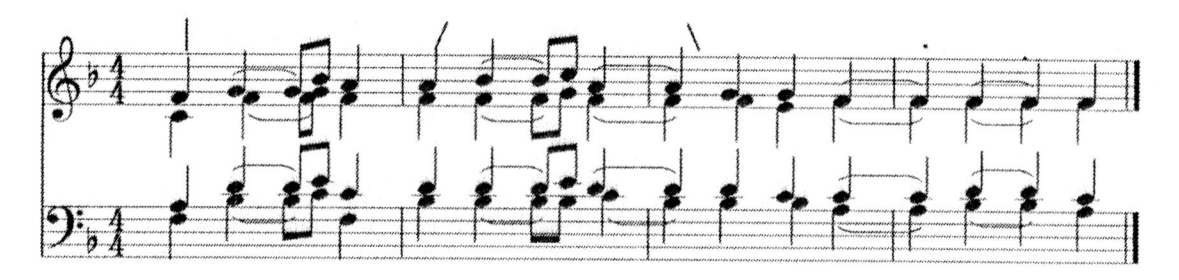

18 On those who keep his / covenant
   and re/member his commandments and / do them.
19 \The Lord has set his throne in \ heaven,
   and his kingship has dominion over \ all.
20 **Bless the Lord, you angels of his,**
   you mighty ones who do his | bidding,
   and hearken to the | voice of his | word.
21 Bless the Lord, all you his / hosts,
   you / ministers of his who do his / will.
22 \Bless the Lord, all you works of his,
   in all places of his do\minion;
   bless the Lord, O my \ soul.

Water Hymn: Commentary To Psalm 104

And darkness was on the face of the deep (Genesis 1:2, NKJ).

Water is the unifying theme of this creation hymn. As we follow the flow of water through the psalm, we follow the work of creation, the miracle of self-organizing complexity. Water ties everything together, profoundly symbolic of the Holy Spirit, the Lord, the giver of life.

    T:HOM KALL:VUSH KISSITHOW   "AL-HÁRIM YA"AMDU-MÁYiM
v.6 You covered it with the Deep as with a mantle;
the waters stood higher than the mountains.

You covered the earth with T:HOM (*the Deep*). Water was there from the beginning, in primeval chaos. We never hear when God created it. From the very first moments it was there, roiling and turbulent. From this chaotic water comes water with limits and boundaries, then water that flows in channels; from channeled water comes life. As we follow this water it becomes subtle, invisible, structured in the cells of the creatures.

The Hebrew is magnificent. Verbs with the archaic ending –UWN carry the movement along and give a tone of grandeur. Let us follow the waters from v. 7, when at your rebuke—Y:NUSUWN (*they fled*)—and from the voice of your thunder— YÉ#ÁPHÉZUWN (*they hastened away*)—and went up into the hills and down into the valleys. The boundaries set by God—BAL-YA"aVORUWN (*they shall not pass over*) and—BAL-Y:SHUVUWN (*they shall not return*) to cover the earth.

You send the springs into the valleys; between the mountains "they keep going" and they quench the thirst of the animals. In v. 13 you "water the mountains"; the creative activity reaches into fruit, flocks, wine, oil, bread. In v. 17 the water is invisible: "the trees of the LORD are full of sap"; now we follow those trees to their tops, where "the stork makes his dwelling," and look out to the rugged surroundings.

In v. 26, we see the ocean, with its innumerable creatures, where the ships continually go; and the sea-monster that you made just for fun! Water now lives in the creatures who "look to you" for food; they "gather it up" and they are "satisfied"; but when you hide your face "they are terrified," and they "breathe out their life" and die, and to dust "they return." When you send back your Spirit, "they are created," that is, restored to health. Life is water. Life flows, becomes turbulent, drains off, disperses, returns. All that appears solid is flow. No two droplets identical. Creation continues.

<u>Suggestions</u>: Sing to the Tone #ÁLIL (*flute*), beginning at v.6.

Compare 24, 29, 65, 93. Consult the Appendix for pronunciation of Hebrew words. Read "Thanksgiving over the Water" in the service of Holy Baptism, pages 306-307 in the Prayer Book. As you follow the spiritual path, seek to be like water: flow where you are needed, bring refreshment to all things and all situations.

Psalm 104 (BCP)

Twentieth Day: Evening Prayer   Tone: #ÁLIL

1 Bless the LORD, O my soul; *
 O LORD my God, how excellent is your greatness!
 you are clothed with majesty and splendor.
2 You wrap yourself with light as with a cloak *
 and spread out the heavens like a curtain.
3 You lay the beams of your chambers in the waters above; *
 you make the clouds your chariot; you ride on the wings of the wind.
4 You make the winds your messengers *
 and flames of fire your servants.
5 You have set the earth upon its foundations, *
 so that it shall never move at any time.

6 **You covered it with the Deep as with a | mantle;**
 the | waters stood higher than the | mountains.
7 At your rebuke they / fled;
 at the voice of your thunder they / hastened away.
8 \They went up into the hills and down to the \ valleys beneath,
 to the places you had ap\pointed for them.
9 You set the limits that they should not . pass;
 they shall not again cover the . earth.
10 **You send the springs into the | valleys;**
 they | flow between the | mountains.
11 All the beasts of the field drink their / fill from them,
 and the wild asses quench their / thirst.
12 \Beside them the birds of the air make their \ nests
 and sing among the \ branches.
13 **You water the mountains from your | dwelling on high;**
 the earth is fully | satisfied by the | fruit of your works.
14 You make grass grow for flocks and / herds
 and plants to serve man/kind;
15 \That they may bring forth food from the \ earth,
 and wine to gladden our \ hearts,
16 Oil to make a cheerful . countenance,
 and bread to strengthen the . heart.

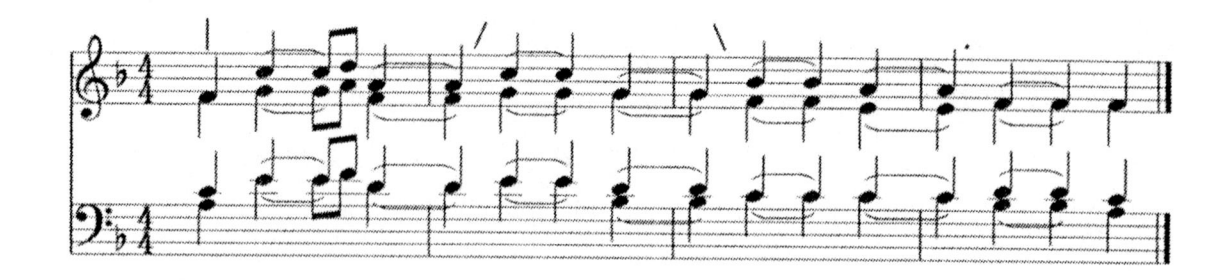

17 **The trees of the L ORD are full of | sap,**
   the cedars of | Lebanon which he | planted,
18 In which the birds build their / nests,
   and in whose tops the stork makes his / dwelling.
19 \The high hills are a refuge for the \ mountain goats,
   and the stony cliffs for the rock \ badgers.

20 You appointed the moon to mark the seasons, *
   and the sun knows the time of its setting.
21 You make darkness that it may be night, *
   in which all the beasts of the forest prowl.
22 The lions roar after their prey *
   and seek their food from God.
23 The sun rises, and they slip away *
   and lay themselves down in their dens.
24 Man goes forth to his work *
   and to his labor until the evening.

25 **O L ORD, how manifold are your | works!**
   in | wisdom you have made them | all;
   the / earth is full of your / creatures.
26 **Yonder is the great and wide | sea**
   with its living | things too many to | number,
   / creatures both small and / great.
27 \There move the ships,
   and there is that \ Leviathan
   which you have made for the \ sport of it.
28 All of them . look to you
   to give them their food in due . season.
29 +You give it to them; they + gather it;
   you open your hand, and they are filled with good + things.
30 You hide your face, and they are + terrified;
   you take away their breath, and they die and return to their ++ dust.
31 +You send forth your Spirit, and they are + created;
   and so you renew the face of the + earth.

Psalm 104 (conclusion)

32 **May the glory of the Lord endure for | ever;**
   may the Lord re|joice in all his | works.
33 He looks at the earth and it / trembles;
   he touches the mountains and they / smoke.
34 +I will sing to the Lord as long as I + live;
   I will praise my God while I have my + being.
35 May these words of mine + please him;
   I will rejoice in the ++ Lord.
36 +Let sinners be consumed out of the + earth.
   and the wicked be no + more.
37 Bless the Lord, O my + soul.
   Hallelu++jah!

Does God Have Faith? Commentary To Psalm 105

ZIKHRUW NIPHL:.OTHÁW .aSHER-"ÁSÁH

v.5   Remember the marvels he has done.

Faith, in a sense, is memory. Compare 78. Images from a lifetime of experience come together to form a picture. Stories from the centuries give that picture depth. Slowly it solidifies and becomes unshakable. We learn to remember what we cannot see. The series on faith continues in this psalm. Does God have faith?

An odd question in English, but an absurdity in Hebrew. The English word *faith* has broken off from its roots. We think of it as a kind of emotion: *If I just try real hard and have more faith, it will all work out!* We talk about *enough faith* and *more faith* as though a little more holy adrenaline would do the trick. If only we could muster a few more drops! Does God do that? Does he work himself up into believing—once again — that it just might work out? Remember that the Hebrew word .eMUNÁH means faithfulness, not an emotion but constancy. God is the One who makes a covenant for a thousand generations. His faith(fulness) is utterly reliable.

ZÁKHÁR L:"OLÁM BRITHOW

v.8   He has remembered his covenant to eternity. His constancy transcends my lifetime. His plan for me goes far beyond me. From Abraham to Isaac, from Isaac to Jacob, and from Jacob to Israel, a new identity. From Israel to Rome, from Rome to Poland, from Poland to America. And from me to my children's children, to children who will never have heard of me. My part in his plan may be small, my place in it unclear. Things I will never be told, he has remembered.

v.15 Do not touch my anointed (ones)
and do my prophets no harm.

He has followed us down through the centuries, his "anointed ones," appointed to his plan, not ours. There was no great vision for most of us, no public acclaim, no anointed feeling. Just our family, difficult at best, with all our faults. We were sent and we went. There were some really bad days along the way. Like Old Joseph rotting in jail, somewhere in Egypt. "The iron entered into his soul," says the 1928 Prayer Book, and he changed. He lost his abrasive ways and became a little more humble. He never knew the whole plan, but God remembered. Does God have faith?

Notes: Verses 1-15, compare 1 Chronicles 16:8-22. Historical references in Genesis 12, 15, 20, 26, 37, 39, 41, 46-47; and in Exodus 1, 7-10, 12-14, 16-17.

Suggestions: Sing refrains. Walk in a slow metrical way as in 26 and 78. Note the extra steps of "sojourning" in v. 23. Stand in place for the sung refrains and where so instructed.

Memorize a verse or line each day as you meditate. Reflect on your verse or line all through the day. When you find that you cannot settle down, or cannot stay awake, you may *stand* to meditate, or *walk*, in that same slow metrical way.

Psalm 105 (BCP)

Twenty-first Day: Morning Prayer Tone: KINNOR (2)

1 **Give thanks to the L<small>ORD</small> and call upon his | Name;**
   make known his deeds among the | peoples.
                              [Walk]
2 Sìng to him, sing pràises to hìm, `
   and spèak of all his màrvelous wòrks. `
3 **/Glory in his holy / Name;**
   let the hearts of those who seek the L<small>ORD</small> / rejoice.
4 Sèarch for the L<small>ORD</small> and his strèngth; `
   continually sèek his fàce. `
5 Remèmber the màrvels he has dòne, `
   his wònders and the jùdgments of his mòuth. `
6 O òffspring of Àbraham his sèrvant, `
   O chìldren of Jàcob his chòsen. `
7 Hè is the L<small>ORD</small> our Gòd; `
   his jùdgments prevàil in all the wòrld. `
8 **He has always been mindful of his | covenant,**
   the promise he made for a thousand gene | rations:
9 The còvenant he màde with Àbraham, `
   the òath that he swòre to Ìsaac. `
10 **/Which he established as a statute for / Jacob,**
   an everlasting covenant for / Israel,
11 Saying, "To yòu will I gìve the land of Cànaan `
   to bè your allòtted inhèritance." `
12 Whèn they were fèw in nùmber, `
   of little accòunt, and sojòurners in the lànd, `
13 Wàndering from nàtion to nàtion `
   and fròm one kìngdom to anòther, `
14 He lèt nò one opprèss them `
   and rebùked kìngs for their sàke, `
15 Sàying, "Do not tòuch my anòinted `
   and dò my pròphets no hàrm. `
16 Then he càlled for a fàmine in the lànd `
   and destròyed the supply of brèad. `
                              [Stand]
17 **He sent a man be | fore them,**
   Joseph who was sold as a | slave.

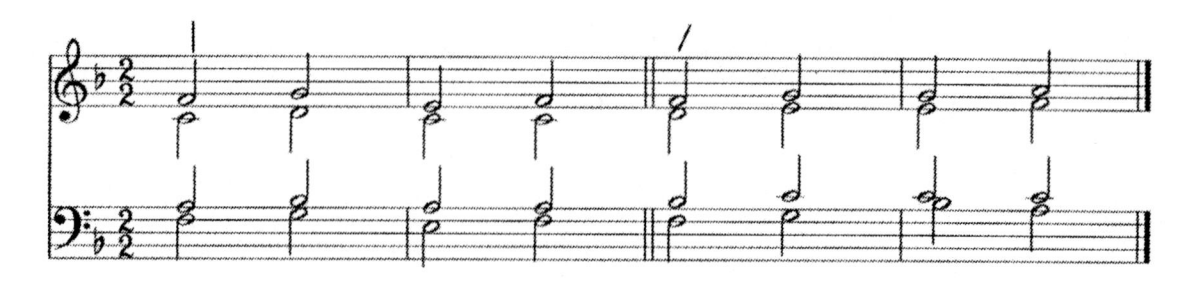

18 They bruised his feet in fetters; *
    his neck they put in an iron collar.
19 Until his prediction came to pass, *
    the word of the LORD tested him.
20 **/The king sent and re/leased him;**
    the ruler of the peoples set him / free.
21 He set him as a master over his household, *
    as a ruler over all his possessions.
22 To instruct his princes according to his will *
    and to teach his elders wisdom.

Part II

[Walk]

23 Ìsrael càme into Ègypt, `
    and Jàcob becàme a sojòurner `` in the lànd of Hàm. `
24 The LORD made his pèople excèedingly frùitful; `
    he màde them strònger than their ènemies; `
25 Whose heart he tùrned, so that they hàted his pèople, `
    and dèalt unjùstly with his sèrvants. `
26 **He sent Moses his | servant,**
    and Aaron whom he had | chosen.
27 They wòrked his sìgns amòng them, `
    and pòrtents in the lànd of Hàm. `

[Stand]

28 **He sent darkness, and it grew | dark;**
    but the Egyptians rebelled against his | words.
29 He turned their waters into blood *
    and caused their fish to die.
30 Their land was overrun by frogs, *
    in the very chambers of their kings.
31 **He spoke, and there came swarms of | insects**
    and gnats within all their | borders.
32 He gave them hailstones instead of rain, *
    and flames of fire throughout their land.
33 He blasted their vines and their fig trees *
    and shattered every tree in their country.

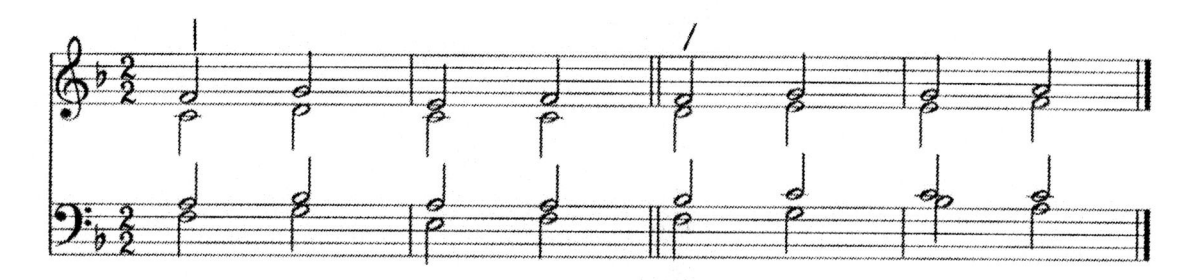

34 **He spoke, and the locust | came,**
   and young locusts without | number,
35 Which ate up all the green plants in their land *
   and devoured the fruit of their soil.
36 He struck down the firstborn of their land, *
   the firstfruits of all their strength.
37 **He led out his people with silver and | gold;**
   in all their tribes there was not one that | stumbled.

[Walk]

38 Ègypt was glàd of their gòing, `
   becàuse they were afràid of thèm. `
39 He sprèad out a clòud for a còvering `
   and a fìre to give lìght in the night sèason. `
40 They àsked, and quàils appèared, `
   and he sàtisfied them with brèad from hèaven. `
41 He òpened the ròck, and water flòwed, `
   so the rìver ràn in dry plàces. `
42 For God remèmbered his hòly wòrd `
   and Àbraham ` his sèrvant. `

[Stand]

43 **/So he led forth his people with / gladness,**
   his chosen with shouts of / joy.
44 He gave his people the lands of the nations, *
   and they took the fruit of others' toil
45 That they might keep his statutes *
   and observe his laws.
   Hallelujah!

But They Soon Forgot: Commentary To Psalm 106

#ÁtÁ.NU "IM-.aVOTHEYNU   HE"eWINU HIRSHÁ"NU
v.6 We have sinned as our forebears did;
we have done wrong and dealt wickedly.

The series on faith continues. Formative events of Israel's history are reviewed—not the familiar Bible stories of my childhood, but events that may seem obscure. For this is not history as trivia or patriotism, but as penitence. We study it to understand that we are not getting any better. We are the same sinners as our parents.

The heart of the psalm (for me) is found in the following sequence: "They did not consider ... nor remember ... but he saved them ... then they believed his words ... but they soon forgot." The sequence is repeated over and over, as we (yes, we) descend into depravity. We were not spiritually naive. We had had personal experiences with God. But we did not consider nor remember. And he saved us anyway—more evidence — and for a short time we believed, we sang his praises. But we soon forgot.

We kept forgetting. We were constantly distracted, restless, unwilling to take direction, complaining. We were bright, but undisciplined. We were dominated by thoughts and emotions. We developed cravings that nothing could satisfy. We knew all the answers even as our lives were in shambles. This is my own story as well. I have experienced communication with God; he has helped me. Yet I remember only till the next crisis. Can he solve this one? At times it seems I can hardly remember from one day to the next. I could tell you what "the LORD told me," but I quickly forget.

Psalm 106 is about faith. Remember that faith in Hebrew is not an emotional state or enthusiasm. *Faith* and *faithfulness* are the same word [.eMUNÁH] and closely related to the words for *truth* and *to believe*. All refer to steadiness or constancy. Loyalty. In intimate relationships, what psychiatrists call object constancy, my ability to appreciate you whether or not you are meeting my needs at the moment.

While we often think of faith as ignorant belief, or "blind faith," Scripture describes it as enlightened constancy. You have an experience with God and you are directed to follow a certain path. Such direction is not lightly taken. You don't just hear the word *Saskatoon* one day, quit your job, leave Oklahoma and move to Canada. God's messages are subtle and gentle, paced to what you are able and willing to receive. When you receive them, you test them against Scripture, against common sense, and against the wisdom of your church community.

Once you are convinced that the directions are from God, you know they are reliable, and you follow them reliably. You keep going where God has sent you, even though you receive no further encouragement. Outward circumstances may seem to go against you. It may be months or years before you receive further word, but you hold steady. That is faith. Not the evidence of things never seen, but rather the evidence of things not seen at the moment. When I decide to travel on U.S. 1, I look for the sign "U.S. 1." But once I have found it, I don't need constant reassurance. As long I stay on the road, I trust it is still U.S. 1.

This is what the people of Israel (read "our community") were lacking, in Psalm 106. They were excited when they saw miracles, but they quickly forgot when things became difficult. It was the same way in Jesus' day. People were filled with enthusiasm when they saw a miracle, but soon they were asking for another sign. That is why he chastised them for their lack of faith — not because they lacked religious enthusiasm, but because they lacked constancy. They were wonderful religious people until the next thought carried them away.

Faith is not something whipped up or stirred up by charismatic preachers. It is a discipline that can be developed. It is the quality of unchanging steadfastness. In practice it may appear plodding, like inspired stubbornness. How is it acquired? Not by jumping up and following every spiritual hunch. It is developed like any other form of discipline, by practice. We hear, we listen, we do, and we keep doing, even though there is no outward encouragement.

Jesus said that if we had only as much faith as a mustard seed we could perform miracles (Matthew 17:20). How much faith, then, does a mustard seed have? If we think of it as a bit of religious enthusiasm, then the saying is puzzling. The mustard seed is tiny, and we feel that we have plenty of faith. But think of it this way: the mustard seed is faithful enough to produce the mustard plant, reliably, in perfect detail, every single time. It needs no encouragement, only water and light. No miracles are needed to refresh its faith. If we were only that faithful, we could do anything.

Notes: For historical references see Exodus 32; Numbers 11, 16, 19, 20, 25. (*) = translation modified by the author.

Suggestions: Read in a steady, deliberate pace, and sing the refrains.

Develop a rule of life, a regular rhythm of work, rest, sleep, meals and meditation. Keep these things as constant as you can. Remember, though, that constancy, a discipline of the heart, is more important than a rigid procedure. Practice your meditation in a way that does not call attention to you or cause inconvenience to others. If circumstances make it difficult to meditate in your usual way, do whatever you can. If nothing else, observe some moments of silence and direct your attention to God.

Continue your spiritual practice year after year, with or without encouragement. At times it will be your greatest delight and pleasure; at other times it will be tedious and dry. Continue faithfully and you will grow in faith.

Psalm 106 (BCP)

Twenty-first Day: Evening Prayer **Tone: HIGÁYON (2)**

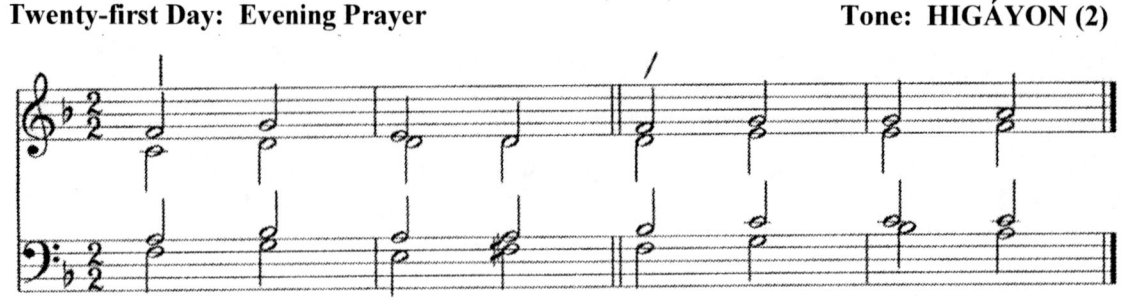

1 Hallelujah!
    Give thanks to the LORD, for he is good, *
    for his mercy endures for ever.
2 /Who can declare the mighty acts of the / LORD
    or show forth all his / praise?
3 Happy are those who act with justice *
    and always do what is right!
4 Remember me, O LORD, with the favor you have for your people, *
    and visit me with your saving help;
5 That I may see the prosperity of your elect
    and be glad with the gladness of your people, *
    that I may glory with your inheritance.
6 We have sinned as our forebears did; *
    we have done wrong and dealt wickedly.
7 In Egypt they did not consider your marvelous works,
    nor remember the abundance of your love; *
    they defied the Most High at the Red Sea.
8 But he saved them for his Name's sake, *
    to make his power known.
9 He rebuked the Red Sea, and it dried up, *
    and he led them through the deep as through a desert.
10 He saved them from the hand of those who hated them *
    and redeemed them from the hand of the enemy.
11 The waters covered their oppressors; *
    not one of them was left.
12 /Then they believed his / words
    and sang him songs of / praise.
13 But they soon forgot his deeds *
    and did not wait for his counsel.
14 A craving seized them in the wilderness, *
    and they put God to the test in the desert.
15 He gave them what they asked, *
    but sent leanness into their soul.

16 They envied Moses in the camp, *
   and Aaron, the holy one of the LORD.
17 The earth opened and swallowed Dathan *
   and covered the company of Abiram.
18 Fire blazed up against their company, *
   and flames devoured the wicked.

Part II

19 Israel made a bull-calf at Horeb *
   and worshiped a molten image.
20 And so they exchanged their Glory *
   for the image of an ox that feeds on grass.
21 They forgot God their Savior, *
   who had done great things in Egypt,
22 Wonderful deeds in the land of Ham, *
   and fearful things at the Red Sea.
23 So he would have destroyed them,
   had not Moses his chosen stood before him in the breach, *
   to turn away his wrath from consuming them.
24 They refused the pleasant land *
   and would not believe his promise.
25 They grumbled in their tents *
   and would not listen to the voice of the LORD.
26 So he lifted his hand against them, *
   to overthrow them in the wilderness,
27 **To cast out their seed among the | peoples, (*)**
   and to scatter them throughout the | lands.
28 They joined themselves to Baal-Peor *
   and ate sacrifices offered to the dead.
29 They provoked him to anger with their actions, *
   and a plague broke out among them.
30 Then Phinehas stood up and interceded, *
   and the plague came to an end.
31 This was reckoned to him as righteousness *
   throughout all generations for ever.
32 Again they provoked his anger at the waters of Meribah, *
   so that he punished Moses because of them;
33 For they so embittered his spirit *
   that he spoke rash words with his lips.

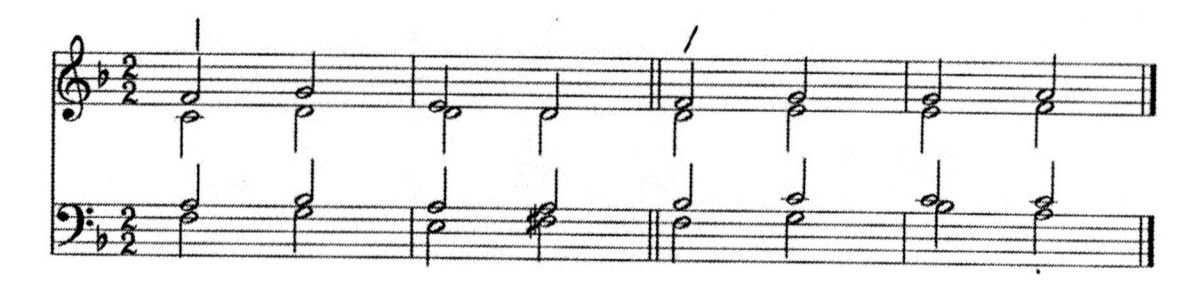

34 They did not destroy the peoples *
    as the LORD had commanded them.
35 **They intermingled with the | peoples** (*)
    and learned their pagan | ways,
36 So that they worshiped their idols, *
    which became a snare to them.
37 They sacrificed their sons *
    and their daughters to evil spirits.
38 They shed innocent blood,
    the blood of their sons and daughters, *
    which they offered to the idols of Canaan,
    and the land was defiled with blood.
39 Thus they were polluted by their actions *
    and went whoring in their evil deeds.
40 Therefore the wrath of the LORD was kindled against his people *
    and he abhorred his inheritance.
41 **He gave them over to the hand of the | peoples,** (*)
    and those who hated them ruled | over them.
42 Their enemies oppressed them, *
    and they were humbled under their hand.
43 Many a time did he deliver them,
    but they rebelled through their own devices, *
    and were brought down in their iniquity.
44 Nevertheless, he saw their distress, *
    when he heard their lamentation.
45 He remembered his covenant with them *
    and relented in accordance with his great mercy.
46 He caused them to be pitied *
    by those who held them captive.
47 Save us, O LORD our God,
    and gather us from among the peoples, * (*)
    that we may give thanks to your holy Name
    and glory in your praise.
48 **/Blessed be the LORD, the God of Israel,**
    from everlasting and to ever/lasting;
    and let all the people say, "Amen!"
  Hallelu/jah!

Book Five

In Desert Wastes: Commentary To Psalm 107

Four groups of people wander and struggle through various ordeals. The problems sound familiar to a psychiatrist. There are confusion and alienation, depression, rebellion, addiction, eating disorder, mood swings, alcoholism. The subjects are lost and helpless. All find themselves in self-inflicted misery from which they cannot get free. Who are they? Ourselves, of course.

No matter how hard they struggle, they cannot extricate themselves. Not by effort or intellect, by will power, by therapy, by consulting experts; certainly not by spiritual magic. They cry out helplessly, and God rescues them. They experience grace. And what are they to do in response? "Let them thank the LORD for his love ... Let them offer a sacrifice of thanks." Do they ever figure it out? No, for it is a mystery and God does not explain himself.

I believe that most recovery from mental disorders is like that. The medications I prescribe do help some, the therapeutic relationship gives encouragement and acceptance, but mostly patients recover by means of grace. They reach a point where they know they don't have the answers, they know they have lost the game, and they are ready to surrender control. They are well past responding to suggestions with *Anything but that*.

> WAYI3"aQUW .EL-YHWH BA33AR LÁHEM   MIMM:3UQOTHEYHEM YA33ILÉM
> v.6 Then they cried to the LORD in their trouble
> and he delivered them from their distress.

The patients (travelers, wanderers, exiles) in Psalm 107 do not pray to God in any conventional way. They begin to cry to him like helpless children in the midst of their stress. That is, in their 3AR (*straits*), the narrow and confining places where they find themselves. And immediately, from their troubles he "begins to rescue them ... begins to save them ... begins to bring them out." A slightly different Hebrew word in each refrain creates the four variations.

Ups and downs, exile and return. I find no support here for a dualistic or prosperity theology, a world view in which only health and wealth come from God. God will or must respond to our requests if we present them in the proper form. All the unpleasant things—illness, suffering, poverty—come from the *other* God—Satan. In its extreme form this theology puts man in a controlling position between the two cosmic Powers. Then religion becomes a chess game of manipulating God and challenging Satan; reminding God of his promises; rebuking and admonishing Satan.

Psalm 107 makes it clear that there is only one God, who is responsible for the downs as well as the ups. The LORD is the one who "rescued them from their distress" and the one who "crushed their spirit with toil." The LORD who "stilled the storm to a whisper" is also the LORD who "summoned the gale." He "changes deserts into streams" and "streams into a desert." This is a complex and difficult God!

This God, the real God, is in control of everything. He is there in the prisons and in the trackless wastes, just as he is in the straight path, the healing, the calm, and the good harbor. How do I respond to such a God? I learn to accept his grace, to give up control, to turn my will over to him, to offer the sacrifice of thanksgiving.

I accept the truth that life is cyclical. I oscillate between joy and despair, success and failure. I cannot go from one high to a higher high. It is good to praise the LORD, but I cannot by praising achieve permanent euphoria. I may wish to lose weight, but I will not achieve heaven by getting thinner and thinner. God is also in the valleys. The downfalls are as important as the mountaintops. If I refuse to accept this truth, if I think I know better, I soon find myself in the trackless wastes, in darkness and deep gloom.

KI-HIS<u>BI</u>a" <u>NE</u>PHESh SHOQÉQÁH   W:<u>NE</u>PHESh R:"ÉVÁH MILLÉ.-tOV
v.9 For he satisfies the thirsty soul,
and fills the hungry soul with good things.

He satisfies, as in 103, the soul (breath, breathing, life) which is running about in search of—who knows what? He brings that yearning life to the experience of *enough*. And the hungry soul (breath, breathing, life) he fills with good. My restless, driven life he brings to balance, to peace.

YODUW LAYHWH #ASDOW
v.15 Let them give thanks to the LORD for his love.

Let them continue to give thanks to the LORD for his devoted love. The healing was miraculous, but the real healing is a process. It begins with thanksgiving, with learning to affirm and be grateful, no matter what. The real and continuing healing is freedom from circumstance. There will be ups and downs, terrible downs, but they will continue to give thanks.

v.43 Whoever is wise will ponder these things. Go back to verse 1 and start over. Study these verses again and again. Recall that Jesus read this psalm as a young man, lived it in the desert (Matthew 4:1-2), and left his signature on it in v. 29.

<u>Suggestions</u>: Sing refrains. In group study, as always, let each member read a verse in turn, but sing the refrains in unison.

On the four groups and four directions, compare 115, 118. The number four in Scripture is symbolic of creation, the created world or things. Think of it here as the world of thoughts and emotions, a good world but a limited one. They *and you* cannot find the way out by thinking or reasoning. Sometimes, the only escape is to step out of that world completely for a moment and cry out helplessly. Follow this teaching in your own hopeless situations. Cry to God helplessly; give thanks to God for his mercy. Practice moments of silence and allow God to guide you.

Psalm 107 (BCP)

Twenty-second Day: Morning Prayer Tone: **KINNOR**

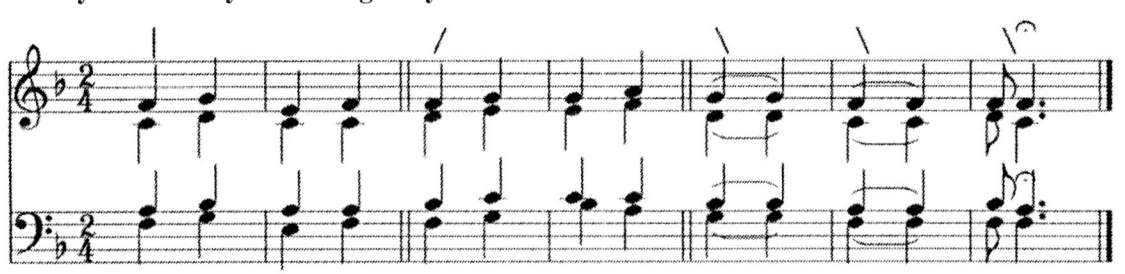

1 Give thanks to the LORD, for he is good, *
 and his mercy endures for ever.
2 Let all those whom the LORD has redeemed proclaim *
 that he redeemed them from the hand of the foe.
3 He gathered them out of the lands; *
 from the east and from the west,
 from the north and from the south.
4 Some wandered in desert wastes; *
 they found no way to a city where they might dwell.
5 They were hungry and thirsty; *
 their spirits languished within them.
6 **Then they cried to the LORD in their | trouble,**
 and he delivered them from their dis | tress.
7 He put their feet on a straight | path
 to go to a city where they might | dwell.
8 / Let them give thanks to the LORD for his / mercy
 and the wonders he does for his / children.
9 For he satisfies the thirsty *
 and fills the hungry with good things.
10 Some sat in darkness and deep gloom, *
 bound fast in misery and iron;
11 Because they rebelled against the words of God *
 and despised the counsel of the Most High.
12 So he humbled their spirits with hard labor; *
 they stumbled, and there was none to help.
13 **Then they cried to the LORD in their | trouble,**
 and he delivered them from their dis | tress.
14 He led them out of darkness and deep | gloom
 and broke their bonds a | sunder.
15 / Let them give thanks to the LORD for his / mercy
 and the wonders he does for his / children.
16 For he shatters the doors of bronze *
 and breaks in two the iron bars.
17 Some were fools and took to rebellious ways; *
 they were afflicted because of their sins.

18 They abhorred all manner of food *
   and drew near to death's door.
19 **Then they cried to the Lord in their | trouble,**
   and he delivered them from their dis | tress.
20 He sent forth his word and | healed them
   and saved them from the | grave.
21 / Let them give thanks to the Lord for his / mercy
   and the wonders he does for his / children.

22 \ Let them offer a sacrifice of thanksgiving
   \ and tell of his acts
   with shouts of \ joy.

23 Some went down to the sea in ships *
   and plied their trade in deep waters;
24 They beheld the words of the Lord *
   and his wonders in the deep.
25 Then he spoke, and a stormy wind arose, *
   which tossed high the waves of the sea.
26 They mounted up to the heavens and fell back to the depths; *
   their hearts melted because of their peril.
27 They reeled and staggered like drunkards *
   and were at their wits' end.

28 **Then they cried to the Lord in their | trouble,**
   and he delivered them from their dis | tress.
29 / He stilled the storm to a / whisper
   and quieted the waves of the / sea.
30 **Then were they glad because of the | calm,**
   and he brought them to the harbor they were | bound for.
31 / Let them give thanks to the Lord for his / mercy
   and the wonders he does for his / children.

32 \ Let them exalt him in the congregation of the people
   \ and praise him
   in the council of the \ elders.

Part II

33 The Lord changed rivers into deserts, *
    and water-springs into thirsty ground,
34 A fruitful land into salt flats, *
    because of the wickedness of those who dwell there.
35 He changed deserts into pools of water *
    and dry land into water-springs.
36 He settled the hungry there, *
    and they founded a city to dwell in.
37 They sowed fields, and planted vineyards, *
    and brought in a fruitful harvest.
38 He blessed them, so that they increased greatly; *
    he did not let their herds decrease.
39 Yet when they were diminished and brought low, *
    through stress of adversity and sorrow,
40 (He pours contempt on princes *
    and makes them wander in trackless wastes)
41 He lifted up the poor out of misery *
    and multiplied their families like flocks of sheep.
42 The upright will see this and rejoice, *
    but all wickedness will shut its mouth.

43 Whoever is wise will ponder these things, *
    and consider well the mercies of the Lord.

Wake Up, Lute And Harp: Commentary To Psalm 108

The Hebrew differs slightly from 57:7-11, the Prayer Book version is identical. It is a song of progressive elevation—of mood, energy, hope, and alertness. It is the positive transformation of consciousness.

      NÁKHON LIBBIY .eLOHIM   .ÁSHIRÁh WA.aZAMM:RÁH .APH-K:VODIY

v.1 My heart (attitude) is firm (sure, prepared); I begin to sing and praise; even my glory—my highest self—me at my very best.

      "URÁh HANNEVEL W:KHINNOR   .Á"IRÁh SHÁ#AR

v.2 Wake up, lute and harp: I begin to wake up the dawn (or, at dawn). In these few short phrases, a cascade of awakenings. The NÉVEL and KINNOR might be taken as musical instruments, or as states of consciousness, moods, or faculties. One by one I call upon my inner potentials to wake up. And the greatest single awakening is the awakening to affirmation—praise or gratitude.

v.3 I will give thanks to you among the peoples, O LORD. I lose myself in the praise of God, "for your love (or mercy) is greater than even the heavens; and your faithfulness (constancy, reliability) is as high as the clouds." My attention rises up and out of my self, my inner world. It is the way of praise, the transforming path, and the highest form of prayer.

There are different strategies of personal growth and spiritual development. One approach is to sit quietly, keep calm, think of green meadows, let a mantra roll over and over in my thoughts, or tell myself passively, "I am... relaxed." Compare 27. This is what happens in hypnosis or self-hypnosis. Attention is narrowly focused on a thought or image and I go "deeper and deeper relaxed." These methods are not necessarily bad, but they are not as powerful as they appear. They are all based upon thoughts, the power of a thought—*calm* or *relaxed* or *green meadows*—to lead me in a certain direction. And so it will, until another thought comes along, or a wave of emotion takes me in some other direction.

The other path is to get "wider and wider awake"; to give up my own personal agendas and listen to God; to listen silently and let him direct me; to become aware of others and their otherness. Their needs may not be my needs, their feelings may surprise me. I become aware of the complexity of things and of how little I really control. I become aware of my sin and my helplessness. Of my own instability and of his constancy. I become aware of goodness and I learn to praise. And as I begin to praise God I become wider and wider awake.

Suggestions: Stand. Sing the refrains as marked. Giving yourself suggestions—*cheer up -- calm down—relax—green meadows*—is a waste of time. In your practice of meditation, lift your attention to God. Praise God and thank him. Clear your thoughts, all thoughts, and be silent in his presence, as often and as long as you can.

Psalm 108 (BCP)

Twenty-second Day: Evening Prayer　　　　　　　　　　　　　　　　　　Tone: GITTITH

1 My heart is firmly fixed, O God, my heart is fixed; *
    I will sing and make melody.
2 Wake up, my spirit;
    awake, lute and harp; *
    I myself will waken the dawn.
3 **I will confess you among the | peoples, O LORD;**
    I will sing praises to you among the | nations.
4 \For your loving-kindness is greater than the \ heavens,
    and your faithfulness reaches to the \ clouds.
5 **Exalt yourself above the | heavens, O God,**
    and your glory over all the | earth.
6 \So that those who are dear to you may be de\livered,
    save with your right hand and \ answer me.
7 God spoke from his holy place and said, *
    "I will exult and parcel out Shechem;
    I will divide the valley of Succoth.
8 Gilead is mine and Manasseh is mine; *
    Ephraim is my helmet and Judah my scepter.
9 Moab is my washbasin,
    on Edom I throw down my sandal to claim it, *
    and over Philistia will I shout in triumph."
10 Who will lead me into the strong city? *
    who will bring me into Edom?
11 **Have you not cast us | off, O God?**
    you no longer go out, O God, with our | armies?
12 \Grant us your help against the \ enemy,
    for vain is the help of \ man.
13 /With God we will do valiant / deeds,
    /and he shall tread our enemies under / foot.

The Trial: Commentary To Psalm 109

This is a difficult psalm for many Christians. It is all too easily dismissed as "Old Testament." The difficulty relates to a superficial understanding of verses like Matthew 5:44 --
But I say to you, love your enemies, bless those who curse you, do good to those
 who hate you, and pray for those who spitefully use you and persecute you (NKJ).

Christians who have heard these verses since childhood may attempt to live them by a sort of "be nice" approach to life. They convince themselves they have no negative feelings toward others, or project them (as psychiatrists like to say) onto some other person or group. The Pharisees. *They* were vengeful, merciless, and didn't know about forgiveness. They believed in "an eye for an eye and a tooth for a tooth." *Their* God was a God of vengeance, the Old Testament God. *Our* God is a God of love and forgiveness, the New Testament God. Compare 137, 139.

As a psychiatrist I have seen where such thinking can lead: a person who is seething with hostility and crippled with resentment. Who is isolated because all the relatives and friends have been alienated. Who piously denies hurt feelings and repeats blandly, "I have forgiven everyone. I love everyone." That is what I heard Scott Peck (borrowing I'm sure from Bonhoeffer) call "cheap forgiveness," meaningless, because there has been no acknowledgement of the offense, no trial, no penalty, and no repentance.

Yet I must admit that, even though I was not raised in such a tradition, I still find this a difficult Scripture. For a long time I would only read verses 1-4 and 20-30, skipping over the middle section; it was too full of self-righteous hatred even for me. Then one day these words lit up for me:

YA"AN .aSHER LO.-ZÁKHÁR "aSOTH #ÁSED
v.15 Because he did not remember to show mercy.

Could that be me? Suddenly I am no longer the prosecutor in this trial, but the defendant. They are saying those terrible things about me; and they might be true. I was feeling so puffed up and self-righteous. I was saying those cutting things about my persecutors that I had been rehearsing for years. It felt good at first; I was sure that

v.3 Despite my love they accuse me;
but as for me, I pray for them (literally *I am prayer*).

Then to my horror I am on trial myself, forced to listen to things I never wanted to hear. They are telling me how thoughtless, uncaring, and cruel I really am. I can't run away from it because I have just said those cruel things. I just finished saying that his children should be orphans and his wife a widow. His whole family should be consigned to Skid Row! I am condemned out of my own mouth. I, I am the one who repays evil for good and hatred for love. With the beautiful ambiguity of Hebrew dialogue, subject and object keep switching. It is a surreal trial in a dream-like court, where accuser and accused keep changing places; the lawyers also change sides; the Judge is absolutely impartial.

v.3b   but I am prayer.

When I became a Christian I found it easy to pray for my enemies. It was a wonderful new toy, like spiritual voodoo. See how spiritual I am, I even pray for—*him*. Yes, LORD, bless him and bring him around, bless her—and show her how to treat me. Later I came to realize how difficult it is to recognize true enemies, acknowledge how badly they hurt me, and then to pray for them and really mean it.

Then I can say, "LORD, I praise you and thank you that you have made him (or her) exactly the way you did. I don't understand why he (or she) dislikes me so intensely, and I don't like it one bit. But nevertheless, LORD, I praise you and thank you. I lift up my enemy to you, to bless him and keep him, shine your light upon her, give them their heart's desire. I don't know what you are trying to teach me here but I know that you are in control. I know you are bringing something good out of this." That is a hard prayer, but a prayer that truly sets me free.

Undoing projection is a life-long task of personal growth. Acknowledging that what I hate in others is what I hate in myself. The enemy is not you but myself. The enemy is here, my shadow side.

<u>Suggestions</u>: Here is a beautiful way to make use of these "enemy" psalms. Read as though speaking to *them*, the enemies; then read again as though listening to them. Notice the difference. How much easier it is when they are the enemy, not me. In group study, let some of the members be *us* and others *them* as everyone takes turns reading. Look for projection, that psychological trick of finding your worst characteristics in the other person. Look for it in yourself, and whenever you find it, let it go.

Be aware of righteous indignation, that most deceptive of all inner states. What they are doing is outrageous, inexcusable, yes. Look more deeply and you may find they are doing it for you! They are acting out your deepest impulses and your most secret fantasies. When you find yourself righteously indignant, outraged at some person or group, look for the evil in yourself. And when you find it, let it go.

Read vv. 5-19 in a low whisper.

Psalm 109 (BCP)

Tone: N:GINOTH

1 \Hold not your tongue, O God of my \ praise;
   for the mouth of the \ wicked,
   the mouth of the deceitful, is opened a\gainst me.
2 \They speak to me with a lying \ tongue;
   they encompass me with hateful \ words
   and fight against me without a \ cause.
3 \Despite my love they ac\cuse me;
   but as for me, I \ pray for them.
4 They repay evil for \ good
   and hatred for my \ love.
              [Read softly]
5 Set a wicked man against him, *
   and let an accuser stand at his right hand.
6 When he is judged, let him be found guilty, *
   and let his appeal be in vain.
7 Let his days be few, *
   and let another take his office.
8 Let his children be fatherless, *
   and his wife become a widow.
9 Let his children be waifs and beggars; *
   let them be driven from the ruins of their homes.
10 Let the creditor seize everything he has; *
   let strangers plunder his gains.
11 Let there be no one to show him kindness, *
   and none to pity his fatherless children.
12 Let his descendants be destroyed, *
   and his name be blotted out in the next generation.
13 Let the wickedness of his fathers be remembered before the LORD, *
   and his mother's sin not be blotted out;
14 Let their sin be always before the LORD; *
   but let him root out their names from the earth;
15 Because he did not remember to show mercy, *
   but persecuted the poor and needy
   and sought to kill the brokenhearted.

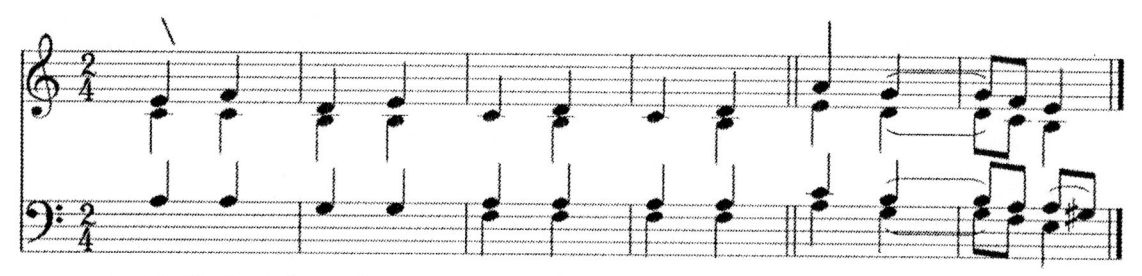

16 He loved cursing;
    let it come upon him; *
    he took no delight in blessing,
    let it depart from him.
17 He put on cursing like a garment, *
    let it soak into his body like water
    and into his bones like oil;
18 Let it be to him like the cloak which he wraps around himself, *
    and like the belt that he wears continually.
19 Let this be the recompense from the LORD to my accusers, *
    and to those who speak evil against me.

[Sing]

20 **But you, O LORD my God,**
    oh, deal with me according to your | Name;
    for your | tender mercy's sake, de | liver me.
21 \For I am poor and \ needy,
    and my heart is wounded with\ in me.
22 I have faded away like a shadow when it \ lengthens;
    I am shaken off like a \ locust.
23 \My knees are weak through \ fasting,
    and my flesh is wasted and \ gaunt.
24 I have become a re\proach to them;
    they see and shake their \ heads.
25 **Help me, O LORD my | God;**
    | save me for your | mercy's sake.
26 \Let them know that this is your \ hand,
    that you, O LORD, have \ done it.
27 \They may curse, but you will \ bless;
    let those who rise up against me be put to \ shame,
    and your servant will re\joice.
28 **Let my accusers be clothed with dis | grace**
    and | wrap themselves in their shame as in a | cloak.
29 \I will give great thanks to the LORD with my \ mouth;
    in the midst of the multitude will I \ praise him;
30 Because he stands at the right hand of the \ needy,
    to save his life from those who would con\demn him.

The LORD Said To "My Lord": Commentary To Psalm 110

N:.UM YHWH LA.DONIY

v.1 The oracle of YHWH to my Lord.

Psalm 110 is called in Hebrew N:.UM (*oracle*), that is, a mysterious divine revelation. As a window into mystery an oracle has no fixed or final meaning. It is a channel for God to communicate with me. One day Rabbi Jesus was teaching this psalm to his students (Mark 12:35-36, NKJ): "How is it that the scribes say that the Christ is the Son of David? For David himself said by the Holy Spirit... "

David, centuries before, had written by the Holy Spirit, "The oracle of YHWH to my Lord." Jesus, teaching by the Holy Spirit, explained that the mysterious "my Lord" referred to himself as Messiah or Anointed One: one anointed, commissioned for some great work.

I like to think of it this way: God himself has spoken to someone I call "my Lord." In this little song of delight, I am absolutely delighted with "Someone." I am saying to this Someone, "I am so happy to be your follower, I believe in you, I will follow you anywhere!" In this lyrical rhyming poem, I am saying to the one I call my Lord, "I will obey you without question. I will follow you into any danger. I commit myself to you and everything you stand for; You are worthy to sit at the right hand of God." I am singing about a relationship with a Lord.

In a world where leadership is rare enough, "Lordship" is almost unheard of. We yearn for it and search for it without finding it. Not in the *Guru* from India or Pastor Wonderful or Great Evangelist. Leaders betray us and wise men do foolish things, yet followers continue to follow. We see them through an image of a Lord. And though they always disappoint we continue to yearn. It is our deepest wish, to surrender ourselves to a Lord—to one who is absolutely faithful, unshakable, totally without self-interest, holy.

No human breathing can fulfill this wish. There is only One who can. To the early Christians this was unquestionably a song about Jesus. To others, this beautiful psalm may have other meanings. Please respect them. An oracle has no fixed or final meaning. It is a window, a channel. Read this beautiful poem for yourself. Who is that Someone for you? Who is the one you call, "my Lord"?

Notes: Psalm 110 is more extensively quoted and reinterpreted in the New Testament than any other. Verse 1, see for example Matthew 22:41-46, Mark 12:35-37, Acts 2:33-36 and Hebrews 1:13; Verse 4, see Hebrews 4:14 to 7:28.

Suggestions: Sing in an easy flowing manner. Recognize in yourself that need to make someone your "Lord." Respect pastors, teachers, and scholars; listen to them, but do not make them Lords. Learn to read the oracles of God as oracles, windows to God's wisdom. You do not know the whole truth of the Scriptures and neither does any human breathing. Study in the fear of God and respect the interpretations of others.

Psalm 110 (BCP)

Twenty-third Day: Morning Prayer Tone: #a3O3:ROTH

1 +The LORD said to my + Lord,
   "Sit at my right / hand,
      until I make your enemies your \ footstool."
2 +The LORD will send the + scepter
   of your power out of / Zion,
      saying "Rule over your enemies round \ about you.
3 +Princely state has been yours from the day of your + birth;
   in the beauty of holiness have I be/gotten you,
      like dew from the womb of the \ morning."
4 +The LORD has sworn and he will not re+cant;
   "You are a priest for / ever
      after the order of Mel\chizedek."
5 +The Lord who is at your right + hand
   will smite kings in the day of his / wrath;
      he will rule over the \ nations.
6 He will heap high the corpses;
      he will smash heads over the wide \ earth.

7 **He will drink from the brook beside the | road;**
   /therefore he will lift high his / head.

On And On To Eternity: Commentary To Psalm 111

v.1 I will give thanks to the LORD with my whole heart. Compare 9. I will begin and continue to lift up my hands toward God in the gesture of thanks and praise. And I will do this openly, in the presence of the whole congregation. As I begin and continue to do this, my consciousness is transformed, from fragmented thoughts and feelings to continuity and meaning.

W:3IDQÁTHOW "OMEDETh LÁ"AD

v.3 and his righteousness is standing for ever. The word LÁ"AD comes from a root that means to pass over or go on (Gesenius, p. 605), hence passing, progress, duration, and perpetuity. His righteousness stands continuing, it is going on and on. As long as time endures, his praise goes on.

YIZKOR L:"OLÁM BRITHOW

v.5 He keeps remembering his covenant for ever.

The word "OLÁM (*eternity*) derives from a root that means hidden or unseen. The hidden or invisible realm where he lives and reigns. Where his covenant is established. More than a very long time. Outside yet interpenetrating our world, it is his timeless world, his kingdom. In vv.7-8 we learn that "all his commandments are sure (faithful), they stand fast (upheld, supported) for ever, for eternity." In v. 9 "He has commanded his covenant for ever," and in v.10, "His praise is standing for ever."

As children we love to hear about forever, forever and ever, and happily ever after. Eternity sounds grand. There is something romantic about always and forever. As we grow older these terms have a different cast. Time moves faster for us. We experience the fragmentation of life. We are torn, pulled in different directions by the demands of this world. We question whether life has meaning.

I do not understand eternity. I am a creature of time, driven by thoughts and emotions. I have had glimpses of eternity—on that road in eastern Oklahoma on a rainy day, where a car had spun out of control and a mother and her young sons lay suddenly still. When—rarely—I can be silent. When I have awakened in the night to realize I am already awake, just breathing quietly without thoughts. When I visit my parents in the cemetery and see the adults of my childhood lying under stones. I feel the cold breath of eternity and I shudder. I do not understand eternity.

Yet I know that in relationship to God I am part of that invisible realm. In his word, precepts, teaching, eternity breaks through into this world. His covenant, grounded in that other world, is faithful and constant. I understand only this: an unseen reality upholds me, forever.

Suggestions: Sing this beautiful alphabetic psalm, and the next one, to the short version of *Alphabet*. Practice the teaching of the psalms and praise God continually, with your whole heart. Be thankful and grateful, remembering his faithful goodness with your whole heart, and you will begin to have glimpses of eternity.

Psalm 111 (BCP)

Tone: *Alphabet*

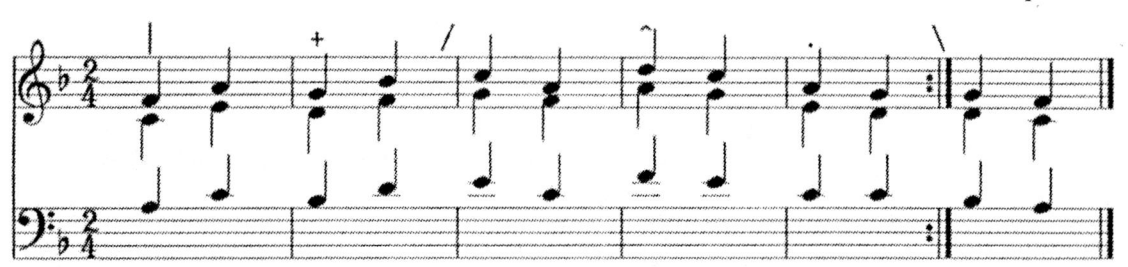

1 Hallelujah!
   I will give thanks to the LORD with my whole | heart,
   in the assembly of the upright, in the + congregation.
2 Great are the deeds of the / LORD!
   they are studied by all who ^ delight in them.
3 His work is full of majesty and . splendor,
   and his righteousness endures for | ever.
4 He makes his marvelous works to be + remembered;
   the LORD is gracious and full of / compassion.
5 He gives food to those who ^ fear him;
   he is ever mindful of his . covenant.
6 \He has shown his people the power of his \ works
   in giving them the lands of the | nations.
7 The works of his hands are faithfulness and + justice;
   all his commandments are / sure.
8 They stand fast for ever and ^ ever,
   because they are done in truth and . equity.
9 **He sent redemption to his | people;**
   he commanded his covenant for + ever;
   holy and awesome is his / Name.
10 The fear of the LORD is the beginning of ^ wisdom;
   those who act accordingly have a good . understanding;
   \his praise endures for \ ever.

Fearing, He Will Not Be Afraid: Commentary To Psalm 112

.ASHREY-.IYSH YÁRÉ. .ETH-YHWH   B:MI3WOTHÁW #ÁPHÉ3 M:.OD
v.1 Happy (is) a man fearing the LORD,
in his commandments delighting very much.

MISSH:MU"ÁH RÁ"ÁH LO. YIYRÁ.   NÁKHON LIBBOW BÁtUa# BAYHWH
v.7 He will not be afraid of any bad news;
his heart established, trusting in the LORD.

He does not continue to be afraid of bad news, because his heart is established (firm, steady, prepared). Fearing the LORD, he will no longer be afraid of the bad news. He hears the bad news daily and hourly, in the newspaper, in his office, on the radio driving home, and from his family when he arrives at home. Yet he knows that this news may change within the hour. He knows it is not truth. It arises from the hearts of men, where thought leads to thought, rumor to rumor, reaction to reaction.

Fearing God, I know where I stand. Fearing God, I do not ask *What if...* ? Whatever it may be, I will know it when I know it, when I need to know it. I already know where my life is coming from. He breathes into me this breath I take, now. I know he may take it from me, now. I know that I can do nothing to secure my life or to increase his favor. He loves me as he loves me because he loves me. His choice and pleasure, not mine. Fearing the LORD, I need not be afraid.

Two kinds of fear. *To fear* is cognitive; it is to see and understand the dangers. Even to see what others choose not to see. To fear is unemotional and clear; there is no doubt as to its object. *To be afraid* is emotional. It is to be flooded with adrenaline, even when the danger is trivial, or the object unknown. To be afraid or scared is passive; to fear is a choice, and may be wisdom.

v.8 His heart supported (sustained, upheld), he will not continue to be afraid.

The fear which is not an emotion has been called the beginning of wisdom (see 111:10). Real happiness is to fear this wise fear and not be afraid. When I truly assimilate this teaching, I will not react to every rumor nor panic at every headline in the newspaper. I will be supported and sustained. I will fully understand the dangers that surround me, but I will not panic. I will not waste my days worrying.

Like Psalm 1 this one begins with the word .ASHREY (*happy* or *blessed*) and ends with TO.VÉD (*shall perish*). Real happiness is to fear the LORD wisely. As for the wicked, those who keep the world in confusion, their plans are already doomed.

<u>Suggestions</u>: Sing, like 111, to the short version of *Alphabet*. Practice the fear of the LORD — that awareness of helpless dependence on God, of having no real control. Enjoy each breath as it comes. Do not be afraid of bad news or upsetting rumors. Do not make a practice of asking, *What if...* ?

Psalm 112 (BCP)

1 Hallelujah!
 Happy are they who fear the | Lord
 and have great delight in his com+mandments!
2 Their descendants will be mighty in the / land;
 the generation of the upright will be ^ blessed.
3 Wealth and riches will be in their . house,
 and their righteousness will last for | ever.
4 Light shines in the darkness for the + upright;
 the righteous are merciful and full of com/passion.
5 It is good for them to be generous in ^ lending
 and to manage their affairs with . justice.
6 \For they will never be \ shaken.
 The righteous will be kept in everlasting re|membrance.
7 They will not be afraid of any evil + rumors;
 their heart is right;
 they put their trust in the / Lord.
8 Their heart is established and will not ^ shrink
 until they see their desire upon their . enemies.
9 **They have given freely to the | poor,**
 and their righteousness stands fast for + ever;
 they will hold up their head with / honor.
10 The wicked will see it and be ^ angry;
 they will gnash their teeth and pine . away;
 \the desires of the wicked will \ perish.

Passover Wine: Commentary To Psalm 113

Psalms 113-118 are called in Hebrew *Hallel* (Praise Songs), or Egyptian *Hallel* (Praise Songs of Egypt). They are sung at *seder*, the fellowship meal of Passover. It is the symbolic re-living of the spiritual journey. It is our family story, our passage from slavery to freedom, re-created with traditional symbols: the breaking of unleavened bread, symbolic of new life; the drinking of wine to signify renewal and refreshment. So Rabbi Jesus broke and drank with his friends, on the last night of his life, his actions memorialized in every communion service. So every Jewish father breaks and drinks, telling our family story and singing this song:

v.5 Who is like YHWH our God who exalts himself to reign, who lowers himself to see, in the heavens and on the earth? From the exalted place where he really reigns; from somewhere outside of creation, beyond time and space, he comes down. Down to heaven! And from heaven he comes down to earth, lowering himself progressively, scaling back his terrible energy fields to a level that will not destroy us.

v.6 He raises up from the dust the weak (or sick; Compare 30)
and from the ash-heaps he lifts up the poor. He lowers himself down to our level, down to the dust-heaps and trash-heaps, to the hospital bed where the sick one is lying, and he begins to lift him (or her) up.

v.7 To return (restore) him (to sit) with the leaders,
with the leaders of his people. He does not shower down money on the poor, or drugs on the sick, but he lowers himself into their poverty and their illness, and he restores them to social acceptance. Entering into their sad estate, he leads them out to freedom, self-respect. He gives them new life. They are sitting with the community leaders.

MOSHIVIY "aQERETh HABBAYITh .ÉM HABBÁNIM SMÉ#ÁH
v.8 Returning (restoring) the barren woman of the house,
(to be) a mother of children, happy.
The barren woman—from a root that means something damaged and rendered useless (Gesenius, p. 650). This woman who feels useless because she cannot bear children, he turns completely around. He transforms her, correcting the biological defect; more important, he transforms her heart: she is "happy."

Note: The second *Hallelujah* is sometimes assigned to Psalm 114.

Suggestions: Stand. Sing to the movement Reverential Praise (see Appendix). The music for 113 and 114 is the same. Attend a *seder* if you can. Read *Rediscovering Passover* (see 136) and the *New Union Haggadah* (Central Conference of American Rabbis, New York, 1974, 1975).
As helper or healer, humble yourself. Enter into the suffering of the sufferer without judging or giving advice. Let the sufferer teach you and change you.

Psalm 113 (BCP)

Tone: SHOPHÁR

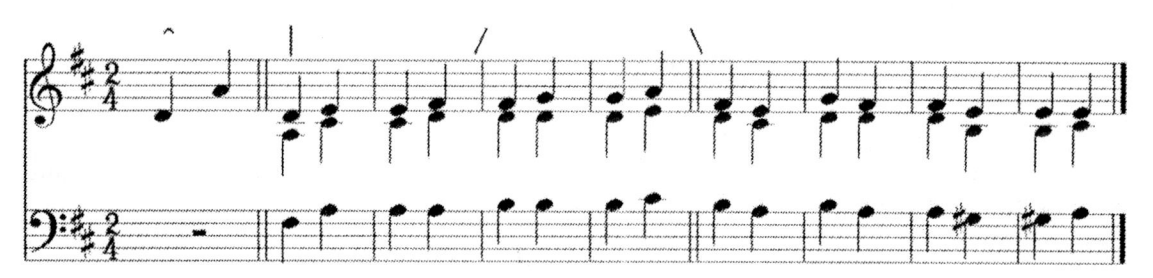

1 ^Hallelu^jah!
   Give praise, you servants of the | LORD;
   praise the Name of the | LORD.
2 /Let the Name of the LORD be / blessed,
   from this time forth for / evermore.
3 **From the rising of the sun to its | going down**
   let the Name of the LORD be | praised.
4 /The LORD is high above all / nations,
   and his glory above the / heavens.
5 \Who is like the LORD our God, who sits enthroned on \ high,
   but stoops to behold the heavens and the \ earth?
6 He takes up the weak out of the \ dust
   and lifts up the poor from the \ ashes.
7 **He sets them with the | princes,**
   with the princes of his | people.
8 /He makes the woman of a childless / house
   to be a joyful mother of / children.
^Hallelu^jah! (*)

When Our Family Broke Free: Commentary To Psalm 114

B:3É.TH YISRÁ.ÉL MIMMI3RÁYiM   BEYTH YA"aQOV MÉ"AM LO"ÉZ
v.1 At the going forth of Israel (our community) from Egypt,
the house of Jacob (our family) from a people of alien speech.

When our little group went forth out of Egypt ("house of slaves"), when our family broke free from those who speak a barbaric foreign language, it was an event that would change the whole world. You would never have read it in the papers, but the ocean knew it, the river knew it, the mountains and the hills knew it. The entire world order was excited, when our family broke free out of Egypt.

From Egypt, the house of slaves, my family broke free. From the comfortable complaining of slavery, good food, meat, garlics and leeks, guaranteed job, structured time, few big decisions. From security and all that was familiar, from the bondage of all the things they owned. From the ultimate excuse for failure, "We are just slaves." Complaining and worrying every step of the way, my family broke free.

From Russia and Poland, in horse-drawn wagons hiding under straw, then huddled together in ships, my family broke free. From familiar villages and familiar troubles, my family broke free. My family and thousands of families, changing the world.

v.1 from a people speaking jargon.

From Egypt, a state of mind, a state of bondage. In Scripture one always goes *down* into Egypt, for it symbolizes spiritual darkness. It is the state of enslavement—to needs, impulses, expectations of others, rewards that never satisfy, the illusion of security. It is the state of speaking jargon—words like *excellence* and *quality* and *cost-effectiveness; freedom of choice* and *freedom of speech; the right to life* and *the right to die*. A slogan for every situation, but no communication.

When a human breathing breaks forth out of Egypt, it is such a wonderful, transforming event, that the sea rolls back, the river turns and runs upstream, the mountains and hills jump around like frolicking lambs. When I break forth out of Egypt, even for a moment, all is changed. When I transcend a "need" or an impulse, when I act unselfishly because I really want to, when I give something away that I would have enjoyed, when I stop complaining and help someone else stop complaining. When I think about an issue deeply, and say what no one wants to hear. When I do these things I am changed. It is like finding Christ living within me. It is me at my very best.

<u>Suggestions</u>: Stand. Sing to the movement Reverential Praise (see Appendix). The music is the same as for 113.

In your practice of meditation you are learning to break free from thoughts. Old thoughts that have kept you in chains; new thoughts that would enslave you anew. Now continue to practice moments of silence; let go of thoughts old and new, the jargon of Egypt and the jargon of New York City. Jargon of *gurus* and of preachers. Listen to God and he will set you free.

Psalm 114 (BCP)

Twenty-Third Day: Evening Prayer

1 ^Hallelu^jah! (*)
   When Israel came out of | Egypt,
   the house of Jacob from a people of strange | speech,
2 /Judah became God's / sanctuary
   and Israel his do/minion.
3 **The sea beheld it and | fled;**
   Jordan turned and went | back.
4 /The mountains skipped like / rams,
   and the little hills like young / sheep.
5 \What ailed you, O sea, that you \ fled?
   O Jordan, that you turned \ back?
6 You mountains, that you skipped like \ rams?
   you little hills like young \ sheep?
7 **Tremble, O earth, at the presence of the | Lord,**
   at the presence of the God of | Jacob,
8 /Who turned the hard rock into a pool of / water
   and flint-stone into a / flowing spring.

Their Idols: Commentary To Psalm 115

"a3ABBEYHEM <u>KE</u>SEPh W:ZÁHÁV MA"aSEH Y:DEY .ÁDÁM

v.4 Their idols are silver and gold,

the work of human hands. I have often heard idolatry taken as a metaphor for attachment, the fascination with things such as clothes, cars, money or power. I have to remind myself that idolatry was a form of worship. Carved images of human-like beings and animals were actually worshiped. That was as normal for those times as praying with the Prayer Book for ours. The worship of images, objects or animals was serious religion. More importantly, it was different. Not just another way of seeking God. Idolatry is absolutely alien to biblical religion.

It was powerful and fascinating. People believed in it. Idols were made with great artistry, bought, sold, cared for, treasured. The believers knew that these carved figures could neither move nor talk. They believed that their idols gave access to spiritual forces. Through worship of the idols, man could control and manipulate those forces to gain power over others. See Feuer, pp. 1377-1379.

Idolatry has not been the common religion for centuries, and so it is unfamiliar to us. We get a sense of it in the occult. It is the age-old dream of control—the ability to determine the outcome of events and the behavior of others. The Great Fantasy. Now it appears in the form of New Age teaching, fascination with ESP, the paranormal, supernatural powers. *Secrets known to the few, but I can reveal them to you.* And when I do you will have power! Some of it is inspired nonsense, some may be true. Unfortunately the power comes with a price: enslavement to the forces of darkness.

The Hebrew Bible makes it clear that there is only one God. The real God does not give power to us; he is himself power. The other gods are deceptive and illusory; their apparent power is based on lies and confusion. We cannot control the real God, we can only surrender to him and trust him. Hebrew religion demands that we choose. We can worship God or false gods, but not both.

The choice may not be obvious. Idolatry is fascinating and promises so much. God is demanding, he wants total commitment. God is invisible, hard to grasp, hard to find when we need him. And yet, we are told, God created heaven and earth; he is in total control; whatever he wills to do, he does. God remembers us, cares for us, blesses us. Everything belongs to him. The dead in their shadowy world cannot praise him, but we who fear him, in some unexplainable way, are part of eternity. Think about the choice: Have you committed yourself to the one real God? How did you decide?

<u>Notes</u>: This psalm is sometimes considered a continuation of 114. Verse 4 ("their idols"), compare 135:15-18. On the four-fold "He will bless" (vv. 12-13), compare 107, 118.

<u>Suggestions</u>: Stand. Sing to the movement Standing Drum (see Appendix). In your spiritual search, take care to avoid magic, especially religious magic. Do not ask for special gifts or powers. Be especially careful in worship, that you worship only God.

Psalm 115 (BCP)

Tone: #a3O3:ROTH

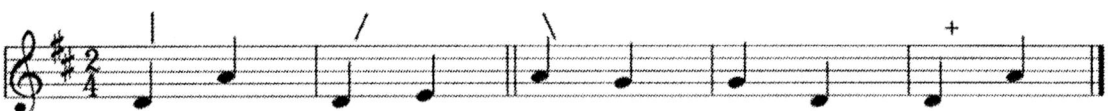

1 ` ` ` ` **Not to ùs, O LÒRD, not to | ùs,** `
   but to your Nàme give | glòry; `
   /becàuse of your lòve and becàuse of your / faìthfulnèss. `

2 **Why` should the hèathen | sày,** `
   /"Where thèn is their / Gòd?" `

3 Òur Gòd is in | hèaven; `
   /whatèver he wills to dò he / dòes. `

4 \Their idols are silver and \ gold,
   the work of human \ hands.

5 They have mouths, but they cannot + speak;
   \eyes have they, but they cannot \ see;

6 They have ears, but they cannot \ hear;
   noses, but they cannot + smell;

7 **They have hànds, but they cànnot | fèel;** `
   fèet, but they cànnot | wàlk; `
   /they màke no sòund with their / thròat. `

8 Thòse who màke them are | lìke them, `
   /and so are àll who pùt their / trùst ìn thèm.

9 \O Israel, trust in the \ LORD;
   he is their help and their \ shield.

10 O house of Aaron, trust in the + LORD;
   \he is their help and their \ shield.

11 You who fear the LORD, trust in the \ LORD;
   he is their help and their + shield.

12 **The LÒRD has been mìndful of ùs, and he will | blèss us;** `
   he will blèss the hòuse of | Ìsrael; `
   /he will blèss the hòuse of / Àaron; `

13 **He will blèss those who fèar the | LÒRD,** `
   /both smàll and grèat to/gèther.

14 \May the LORD increase you more and \ more,
   you and your children \ after you.

15 May you be blessed by the + LORD,
   the maker of heaven and \ earth.

16 The heaven of heavens is the \ LORD's,
   but he entrusted the earth to its + peoples.

17 **The dèad do not pràise the | LÒRD,** `
   /nor all thòse who go dòwn into / sìlence; `

18 **But wè will blèss the | LÒRD,** `
   /from thìs time fòrth for / èvermore.
   Hàllelù/jàh!

And Call Upon The Name: Commentary To Psalm 116

Over a three year period we meditated this psalm many times in group therapy at Christian Hill.* Each time I came away with new insights. It is a therapeutic journey, from despair to victory. It begins with an unusual statement of faith: I love how the LORD keeps listening *or* always listens. It is somewhat different from *the LORD always answers prayer*. He is listening. He leans his ear, bends over to hear me. Meanwhile I am in despair. The cords of death entangled me; the grip of the grave took hold of me.

ЗÁRÁH W:YÁGON .EM3Á.   UV:SHÉM-YHWH .EQRÁ.

v.2-3   I keep finding grief and sorrow; and I begin to call upon the Name of the LORD. Each time I find grief and sorrow; each time I will call upon the LORD. The process of healing takes place in little leaps—small, decisive changes of direction. I begin to call. I struggle no more with those cords, but I cry out to him. Then healing begins, but is not final, for I continue to struggle and relapse.

SHUVIY NAPHSHIY LIM:NU#ÁY:KHI   KI-YHWH GÁMAL "ÁLÁY:KHI

v.6   Turn again to your rest, O my soul (breath, breathing, life). I talk to my soul, my inner Other. "Return to your rest, my inner self, my breathing, for the LORD has treated us well." I had worked myself up into a fierce tantrum; then as I spoke gently to my self, my breathing began to settle down: He really has treated me well. I feel my irritation beginning to subside.

v.9   I believed even when I was saying, "I have been brought very low," or, "I am very depressed." To believe, in Hebrew, does not mean to think, but to be committed. As when a person says, "I believe in you." I had already made my commitment to you, LORD, yet I was still talking about how bad I felt. And in my haste I even said, "No one can be trusted" (Everyone lies). I am embarrassed at this now, but at the time it seemed all too true. In the depths of my depression, I saw through dark glasses.

Another therapeutic leap is found in v. 10. "How shall I repay the LORD for all the good things he has done for me?" The answer marks my decisive turn toward recovery:

KOS-Y:SHU"OTH .ESSÁ.   UV:SHÉM YHWH .EQRÁ.

v.11   I will lift up the cup of salvation
and call upon the Name of the LORD.

The cup of victories. The biblical metaphor of lifting a cup signifies receiving or acceptance. I begin to receive the victories and not reject them. I take them joyfully, lifting them up into the vertical—the spiritual—dimension, like the cup at Eucharist. I receive and I learn to be grateful. I receive because he chooses to give to me, and I begin to call upon the Name of the LORD.

v.12b   Let it be, please, in the presence of all his people. That is, the fulfilling of my vows to the LORD. Let me commit myself in public. Telling my community makes it real. My conversion is solid and my healing complete when I begin to share them with others.

L:KHÁ-.EZBA# ZEVA# TODÁH   UV:SHÉM YHWH .EQRÁ.

v.15 I will offer you a sacrifice of thanksgiving
and call upon the Name of the LORD.

My sacrifice is thanksgiving itself. Eucharist. Gratitude. Compare 34. Sometimes it is the most difficult sacrifice of all. The Hebrew concept of sacrifice does not imply self-deprivation; but sometimes I don't want to say thank you. I would rather brood and complain! The sacrifice of thanksgiving is an act of affirmation that brings me into communion with God. Let it be, please, in the presence of all his people. In the courts of the LORD's house, in Jerusalem, holy community. Healing completed. And I continue to call upon the Name.

The journey is not over. It is cyclical. I will go through these passages over and over again: from the "cords of death" to "grief and sorrow" to "brought very low" to walking "in the presence of the LORD," to lifting up "the cup of salvation." The spiritual path is very much like that. I face the same problems, and make the same astonishing discoveries, over and over. I do not achieve a final state of enlightenment, at least not in this lifetime. I will gladly keep walking, but I will never have arrived. I accept this, more or less, for myself. I am learning to accept it for others.

Suggestions: Sing refrains with the hand movements for KINNOR (see Appendix). At v.11 ("I will lift up the cup") and v. 15 ("I will offer you the sacrifice"), the right hand, slightly cupped, may rest upon the left, as when receiving communion. The wave gesture for thank offerings may be combined with the hand movements if desired. Beginning with the praise gesture, lift and lower the arms on "I will lift up the cup" and "I will offer the sacrifice." Move them gracefully leftward and rightward on "and call upon the Name," ending in the original position. For a discussion of the sacrifice of thanksgiving, see Edersheim.**

Practice the sacrifice of thanksgiving at every opportunity. Receive gifts, favors and compliments with simple gratitude. Do not make speeches about your unworthiness, but practice true humility, that is, gracious receiving.

---

*Christian Hill was an institution where medicine and prayer were practiced in complete integration. Although it is now closed, the vision lives on. See also 62, 119.
**Alfred Edersheim: *The Temple, Its Ministry and Services*. Updated Edition. Hendrickson Publishers, Peabody, MA, 1995.

Psalm 116 (BCP)

Twenty-fourth Day: Morning Prayer Tone: KINNOR

1 I love the LORD, because he has heard the voice of my supplication, *
 because he has inclined his ear to me whenever I called upon him.
2 The cords of death entangled me; the grip of the grave took hold of me; *
 I came to grief and | sorrow.
3 Then I called upon the Name of the | LORD:
 "O LORD, I pray you, save my life."
4 Gracious is the LORD and righteous; *
 our God is full of compassion.
5 The LORD watches over the innocent; *
 I was brought very low, and he helped me.
6 Turn again to your rest, O my soul, *
 for the LORD has treated you well.
7 For you have rescued my life from death, *
 my eyes from tears, and my feet from stumbling.
8 I will walk in the presence of the LORD *
 in the land of the living.
9 I believed, even when I said, "I have been brought very low." *
 In my distress I said, "No one can be trusted."
10 How shall I repay the LORD *
 for all the good things he has done for me?
11 **I will lift up the cup of sal | vation**
 and call upon the Name of the | LORD.
12 /I will fulfill my vows to the / LORD
 in the presence of all his / people.
13 Precious in the sight of the LORD *
 is the death of his servants.
14 O LORD, I am your servant; *
 I am your servant and the child of your handmaid;
 you have freed me from my bonds.
15 **I will offer you the sacrifice of thanks | giving**
 and call upon the Name of the | LORD.
16 /I will fulfill my vows to the / LORD
 in the presence of all his / people.
17 \In the courts of the LORD's house,
 \in the midst of you, O Jerusalem.
 Hallelu\jah!

Psalm 117 (BCP)

Tone: SHOPHÁR

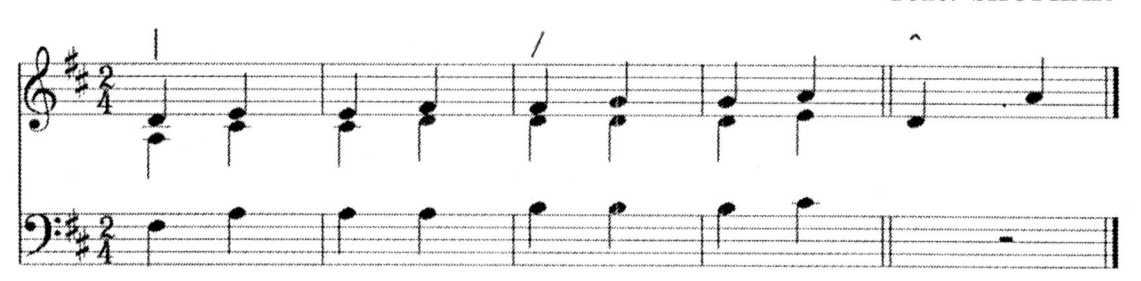

1 **Praise the LORD, all you | nations;**
   laud him, all you | peoples.
2 /For his loving-kindness toward us is / great,
   and the faithfulness of the LORD endures for / ever.
   ^Hallelu^jah!

All You Nations: Commentary To Psalm 117

KI-GÁVAR "ÁLEYNU #ASDOW
v.2 for his merciful kindness is ever more and more toward us.*

The verb means "to be strong, prevail" (Gesenius, p. 156). His merciful devotion toward us is stronger than we are. It over-powers our stubborn resistance. It is a strange way to think about grace. I had just gotten used to the idea that it comes undeserved, unmerited. I could almost accept the idea that I cannot work for grace. And now I learn that it is thrust upon me, in spite of my stubborn pride. Unless I deliberately refuse it, it is given to me.

All nations and all peoples are included in this fierce, devoted, possessive, insistent love. All of us together, whether I would have chosen them or not! Now as we stand and praise, we must include them, too. Real praise embraces all, for all is of God. Genuine praise does not classify. *Is he spirit-filled? Is she really a Christian?* The true service of God is known by this: it draws us together as God draws us together. Including those who classify. Including me. Compare 47, 87.

Suggestions: Stand. Sing worshipfully to the movement Reverential Praise (see Appendix). If desired repeat up to four times, using different singers or facing in different directions. In your group study of the psalms, exclude no one, no one who wants to be included. Accept everyone and respect all opinions.

The Book of Common Prayer and Administration of the Sacraments and Other Rites and Ceremonies of the Church. According to the Use of the Protestant Episcopal Church in the United States of America. The Church Pension Fund, New York, 1945, (the 1928 Prayer Book).

Dancing Procession Of Life: Commentary To Psalm 118

I call heaven and earth as witnesses today against you, that I have set before you
life and death, blessing and cursing; therefore choose life (Deuteronomy 30:19 NKJ).

I like to think of this psalm as a procession with dancing, jumping, and singing. Like a Mardi Gras parade in New Orleans on a sultry night; sinewy young men carry blazing *flambeaux*, weaving and turning as they march through screaming crowds. The message is coded in the rhythm: I belong to life, not death!

        LO. .ÁMUTH KI-.E#:YEH   WA.aSAPPÉR MA"aSEY YÁH'

v.17 I shall not die but live,
and declare the works of the LORD.

I shall not begin to die for I have decided to live. And I renounce all ties to death. All suicide clauses: *I can always commit suicide if... I will end it all unless...* I will not be like those who are addicted to the thought of suicide as an alcoholic to alcohol. One day, if he is fortunate, the alcoholic simply stops drinking; and the suicide patient decides, *I shall not die but live*, and is born again to life.

I shall not go on dying; no longer among the living dead or the merely existing, I shall begin to really live! So you will no longer hear me saying, *I can't go on* or *I can't stand it anymore*. I won't be threatening to resign from my job or my life. I will live no matter what. I will live to tell a story—the works of the LORD. Life and love do not work on a conditional basis. Divorce as an option means that the marriage is over. Death as an option may sound enlightened, but psychologically it is just death. Death as an option means that life has stopped.

v.18 The LORD has punished me (disciplined me) sorely,
but he did not hand me over to death.

The LORD has training trained me. Corrected me, chastised me. Like my one-time karate instructor who yelled "Training! Training!" at his sore, aching students, as we lay gasping on the floor. Training for the mountain, for life. Belonging to him I belong to life, not death.

Notes: Verse 1, compare 106, 136. "The LORD is my strength and my song," compare Exodus 15:2, the Song of Moses. "The same stone which the builders rejected," compare Matthew 21:42. "Hosanna," compare John 12:13.

Suggestions: Sing to the movement Marching and Swaying Dance (see Appendix). Music is the same as for 115. At every opportunity, choose life. Listen for those terminal clauses in your thinking: *I can't stand it any more* or *I can't go on*—and let them go.

On the four-fold invocation, compare 107 and 115. As noted earlier the number four in Scripture may symbolize the created world, things, the world of thoughts and emotions. It is a good world, a world of vast potential, but there is more.

Psalm 118 (BCP)

Tone: #a3O3:ROTH

1 **Give thànks to the LORD, for he is | gòod;** `
  /his mèrcy endùres for / èver. `
2 **Let Ìsrael nòw pro|clàim,** `
  / "His mèrcy endùres for / èver." `
3 **Let the hoùse of Àaron now pro|clàim,** `
  / "His mèrcy endùres for / èver." `
4 **Let thòse who fear the LORD now pro|clàim,** `
  / "His mèrcy en|dùres for / èver."

5 \I called to the LORD in my dis\tress;
  the LORD answered by setting me \ free.
6 The LORD is at my side, therefore I will not + fear;
  \what can anyone \ do to me?
7 The LORD is at my side to \ help me;
  I will triumph over those who + hate me.

8 **It is bètter to rely on the | LORD** `
  /than to pùt any trùst in / flèsh. `
9 **It is bètter to rely on the | LORD** `
  /than to pùt any trùst in / rùlers. `

10 \All the ungodly en\compass me;
   in the name of the LORD I will re\pel them.
11 They hem me in, they hem me in on every + side;
   \in the name of the LORD I will re\pel them.

12 **They swàrm abòut me like | bèes;** `
   they blàze like a fìre of | thòrns; `
   /in the nàme of the LORD I will / repèl thèm.

13 \I was pressed so hard that I almost \ fell,
   but the LORD came to my \ help.
14 The LORD is my strength and my + song,
   \and he has become my sal\vation.
15 There is a sound of exultation and \ victory
   in the tents of the + righteous:

16 "The rìght hand of the Lòrd has | trìumphed! `
    the rìght hand of the Lòrd is | exàlted! `
    /the rìght hand of the Lòrd has / trìumphed!"

17 \I shall not die but \ live,
    and declare the works of the \ Lord.

18 The Lord has punished me + sorely,
    \but he did not hand me over to \ death.
19 Open for me the gates of \ righteousness;
    I will enter them;
    I will offer thanks to the + Lord.

20 "Thìs is the gàte of the | Lòrd; `
    /hè who is rìghteous may / ènter."

21 \I will give thanks to you, for you \ answered me
    and have become my sal\vation.
22 The same stone which the builders re+jected
    has become the chief \ cornerstone.
23 This is the Lord's \ doing,
    and it is marvelous in our + eyes.

24 **Òn this dày the Lòrd has | àcted;**
    /wè will rejòice and be / glàd ìn ìt.

25 \Hosannah, Lord, ho\sannah!
    Lord, send us now suc\cess.
26 Blessed is he who comes in the name of the + Lord;
    \we bless you from the house of the \ Lord.

27 **Gòd is the Lòrd; he has shìned u|pòn us;**
    fòrm a procèssion with | brànches
    /ùp to the hòrns of the / àltar. `
28 **"Yòu are my Gòd, and Ì will | thànk you;**
    /yòu are my Gòd, and Ì will / exàlt you." —
29 **Give thànks to the Lòrd for he is | goòd; `**
    /his mèrcy endùres for / èvèr.

328

Heavenly College: Introduction To Psalm 119

I remember when a patient at Christian Hill, after a long period of confusion and turmoil, was finally able to attend groups. In the classes of George Parkhurst, M.D., Christian psychiatrist and biblical scholar, mental illness and problems of living were discussed. Biblical concepts provided the foundation, yet there was much good humor, brainstorming, and sharing of different points of view. "I feel as though I've gone from the locked ward to Heavenly College!" she told me.

I think of psalm walking as climbing a spiritual mountain, and I still refer to Psalm 119 as Heavenly College. I picture it as an academy shrouded in mist, or a cloud-hidden abbey, high on the slopes of that mountain. Here the deep mysteries of God are taught, but only to those who are ready to follow them. The casual student who hopes to learn spiritual techniques will find nothing here but words repeated over and over. But the student who is already committed to the path will find untold wisdom. Such a student has already come far in surrender and has given up much control, the secret of maturity. Most of all, he or she has learned to meditate—that is, be silent and listen.

More than any other, Psalm 119 is meditation. It consists of twenty-two stanzas, each with eight lines; each line has two parts, and each part has two or three rhythmic beats. This format creates a slow, soothing, contemplative rhythm. And within this rhythmic pattern, certain key words are heard again and again: Teaching. Way. Laws. Precepts. Righteousness. This is an alphabetic psalm—each stanza features one letter of the Hebrew alphabet as the first letter of every line. As we work our way through the alphabet, we symbolically walk the steps of spiritual development.

"O the happiness!" Like Psalm 1, instructional. Real happiness is like this. Heavenly College reaches back to Psalm 1, and forward to the Sermon on the Mount. But this is strange instruction indeed. We find ourselves meditating certain words and phrases again and again. We sense a profound meaning, yet we cannot penetrate the logic. We find neither beginning nor end. There is no sequence of basic and advanced information. There is no gnosis here, no esoteric technique of enlightenment. Rather, it is the mysterious wisdom of God, mysteriously infused into us from within. I think of it as inspiration, in a very literal sense, or instillation. It is learning by the slow infusion of Spirit, and we learn it by our willingness to obey it.

<u>Suggestions</u>: Read or sing slowly, rhythmically, maintaining a steady pace. Stay alert, as the notes may change at odd places. The Tone NÉVEL (*lyre*) is sung in this way: the first Order (first two measures) is sung three times, then the second Order (last two measures) once. You may wish to sing all verses, or you may choose to alternate singing and reading. You may also wish to do parts of this psalm as walking meditation, like 26.

Heavenly College: Commentaries To Psalm 119

.ÁLEPh — The First Letter

.ASHREY TH:MIMEY-DÁREKh   HAHOL:KHIM B:THORATH YHWH

v.1 Happy are the innocently simple in the path, those walking in the teaching of the LORD.

Real happiness begins with innocent simplicity, that naive integrity that has no ulterior motives or hidden agendas. Compare 1, 26, 101. It begins as a walk, walking in the teaching of the LORD. Not knowing about that teaching as information, but being willing to follow it. A process of willing surrender, seeking his will without knowing what he will ask.

v.5 Oh, that my ways were made so direct (established, stabilized).

This walk of willingness is easy to start, but hard to maintain. Put another way, it is hard to continue in this way, yet it is always possible to start over. With every breath, with every moment of silence, I begin anew, seeking his will and his ways.

In a very literal way, this walk begins with .ÁLEPh — the letter that is silent. We might think of it as silence itself, the energized potential that underlies all possibilities, the listening moment. Compare 62. Spiritual growth begins in those moments of silence, tiny gaps in my system of thinking, my certainty, my self-righteous conviction that I know the answers or even that I know who I am. In those moments, of intimacy, of real awareness, I break out of trance. I begin to awaken from an automatic, machine-like manner of living. I begin to hear.

As a verbal prefix the first letter signifies the first person singular, imperfective: *I will begin*, or, *I will continue*. Small beginnings, repeated daily and hourly, small choices with immeasurable consequence. The spiritual walk begins with these tiny choices quite as much as with great experiences. While some traditions emphasize the conversion moment, I would rather point to the little decisions. Psalm 119 speaks to the walk, the process. A lifetime of tiny openings to God.

Suggestions: Sing slowly, in a reflective way, listening more than analyzing. Remember that *Torah* is more like teaching than law and certainly not legalistic. Listen and let it teach you in its own way and timing. When you have the opportunity, study the commentary of Bonhoeffer,[*] tragically unfinished though it is. Meditate as he taught, going slowly from word to word.

---

[*]Dietrich Bonhoeffer: *Meditating on the Word*, Ed. and Trans. by David McI. Gracie, Cowley, Cambridge MA, 1986, pp. 103-146.

Psalm 119 (BCP)

Twenty-fourth Day: Evening Prayer Tone: NÉVEL

ÁLEPh

1 Happy are they whose way is | blameless,
  who | walk in the law of the | LORD!
2 Happy are they who observe his | decrees
  and | seek him with all their | hearts!
3 Who never do any | wrong,
  but always | walk in his | ways.
4 \You laid down your com\mandments,
  that \ we should fully \ keep them.
5 Oh, that my ways were made so di|rect
  that I might | keep your | statutes!
6 Then I should not be put to | shame,
  when I | regard all your com|mandments.
7 I will thank you with an unfeigned | heart,
  when I have | learned your righteous | judgments.
8 \I will keep your \ statutes;
  do not \ utterly for\sake me.

BEYTH — The Second Letter

BAMMEH Y:ZAKKEH <u>NA"AR</u> .ETH .OR#OW

v.9 How shall a young man keep his way pure (clean, clear)? Already we sense complications. The simplicity of the path is deceptive. Seeds of disorder are hidden in those three negative pleas — not stray, not sin, not forget. It is like Newton's Third Law: "For every action there is an equal and opposite reaction." For every moment of simple innocence, an attack of selfish entitlement. For every hour of joy there is a wave of depression. For every step of spiritual progress there will be a "sinking spell," back to me at my worst! How can I keep the way pure?

The literal meaning of BEYTH is house, hence where I live. The spiritual way seems easy on a weekend retreat. But how do I keep my way pure at home, where I live? I can be "high" when I meditate. But how do I live it in the bedroom or the office? And if I manage it occasionally with strangers, how do I live it with my wife?

From BEYTH comes B: (*in* or *with*). Seven of these eight verses begin with it. "In (or *with*) my whole heart ... in my heart I have treasured ... in (or *with*) my lips I have told." I love to read spiritual truth, I love to discuss it. The challenge is to internalize it, bring it into a context, the place where I live.

<u>GIMEL</u> — The Third Letter

v.17 Deal bountifully with your servant, I shall live.

Do something good for your servant, (so that) I may continue to live. The contemplative tone gives way to restless stirrings. I cry to God again and again: Open my eyes that I may see, roll away from me shame and rebuke. My soul (breath, life) is crushed, longing for your judgments, for order and meaning.

I am a stranger on earth, a person *from all over the place*, wandering about in confusion. I seem permanently disoriented. I do not understand the game of life; I only know that the written rules are not the real rules. I long for order and direction. I start each day with high resolve and come home drained and dispirited.

It is the place of emptiness, where religion and spirituality part company. Disorder wells up within and without, and I know that I have no answers. If at first I drew great refreshment from my meditation, now I have spells of dryness, doubt and confusion. I begin to question the path. Have I wasted my life?

The focus has shifted from inward contemplation to outward desperation. To reaching and flailing, feeling needy and helpless. It is a painful but necessary phase. The answers are not within me and never were. Open my eyes that I may see.

<u>Suggestions</u>: Continue your practice of silence, informal meditation, in everyday activities: a moment of silence when you wash your hands, when you put on a shirt, when you start your car. Clear your thoughts and listen, if only for a moment.

BEYTH

9 How shall a young man cleanse his | way? *
    By | keeping to your | words.
10 With my whole heart I | seek you; *
    let me not | stray from your com | mandments.
11 I treasure your promise in my | heart, *
    that I | may not sin | against you.
12 \Blessed are you, O \ Lord; *
    in\struct me in your \ statutes.
13 With my lips will I re | cite *
    all the | judgments of your | mouth.
14 I have taken greater delight in the way of your de | crees *
    than in all | manner of | riches.
15 I will meditate on your com | mandments *
    and give at | tention to your | ways.
16 \My delight is in your \ statutes; *
    I will \ not forget your \ word.

GIMEL

17 Deal bountifully with your | servant, *
    that I may | live and keep your | word.
18 Open my eyes that I may | see *
    the | wonders of your | law.
19 I am a stranger here on | earth; *
    do not | hide your com | mandments from me.
20 \My soul is consumed at all \ times *
    with \ longing for your \ judgments.
21 You have rebuked the | insolent; *
    cursed are they who | stray from your com | mandments!
22 Turn from me shame and | rebuke, *
    for I have | kept your de | crees.
23 Even though rulers sit and plot a | gainst me, *
    I will | meditate on your | statutes.
24 \For your decrees are my de\light, *
    and \ they are my \ counselors.

DÁLETh — The Fourth Letter

The key word is DEREKh (*road, path,* or *way*). It appears in five of the eight verses — five paths or ways, as I rise from turmoil to peace. I begin in self-absorbed misery, for "My soul (breath, breathing, life) cleaves to the dust," and, "melts away for sorrow." My soul is at a low ebb; "My ways I have told," I cry, "and you begin to answer." Now, "Teach me your statutes." I am crawling in the dirt, helpless; I acknowledge that I am powerless. I tell you how I have lived.

It takes a long time for me to say, "The way of your commandments make me understand," admitting my ignorance and accepting direction. Harder still, "The way of falsehood put away from me," as I come to recognize my own dishonesty and self-deception. Then and only then, "The way of faithfulness I have chosen," the way of constancy and stability. The way of balance. Finally, "The way of your commandments I will run!" I have come a long way: from "My ways I have told" — that's the way I am — to "the way of your commandments I will run."

I am indebted to Charles Kaldahl* for illuminating a recurrent pattern in 119 — the contrast of order and disorder. The forces of disorder (disharmony, entropy) swirl about and within me; the ways of God are orderly and bring me to order. The verses are orderly and soothing, yet disorder tries to break in at all times. "My soul cleaves to the dust," and, "the way of lying turn away from me." My thinking is basically dishonest. Thrashing about in misery, I may convince myself that all is lost, or insist that I am all right, and blame my suffering on others. Yet I keep calling to God: "Give me life ... instruct me ... make me understand." The orderliness of God floods into me, and I cling to it for life.

The word DÁLETh means a door. We might think of it as a boundary or phase transition. So each of these roads or paths may be thought of as a door, a boundary, a new phase of development. As I cross each boundary, I progress to a higher level of order: from telling my ways to learning your ways to becoming honest with myself and others, but only with your help; to choosing the way of faithfulness, the ability to make a commitment; to running — to active, willing, positive, enlightened surrender.

<u>Suggestions</u>: Pray constantly for direction, in every decision, in every action of life. Seek to know God's will for you each moment. How will you know it? By your willingness to do it, whatever it may be. Do not wait for some great revelation, but go about your work with that willing, listening attitude. Practice that listening disposition in everything that you do, without exception.

Do not concern yourself with stages of spiritual development. At times you will see them clearly; at others you will feel you are going nowhere. As long as fruit of the Spirit is present (*love, joy, peace, patience...*), at least on occasion, your practice is correct and your progress as it should be.

---

*The Journal of Christian Healing, Vol. 13, No. 4, pp. 3-10, Winter, 1991.

DÁLETh

25 My soul cleaves to the | dust; *
    give me life ac|cording to your | word.
26 I have confessed my ways, and you | answered me; *
    in|struct me in your | statutes.
27 Make me understand the way of your com|mandments, *
    that I may | meditate on your | marvelous works.
28 \My soul melts away for \ sorrow; *
    \strengthen me according to your \ word.
29 Take from me the way of | lying; *
    let me find | grace through your | law.
30 I have chosen the way of | faithfulness; *
    I have set your | judgments be|fore me.
31 I hold fast to your | decrees; *
    O Lord, let me | not be put to | shame.
32 \I will run the way of your com\mandments, *
    for you have \ set my heart at \ liberty.

HE. — The Fifth Letter

HA"aVÉR "EYNAY MÉR:.OTH SHÁW.

v.37 Turn my eyes from watching what is worthless.

Every verse but one begins with a causative: Teach me, make me understand, direct me, incline my heart or attitude, make to pass over from my eyes. The paths and phases of the previous section will not be achieved by personal effort. My only contribution is the willingness. Yet this can be deceptive. If I tell God to wake me when I'm fixed, I know quite well that nothing will happen. Each tiny step takes willingness — to ask for it, to plead for it, to give up control of it, to receive it, to be grateful for it. Teach me, O LORD. Take me. Transform me.

Cause to pass over from my eyes the looking at what is vain. Help me to redirect my attention. Turn my eyes from all I have been looking at — the evening news, the empty wisdom of commentators, the exotic wisdom of *gurus*, the catalogs full of marvelous toys, the opposite sex, the approval of those I work for. Cause to pass over (from me) the reproach (scorn, contempt) which I dread, and most likely deserve.

WÁW — The Sixth Letter

WIYVO.UNI #aSÁDEKHÁ YHWH

v.41 And let your acts of devotion come to me, O LORD.

The word WÁW means a hook or nail. The word W:- (*and*) is a connector, not only of words, but of ideas, times, and states. It links in sequence, in consequence, or in contrast. It asks the question, "How are these things related?" It suggests connection itself, the meaningful relatedness of all things.

The entire stanza is a tissue of connections: "And (then) I will begin to answer ... but do not (then) take from my mouth the word of truth ... and I will continue to guard, watch, or preserve ... and I will begin to walk in freedom ... and I will begin to speak ... and I will be delighted ... and I will begin to lift up my hands." It is a progression of states, again. Step by step with God, from my first feeble responses, to walking in freedom, to delight, to worship. As I grow in my life with God, one step leads to the next. Chance meetings bring new insight. All that happens is part of a plan. There is no coincidence.

Suggestions: Lift the arms, palms up, at v. 48 ("I will lift"); press the palms together in front of the chest, and bow slightly at "and I will meditate."

As you follow the spiritual path, be prepared to go wherever it may lead, for all things are connected. Remind yourself that the path is not *your* path, and you have no idea how one step may connect with the next. Be prepared to change your plans at a moment's notice.

Psalm 119 (BCP)

Twenty-fifth Day: Morning Prayer Tone: NÉVEL

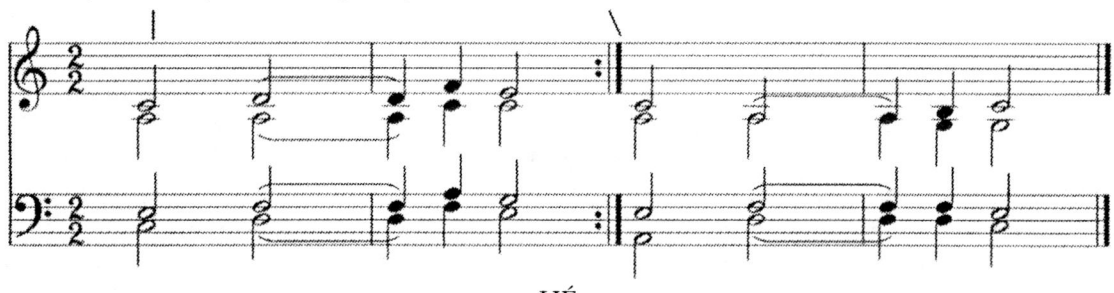

HÉ.

33 Teach me, O LORD, the way of your | statutes,
    and I shall | keep it to the | end.
34 Give me understanding, and I shall | keep your law;
    I shall | keep it with all my | heart.
35 Make me go in the path of your com | mandments,
    for | that is my de | sire.
36 \Incline my heart to your de\crees
    and \ not to unjust \ gain.
37 Turn my eyes from watching what is | worthless;
    give me | life in your | ways.
38 Fulfill your promise to your | servant,
    which you | make to those who | fear you.
39 Turn away the reproach which I | dread,
    because your | judgments are | good.
40 \Behold, I long for your com\mandments;
    in your \ righteousness preserve my \ life.

WÁW

41 Let your loving-kindness come to me, O | LORD,
    and your salvation ac | cording to your | promise.
42 Then shall I have a word for those who | taunt me,
    because I | trust in your | words.
43 Do not take the word of truth out of my | mouth,
    for my | hope is in your | judgments.
44 \I shall continue to keep your \ law;
    I shall \ keep it for ever and \ ever.
45 I will walk at | liberty,
    because I | study your com | mandments.
46 I will tell of your decrees before | kings
    and will | not be a | shamed.
47 I delight in your com | mandments,
    which I have | always | loved.
48 \I will lift up my hands to your com\mandments,
    and I will \ meditate on your \ statutes.

ZAYiN — The Seventh Letter

Z:MIROTH HÁYU-LIY #UQQEYKHÁ   B:VEYTH M:GURÁY

v.54 Your statutes have been like songs to me
wherever I have lived as a stranger.

In the house of my sojournings. Wherever I traveled for many years, I carried these psalms with me, in a big white three-ring notebook. In every motel room, on every airplane, in every retreat house, on every vacation. To St. Helena's convent in Georgia, and to Kanuga Conference Center in North Carolina; to the Outer Banks and Colonial Williamsburg, to New York City and to Montreal. Wherever we drove our big yellow van, the notebook rested beside me between the front seats. I have come to depend on these psalms like food and drink. I meditate them twice a day, and they nourish me. Each month I complete the cycle of the psalms and turn my notebook back to the beginning.

Sometimes I equate that cycle of readings to the *remembering* of these verses. "Remember your word to your servant," and, "When I remember your judgments ... I take great comfort." Sometimes, I "remember your name in the night, O LORD," when I have trouble sleeping. Coming back through your word, your teaching, again and again, I am slowly changed. I may not remember the exact words, but traces remain with me. A faint imprint of your word, your way of thinking, becomes part of me.

Although I love the Bible, I can rarely quote chapter and verse. There is so much of Scripture that I simply do not understand. Some parts I find troubling or even annoying. And yet, this Word is part of me. Little by little it has worked its way into the very structure of my thinking. Disorder rages around me, but "This is my comfort in my trouble."

<u>Suggestions</u>: Continue to meditate the psalms appointed for each morning and evening. Read them, sing them, carry out the suggested movements. Immerse yourself in the experience of the psalms, without trying to analyze them or take them apart. Always conclude your study with silence, and let the verses you have read echo within you. Memorize a verse whenever you can, and reflect on your verse as you go through the day.

Continually redirect your attention, from worthless thoughts that disturb and agitate, to thoughts that uplift and transform. What are they? Not any thoughts of your own, not *relax* or *calm* or *green meadows*, but the words of these psalms. Reflect on them over and over, and then be silent.

ZAYiN

49 Remember your word to your | servant,
      because you have | given me | hope.
50 This is my comfort in my | trouble,
      that your | promise gives me | life.
51 The proud have derided me | cruelly,
      but I have not | turned from your | law.
52 \When I remember your judgments of \ old,
      O \ Lord, I take great \ comfort.
53 I am filled with a burning | rage,
      because of the | wicked who for|sake your law.
54 Your statutes have been like | songs to me
      wher|ever I have | lived as a stranger.
55 I remember your Name in the | night, O Lord,
      and | dwell upon your | law.
56 \This is how it has \ been with me,
      because I have \ kept your \ commandments.

#EYTH — The Eighth Letter

v.59 I have considered (thought about) my ways
and I begin to turn my feet toward your decrees.

I have waited ... I have considered ... I have hastened — three verbs suggesting an outward movement, a turn from inner reflection to changed behavior. I have thought deeply about my ways, my behaviors, how I hurt people, how I try to change and control them. I come to this realization in part because I have already begun to change. From the day I became a Christian, something has been happening, not always smoothly or easily, but happening, like it or not. Your ways, LORD, and your thoughts are becoming part of me. Immersing myself in your ways I am challenged to consider my own. And considering them I cannot but change them.

I have considered my ways. Not yours or anyone else's, but my own. It is uncomfortable at best. I would rather talk about my "spiritual journey" or give you advice about yours. But I find myself considering my ways and turning my feet. And you draw me toward you, changing me from within. You draw me from self-absorption to servant ministry, to community, for I am a companion of all who fear you.

tEYTH — The Ninth Letter

v.65 Good you have done with your servant.

Five of the eight verses begin with tOV (*good* or *It is good*). Compare 92. Let us follow the literal meaning: "Good you have done with your servant ... Good discernment (taste) and knowledge, teach me ... Good are you, and causing to be good." The stanza concludes with "Good for me that I have been afflicted," and, "Good for me is the teaching of your mouth."

Is there a subtle progression here? Good is not always the same. What is good in a relationship changes as the relationship evolves. So I advance, not always happily, from a self-centered valuing of God to a God-centered life. As a new believer I might have said, "Thank you for the miracles!" Down the road there may be fewer miracles, more questions, yet God is still good. For the nature of this path is to give up control of the process. The steps of the path are good steps, leading to other steps. Good ways of understanding are good for me, for a time, then left behind. I began with a miracle God, the focus on me and my needs. I evolve toward God as God, center of everything. Good for me is the teaching of your mouth, wherever it may lead me.

v.71 It is good for me that I have been afflicted.

It is good -- a statement of faith. Saying, "It is good," I see as God sees (Genesis 1:4), and think as God thinks. I bring into harmony what is and what ought to be — one and the same. It is a hard surrender following these steps, going where I am taken. It is hard to give up knowing what *ought* to be done, knowing how things *should be*, improving myself and my family. But this is what I learn. It is good.

#EYTH

57 You only are my | portion O Lord;
    I have | promised to | keep your words.
58 I entreat you with all my | heart,
    be | merciful to me, ac|cording to your promise.
59 I have considered my | ways
    and turned my | feet toward your de|crees.
60 \I hasten and do not \ tarry
    to \ keep your com\mandments.
61 Though the cords of the wicked en|tangle me,
    I do | not forget your | law.
62 At midnight I will rise to give you | thanks,
    because of your | righteous | judgments.
63 I am a companion of all who | fear you
    and of | those who | keep your commandments.
64 \The earth, O Lord, is full of your \ love;
    in\struct me in your \ statutes.

tEYTH

65 O Lord, you have dealt graciously with your | servant,
    ac|cording to your | word.
66 Teach me discernment and | knowledge,
    for I have be|lieved in your com|mandments.
67 Before I was afflicted I went a|stray
    but | now I keep your | word.
68 \You are good and you bring forth \ good;
    in\struct me in your \ statutes.
69 The proud have smeared me with | lies,
    but I will keep your com|mandments with my | whole heart.
70 Their heart is gross and | fat,
    but my de|light is in your | law.
71 It is good for me that I have been af|flicted,
    that I might | learn your | statutes.
72 \The law of your mouth is \ dearer to me
    than \ thousands in gold and \ silver.

YOD — The Tenth Letter

YÁDEYKHÁ "ÁSUNI WAY:KHON:NUNI

v.73 Your hands have made me and they continue to direct me (establish me, keep me stabilized).

If the previous stanza seemed to lead away from me, toward a good but silent God, here I experience a movement of return, things turning toward me, comforting me. "Those who fear you will see me and be happy ... Let now your devoted love come to comfort me ... Let your mercies come to me ... Let those who fear you return to me."

Surrender is not abandonment. Giving up control, even a little control, is frightening; but when I do, it is painless. When I do give up control, even a little control, I have a sense of freedom and lightness. Fresh air blows in where prison was; situations that were frozen begin to move my way.

Disorder lurks in "the arrogant" who tell lies about me, but, "Let my heart be sound (whole, innocently simple) in your statutes." Your hands are still in control.

KAPH — The Eleventh Letter

KÁL:TÁH LITH:SHU"ÁTH:KHÁ NAPHSHIY

v.81 My soul (breath, breathing, life) has longed for your salvation ... my eyes have longed for your word ... for I have become like a leather flask in the smoke — like a wineskin stretched out to dry over a smoking fire (Feuer, p. 1455).

Disorder from within — weariness and longing overwhelm me, and I ask, "How many are the days?" I begin to sound self-pitying, if not paranoid, for "the proud have dug pits for me ... persecute me with lies ... had almost made an end of me on earth."

Me at my worst, at the end of a hard day or in a hopeless situation. Me "coming apart at the seams." Yet I have not lost everything from my lessons, for "I have put my hope in your word ... I have not forgotten your statutes."

Suggestions: Try reading only the disorder lines — 82a, 83a, 84, 85a, 86b; then the contrasting lines that speak of God's orderliness. What a striking contrast, like reading two different, unrelated poems! Then read the verses together, in the normal way. What do you learn?

Acknowledge the disorder and confusion in your own life. *You at your absolute worst* continues to make appearances, and always will. The dark side of your nature will always be part of you. Continue to meditate, good days and bad.

Psalm 119 (BCP)

Twenty-fifth Day: Evening Prayer   Tone: NÉVEL

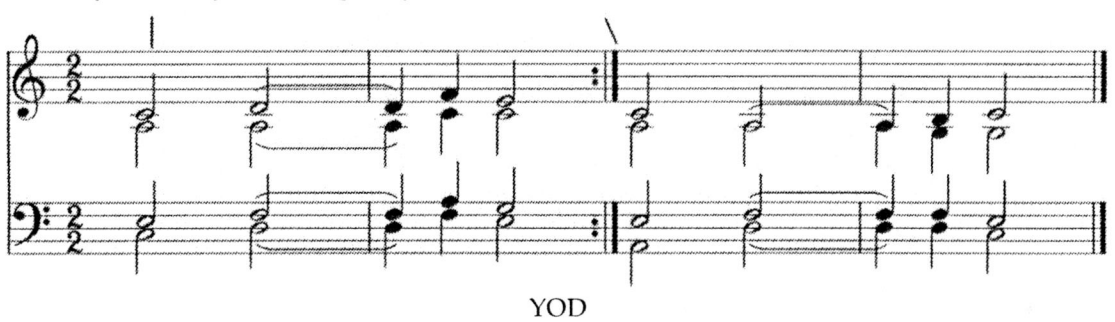

YOD

73 Your hands have made me and | fashioned me;
    give me under|standing, that I may | learn your commandments.
74 Those who fear you will be glad when they | see me,
    because I | trust in your | word.
75 I know, O LORD, that your judgments are | right
    and that in | faithfulness you have af|flicted me.
76 \Let your loving-kindness be my \ comfort,
    as you have \ promised to your \ servant.
77 Let your compassion come to me, that I may | live,
    for your | law is my de|light.
78 Let the arrogant be put to shame, for they wrong me with | lies;
    but I will | meditate on your com|mandments.
79 Let those who fear you | turn to me,
    and also those who | know your de|crees.
80 \Let my heart be sound in your \ statutes,
    that \ I may \ not be put to shame.

KAPH

81 My soul has longed for your | salvation;
    I have put my | hope in your | word.
82 My eyes have failed from watching for your | promise,
    and I say, | "When will you | comfort me?"
83 I have become like a leather flask in the | smoke,
    but I have not for|gotten your | statutes.
84 \How much longer must I \ wait?
    when will you give \ judgment against those who \ persecute me.
85 The proud have dug | pits for me;
    they do not | keep your | law.
86 All your commandments are | true;
    help me, for they | persecute me with | lies.
87 They had almost made an end of me on | earth,
    but I have not for|saken your com|mandments.
88 \In your loving-kindness, re\vive me,
    that I may \ keep the de\crees of your mouth.

LÁMED — The Twelfth Letter

L:"OLÁM YHWH D:VÁR:KHÁ   NI33ÁV BASSHÁMÁYiM

v.89 To eternity, O LORD, (is) your word;
standing firm in the heavens.

Seven of the eight verses begin with L: (*to* or *toward*); hence for, belonging to, of. "To eternity, O LORD, (is) your word ... to generation after generation is your faithfulness ... to eternity I will not forget ... toward you am I; save me!"

If the previous verses implied holding or endurance, these suggest a kind of movement. To the seemingly random activity of this world there is, after all, direction. We cannot see it because it leads nowhere within this world. It leads to eternity, the world unseen. My existence is directed toward you.

Everything I do, I do in time — on earth, with my family, friends, colleagues, patients. And everything points beyond, to the timeless world. For "I have seen (that there is) an end to every purpose, (but) your commandment is very broad." Exceedingly broad (Feuer, p. 1461), without limit, infinite.

"What difference will it make in fifty years?" I said. I was pretending to be philosophical. Why be upset about some momentary crisis? In fifty years who will remember? In a sense it is true: the exact events may be forgotten. I am also convinced that everything I do lives on — in those I have hurt or encouraged, in the attitudes of my child, in the children of my patients, and the patients of those I have trained. My existence is directed toward you. My walk on earth leaves footprints in eternity.

Nothing stands alone upon the earth, for all things lead to other things; thought leads to thought and emotion to emotion. Things, people, events are connected, linked in remarkable ways we cannot imagine. And all things lead beyond things, to another reality. That other universe is what we call eternity, or the Kingdom of God, or the realm of Spirit. It is my nature as a human breathing to live in both worlds, never quite at home in either. And yet, the more I come to know that other world, the more I am reconciled to this one.

Suggestions: Do not daydream about forever after, nor lose yourself in daily life. Live where you are placed — in work, relationships, conflicts, good and bad experiences. Practice your moments of silence, tiny openings to eternity. Listen to the word of God, the language of eternity, as you walk in your life.

LÁMED

89 O Lord, your word is ever | lasting;
   it stands | firm in the | heavens.
90 Your faithfulness remains from one gene | ration to another;
   you es | tablished the | earth, and it abides.
91 By your decree these con | tinue to this day,
   for all | things are your | servants.
92 \If my delight had not been in your \ law,
   I should have \ perished in my af\fliction.
93 I will never forget your com | mandments,
   because by | them you give me | life.
94 I am yours; oh, that you would | save me!
   for I | study your com | mandments.
95 Though the wicked lie in wait for me to de | stroy me,
   I will apply my | mind to your | decrees.
96 \I see that all things come to an \ end,
   but your com\mandment has no \ bounds.

MEM — The Thirteenth Letter

Half-way through Heavenly College and, "Oh, how I love your teaching." It is what I talk about and think about all day long.

MIKKOL-M:LAMM:DAY HIS<u>K</u>ALTI

v.99   I have more understanding than all my teachers.

I have more understanding than all who have taught me, more than Great Evangelist and Pastor Wonderful and the *Guru* from India. Wiser than all of them, though I know nothing. Wiser with a wisdom not my own but yours, when I seek your will, when I turn to you humbly. When you show me what to do at each moment. And all the books ever written would never have suggested that elegant solution you gave me. Wiser than all my teachers, for that moment alone.

from all my teachers I grew wise (Feuer, p. 1463).

I grew wise as I learned to surrender. As I learned to learn from everyone and from all situations. Whomever you bring into my life may be my teacher. Learning to say *I don't know* I learned to listen. Your word is everywhere.

It is a great paradox: I no longer need *guru* or mentor, not because I know all the answers, but because I know nothing. The information I have saved on little cards since medical school is mostly obsolete. I still love to wander in bookstores. I glance with momentary fascination at books about life in the Spirit, strange experiences, visions of Indian monks and English vicars, books that would tell me how to live, how to have powers and riches. I look at these books and wander on, for this I know: I have more understanding than all my teachers. More than all these wonderful books, I have your presence. I learn from everyone I meet, knowing less and less.

Jesus said, "Blessed are the poor in spirit" (Matt. 5:3), those who know they do not know. Their eyes are open, really open; they see what most of us cannot.

<u>Suggestions</u>: Learn from each person you meet today. Study the Book of Proverbs. If possible study these psalms in groups. Read or sing by turns or in unison, or alternating leader and chorus, or in any other way that seems comfortable. Then let each member share impressions, understandings, reactions, personal associations. Every contribution is acceptable and good. Led by the Holy Spirit, we are all experts!

MEM

97 Oh, how I love your | law!
    all the day | long it is in my | mind.
98 Your commandment has made me wiser than my | enemies,
    and it is | always | with me.
99 I have more understanding than all my | teachers,
    for your de|crees are my | study.
100 \I am wiser than the \ elders,
    because I ob\serve your com\mandments.
101 I restrain my feet from every evil | way,
    that I may | keep your | word.
102 I do not shrink from your | judgments,
    because | you yourself have | taught me.
103 How sweet are your words to my | taste!
    they are sweeter than | honey to my | mouth.
104 \Through your commandments I gain under\standing;
    therefore I \ hate every lying \ way.

NUN — The Fourteenth Letter

NÉR-L:RAGLIY D:VÁREKHÁ   W:.OR LIN:THIVÁTHIY

v.105 Your word is a lantern to my feet
and a light upon my path.

The expression "your word" is found twenty times in Psalm 119. Your word, including but more than Scripture, is compared here to a light or candle. Light in Hebrew signifies enlightenment, clarity, order. It is the light that enlightens me to seek your will. What kind of light, what kind of enlightenment is this? Light for the foot, for the road. Not some great understanding or academic knowledge, but light for walking. Light for the next step.

I am walking in darkness, confusion. My own light flickers dimly in the inner storm. Thought leads to thought and emotion to emotion. I am beset by the forces of disorder, within and without. Your word is my only light upon the path, a subtle and pale light, pleasant but easily missed. Yet if I look for it, it will guide me.

v.107 I am troubled very much, O LORD;
Give me life, according to your word.

Trouble and turmoil will not end in this lifetime. My soul (breath, life) is in my hands, a place where nothing is secure. The wicked have set traps for me in the darkness. Your word is my light in that darkness but only if I search for it and follow it.

SÁMEKh — The Fifteenth Letter

SÉ"aPHIM SÁNÉ.THI   W:THORÁTH:KHÁ .ÁHÁVTI

v.113 I hate those who have a divided heart,
but your law (your teaching) do I love.

The Hebrew root means branch. Those who branch, divide and vacillate, I hate. Compare 94, 139. They are unable to make lasting commitments. They swing wildly from one extreme to another. Nothing is reliable for them. They live by thoughts and feelings. I do not hate them as individuals for they make delightful company, but their instability is frightening. I hate that quality, especially in myself. Let me be grounded, stable and steady. How do I achieve this amid constant change, stress and pressure? By your support. By your holding me up.

v.116 Sustain (support) me according to your promise, and I will continue to live.

Suggestions: Ask God for direction constantly, in every situation. Do not rely upon your feelings, no matter how intense or convincing, for God is more like light than emotion. Look for that subtle, pale light, and follow it as faithfully as you can.

Psalm 119 (BCP)

Twenty-sixth Day: Morning Prayer Tone: NÉVEL

NUN

105 Your word is a lantern to my | feet
   and a | light upon my | path.
106 I have sworn and am de | termined
   to | keep your righteous | judgments.
107 I am deeply | troubled;
   preserve my life, O LORD, ac | cording to your | word.
108 \Accept O LORD, the willing tribute of my \ lips,
   and \ teach me your \ judgments.
109 My life is always in my | hand,
   yet I do | not forget your | law.
110 The wicked have set a | trap for me,
   but I have not | strayed from your com | mandments.
111 Your decrees are my inheritance for | ever;
   truly, they are the | joy of my | heart.
112 \I have applied my heart to fulfill your \ statutes
   for \ ever and to the \ end.

SÁMEKh

113 I hate those who have a divided | heart,
   but your | law do I | love.
114 You are my refuge and | shield;
   my | hope is in your | word.
115 Away from me, you | wicked!
   I will keep the com | mandments of my | God.
116 \Sustain me according to your promise that I may \ live,
   and let me not be disap\pointed in my \ hope.
117 Hold me up, and I shall be | safe,
   and my de | light shall be | ever in your statutes.
118 You spurn all who | stray from your statutes;
   their de | ceitfulness is in | vain.
119 In your sight all the wicked of the earth are but | dross;
   therefore I | love your de | crees.
120 \My flesh trembles with \ dread of you;
   I am a\fraid of your \ judgments.

"AYiN — The Sixteenth Letter

"ÁSITHI MISHPÁt WÁ3EDEQ

v.121 I have done what is just and right.

I have acted; I have done what I could. I went to work today. My life on the spiritual path is not lived in a remote monastery but in a busy hospital; in meetings and conferences, talking with difficult patients, arguing with staff and students. And although I may dream of retreat, I must admit that work enriches me. It is in work, however difficult, that I see the fruits of the path and experience the growth. If only I can remember that this is not *my* work or *my* path. "My eyes have failed from watching for your salvation"; I turn to you yearning for guidance. "Deal with your servant," I say, "according to your loving-kindness," and, "grant me understanding." My work in this world is but a temporary assignment; I am your servant, on the way of surrender. I will not eliminate mental illness or stamp out evil in my short career. The ultimate action is yours, O LORD, and always has been.

The way of surrender is not passive or lazy. It is, however I may resist, the way of demands and commitments. I am your servant. Here I am. Send me.

PÉ. — The Seventeenth Letter

v.133 Steady my footsteps in your word;
let no iniquity have dominion over me.

Establish (direct, stabilize) my footsteps on this path. My nature is so unstable. I react to everything, then I react to my own reactions. I live in emotions, memories, primitive thoughts from childhood. *Should. Ought to. Have to. Guess what I did. Look at me! What if? Why did I say that? What is wrong with me?* Then, a moment of closeness with God, and I know it all. I remember it over and over, listening no longer. A little spiritual insight, I am ready to be your *guru* in a long white robe!

Stabilize my footsteps in your word, so that evil does not take control of me. So that pride does not creep in and take over when I do something right. So that resentment does not overshadow my thinking. Keep me steady on the path in all situations. When my patients are grateful and when they blame me for everything. Iniquity can take dominion over anyone, anyone at all, at any time. LORD, stabilize my footsteps in your word. Keep me steady.

Suggestions: The spiritual practice taught in this book is not retreat or escape. It is a practice for everyday life. Practice formal meditation morning and evening, go to work, practice informal meditation all through the day. Practice with your eyes open, moments of silence and listening, while driving your car, while meeting with your boss, in a difficult conversation, when others are unreasonable. This meditation is not reverie, in which thought leads to thought or image to image. Practice the continual, repeated stepping back from thoughts, the balancing of thoughts with silence. This will be your pathway to internal stability.

"AYiN

121 I have done what is just and | right;
    do not de|liver me to my | oppressors.
122 Be surety for your servant's | good;
    let not the | proud op|press me.
123 My eyes have failed from watching for your | salvation
    and for your | righteous | promise.
124 \Deal with your servant according to your loving\kindness
    and \ teach me your \ statutes.
125 I am your servant; grant me under|standing,
    that I may | know your de|crees.
126 It is time for you to | act, O LORD,
    for they have | broken your | law.
127 Truly, I love your comm|mandments
    more than | gold and precious | stones.
128 \I hold all your commandments to be \ right for me;
    all paths of \ falsehood I ab\hor.

PÉ.

129 Your decrees are | wonderful;
    therefore I o|bey them with all my | heart.
130 When your word goes forth it gives | light;
    it gives under|standing to the | simple.
131 I open my mouth and | pant;
    I | long for your com|mandments.
132 \Turn to me in \ mercy,
    as you always \ do to those who \ love your Name.
133 Steady my footsteps in your | word;
    let no in|iquity have do|minion over me.
134 Rescue me from those who op|press me,
    and I will | keep your com|mandments.
135 Let your countenance shine upon your | servant
    and | teach me your | statutes.
136 \My eyes shed streams of \ tears,
    because \ people do not keep your \ law.

3ÁDE — The Eighteenth Letter

3ADDIYQ .ATTÁH YHWH   W:YÁSHÁR MISHPÁtEYKHÁ

v.137 Righteous are you, O Lord,
and straight are your judgments.

Forms of the word 3EDEQ (*righteousness*) occur five times in this lesson. The root meaning is straight. Although there are few straight lines in nature we have a natural affinity for them. An internal geometry equates straight (physical) with right (moral). Perhaps because straight is simple, credible; because it goes to the heart of a matter, to the need. A straight look. A straight answer. It goes from the person to the person, without evasions or exceptions. Straight feels safe because I can see where it is going; I do not have to fear a surprise appearance, ambush or betrayal. I can relax with the straight, because I know where I stand.

I would like to be straight and straightforward. I like to think of myself as a person who comes straight to the point, who goes to the heart of a matter. If I have something to ask, I ask it. If I see something wrong, I say it. I would like to think of myself that way, but the truth is otherwise. I am often amazed at my avoidance, evasiveness, and manipulating. I pout instead of asking, and glance away instead of seeing. I have missed so much in life, playing these games. Lord, help me to be straight.

You are righteous, O Lord. You are the very source and paradigm of righteousness. You are the embodiment of playing straight, with me and with all human breathings. Your righteousness is not self-righteousness, but real righteousness. It is without self-consciousness, constant, faithful and reliable. Your law is the truth. I can rely on your righteousness in time of crisis, for your commandments are my delight, and the righteousness of your decrees is everlasting. Let me live within your righteousness, O Lord, let me embody and bear witness to it.

<u>Suggestions</u>: Do not strive to be or appear righteous, but live in the righteousness of God, day by day. How can you do this? By listening, by the practice of silence, day after day, until it becomes second nature. Real righteousness is the right ordering of things, always in harmony with the will of God. In your communing with God, seek understanding, seek to understand his ways, that you may live in his righteousness.

Practice the straight way in your daily life. Look straight at me when you talk. Look straight into my eyes. Speak straight without flowery phrases or euphemisms. Tell it to me straight, whether it is good or bad. When you pray for me, pray simple and straight; pronounce my name and ask God to bless me.

3 ÁDE

137 You are righteous, O | Lord,
    and | upright are your | judgments.
138 You have issued your | decrees
    with | justice and in perfect | faithfulness.
139 My indignation has con|sumed me,
    because my | enemies for|get your words.
140 \Your word has been tested to the \ uttermost,
    and your \ servant holds it \ dear.
141 I am small and of little ac|count,
    yet I do not for|get your com|mandments.
142 Your justice is an everlasting | justice
    and your | law is the | truth.
143 Trouble and distress have | come upon me,
    yet your com|mandments are my de|light.
144 \The righteousness of your decrees is ever\lasting;
    grant me under\standing that I may \ live.

QOPH — The Nineteenth Letter

QÁRÁ.THI V:KHOL-LÉV "aNÉNI

v.145 I have called with my whole heart; answer me!

I have called or cried from the heart, not with elegant prayers, but with cries of yearning, frustration and despair. I am awake early in the morning, before the alarm clock sounds, seeking an answer from you. I have been awake in the night, at two o'clock, three o'clock, four o'clock; my eyes wide open as I thought about your promises, and longed for an answer from you.

I feel profoundly insecure. Nothing seems solid any more, nothing. Not my job, career, marriage, health, relationships. I question my own abilities, even basic competence seems doubtful. The enemies, the forces of disorder, are on the move again. The mountain top experience seems very insubstantial now. And this too is part of the path. Yet I know that you are near, your commandments are true — that is, reliable, constant, consistent — established for all eternity.

REYSH — The Twentieth Letter

RO.SH-D:VÁR:KHÁ .eMETH

v.160 The heart of your word is truth.

The heart, actually *the head*, of your word is truth, that which is constant and reliable. For .eMETH (*truth*) is from the same root as faith or faithfulness. The heart of your word is constancy, faithfulness; it is learning to be constant with God, my family, my patients. That is the heart, the leading value of your word. Not to be excited about miracles, nor zealous about the occult. Not to enthuse over Pastor Wonderful nor to agitate against those who are different. But to assimilate his faithful ways: to be constant, stable, reliable; balanced in any situation. Compare Philippians 4:8,11,12.

It is easy to get carried away. All it takes is a thought, a word, then another thought, then emotion. Soon the crusade is under way. It feels important to lead a crusade, to be part of a movement. But this is the better part: "I do not forget your teaching ... I have not swerved from your judgments ... the heart of your word is truth." The heart of your word is this: a constancy that is never rigid, always reliable, never condemning of anyone.

<u>Suggestions</u>: Read or sing Psalm 119 whenever you can't sleep. Sing slowly, in that steady, flowing rhythm. In group study share from the heart, that is, your deepest concerns and yearnings. Seek the heart of this word, its essential message for yourself; but do not lecture to anyone else. Verse 145 is slightly modified by the author.

Psalm 119 (BCP)

Twenty-sixth Day: Evening Prayer Tone: NÉVEL

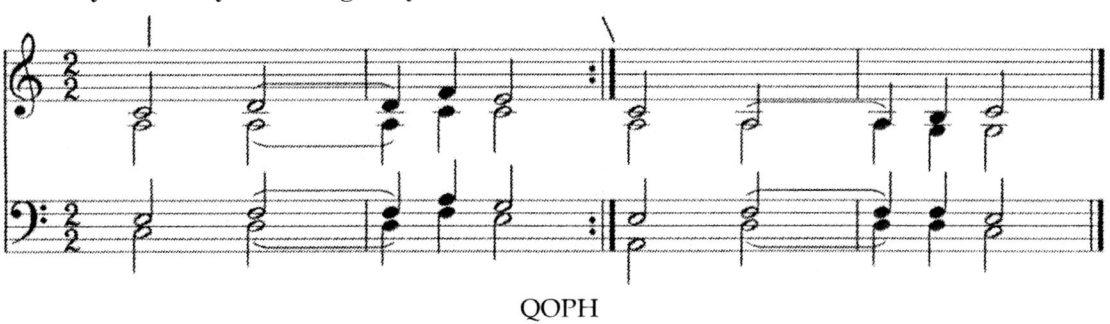

QOPH

145 I call with my whole heart; | answer me, (*)
    O LORD, that I may | keep your | statutes.
146 I call to you; oh, that you would | save me!
    I will | keep your de|crees.
147 Early in the morning I cry | out to you,
    for in your | word is my | trust.
148 \My eyes are open in the night \ watches,
    that I may \ meditate upon your \ promise.
149 Hear my voice, O LORD, according to your loving|kindness;
    according to your | judgments, give me | life.
150 They draw near who in malice | persecute me;
    they are very | far from your | law.
151 You, O LORD, are near at | hand,
    and all your com|mandments are | true.
152 \Long have I known from your de\crees
    that you have e\stablished them for \ ever.

REYSH

153 Behold my affliction and de|liver me,
    for I do | not forget your | law.
154 Plead my cause and re|deem me;
    according to your | promise give me | life.
155 Deliverance is far from the | wicked,
    for they do not | study your | statutes.
156 \Great is your com\passion, O LORD;
    preserve my \ life, according to your \ judgments.
157 There are many who persecute and op|press me,
    yet I have not | swerved from your de|crees.
158 I look with loathing at the | faithless,
    for | they have not | kept your word.
159 See how I love your com|mandments!
    O LORD, in your | mercy, pre|serve me.
160 \The heart of your word is \ truth;
    all your righteous \ judgments endure for \ evermore.

SHIN or SIN — The Twenty-first Letter

SHÁLOM RÁV L:.OHaVEY THORÁTHEKHÁ

v.165 Great peace have they who love your law.

Shalom means completeness, wholeness or health. We tend to think of it as the absence of conflict, or as a calm feeling. That kind of peace can be achieved, temporarily, by ignoring unpleasantness; by insisting, at any cost, that all is well. Sometimes the word is used as a spiritual cloak: A person says, "I have peace about it," after deciding something terribly misguided. In this sense, *I have peace about it* might mean, *I am a very spiritual person, so don't question me!*

Godly peace, true peace, is not like that at all. It is wholeness, doing what I was called to do with all that is in me, but it is not always peaceful or comfortable. Jesus said, "My peace I give unto you" (John 14:27, KJV), but he added, "not as the world giveth." He also said, "Suppose ye that I am come to give peace on earth? I tell you, Nay; but rather division" (Luke 12:51). Great peace have they who love your law, but not a feeling of peace, or a peaceful appearance. Peace in difficulty, even in conflict.

Those who love your *Torah* will increasingly understand and accept differences, and harmonize contradictions; they will become ever more complete. But they will not always be comfortable and they will not always bring comfort. Sometimes they will be known as troublemakers.

Suggestions: Seek peace (*shalom*) in every aspect of your life. Seek to be complete, balanced, fully aware of your potential for evil as well as good. Do not strive to be or appear peaceful, serene, calm. Remember that peace is a fruit of the Spirit, a natural outgrowth of genuine spiritual life. In your meditation, remain awake, alert, and balanced; clear your thoughts and be silent, over and over.

SHIN / SIN

161 Rulers have persecuted me without a | cause,
    but my | heart stands in | awe of your word.
162 I am as glad because of your | promise
    as one who | finds great | spoils.
163 As for lies, I hate and | abhor them,
    but your | law is my | love.
164 \Seven times a day do I \ praise you,
    be\cause of your righteous \ judgments.
165 Great peace have they who love your | law;
    for | them there is no | stumbling block.
166 I have hoped for your sal|vation, O LORD,
    and I have ful|filled your com|mandments.
167 I have kept your de|crees
    and I have | loved them | deeply.
168 \I have kept your commandments and de\crees,
    for all my \ ways are be\fore you.

TÁW — The Twenty-second Letter

TÁW — the final letter — was anciently an X or cross. Perhaps we could say now, graduating Heavenly College, that we have begun with silence (energized potential, listening, teachable heart) and ended with a sort of cross. With the way of emptiness, surrender and crucifixion. Not a way of obvious harmony or of that peace that the world gives. It is the mysterious way of Christ, the way of plunging into conflict and giving oneself away.

T:#I-NAPHSHIY UTH:HAL:LEKHÁ

v.175   Let my soul (breath, breathing, life) live, and let her continue to praise you. Not just "I," that remarkably tenacious thought of who and how important I am, but my real self, my real existence: self-organizing, unpredictable complexity in breathing, walking, dancing, error and correction, growth and dissolution. Let her live, really live, more than exist. Spending herself in affirmation, praising you.

TÁW is a prefix in six of these eight verses. "Let her begin," or, "Let her continue." No longer what I will do or say, but *Let it happen.* "Let my cry come to your presence ... let my supplication come ... let my lips pour fourth ... let my tongue answer." Let all parts of me begin and continue to respond to you. More and more now I experience myself not as *thing* or *someone who*, but as process. Happening rather than doing. Perhaps this is what the psychologist Carl Rogers calls "fully functioning person" — a person in continual flux, continual development.* A person almost normal, no longer trying to be in control.

TÁ"ITHI K:SEH .OVÉD BAQQÉSH "AVDEKHÁ

v.176   I have gone astray like a sheep that is lost; search for your servant. Wisdom at last. The insight that I have wandered off like a sheep that goes lost, grazing my way to disaster. That I will always be this same wandering sheep and that I will need you to come look for me no matter how far I may go on the path. Indeed, that *is* the path: the growing realization of my need. Come look for me.

Suggestions: Continue to practice the formal meditation morning and evening. Let these teachings distill into your innermost self and transform you. Gradually increase the time you spend in silence. Let the soothing rhythm of Psalm 119 become a part of you. Seek to live in that rhythmic, steady way as you go through the day.

For additional material on the Hebrew alphabet, you may wish to browse Carlo Suarès: *The Sepher Yetzira*, Shambhala, 1976. Or study Feuer's commentary, pp. 1415-1501.

---

*Cited in Daniel Offer and Melvin Sabshin: *Normality. Theoretical and Clinical Concepts of Mental Health.* Basic Books, New York, 1966, pp. 208-210.

Psalm 119 (conclusion)

TÁW

169 Let my cry come before you, O | Lord;
    give me understanding, ac|cording to your | word.
170 Let my supplication come be|fore you;
    deliver me, ac|cording to your | promise.
171 My lips shall pour forth your | praise,
    when you | teach me your | statutes.
172 \My tongue shall sing of your \ promise,
    for all your com\mandments are \ righteous.
173 Let your hand be ready to | help me,
    for I have | chosen your com|mandments.
174 I long for your salvation, O | Lord,
    and your | law is my de|light.
175 Let me live, and I will | praise you,
    and let your | judgments | help me.
176 \I have gone astray like a sheep that is lost;
    search for your \ servant,
    for I do not for\get your com\mandments.

Songs Of The Steps: Commentary To Psalm 120

I think there is a stage of spiritual development when we have come up out of the darkness but in some ways we are even more unhappy than before. We have become sensitized to spiritual issues yet we feel powerless to live a spiritual life. We look around us and see only the negative. We talk about stress and burnout.

I spent a very long time in this stage. I wanted to spend my days meditating and thinking about God, but I kept finding myself in surroundings where that seemed impossible. I kept thinking, *Not here!* How could I become enlightened at Charity Hospital, New Orleans? How could I grow spiritually in places filled with despair and double-talk? How could I be a Christian in a place where no one seemed to care?

Can a person grow spiritually while practicing psychiatry? Can one pray while carrying a beeper? Can I possibly pray to you, LORD, knowing that at any moment the telephone may ring? That someone will be making unreasonable demands? And that, worst of all, I will soon become angry and defensive?

.aNIY-SHÁLOM W:KHI-.aDABBÉR   HÉMMÁh LAMMIL#ÁMÁH
v.7 I am (for) peace, but when I speak,
they are for war.

I can identify with the writer as he complains, "Long has my soul languished here with one who hates *shalom*. Yes, I am of *shalom*, but when I try to tell them, they are for war!" I am of peace (wholeness, health, completeness), but they are all for war. Why can't I interest them in peace? Why won't they listen to my ideas? Is it because they consider me pompous, abrasive? Because what I really want is not peace but recognition? Because I glare at them and think of them as right-wing fanatics or worse? If I were really for peace, I would *be* at peace. I would demonstrate peace. I get so lonely being the only one who knows what to do, and no one, no one at all, will listen to me.

Coming out of Heavenly College I would have liked to stay there in the cool mists and meditate. Like Peter, who wanted to stay on the mountain and build little shrines. But God would not allow me to go on mystical vacation, or to keep saying, *Not here!* Rather, it seems, he is teaching me to say yes. Even in Meshech, even in Kedar. Yes, LORD, what do you want me to do?

Here begin the fifteen psalms called Songs of the Steps. What are these steps? Some scholars liken them to fifteen steps leading up to the temple sanctuary, steps on which the Levites used to sing these psalms. To others they are the steps of spiritual progress. They define a spirituality of everyday life. I begin in darkness, unhappiness, frustration, complaining. All is not well. I have such a long way to go.

Suggestions: Take heed to the personal application in each of these psalms. When you find yourself in this writer's situation, when you know exactly what is needed, but no one will listen to you; remember what you have learned in this book. Stop everything, clear your thoughts, and *listen*! What is it you have failed to hear in this situation? What is God trying to tell you?

Psalm 120 (BCP)

Twenty-seventh Day: Morning Prayer   Tone: N:GINOTH

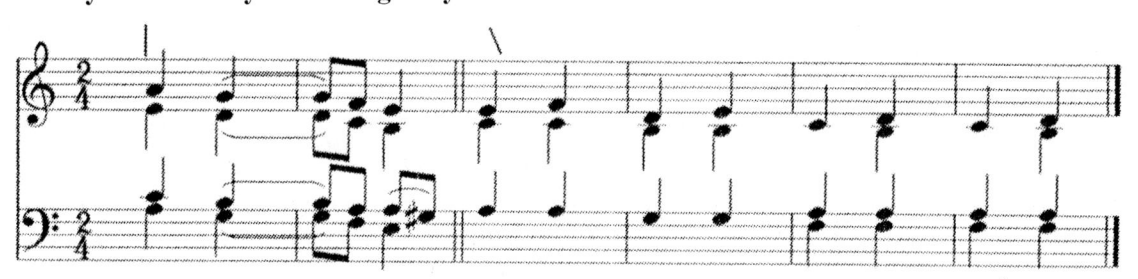

1 **When I was in trouble, I | called to the LORD;**
   I | called to the LORD, and he | answered me.
2 \Deliver me, O LORD, from lying \ lips
   and from the deceitful \ tongue.
3 What shall be done to you, and what \ more besides,
   O you deceitful \ tongue?
4 \The sharpened arrows of a \ warrior,
   along with hot glowing \ coals.
5 **How hateful it is that I must lodge in | Meshech**
   and | dwell among the tents of Ke|dar!
6 \Too long have I had to \ live
   among the enemies of \ peace.
7 I am on the side of \ peace,
   but when I speak of it, they are for \ war.

I Lift Up My Eyes: Commentary To Psalm 121

The lifting up of eyes (soul, hands, heart) can be understood on many levels. Lifting up my eyes I see things differently. If you had asked me how I feel, you might have noticed a downward glance, eyes shadowed as I pondered internal experience. But ask me to *think* (when? where? how?) and you may see my eyes roll up, scanning an unseen horizon. There is a physiologic change as I move from scattered thoughts and emotion to looking for a certain answer. A different part of the brain is being consulted. So we might understand the abrupt transitions of 121.

.ESSÁ. "EYNAY .EL-HEHÁRIM   ME.AYiN YÁVOW. "EZRIY
"EZRIY MÉ"IM YHWH

v.1 I lift up my eyes to the hills.
Where is my help going to come from?
v.2 My help is (coming) from the LORD.

In the previous psalm, I was exiled somewhere in Arabia, with people who wouldn't listen to my ideas or share my values. But when I changed my attitude from self-righteous complaining to submission, I felt better at once. And I thought, "Wait! Where does my help really come from?" And I answered my own question instantly. "My help comes from the LORD!" And with that thought came rest.

Lifting up my eyes is more than looking up, it is raising the level of my vision. Lifting it to a higher perspective. Spiritual vision. I look up and I see things differently. No longer from the perspective of my thoughts and my feelings alone. LORD, what do you want me to see?

I was frustrated and unhappy with you. I felt you were not listening to me. Then, I look up. I lift up my eyes, as it were, and I see you differently. You are no longer a problem I have to deal with. For that tiny moment you are a message from God. You are not there to meet my needs or to frustrate them; you are there because God wants you there, and I can only look deep into your eyes and praise him. Looking into your eyes I see you seeing me. I look into your eyes and God looks back at me.

Working as a psychiatrist I see so many who look down, as though there were answers in the floor. Eyes probing lap or fingernails, they drift into reverie, mired in a gloom from which they cannot get free. *What is the use?* they think. *What good will it do to talk about it?* (Where is my help going to come from?) Some will look up, if asked, but many will not. Lifting up the eyes is a serious thing. It is a tiny but decisive choice. Life, but not control. My help does not come from within me. It is the LORD who will preserve my soul (breathing, life).

Notes: (*) signifies translation modified by the author. Forms of the word SHÁMAR (*to guard* or *preserve*) are found in almost every verse.

Suggestions: Look upward slightly on verses 1-2. Practice lifting the eyes when you find yourself in stress and turmoil. Take a deep breath through the nose and look upward ever so slightly. Experience that movement from feeling to thought to awareness of the moment, here and now.

Psalm 121 (BCP), modified*

Tone: #a3O3:ROTH

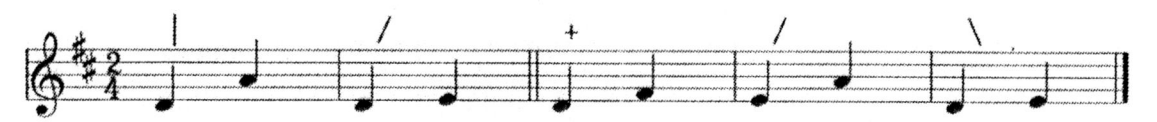

1 **I lift up my eyes to the | hills;**
 /from where is my / help to come?
2 **My help comes from the | Lord,**
 /the maker of heaven and / earth.

3 +He will not let your + foot be moved,
 and he who watches over you will not fall / asleep.
4 Behold, he who keeps watch over Israel
 shall neither slumber nor \ sleep;
5 +The Lord himself watches + over you;
 the Lord is your shade at your right / hand,
6 So that the sun shall not strike you by day,
 nor the moon by \ night.
7 +The Lord shall preserve you from all + evil;
 The Lord shall preserve your / soul. (*)
8 The Lord shall preserve your going out and your coming in,
 from this time forth for \ evermore.

Let Us Go: Commentary To Psalm 122

A few days ago I was languishing in the Arabian desert, but "now our feet are standing within your gates, O Jerusalem!" I was so unhappy then, adrift like a bird without a nest; now, without fully understanding, I have come home—from Meshech to Jerusalem. From a state of self-righteous, lonely complaining to — *community*. To a city at peace with itself, where the tribes come together. There I was a permanent stranger, an outsider with outlandish ideas. But here I experience fellowship.

SÁ<u>MA</u>#TI B:.OM:RIM LIY   BEYTH YHWH NÉLÉKH
v.1 I was glad when they said to me,
"Let us go to the house of the LORD."

I was so happy when they asked me to join them, to go to the LORD's house. They never asked who I was, or what I do for a living, or whether I was saved or spirit-filled. They just said, "Let us go." And I went with them, not even sure what that meant; all I knew for sure was that I was no longer just *me*, but part of an *us*, part of a community.

That's how it was in my first church, a tiny Episcopal church that we called the Chapel. The pastor was a remarkable man, utterly unlike my stereotype of the Christian preacher. He never tried to convert me. He didn't claim to have all the answers. He never acted virtuous. Yet I soon came to recognize his intense awareness of me, and of my spiritual journey, and his caring; and that he saw me without illusions, just as I was, and still accepted me.

One Sunday, during a heated congregational discussion, I said, "Well, I'm not a member of this congregation, but... " and he responded, "No! This is your church. You belong here. This is your church!" The acceptance I experienced at that moment continues to transform my life even years later, for in that moment I had a glimpse of Jesus. This same pastor once remarked to me that Jesus didn't write a book, he founded a community. I thought a great deal about that. Why didn't he write a book? How we would love to have a copy of his book!

I slowly came to understand that Jesus did something far more profound for us than write a book. He seeded himself among us like the mustard seed; he hid himself in our midst like the leaven in three measures of meal; he made us a community, so that he could live among us always.

Spiritual growth is not a private matter; it is more than self-realization. Scripture portrays it as the growth to community. To the place where you belong, no matter who you are; the place where I can say to you, unconditionally, "Let us go."

<u>Suggestions</u>: Sing to the Tone MÁ#OL (*dance*) and the movement Twirling Dance (see Appendix).

Join yourself to a praying community and participate in its life. Commit yourself to this community and stay with it as faithfully as you can. Accept everyone who comes to your community and exclude no one.

Psalm 122 (BCP)

Tone: MÁ#OL

1. \I was glad when they \ said to me,
   "Let us go to the \ house of the LORD."
2. \Now our feet are \ standing
   within your gates, O Je\rusalem.
3. **Jerusalem is | built as a | city**
   that is at unity | with itself;
4. \To which the tribes go up,
   the tribes of the \ LORD,
   the assembly of \ Israel,
   to praise the \ Name of the LORD.
5. \For there are the thrones of \ judgment,
   the thrones of the house of \ David.
6. **Pray for the | peace of | Jerusalem:**
   "May they prosper who | love you.
7. \Peace be within your \ walls
   and quietness within your \ towers.
8. \For my brethren and com\panions' sake,
   I pray for your pros\perity.
9. **Because of the house of the | LORD our | God,**
   I will seek to do | you good."

Up To Helplessness: Commentary To Psalm 123

Submitting yourselves to one another in the fear of God (Ephesians 5:21, NKJ).

HINNÉH KH:"EYNEY "aVÁDIM .EL-YAD .aDONEYHEM
v.2 Behold, like the eyes of slaves toward the hand of their masters.

Again I lift up my eyes—that is, my vision—to the realization of helpless dependency. Ever since I can remember I have been fighting for autonomy. Independence! The state where no one could tell me what to do. All too soon I achieved it, or thought I did, but I never felt free. Freedom began when I accepted helplessness, when I learned to receive.

Helpless dependency is the natural state of man. We tend to confuse this with pathologic dependency—whining and clinging behavior. Natural dependency is inter-dependence. We are the naked animal, noisy but helpless we are born. We live in groups and pairs. It is not good for us to be alone; we were created to need a helper (Genesis 2:18). We like to pretend that we are self-sufficient predators in the social jungle. Deep in our hearts we know better. Soon enough the jungle games are over and we can only hope that someone will call us for supper.

We each depend on each other, and we all depend on God. We lift up our eyes to him, and we realize how vulnerable we are. We cannot control anything or anyone. We are continuously and permanently in danger. There is no security, none. And because there is no security, and never will be, we learn to take care of one another. Submitting ourselves to one another in the fear of God, as Paul says. Literally subordinating, putting ourselves in orderly relationships, giving up control to one another. Accepting authority. Accepting responsibility.

KÉN "EYNEYNU .EL-YHWH
v.3 So our eyes to the LORD.

Subordinating ourselves to one another—putting ourselves in one another's care, as even a slave subordinates himself (or herself) to an owner—is part of the spiritual path. And the second part is subordinating ourselves to God. Putting ourselves under authority, accepting care. It is not necessarily an hierarchical system, for we are all subordinate together. Giving up control to each other, we learn to surrender to God. And to accept his comfort. And to ask for mercy.

<u>Suggestions</u>: Sit or kneel. Look upward slightly on verses 1-3. Always meditate with your eyes open, but let them look about naturally. Do not stare fixedly at any one point, so that you will not slip into reverie or trance. The music for Psalms 123 and 124 is the same.

Practice brief moments of silence in your interactions with each person. Ask God how you are to relate to this person. Recognize that in some way, known or unknown, your life depends on this individual.

Psalm 123 (BCP)

Tone: HIGÁYON

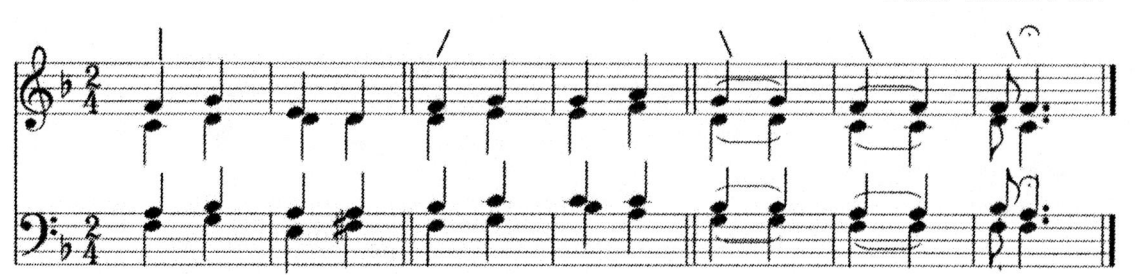

1 **To you I lift up my | eyes,**
   to you enthroned in the | heavens.
2 / As the eyes of servants look to the hand of their / masters,
   and the eyes of a maid to the hand of her / mistress,
3 **So our eyes look to the LORD our | God,**
   until he show us his | mercy.
4 / Have mercy upon us, O LORD, have / mercy,
   for we have had more than enough of con/tempt,
5 \ Too much of the scorn of the indolent rich,
   \ and of the derision
   of the \ proud.

Escaped Like A Bird: Commentary To Psalm 124

NAPH<u>SHE</u>NU K:3IPPOR NIML:tÁH   MIPPA# YOQSHIM
v.7   We have escaped like a bird from the snare of the fowler.

San Diego, 1982. A beautiful spring day. There is a commotion in the house and our cat is unceremoniously thrown out the front door. Cat has just killed a bird in the upstairs bedroom closet. I run upstairs and find a little black bird lying on the floor of the closet. I pick him up and immediately realize he is not dead. He is in some kind of frozen state, as if resigned to his death, unable to move. We discovered the crime just in time.

I open a window in this second story room and gently place the little bird on a roof that slopes down from the ledge. At this very moment, cat is climbing up over the edge of the roof, determined to finish off her prey. Suddenly bird comes to his senses and flies away.

I have often wondered what the little bird thought about this adventure, what he might have told his bird friends. Perhaps he told them, "Yes, there is life after death. It was like a pair of great hands that gently picked me up." Maybe he told them, "It was a miracle. I was snatched from the jaws of death!" Or perhaps he thought he had escaped by being so still and quiet. Maybe he had prayed. What happened to the little bird after that I do not know. Perhaps he was eaten by another cat later that day. Or perhaps his descendants are even now twittering and flying about San Diego.

We interpret our experiences at our own level of wisdom and according to our own needs. A tragic mishap that takes a life is considered a freak accident. Unexpected survival is considered a miracle. Some Christians put great emphasis on miracles. Miracles validate faith. Miracles validate the believer; they show that one is in favor with God. Miracles are the reward for good behavior. This is exhilarating when things are going well. But when the miracles don't seem to come, faith is questioned, and the victim is questioned. Perhaps, after all, he or she was lacking in faith.

Psalm 124 offers a different view. Life itself is a miracle. It has been a miracle all the way along. We have survived another day. At any and every moment we were doomed. Any wave could have taken us down in that stormy sea. What will happen with the next wave, who can say? It has all been grace, all miracles. What can we learn from it? Only to say, "Thank you, LORD!"

<u>Suggestions</u>: Think of yourself as the little bird, "escaped from the snare of the fowler," and be thankful for miracles. For existence itself, for breathing, for waking in the morning, for colors and flavors. When you experience a miracle, tell no one. Do not boast. Do not judge the miracles of anyone else.

Psalm 124 (BCP)

1 **If the L<small>ORD</small> had not been on our | side,**
   let Israel now | say;
2 **If the L<small>ORD</small> had not been on our | side,**
   when enemies rose up | against us;
3 /Then would they have swallowed us up / alive
   in their fierce anger to/ward us;
4 **Then would the waters have over|whelmed us**
   and the torrent gone | over us;
5 /Then would the raging / waters
   have gone right / over us.
6 \Blessed be the L<small>ORD</small>!
   he has not given us over to be a prey for their teeth.
7 \We have escaped like a bird from the snare of the fowler;
   the snare is broken, and \ we have escaped.
8 /Our help is in the Name of the / L<small>ORD</small>,
   the maker of heaven and / earth.

Like Mount Zion: Commentary To Psalm 125

HABBOt:#IM BAYHWH K:HAR-3IYYON   LO.-YIMMOt L:"OLÁM YÉSHÉV
v.1 Those who are trusting in the LORD are like Mount Zion,
it will not be moved (shaken, overthrown), it will stand to eternity.

Those who are trusting in the LORD are like an unshakable fortress, surrounded by protecting mountains; just so are God's people surrounded by his protection, now and forever.

Trusting in the LORD sounds easy. I trust in him and find my security in him. But then I feel insecure. I worry about my job. I worry about my marriage. My patient is doing poorly and I go home with a sinking feeling. I thought I was trusting in him, but I was trusting myself. I thought I was trusting in the LORD, but I was trusting in religion. The Episcopal Church stands round about her people. At least my little church community stands round about me. "I can always pray," I was thinking, trusting in prayers.

I thought I was trusting in the LORD, but I was trusting my faith. I was feeling very spiritual. I was learning all kinds of Scriptures. I was trusting the words "trust the LORD." I was making fantastic spiritual progress, and yet... I was waking up at four in the morning, reaching for my wife and telling her, "I'm a nervous wreck." And she would comfort me, wishing she could get me to relax.

Trusting in the LORD is radical insecurity, the security of having no security at all. Compare 27. I do not have to feel secure. I will not die of anxiety. I do not know where my foot will land. I live from one breath to the next and I hear myself worrying. And if only I could learn to let go. I would soon begin to trust letting go. LETTING GO THERAPY SWEEPING NATION; LGT CLINICS OPENING IN MALLS.

It is so easy to wander off the path. Surround us, LORD, with your protection—from ourselves. It is so deceptively easy to trust in ourselves and our wisdom, our faith, our (apparent) surrender, our overflowing good will, our obvious spirituality, our extensive reading, and our undeniable good intentions. It is so easy to get inflated. Give me a little recognition and I will follow you to hell. Protect me, O LORD, from jumping up and following the evildoers.

And how do I trust in the LORD without trusting in trust?

<u>Suggestions</u>: Practice trusting in the LORD in actual situations. Do the difficult job or face the difficult crisis, now, without knowing how it will turn out. Pray for direction as you proceed and be willing to do whatever he wills.

Psalm 125 (BCP)

Tone: #a3O3:ROTH

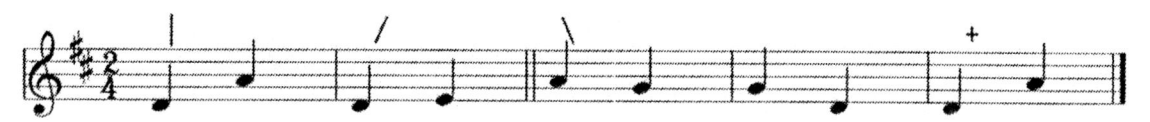

1 **Those who trust in the LORD are like Mount | Zion,**
   /which cannot be moved, but stands fast for / ever.
2 \The hills stand about \ Jerusalem;
   so does the LORD stand round about his \ people,
   from this time forth for + evermore.
3 \The scepter of the wicked shall not hold \ sway
   over the land allotted to the \ just,
   so that the just shall not put their hands to + evil.
4 **Show your goodness, O LORD, to those who are | good**
   /and to those who are / true of heart.
5 \As for those who turn aside to crooked \ ways,
   the LORD will lead them away with the \ evildoers;
   but peace be upon + Israel.

Dance Of Joy: Commentary To Psalm 126

We tend to think of joy as an exuberant, special kind of pleasure or happiness. Intuitively we understand it as a higher or spiritual happiness. Joy is to happiness, we might say, as heaven is to sky, or home to house.

Sometimes I don't know what joy means. For days or weeks I walk in the gray zone, and joy is a meaningless concept. I can make jokes and laugh, but I cannot make myself joyful, no matter how hard I try. I have to remember that joy is a fruit of the Spirit (Galatians 5:22). It comes when it comes, when the wind blows, when the Spirit brings it out of me.

Sometimes I do know the meaning of joy. It is the high delight of returning. Like times when we have quarreled and then we make up, and I hold you in my arms again. It is like rediscovering something precious that I thought was lost. It is what I would feel if I could talk to my mother again. Joy is the experience of restoration. Strangely enough, I can't go home again until I have been lost. I cannot appreciate what was always there until I find it for myself.

HAZOR"IM B:DIM"ÁH   B:RINNÁH YIQ3ORU
v.6 Those who are sowing with tears,
in joy they begin to harvest.

Now I begin to understand why they must sow in tears. Why joy is not harvested from joy but from hard planting, from the agriculture of tears. Searching within myself I could never find it. Sowing my seed in the world, and letting it go, practicing silence, I come home with the harvest. I used to take long, sad walks, wishing and hoping that life could be better. Now I am learning to live moment by moment, harvesting joy.

Joy is not always spectacular or dramatic. Sometimes it is as simple as returning to what I really am: a human breathing, being here, moment by moment. To my real existence, wordless and simple. To the happy, laughing baby that I was before I learned self-consciousness. It is as simple as returning to silence, when the chattering thoughts are still, even for a moment, and I can listen to God.

<u>Suggestions</u>: Sing joyfully to the Tone MÁ#OL (*dance*) and the movement Twirling Dance (see Appendix). Experiment until you find the step that feels joyful, as in 100.

Do not strive to be or appear joyful. Follow the way of surrender, moment by moment, and joy will come. In every difficult situation, give up control and listen. It is not for you to know how this will turn out. Go out with the seed, do the work, return to the silence, enjoy the moment. In your meditation, do not attempt to remain in silence, but return to it, again and again.

Psalm 126 (BCP)

Twenty-seventh Day: Evening Prayer Tone: MÁ#OL

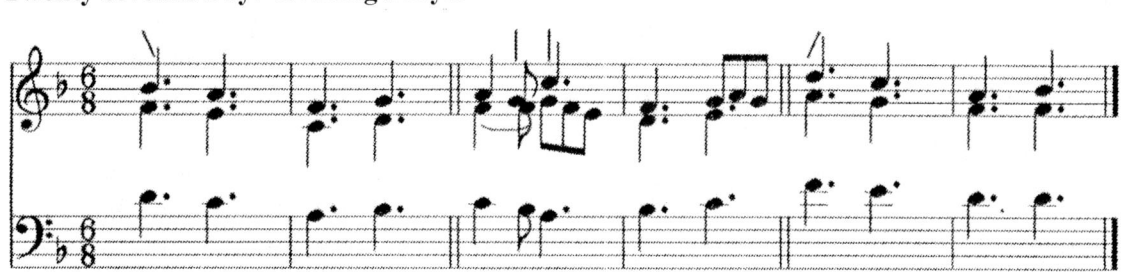

1 \When the LORD restored the fortunes of \ Zion,
 then were we like those who \ dream.
2 **Then was our mouth | filled with | laughter,**
 and our tongue with shouts of | joy.
3 \Then they said among the \ nations,
 "The LORD has done great \ things for them."
4 **The LORD has done great | things for | us,**
 and we are glad in | deed.
5 \Restore our fortunes, O \ LORD,
 like the watercourses of the \ Negev.
6 /Those who sowed with / tears
 will reap with songs of / joy,
7 \Those who go out \ weeping,
 carrying the \ seed,
 will come a | gain with | joy,
 shouldering their | sheaves.

Vain That You Rise So Early: Commentary To Psalm 127

SHÁW. LÁKHEM MASHKIMEY QUM   M:.A#aREY-<u>SHE</u>VETh
.OKHLEY LE#EM HA"a3ÁVIM

v.3 It is vain for you rising up early, staying up late,
eating the bread of toilsome labor.

How silly to get up early and stay late at the office, to worry about professional success and to compete for power. Unless God is in the work, the work is doomed. I cannot control the outcome. It is the same whether I work for a corporation or a church. I cannot be sure of success.

In every profession and occupation we hear the same thing: more stress, more pressure, little joy. The workers worry about their future, the owners about costs. There is more to do, less time to do it right, less help with the burden. The only reward is the money but we have nothing to show for it. We cannot spend time with our children. All vain, says the writer, doomed. And not only for the company, it is doomed for you. It is in vain that you wake up early and stay up late, burning up your life's energy in the pursuit of success. There is something more important.

Like Psalm 90, a treatise on the use of time. I hear a great deal about time management, the efficient use of time; in my own experience it never works very well. I can organize my time, but then someone comes along and steals time from me. I come early and stay late, trying to make up for lost time. I organize time and plan time. Things to do, appointments, goals for the day. A spiritual approach to time is surrendered time. I respond to the person who needs me at the moment of need. Then I respond to the next need. I enjoy the moment, meeting the need; I let go of the moment I had planned. I have great difficulty with this. I am slowly learning that time does not belong to me.

v.6 Happy is the man who has filled
his quiver (full) of them (children).

Real happiness is not success at the office, but receiving from God. Real happiness is taking care of your family. Responding to the need as it arises, here and now. Enjoying the moment as it comes and letting it go. Being there, really there, with your total attention, when your child needs you.

Then you will not be embarrassed at the gate. That is, the city gate, the place where business is conducted, where the men get together to boast and compete. The real world, so-called, of outward friendliness and savage competition. Real happiness is to take care of your children, and to stay with your spouse, and to watch them grow up, together. Those who do these things will have nothing to be embarrassed about when they meet with their competitors in the gate—the real world, the business world, the academic world, any world.

<u>Suggestions</u>: Plan your time, but be ready to change your plans at any moment. Respond to the need of a child before anything else. Practice moments of silence all through the day, and listen for the timing of God. Note that the music for Psalms 127 and 128 is the same.

Psalm 127 (BCP)

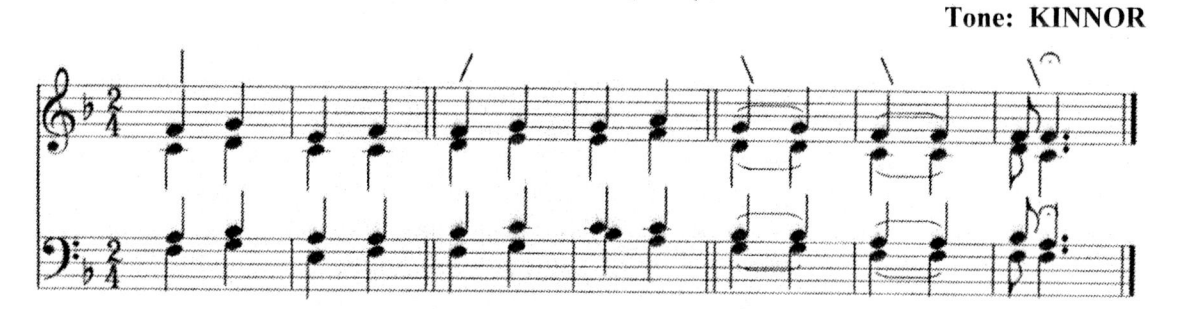

Tone: KINNOR

1 **Unless the LORD builds the | house,**
   their labor is in vain who | build it.
2 /Unless the LORD watches over the / city,
   in vain the watchman keeps his / vigil.
3 \It is in vain that you rise so early, and go to bed so late;
   \vain too, to eat the bread of toil,
   for he gives to his beloved \ sleep.
4 **Children are a heritage from the | LORD,**
   and the fruit of the womb is a | gift.
5 /Like arrows in the hand of a / warrior
   are the children of one's / youth.
6 \Happy is the man who has his quiver full of them!
   \he shall not be put to shame
   when he contends with his enemies in the \ gate.

Your Wife Like A Fruitful Vine: Commentary To Psalm 128

A psalm about the spirituality of marriage. Begin with the fear of God, that awareness of vulnerability; the awareness that you do not own yourself and cannot own anyone else. You begin any relationship as a sinful, distractible human breathing.

v.2 The produce of your hands, when you begin to eat.
When you begin to take care of yourself, feed yourself. When you are ready, emotionally and financially, to leave your parents. All parents. You will not be looking for someone to take care of you and minister to you. And you will not be looking for someone weaker or helpless, someone for you to take care of. You will be self-sustaining looking for self-sustaining. Then how happy you will be.

.ESHT:KHÁ K:GEPHEN PORIYÁH   B:YARKTHEY VEYTHEKHÁ
v.3 Your wife like a fruitful vine
in the innermost recesses of your house.
That is, where you live. Your spouse will be a life-giving partner at the very center of your life. Your spouse will nourish and encourage you at the very core of life, the intimate zone. It will be a life-giving relationship that keeps you healthy. Many good things (fruit) will come out of your marriage, because your spouse believes in you and brings out the best in you, just as you do for your spouse.

BÁNEYKHÁ KISH:THILEY ZEYTHIM   SÁVIV L:SHUL#ÁNEKHÁ
v.3b   your children like olive shoots, round about your table. Around that core of commitment, the family circle, the children growing like olive plants. You do not raise them, really; they grow, drawing from that nourishing center. All this is possible for those who fear the LORD.

Marriage is profoundly touching to me. I am touched when my patients come to see me with their spouses. When I invite their spouses into the sessions, they are invariably grateful. I see the tension in these life-giving partners, and their caring. I am deeply touched when a wife comforts her panicky husband, or a husband encourages his depressed wife. It is not romantic. It is constancy, faith, the Holy Spirit at work.

Marriage is the long conversation, the devoted struggle. It is learning to solve problems together and be defeated together. It is learning to be who you are and let your spouse be other. It is admitting, like the alcoholic, that you are powerless. It is the relentless mirror, yourself at your best and your worst. It is having no defense, no escape, and no mask. Not your career or your ministry, but this: this is your real work. Doing this spiritual work in the heart of your house, you will see good for Jerusalem, that is, your city; and peace upon Israel, that is, your community.

Suggestions: Practice moments of silence with your spouse, seeing your spouse always in new ways. Keep your spouse always at the very center of your life. Study the Song of Songs, with its profound teaching about relationships.

Psalm 128 (BCP)

1 **Happy are they all who fear the | L**ORD**,**
   and who follow in his | ways!
2 /You shall eat the fruit of your / labor;
   happiness and prosperity shall be / yours.
3 **Your wife shall be like a fruitful vine within your | house,**
   your children like olive shoots round about
   your | table.
4 /The man who fears the / LORD
   shall thus indeed be / blessed.
5 \The LORD bless you from Zion,
   \and may you see the prosperity of Jerusalem
   all the days of your \ life.
6 **May you live to see your children's | children;**
   may peace be upon | Israel.

Since My Youth: Commentary To Psalm 129

RABBATH 3:RÁRUNI MIN:"URAY YO.MAR-NÁ. YISRÁ.ÉL
v.1 Greatly have they oppressed me since my youth.

Greatly have they oppressed (constrained, constricted) me since my youth. Life grinds us down. Life wears us down and takes away illusions. And in doing so, it makes us human. Out of that grinding comes a depth. Life grinds away those illusions of our youth, dreams of what we will do and be. Life grinds away that wonderful proud husk and finds the heart.

One day in "my youth" a thick red volume arrived at our house; it was the twenty-fifth annual review of my father's college class. Each alumnus reported on his life, his accomplishments since the last report. The men (yes, in those days they were all men) who wrote those little essays were highly successful—in industry, banking, medicine, the ministry. Yet they sounded disillusioned and weary. They looked back on their lives with regret and a sense of emptiness. I remember that I found this amazing, and was sure I would never be like that.

In my youth I knew better than anyone. I was certain to be rich and famous. I was sure I would find the cure for cancer. After lunch, I could do something else. Reaching the age of fifty things were different. I was learning more about limitations. I was studying a subject called humility.

RABBATH 3:RÁRUNI MIN:"URÁY GAM LO.-YÁKHLU LIY
v.2 Greatly have they oppressed me since my youth,

but they have not prevailed against me. Literally, *they were not able to me*. Hopefully I can give up my illusions without becoming disillusioned. I can know my helplessness and keep on going. I can put my life on the cross and let him use it. I am becoming human now, at last. I am looking at wisdom now, for a moment, here and there.

v.3 The plowmen plowed upon my back.

Plowed me, let us hope, for planting, for fruitfulness. For empathy, for humility, for not knowing all the answers, for the ability to say, "I don't know"; for the ability to laugh at myself; for the depth to understand suffering. For the wisdom of middle age.

Thomas Hawkins* writes, "we cannot really 'read' the psalms with meaning until we have lived through some of life's tragic and exhilarating hours." Until we have been oppressed and plowed and worn down and also lifted up. Until we have acquired some of that wisdom of middle age.

<u>Suggestions</u>: Sing this psalm and the next one to the Tone HIGÁYON (*meditation*). Reflect on your personal history but do not complain or blame. What have you learned from life that no one could have told you? Remember that God has been with you all the way along.

---

*Thomas R. Hawkins: *The Unsuspected Power of the Psalms*, The Upper Room, Nashville, TN, 1985, p.16.

Psalm 129 (BCP)

Tone: HIGÁYON

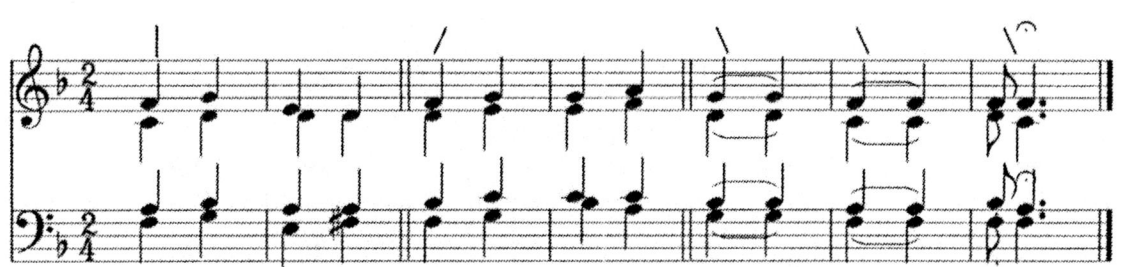

1 "Greatly have they oppressed me since my | youth,"
 let Israel now | say;
2 "Greatly have they oppressed me since my | youth,
 but they have not prevailed a | gainst me."
3 /The plowmen plowed upon my / back
 and made their furrows / long.
4 \The LORD, the Righteous One,
 has cut the cords of the wicked.
5 \Let them be put to shame and thrown back,
 all those who are enemies of \ Zion.
6 **Let them be like grass upon the | housetops,**
 which withers before it can be | plucked;
7 /Which does not fill the hand of the / reaper,
 nor the bosom of him who binds the / sheaves;
8 \So that those who go by say not so much as,
 \"The LORD prosper you.
 We wish you well in the Name of the \ LORD."

My Soul Has Waited: Commentary To Psalm 130

QIW<u>WI</u>THI YHWH QIWW:THÁH NAPHSHIY   W:LID:VÁROW HO#ÁLTI

v.4 I have waited for the LORD, my soul (breath, breathing, life) has waited; and in his word I have hoped. Compare 40.

"I" (my thoughts) have waited; and my inner self, my breathing, my biological self has also waited. My life has been a waiting life, waiting to find a fulfillment I could hardly articulate. At times it has seemed like a drifting life, moving from one easy niche to another. I lived well but with no striking success. A life of restless discontent, varied experiences, rich fantasy, and shallow roots. And at the same time a called life, a waiting life, waiting for *something*.

Waiting to find my true love, and at last I did. Waiting to be "rich and famous," and most likely never will. Waiting for thirteen years for "Cosmic Consciousness," going nowhere. I waited for my ministry, something special to do, and you gave me the psalms. You gave me groups to lead, You let me do workshops. You open doors for me, always after waiting.

Looking back I can see more clearly. LORD, I have been waiting for you. Always for you, to be close to you, to know you! To be in your presence. To be your child. I never knew fully what that meant, yet I knew I was waiting for you.

NAPHSHIY LA.DONÁY MISSHOMRIM LAB<u>BO</u>QER   SHOMRIM LAB<u>BO</u>QER

v.5 My soul is for the LORD more than watchmen for the morning, watchmen for the morning.

My soul (my real self, breathing, life) is to the LORD, yearning and waiting, from among those, as Feuer puts it (p. 1567), who are longing for the dawn, those longing for the dawn. I know I am asleep, yet waiting and longing to wake up. And what is this wakening I wait for? It is wakening from the depths—from the alienation of self-consciousness, from being preoccupied with my feelings and my needs; from doing it my way; from trying harder and self-improvement. From knowing better and needing to be right. From everything that separates me from you, from the stifling oblivion of living for myself. When I awake from all these things, I shall be satisfied, beholding your likeness. Compare 17:16.

<u>Suggestions</u>: Sing vv. 4-6 with exquisite slowness, taking a full minute or more to sing these three verses. Sing this psalm when you find yourself under great pressure, or running out of time. You might be racing for home, for example, but the traffic is backed up for miles. Sing slowly and slow those racing thoughts. Teach yourself to breathe slowly — sharp, deep inhalations; long, slow, effortless exhalations, no more that six breaths in a minute.

When you come home from a stressful day and your thoughts are racing, take a few minutes to slow down before you meditate. Do whatever you must do slowly, Recollect a verse or line you have memorized; say it or think it slowly; let it go and be silent.

Psalm 130 (BCP)

1 **Out of the depths have I called to you, O Lord;**
   Lord, hear my | voice;
   let your ears consider well the voice of my suppli | cation.
2 **If you, Lord, were to note what is done a | miss;**
   O Lord, who could | stand?
3 /For there is / forgiveness with you;
   therefore you shall be / feared.
                    [S l o w l y]
4 \I wait for the Lord;
   \my soul waits for him;
   in his word is my \ hope.
5 **My soul waits for the Lord,**
   more than watchmen for the | morning,
   more than watchmen for the | morning.
6 /O Israel, wait for the / Lord,
   for with the Lord there is / mercy.
                    [Normal tempo]
7 \With him there is plenteous redemption,
   \and he shall redeem Israel
   from all their \ sins.

Like A Kid With Mom: Commentary To Psalm 131

YHWH LO.-GÁVAH' LIBBIY W:LO. RÁMUW "EYNAY
v.1 O LORD, my heart (attitude) has not been high (proud, arrogant), nor my eyes exalted.

Outspoken arrogance is secretly admired in our time; Assertive self-confidence is the ideal. The biblical concept of humility has no place in modern life. Certainly psychiatry has little to say about it.

American kids are taught to be best; if you can't be the best in school, be the best in sports, in something. If you can't be the best at anything, be the worst! American adults expect more of themselves. Not always more money, but something. Better dressed. Better educated. In some circles, false humility is the goal—more self-effacing. For me, it's recognition. To be told that I'm special; that I'm a good speaker or teacher. That I did a wonderful job. But it's never enough. I get high from it but soon I want more.

Jesus taught that real happiness comes with humility. "Blessed (O how happy) are the poor in spirit ... the meek" (Matthew 5:3,5, NKJ). When you are truly humble or meek, there is no need to defend yourself. You are nobody, free just to be there. You don't have to ask, "Why wasn't I told about this?" You and your self are not a big issue.

I struggle with that sense of entitlement. I'm always wondering, "Why wasn't I told about this?" and, "Why wasn't I consulted?" I always feel that I know better. The rare moments of humility have been my happiest times. When I first arrive in a place, and don't know how it is. When I haven't started to complain because I'm still grateful just to be there.

.IM-LO. SHIW<u>W</u>ITHI W:RO<u>MA</u>MTI NAPHSHIY K:GÁMUL "aLEY .IMMOW
v.3 But I have stilled, literally made level or balanced, and raised up my soul (breath, breathing, life), like a child with its mother. I have balanced and lifted up my soul. I have balanced thought with silence, silence with action, action with prayer, prayer with thought. I have become like a little kid with Mom, not worried, not self-conscious. Not worrying who I am or where I belong. Like a little kid at play, I can just be.

<u>Suggestions</u>: Sing this psalm and the next one to the Tone KINNOR. Sing v.4 s l o w l y.

Today for a few seconds, in one situation, act without self-consciousness. Still those troubled thoughts for those few seconds; watch yourself breathing, looking around, steering the car, picking up the telephone. Watch your hands move as you talk; see yourself doing what needs to be done, without that obsessive ruminating. Without that focus on "I" and "myself." It is hard, but you can do it for a few seconds. What is your experience?

Practice this teaching as often as you can. Look for humility, that fruit of the Spirit, to appear in your life. When it does, pay no attention to it!

Psalm 131 (BCP)

Tone: KINNOR

1 **O LORD, I am not | proud;**
   I have no haughty | looks.
2 /I do not occupy myself with great / matters,
   or with things that are too / hard for me.
3 \But I still my soul and make it quiet,
   \like a child upon its mother's breast;
   my soul is quieted with\in me.
                    [S l o w l y]
4 /O Israel, wait upon the / LORD,
   from this time forth for / evermore.

Never Say Never: Commentary To Psalm 132

v.4 I will not give sleep to my eyes,
nor slumber to my eyelids
v.5 Until I find a place for the LORD.

That is, a place for the ark, that marvelous gold-encrusted chest that once embodied God's presence. Its cover was a slab of solid gold surmounted by winged creatures. Between them, under their outspread wings, an awesome energy, a force both powerful and dangerous. Here God met with his people and taught them.

The writer says he will not go home or sleep again until he finds a resting place for this ark, a temple for God to dwell in. Does he mean it? We have all said or heard, "I won't rest until... " We know it is a figure of speech. It makes me think of my own foolish outbursts. What I'll never do unless this or that happens. Usually I have been able to back down. I spoke too quickly. Maybe you won't hold me to my words.

Vows are powerful and dangerous. Rarely do we understand what we have promised. Mostly what we will never do is something we cannot control. Or something we have no right to decide. Vows are romantic and exciting. Children love them. Children bind their lives with vows they may not even remember. *I'll never marry*, or, *I won't be like Dad*, or, *I'll never be happy again*. You and I may be living such vows without knowing it. Vows once spoken assume a life of their own.

Self-denial, too, is powerful and dangerous. Giving up this or that for Lent or for ever. First a little suffering, then a sense of power. That sense is exciting, even addicting. It is like finally being in control. Friends say we have will power. As time goes on we become amusing, then tiresome, then downright unpleasant. Friends back away. Few things are more frightening than a person with will power. We laugh at the dieter and the resolution maker. Most of the time, fortunately, they fail. They go back to doing this or that with the rest of us. Sometimes, though, they never stop. The dieting becomes anorexia nervosa, and will power goes from foolish to fatal.

There is another way to read vv. 3-5. I really won't go home again or rest again, until I find a place for the LORD. Because my home won't be a home and my rest won't be restful. There will be no rest for me in my house or my bed, until I find God. Until I search for him and seek his will. Until he makes my house his resting place.

Never say what you will never do. You are capable of anything, immune to nothing. Life is made up of little choices, hour by hour and day by day. Each moment I can choose to listen, to seek his will. What now, LORD? What next? Day by day I make commitments; day by day I carry them out with his help. But I never say never.

<u>Suggestions</u>: Sing refrains. Stand beginning at v. 5 (second refrain) and bow deeply from the waist at v. 7b ("let us fall upon our knees"). Be seated at v. 11, stand again from v. 17 to the end of the psalm. Find a place for the LORD, that is, a place where the LORD can actually speak to you. Silence. This will be your ark and your temple, your holy of holies. Here you will seek his presence and his power. Continue to meditate the psalms day after day, and listen to his voice.

Psalm 132 (BCP)

Twenty-eighth Day: Morning Prayer

  1 LORD, remember David, *
     and all the hardships he endured;
  2 **How he swore an oath to the | LORD**
     and vowed a vow to the Mighty One of | Jacob:
  3 "I will not come under the roof of my house, *
     nor climb up into my bed;
  4 I will not allow my eyes to sleep, *
     nor let my eyelids slumber;
  5 **Until I find a place for the | LORD,**
     a dwelling for the mighty one of | Jacob."
  6 "The ark! We heard it was in Ephratah; *
     we found it in the fields of Jearim.
  7 Let us go to God's dwelling place; *
     let us fall upon our knees before his footstool."
  8 Arise, O LORD, into your resting-place, *
     you and the ark of your strength.
  9 **Let your priests be clothed with | righteousness;**
     let your faithful people sing with | joy.
10 /For your servant / David's sake,
     do not turn away the face of your An/ointed.
11 The LORD has sworn an oath to David; *
     in truth, he will not break it:
12 "A son, the fruit of your body *
     will I set upon your throne.
13 If your children keep my covenant
     and my testimonies that I shall teach them, *
     their children will sit upon your throne for evermore."
14 For the LORD has chosen Zion; *
     he has desired her for his habitation:
15 "This shall be my resting-place for ever; *
     here will I dwell, for I delight in her.
16 I will surely bless her provisions, *
     and satisfy her poor with bread.
17 **I will clothe her priests with sal | vation,**
     and her faithful people will re | joice and sing.

18 /There will I make the horn of David / flourish;
   I have prepared a lamp for my An/ointed.
19 \As for his enemies I will clothe them with shame;
   \but as for him,
      his crown will \ shine."

Like Fine Oil Upon The Head: Commentary To Psalm 133

And you shall take the anointing oil, pour it on his head, and anoint him (Exodus 29:7 NKJ).

      HINNÉH MAH-ttOV UMAH-NÁ"IYM   SHEVETh .A#IM GAM-YÁ#AD
v.1 Oh, how good and pleasant it is
when brethren live together in unity.

Community, real community, is not only tOV (*a good thing*), but NÁ"IYM (*sweet*), a sensuous experience. Pseudocommunity, as Scott Peck[*] calls it, is easily found in the work place or in church. Compare 100, 122. Say the right things and wear the right clothes if you want to be accepted. Grow up where you will live, learn the rules, conceal your real thoughts, never be different.

Real community is as rare as real love. Community, where I can be who I am. Where it is safe to be different. Where I don't have to pretend. That is so rare, so precious, so wonderful, it is like the finest perfumed oil, symbol of luxury and joy. Like the holy oil of anointing poured on my hair, flowing down my temples, my cheeks, my chin, dripping upon my clothes. It is like fragrant oil poured on the feet of Jesus by a beautiful woman with long, dark hair (Luke 7:38). It is like the morning dew filtering down from heaven to refresh and to bless.

Real community is like being a disciple and walking with Jesus. He saw me under the fig tree (John 1:48), he knew me at once and yet he loved me. He never asked about my Daddy and Granddaddy. He never asked, "Are you Jewish? Are you saved?" He just said, "Follow me!"

We will not achieve community by reciting slogans or by forming a committee, not even by singing "Weave Us Together." We will not achieve it by better communication in English or any other language. Not even if everyone were like us. Not even if all were saved. Community is found in the way of emptiness. When we know we cannot change or improve anyone, ever. When I can stand beside your cross and bear your suffering, without giving a single word of advice. When I can live with you and love you with all my heart without asking you to change. How good and how pleasant that is. And how difficult.

<u>Suggestions</u>: Stand, arms lifted in the praise gesture. Lift them higher at "when brethren." Beginning at v.2, turn the palms inward, bring the arms slowly downward, with a continuous fluttering movement of the fingers, down toward the shoulders. Repeat this movement on vv.3 and 4. On v.5, return to the praise gesture. Lift arms higher on "life for evermore."

Apply the teachings of community whenever you can. Do not attempt to change, fix or heal anyone. Do not attempt to solve anyone's problems, though the solutions may be obvious to you. Learn to recognize the profound differences between people; speak in the first person singular, in your own name, for others may not think as you do.

---

[*]M. Scott Peck, M.D. *The Different Drum. Community Making and Peace.* Simon and Schuster, New York, 1987.

Psalm 133 (BCP)

Tone: KINNOR (2)

1 /Oh, how good and / pleasant it is,
 when brethren live together in / unity!
2 **It is like fine oil upon the | head**
 that runs down upon the | beard,
3 /Upon the beard of / Aaron,
 and runs down upon the collar of his / robe.
4 **It is like the dew of | Hermon**
 that falls upon the hills of | Zion.
5 /For there the LORD has ordained the / blessing:
 life for / evermore.

Standing In The Nights: Commentary To Psalm 134

These are the singers, heads of the fathers' houses of the Levites, who lodged in the chambers, and were free from other duties; for they were employed in that work day and night (1 Chronicles 9:33, NKJ).

HÁ"OMDIM B:VEYTH YHWH BALEYLOTH
v.1 (You) who are standing in the house of the LORD in the nights.

You who continue the work of God by night. You winds, you oceans, animals; you worms preparing the soil, you trees renewing the air. You who sustain the world in its rhythms and seasons. You who are praying in the night while others rest. You who lie very still so your spouse can sleep. You who rise to sing *matins* before it is light. Bless the LORD, you servants of the LORD, who stand in the nights.

You who are standing in the nights because a baby is crying. You who are on call when others sleep. You who are standing by night in hospitals, in emergency rooms, wherever someone is hurting and needs you. Bless the LORD, you servants of the LORD, who stand in the nights.

You who are standing in the night, "when no one can work" (John 9:4, NKJ). In the night of ignorance, when his message is turned on its head, when truth is in hiding, when his cross becomes a symbol of hate. When his followers harden their hearts and know all the answers. When there is only one interpretation. When only a courageous remnant will stand for his truth. Bless the LORD, you servants of the LORD, who stand in those nights.

How awesome to be standing by night in this temple service: the singers have been dead for centuries and the temple lies in ruins. Yet as you chant these words you are indeed servants of the LORD as they were, and your work continues theirs. The work continues by night and every night. And his temple is where you serve him, no longer a building but a state, spirit and truth.

It is the place of silence, the place where you learn to listen, the temple that is eternal. Standing in that house, you are like a servant grounded in eternity; your actions are directed by God, your work shows wisdom, your ways reflect fruit of the Spirit. You can truly bless the LORD, for everything you do will be a blessing.

Suggestions: Stand. Sing to the movement Reverential Praise. If desired, you may repeat four times, turning to each of the four directions. Begin facing east, turn each time on the word *Zion*. Let different groups alternate the singing.

When you find yourself standing in the night, when you must work while others sleep, pray this psalm. Do not complain but bless the LORD, again and again. Practice moments of silence through the night, and let your night-time vigil be a blessing.

Psalm 134 (BCP)

Tone: SHOPHÁR

1 **Behold now, bless the LORD, all you servants of the | LORD,**
   you that stand by night in the house of the | LORD.
2 / Lift up your hands in the holy place and bless the / LORD;
   the LORD who made heaven and earth bless
   you out of / Zion.

For I Myself Have Known: Commentary To Psalm 135

KI .aNIY YÁDA"TI KI-GÁDOL YHWH
v.5 For I myself have known that great is the LORD.

The pronoun .aNIY (I) is superfluous, hence emphatic; the verb is perfective, completed state. I had already known intimately that the LORD is great. I knew God, in this special way of knowing, long before I understood anything "about" God, before I studied the Bible. The knowledge of God is not information but decision. I know God as I desire to know him, seek him, and commit myself to him.

To put it another way, my knowing God is relationship, intimacy. Out of this relationship I learn who he is. I learn of his omnipotence, his sovereignty over heaven, earth, seas, deeps. I learn the stories of the escape from Egypt. I learn about the inheritance, the promised land. I learn about his justice and compassion. I learn that God is different from idols, from the spirits and powers of the occult. I begin to bless the LORD and praise him along with all others who praise him. I seek this knowledge and find it, because I know him.

When I met you I liked you and I felt a closeness with you. I felt safe and good and complete with you. I wanted to know you more and better and you also wanted to know me. I fell in love with you and knew you closer and closer. Not because anyone told me to love you. Not by information or proof. But knowing you, loving you, I want to know more and more. What are you thinking of now? *What do you think about this? Come, look at this with me.*

God searches for us, invisible and gentle. We search for him although we cannot see him. We search for him because part of us is missing, because we have heard of him, because we know there must be something more. We search for him in all our clever ways, and then we surrender. Here I am, LORD. Teach me your ways! By choice we begin to know him as he chooses to be known. Intimacy comes with commitment. We sense his presence. We want to know more and more. We want to hear the story. Tell me about Egypt, LORD. Tell me who you are.

The spiritual path, from its very first step, is a path of decisions. The decision that God is real; that he is a person; that he in fact communicates with human breathings; that he will communicate even with me. That Scripture is actually his Word. That it can speak to my own experience. That meditation, intentional silence, is the way to listen to his voice. There is no reasonable reason to believe any of these things. I decide, and having decided, I know.

Suggestions: Sing to the movement Reverential Praise or Standing Drum. Note that the second measure of the second Order may be repeated in verses 7 and 11.

Choose, and continue choosing, the way of surrender. Continue to meditate daily, choosing to sit in his presence, choosing to listen. Choose to serve God and not idols (spirits, powers), moment by moment. Choose to wake up from trance, from reverie, now. Make these choices again every day of your life.

Psalm 135 (BCP)

Tone: SHOPHÁR

1 ^Hàllèlù^jàh!
   Praìse the Nàme of the | LÒRD; `
   give praìse, you sèrvants of the | LÒRD, `
2 /You who stànd in the hòuse of the / LÒRD, `
   in the còurts of the hòuse of our / Gòd. `
3 /Praise the LÒRD, for the LÒRD is / gòod; `
   sing praìses to his Nàme, for it is / lòvely.
4 \For the LORD has chosen Jacob for him\self
   and Israel for his own pos\session.
5 For I know that the LORD is \ great,
   and that our Lord is above all \ gods.
6 **The LÒRD does whatever plèases him, in hèaven and on | èarth, `**
   in the sèas and àll the | dèeps. `
7 /He brings up ràin clouds from the ènds of the / èarth; `
   he sènds out lìghtning with the / ràin, `
   and brìngs the winds òut of his / stòrehouse.
8 \It was he who struck down the firstborn of \ Egypt,
   the firstborn both of man and \ beast.
9 He sent signs and wonders into the midst of you, O \ Egypt,
   against Pharaoh and all his \ servants.
10 **He òverthrèw many | nàtions `**
   and pùt mighty kìngs to | dèath. `
11 /Sìhon, kìng of the / Àmorites, `
   and Òg, the kìng of / Bàshan, `
   and àll the kìngdoms of / Cànaan. `
12 **He gave their lànd to bè an in | hèritance, `**
   an inhèritance for Ìsrael his | pèople. `
13 /O LÒRD, your Nàme is ever/làsting; `
   your renòwn, O LORD, endùres from age to / àge. `
14 /For the LÒRD gives his pèople / jùstice `
   and shòws compàssion to his / sèrvants.
15 \The idols of the heathen are silver and \ gold,
   the work of human \ hands.

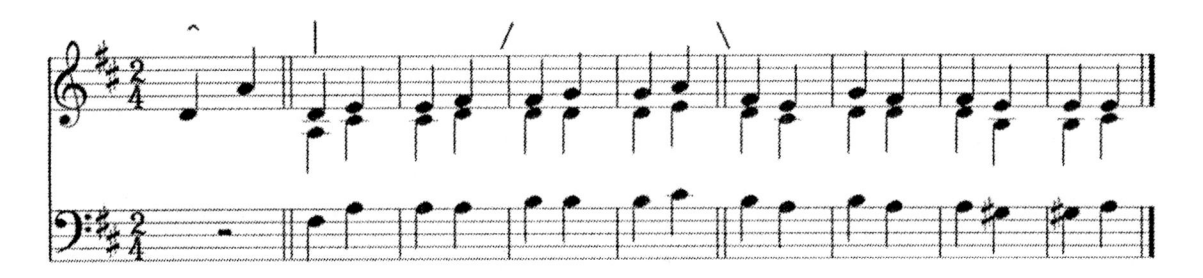

16 They have mouths, but they cannot \ speak;
   eyes have they, but they cannot \ see.
17 **They have èars, but they cànnot | hèar;** `
   nèither is there any brèath in their | mòuth. `
18 /Thòse who màke them are / lìke them, `
   and so are àll who pùt their / trùst in thèm.
19 **Bless the LÒRD, O hòuse of | Ìsrael;** `
   O house of Àaron, blèss the | LÒRD. `
20 /Bless the LÒRD, O hòuse of / Lèvi; `
   you who fèar the LORD, blèss the / LÒRD. `
21 /Blèssed be the LÒRD out of / Zìon, `
   who dwèlls ìn Je/rùsalem.

   ^Hàllèlù^jàh!

Passover Wine: Commentary To Psalm 136

HODUW LAYHWH KI-tOV   KI L:"OLÁM #ASDOW
v.1 Give thanks to the LORD for he is good.

Note the three-fold invocation, the number three signifying perhaps the attributes or perfection of God, or God himself. Behind the endless repetitions, an unfolding progression—creation, redemption, remembering; and continuing presence. First the creation out of nothing—dividing of waters and lights, establishing order. Then the redemption of creation from its innate tendency to self-destruction, from debasement or entropy (Egypt); then the continuing miracle of his presence among us, and feeding.

It is like the story told at a *seder*, as in 113, the history of redemption. Think of Rabbi Jesus and his students and their families in a room in Jerusalem. They have prepared and come together, they celebrate, they pray, they read the long story of deliverance, how our family came up out of Egypt. And they drink four cups of wine, symbolic of refreshment and renewal. They re-live the family story from slavery to freedom, distilling the central message from centuries of experience. After the meal and the wine they sing this song, retelling the miracles again. It is a distillation of all that has gone before, wine distilled from history.

And he lifts up bread and wine, and teaches them as they have never been taught before. He says, "This is my body," and, "This is my blood." And after they sing a hymn, perhaps even this one, they go out (Mark 14:26).

Give thanks (praise, affirmation) to the LORD, for (he is) good! For his love is eternal. #ESED (*love* or *mercy*), from a root that means zeal, passion; whether for good or ill (Gesenius, pp. 293-294). For God is devoted to us in an intense and passionate way. His love for us is not sentimental love. His mercy, if we translate it that way, is not soft mercy. It is a fierce, protective love, like a mother's love.

v.25 He gives bread to all flesh.

The ultimate and continuing miracle is that God feeds me. He brings me into existence, gives me breath, brings me to consciousness. He provides order, meaning and light. And he gives food, good things to eat, to me and my fellow creatures. He feeds me at *seder* meal, at Eucharist, in prayer, in trouble, in miracles and in daily experience. And he delivers me. He sets me free from the bondage of thoughts and emotions, from attachments and addictions.

Suggestions: Sing to the movement Marching and Swaying Dance. Attend or conduct a *seder* if you can. Study the book *Rediscovering Passover, A Complete Guide for Christians,* by Joseph Stallings (Resource Publications, Inc., 160 E. Virginia Street # 290, San Jose, CA 95112, 1988) and the *New Union Haggadah* (Central Conference of American Rabbis, New York, 1974, 1975). Search for the deeper meaning of Passover—liberation from every enslavement.

Psalm 136 (BCP)

Twenty-eighth Day: Evening Prayer   Tone: **SHOPHÁR**

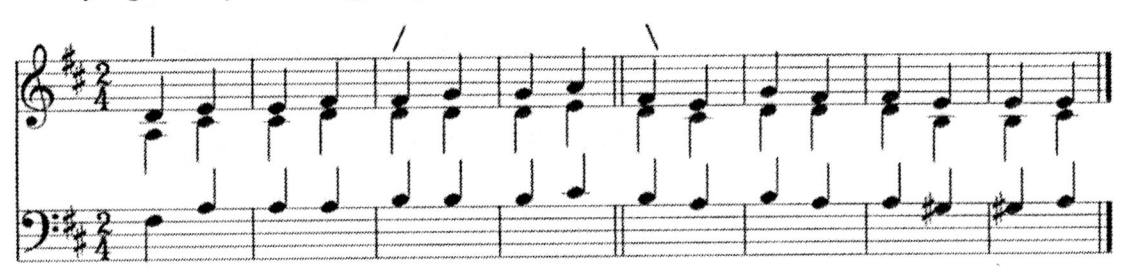

1 **Give thànks to the LÒRD for he is | gòod,** `
  for his mèrcy endùres for | èver. `
2 /Give thànks to the Gòd of / gòds, `
  for his mèrcy endùres for / èver. `
3 /Give thànks to the Lòrd of / lòrds, `
  for his mèrcy endùres for / èver. `
4 **Who ònly dòes great | wònders,** `
  for his mèrcy endùres for | èver; `
5 /Who by wìsdom màde the / hèavens, `
  for his mèrcy endùres for / èver; `
6 /Who sprèad out the èarth upon the / wàters, `
  for his mèrcy endùres for / èver. `
7 **Who creàted grèat | lìghts,** `
  for his mèrcy endùres for | èver; `
8 /The sùn to rùle the / dày, `
  for his mèrcy endùres for / èver; `
9 /The moon and the stàrs to gòvern the / nìght, `
  for his mèrcy endùres for / èver. `
10 \Who struck down the firstborn of \ Egypt,
  for his mercy endures for \ ever;
11 And brought out Israel from a\mong them,
  for his mercy endures for \ ever;
12 **With a mìghty hànd and a strètched-out | àrm,** `
  for his mèrcy endùres for | èver; `
13 /Who divìded the Rèd Sea in / twò, `
  for his mèrcy endùres for / èver; `
15 **But swept Phàraoh and his àrmy into the | Rèd Sea,** `
  for his mèrcy endùres for | èver; `
16 /Who lèd his pèople through the / wìlderness, `
  for his mèrcy endùres for / èver. `
17 **Who strùck dòwn great | kìngs,** `
  for his mèrcy endùres for | èver; `
18 /And slèw mìghty / kìngs, `
  for his mèrcy endùres for / èver; `

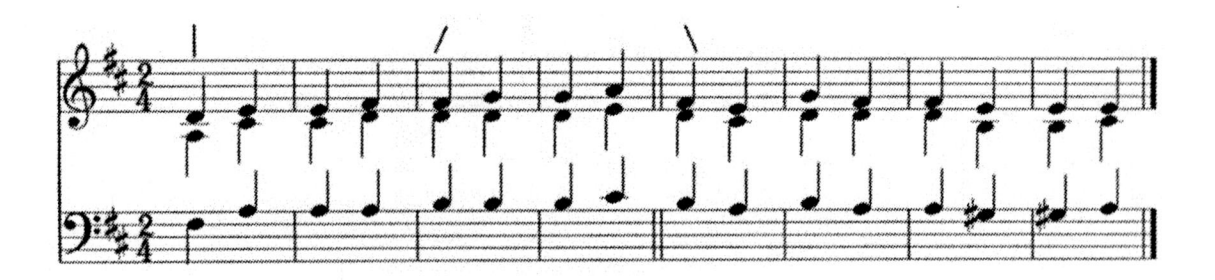

19 Sìhon, kìng of the / Àmorites, `
    for his mèrcy endùres for / èver; `
20 And Òg, the kìng of | Bàshan, `
    for his mèrcy endùres for | èver; `
21 / And gàve away their lànds for an in/hèritance, `
    for his mèrcy endùres for / èver. `
22 / An inhèritance for Ìsrael his / sèrvant, `
    for his mèrcy endùres for / èver.
23 \ Who remembered us in our low \ estate,
    for his mercy endures for \ ever;
24 And delivered us from our \ enemies,
    for his mercy endures for \ ever;
25 Who gives fòod to àll | crèatures, `
    for his mèrcy endùres for | èver. `
26 / Give thànks to the Gòd of / hèaven, `
    for his mèrcy endùres for / èvèr.

I, Babylonian: Commentary To Psalm 137

One of the most difficult psalms, because it deals with a forbidden impulse—revenge. Christians go through terrible struggles with it, as I noted in 109. This is me at my worst. Living in the past, I have decided that I will "never forget!" Worse yet, "never forgive!" Never mind the reasons, let's just say it was justified. Something has been done that I must not forgive or forget, never! It is justified, but unfortunately it will destroy me.

I have seen my Jewish brothers go down this path. My father was deeply imbued with it. Never forgive the Germans, the Romans. Never forget what Titus did to us in 70 A.D. They still allow no instrumental music in synagogues, lest they forget this bitter memory. And who can blame them? Never again! It's important. But how long? When do we move on? We were deported to Babylonia saying "Never forget!" Now we are back in the homeland, and the Palestinians are saying "Never forget!" How long?

The last verses are the hardest, as I descend into murderous fantasy. We hate to read these verses yet we live by them. We live by revenge, and pretend we have outgrown it. We may piously repeat "Forgive your enemies," but what does it mean? Are there limits to forgiveness? Is evil itself forgivable? Is Satan? To ask these questions is to know our ignorance. Yes, we must forgive, like the unforgiving servant in Matthew 18:21-35; but ultimate forgiveness belongs to God.

It is easy for Christians (non-Jewish) to ask a Jew (non-Christian), "Shouldn't we forgive the Nazis?" But can "we" forgive (without trial) what happened to someone else? That is indeed "cheap forgiveness," as Scott Peck says—meaningless forgiveness. Can we even forgive our own enemies until we truly understand what they did? Can one abused as a child forgive her abuser until she remembers what he did, and understands how she has been injured? And if not, can I forgive him for her?

We must forgive, so that we can grow. Because unless we forgive, we cannot be forgiven. Because the unforgiven injury lurks within us like a virus—the last and cruelest legacy of the abuser. Buried within the victim, it is the seed of self-destruction. But forgiveness will never be easy. And we must never tell someone lightly, "Shouldn't you forgive them?" Never, never, never be so cruel!

Turn back to Psalm 137. The Jews are deported to Babylonia in waves, from 597 to 582 B.C. It is an ancient method of subjugation, but this conquest is enlightened for its time. The Jews are allowed to stay together and maintain their culture. They have their former king with them, so there is a link to the house of David. Eventually they flourish in their new homes.*

The writer doesn't see it that way, of course. He is bitter and depressed. The people he encounters seem friendly. "Tell us about your country," they say, "sing us one of your songs." But he answers bitterly, "How can I sing the song of the LORD in a foreign country?" And he takes his KINNOR—the harp so exquisite that the wind blowing through its strings creates music—and leaves it in the crotch of a tree, never to be played again. He would rather forget how to play than forget his home.

Up to now, we have identified with this Jewish writer, and it has been hard. How can we possibly identify with that horrible last verse? So let us imagine that we are the Babylonians, and we are hearing these words! Imagine how it would feel. Could anyone feel that way toward me? What about the black American, whose ancestors were dragged out of Africa? What about the Cherokees, taken from North Carolina on a Trail of Tears? One fourth of the people died along the way. What about the Jews of today, those seemingly well-off people we have just lectured about forgiveness?

How does it feel? Perhaps I was a bit insensitive asking them to sing when they first arrived. Perhaps I didn't understand how they felt. Yet why do they hate me like this? Why do they brood and dream of revenge? I am trying to help them! And they dream of the day when they can take my child and grandchild and smash their heads against a rock!

You see, every one of us is a Babylonian to someone, at some level, at some time. Every one of us, some time, some way, is experienced as persecutor and oppressor. And the more we ourselves have been persecuted and oppressed the easier it is for us to persecute and oppress. It is often when we are trying our best to be helpful that we are so experienced. Then we are shocked and surprised. I was trying to help him (or her) and suddenly I realize that to him (or her) I am the Babylonian.

Sometimes I realize this when I am trying very hard with a patient: I have become a Babylonian to this patient, and nothing good will happen in treatment until I can change that perception. Because I really can't help anyone unless God decides to help them through me. And when I feel very clever and sure about helping someone I may just have become their Babylonian, their music-silencer. Sometimes to my wife or child I am the Babylonian! I know what's best for them, right? But they don't experience it that way. To them, I have become the Babylonian, the spirit-crusher.

Knowing this I can go back to Matthew 5:23-24 and apply it. "If you bring your gift to the altar, and there remember that your brother has something against you ... first be reconciled to your brother, and then come and offer your gift" (NKJ).

<u>Suggestions</u>: Kneel and read softly without music. Read vv. 8-9 in a whisper. Listen to this psalm as though they are talking about you. Notice how differently the words sound when you are the persecutor. Watch yourself carefully whenever you begin to think of yourself as helper.

---

*Chaim Raphael: *The Road from Babylon. The Story of Sephardi and Oriental Jews*. Harper & Row, New York, 1985.

Psalm 137 (KJV)

1 By the rivers of Babylon, there we sat down, yea, we wept, when we remembered Zion.
2 We hanged our harps upon the willows in the midst thereof.
3 For there they that carried us away captive required of us a song; and they that wasted us required of us mirth, saying, Sing us one of the songs of Zion.
4 How shall we sing the LORD's song in a strange land?
5 If I forget thee, O Jerusalem, let my right hand forget her cunning.
6 If I do not remember thee, let my tongue cleave to the roof of my mouth; if I prefer not Jerusalem above my chief joy.
7 Remember, O LORD, the children of Edom in the day of Jerusalem; who said,
Rase it, rase it, even to the foundations thereof.
[Whispering]
8 O daughter of Babylon, who art to be destroyed; happy shall he be that rewardeth thee as thou hast served us.
9 Happy shall he be, that taketh and dasheth thy little ones against the stones.

You Increase My Strength: Commentary To Psalm 138

B:YOM QÁRÁ.THI WATA"aNÉNI TARHIVÉNI V:NAPHSHIY "OZ
v.4 In the day that I have called, then you begin to answer me,
you continue to enlarge strength within my soul (breath, breathing, life).

The conversion moment again, that radical leap. From the very day, the moment, that I first called on you, then, from that moment, you began to enlarge strength within my soul (breath, breathing, life). It is the *and* or *then* of disjunction -- the complete change of perspective.

I had tried every solution, every expert. I had gone from Dale Carnegie* to the *Guru* from India. Then I acknowledged I was powerless. I cried out to you, "LORD, what shall I do?" And from that moment, and every such moment, I began to grow. There was no sudden light. Only in hindsight can I see it. Something began that day that was real and continues. A strength that is not my own you continue to enlarge.

KI-RÁM YHWH W:SHÁPHÁL YIR.EH
v.7 For God is high and yet he cares for (looks after) the lowly. This is a rather odd strength, for I cannot always use it at will. It is not an occultic power or even a learned skill. Rather, it is the strength of weakness. When I let go of it I have it. And the instant, the very microsecond, that I start to take pride in it, it vanishes.

YHWH YIGMOR BA"aDIY
v.9a The LORD will make good his purpose for me.

The LORD will bring to completion for me. What he began that day, and each such day, may he continue and complete. For your (fierce, protective) love is eternal. On one level I am the same nervous wreck I have always been. I am still looking for enlightenment, hoping to be rich and famous. And if I can't be rich and famous, at least let someone like me today. On a deeper level I find myself growing stronger, more stable, more balanced. A transforming work goes on in me, without my knowledge or direction. May the LORD continue this work.

I do not myself do this growing and completing. It is not an achievement or accomplishment. It will never be attained by moral exhortation, will-power, trying harder, legalistic rules, abstaining from this or that. It is not achieved by meditation or prayer. It is received, if I am open to receive it, willing, flexible, poor in spirit. Meditation and prayer open doors. God performs this work in me, God alone.

<u>Suggestions</u>: Sing slowly to the movement Reverential Praise. Bow deeply from the waist on v.2a. Give up, completely, the dream of self-improvement, and allow God to work with you.

---
*Dale Carnegie: *How to Win Friends and Influence People*, Simon and Schuster, New York, 1936.

Psalm 138 (BCP)

Tone: SHOPHÁR

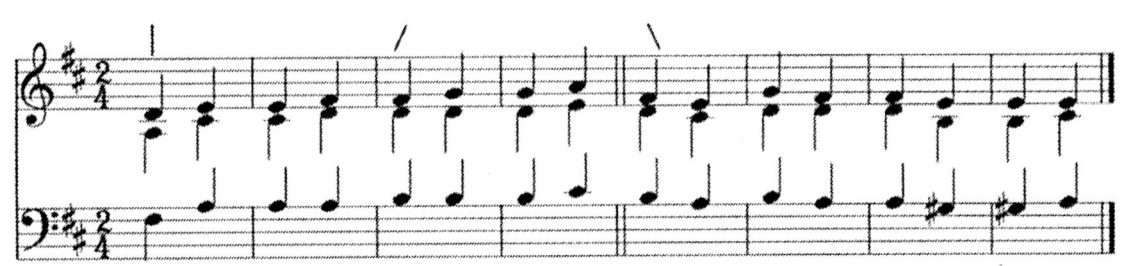

1 **I will give thanks to you, O LORD, with my whole | heart;**
   before the gods I will sing your | praise.
2 /I will bow down toward your holy temple and praise your / Name,
   because of your love and / faithfulness.
3 \For you have glorified your \ Name
   and your word above all \ things.
4 When I called, you \ answered me;
   you increased my strength \ within me.
5 **All the kings of the earth will praise you, O | LORD,**
   when they have heard the words of your | mouth.
6 /They will sing of the ways of the / LORD,
   that great is the glory of the / LORD.
7 \Though the LORD be high, he cares for the \ lowly;
   he perceives the haughty from a\far.
8 Though I walk in the midst of trouble, you keep me \ safe;
   you stretch forth your hand against the fury of my \ enemies;
   Your right hand shall | save me.
9 The LORD will make good his | purpose for me;
   /O LORD, your love endures for / ever;
   do not abandon the works of your / hands.

Search Me Out ... And Know: Commentary To Psalm 139

Forms of the word YÁDA" (*to know intimately*) occur seven times. The word suggests insight (seeing in), or self-knowledge, the golden elixir of psychiatry. On closer examination, the psalm is not about self-knowledge at all, but God-knowledge, God-sight. Seeing myself as God sees me.

v.1 LORD, you have searched me out and (yet) you continue to know me intimately.

You have searched me out thoroughly, yet you continue in that intimate fellowship with me. You have completely understood, from within as it were, my ups and downs, my highs and lows (Feuer). You know every word in my tongue, while it is still in my tongue, before it rolls off my tongue. Even before I hear it in my head.

v.5 (Such) knowledge is (too) wonderful for me,
it is (so) high, I cannot attain to it.

Closer than my tongue and yet, you love me. Literally, *I am not able to it!* I cannot handle this. And I cannot get away from it. I cannot escape from your Spirit (breath) or your presence (face). You know me inside and out, because you made me. You "covered me" in my mother's womb. I have no secrets.

I will praise thee, for I am fearfully and wonderfully made: marvelous are thy works; and that my soul knoweth right well (KJV). The fifth *know*: all your works are awesome, even this work, me. My soul (breath, breathing, life) understands this. She knows how wonderful is this piece of creation, this me. It is only "I" that can say egotistical things like, "I'm not supposed to like myself." True self-knowledge is neither explanation nor condemnation; more than anything it is self-transcendence, losing my self's sense of self, the alienation. I begin to experience a subtle detachment. I actually begin to see myself — standing, walking, moving my hands. And with that detachment comes a kind of love. A compassion for this fragile, impermanent being that is me.

Search me out, O God, and know my heart (attitude), test me and know my (branching) thoughts. My thoughts that branch and bifurcate continually, as in 94. For every good thought an evil thought; for every bad thought — surprise! — a beautiful thought. Come in and know this, LORD, transforming me!

We know that intellectual insight has little value. Emotional insight, the Aha! experience, is better. But the most important insight is not what I know about myself, but what I am willing to know. What God already knows. Look into me and tell me what you see: the good, the bad and the ugly. Search me out, O God, and show me in your good timing. I may be surprised. I expect to look within and find darkness, rage, childish demands to have it all, obscene desires, murder. You will find these things in me if I let you look. And you will also find *love, joy, peace, patience, kindness* (Galatians 5:22). You will find Christ in me. Search me out, O God, and know me.

<u>Suggestions</u>: Sing to the Tone #ÁLIL (*flute*), as in 65 and 92. Verses 18-21 are sung to the special descending form. Do not attempt to explain yourself; ask God to search you and know you and show you who you are. See yourself with compassion, as God does. With your fellow creatures, as much as you can, do the same.

Psalm 139 (BCP)

Twenty-ninth Day: Morning Prayer Tone: #ÁLIL

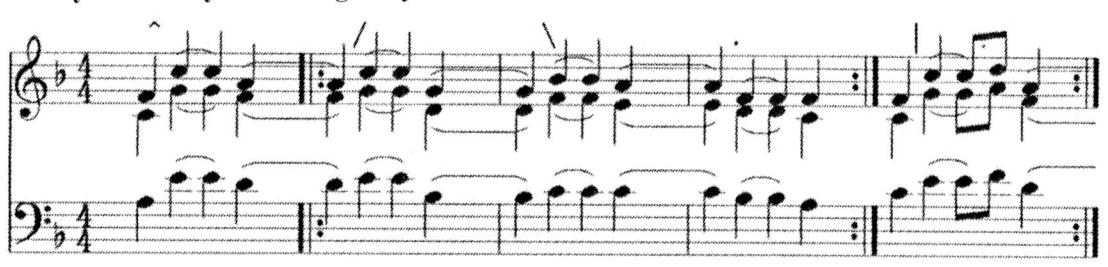

1 ^ LORD, you have searched me out and ^ known me;
   you know my sitting down and my rising up;
   you discern my thoughts from ^ afar.
2 You trace my journeys and my / resting-places
   and are acquainted with all my / ways.
3 \Indeed, there is not a word on my \ lips,
   but you, O LORD, know it \ altogether.
4 You press upon me behind and be.fore
   and lay your . hand upon me.
5 **Such knowledge is too | wonderful for me;**
   it is so | high that I cannot at | tain to it.
6 Where can I go then from your / Spirit?
   where can I flee from your / presence?
7 \If I climb up to heaven, you are \ there;
   if I make the grave my bed, you are there \ also.
8 If I take the wings of the . morning
   and dwell in the uttermost parts of the . sea,
9 ^Even there your hand will ^ lead me
   and your right hand will ^ hold me fast.
10 If I say, "Surely the darkness will / cover me,
   and the light around me turn to / night,"
11 \Darkness is not dark to you;
   the night is as bright as the \ day;
   darkness and light to you are both a\like.
12 For you yourself created my inmost . parts;
   you knit me together in my mother's . womb.
13 **I will thank you because I am marvelously | made;**
   your works are | wonderful, and I | know it well.
14 My body was not / hidden from you,
   while I was being made in secret
   and woven in the depths of the / earth.
15 \Your eyes beheld my limbs, yet unfinished in the \ womb;
   all of them were written in your \ book;
   they were fashioned day by. day,
   when as yet there was . none of them.

Psalm 139 (conclusion)

16 **How deep I find your | thoughts, O God!**
   how | great is the | sum of them!
17 If I were to count them, they would be more in number than the / sand;
   to count them all, my life span would need to be like / yours.
18 +Oh, that you would slay the + wicked, O God!
   You that thirst for blood, de+part from me.
19 They speak despitefully a+gainst you;
   your enemies take your ++ Name in vain.
20 +Do I not hate those, O LORD, who + hate you?
   and do I not loathe those who rise up a+gainst you?
21 I hate them with a perfect + hatred;
   they have become my own ++ enemies.

22 ^Search me out, O God, and know my ^ heart;
   try me and know my restless ^ thoughts.
23 Look well, whether there be any / wickedness in me
   and lead me in the way that is ever/lasting.

They Sharpen Their Tongues: Commentary To Psalm 140

v.1 Deliver me, O LORD, from evil men; Preserve me from violent men.

It was a violent time but not, I think, as our own time is violent. Violent acts were more personal in those days. There were no assault rifles then, no weapons of mass destruction. One did not speak of "senseless" violence, but of wickedness and evil. Everyone knew where it came from—the wicked thoughts of men. It was planned, deliberate violence. And the violent openly boasted of their violent acts.

SHÁN:NUW L:SHONÁM K:MO-NÁ#ÁSh

v.3 They have sharpened their tongues like a snake.

Images burst from this little phrase. I try to picture them sharpening their tongues. How? With what instrument? How sharp? They have sharpened their tongues to hurt—to discredit and dehumanize their opponents. They have sharpened their tongues to split hairs, to make technical distinctions. They can do what is wrong because it is legal. They can do it until a court tells them to stop.

They gather in offices and board rooms, sharpening their tongues. They plot the demise of others, of some other group. If they win, someone loses, someone goes out of business, people lose jobs. Violence may come later, but is not their concern. They have sharpened their tongues to a fine point. They are technically innocent.

v.5 The proud have hidden a snare for me, and cords ...
they have set traps for me.

Deliver me, LORD, from their snares and cords. Let me not fall into their traps. Above all, let me not fall into their ways. Keep me from the way of the sharp tongue—the clever and technical tongue that leads to death. Keep me straight and simple. Compare 15.

.IYSH LÁSHON BAL-YIKKON BÁ.ÁRE3

v.11 Let not a slanderer (man of tongue) be established in the earth.

The sharpened tongues will not always deceive. The cause of the afflicted will not always be forgotten. Compare 9, 10. The evil set in motion by the wicked will come back to destroy them. And "the righteous shall give thanks to your name."

Suggestions: Sing refrains to the Tone "UGÁV (*pipe*). Observe the silences.

Notice that the evil of evil men begins in their hearts, that is, in their inmost thoughts. They "plan evil things in their hearts" and they "have purposed" to make me stumble. Learn to recognize those evil thoughts in your own heart just as in theirs. When you recognize them, let them go. Pay special attention to those thoughts that make you feel righteously indignant; when you find them, clear your mind and practice moments of silence.

Psalm 140 (NKJ)

Tone: "UGÁV irregular

1 **Deliver me, O LORD, from evil | men;**
　　Pre | serve me from violent | men,
2 who plan | evil things in their | hearts;
　　They continually gather together for war.
3 They sharpen their tongues like a serpent; *
　　the poison of asps is under their lips.
　　　　　　　　[Silence...]
4 **Keep me, O LORD, from the hands of the | wicked;**
　　Pre | serve me from violent | men,
　　who have | purposed to make my steps | stumble.
5 The proud have hidden a snare for me, and cords; *
　　they have spread a net by the wayside;
　　they have set traps for me.
　　　　　　　　[Silence...]
6 I said to the LORD: "You are my God; *
　　Hear the voice of my supplications, O LORD.
7 O God the LORD,
　　the strength of my salvation, *
　　You have covered my head in the day of battle.
8 Do not grant, O LORD, the desires of the wicked; *
　　Do not further his wicked scheme,
　　lest they be exalted.
　　　　　　　　[Silence...]
9 "As for the head of those who surround me, *
　　Let the evil of their lips cover them;
10 Let burning coals fall upon them; *
　　Let them be cast into the fire,
　　into deep pits, that they rise not up again.
11 Let not a slanderer be established in the earth; *
　　Let evil hunt the violent man to overthrow him."
12 I know that the LORD will maintain
　　the cause of the afflicted, *
　　and justice for the poor.
13 Surely the righteous shall give thanks to Your name; *
　　the upright shall dwell in Your presence.

From The Traps Of The Evildoers: Commentary To Psalm 141

TIKKON T:PHILLÁTHIY Q:tORETh L:PHÁNEYKHÁ

v.2 Let my prayer be established (as) incense in your presence,

the lifting up of my hands (as) an evening sacrifice. Let my prayer be like the incense burned in the temple, morning and evening, on a golden altar at the entrance to the holy of holies. That offering comes to symbolize prayer itself, the fragrant offering of myself, the responding to God. The lifting of my hands is like sacrifice—the act of lifting to God and letting go. Compare 20, 50, 66. The lifting of my hands from doing to surrender. I cannot save myself. For more on the incense, study Malachi 1:11, Revelation 5:8 and 8:3-4.

SHITHÁH YHWH SHÁMRÁH L:PHIY

v.3 Set, O LORD, a guard on my mouth,

keep watch on the door of my lips;

Do not incline my heart to an evil thing.

Keep me straight, LORD, beginning with my speech, that is, my thoughts. I know that any thought can come to anyone. I have learned that almost anyone, following a sequence of thoughts, can do almost anything. No one is immune to evildoing. Protect my heart (attitude) and let it not lean toward evil.

v.4 to practice wicked works with men that work iniquity:

and let me not eat of their dainties (KJV). I am not too pure to fall away. As I progress in the way of surrender I am more vulnerable, not less. Into the purest life pride comes, the obsession with self. Every day some "law-abiding citizen" is doing unspeakable things. And I am no better. Keep me away from the evildoers, LORD, lest I get caught up in their fascinating schemes. Let me not even have lunch with them.

How fortunate for me if the righteous rebuke me, even hit me, to get my attention, to keep me out of trouble. Better that blow from the righteous than the gourmet lunches of the evildoers. Let me listen to them even if it hurts. Let me listen to my wife. Is it a word from the LORD? More than likely, if I don't want to hear it.

The wicked live fascinating lives, engaged in the most ingenious machinations. They seem to understand the system so much better than I do. They understand the power games of this world. They know whom to call. Yet I see them laying snares for the unwary that will ultimately trap themselves. LORD, keep me from getting too interested in their schemes, and save me from their nets.

<u>Suggestions</u>: Extend hands in the praise gesture at v.2 ("let my prayer"); Lift them higher at "the lifting up"; bring the right hand in front of the mouth in a gesture of silence at v. 3 ("set a watch"); fold arms in the heart gesture at "let not my heart." Lift eyes slightly at v. 8 ("But my eyes") and lift the arms as above. Return to the heart gesture at "In you I take refuge."

Psalm 141 (BCP)

Twenty-ninth Day: Evening Prayer Tone: SH:MINITH

1 O Lord, I call to you; come to me quickly; *
    hear my voice when I cry to you.
2 Let my prayer be set forth in your sight as incense, *
    the lifting up of my hands as the evening sacrifice.
3 Set a watch before my mouth, O Lord,
    and guard the door of my lips; *
    let not my heart incline to any evil thing.
4 **Let me not be occupied in wickedness with | evildoers,**
    nor | eat of their choice | foods.
5 Let the righteous smite me in friendly rebuke;
    let not the oil of the unrighteous anoint my head; *
    for my prayer is continually against their wicked deeds.
6 Let their rulers be overthrown in stony places, *
    that they may know my words are true.
7 As when a plowman turns over the earth in furrows, *
    let their bones be scattered at the mouth of the grave.
8 But my eyes are turned to you, Lord God; *
    in you I take refuge; do not strip me of my life.
9 **Protect me from the snare which they have | laid for me**
    and from the | traps of the | evildoers.
10 Let the wicked fall into their own nets, *
    while I myself escape.

My Breath From Prison: Commentary To Psalm 142

B:HITH"AttÉPH "ÁLAY RU#IY   W:.ATTÁH YÁ<u>DA</u>"TÁ N:THIVÁTHIY
v.3   When my spirit was overwhelmed within me,
then you knew my path.

HITH"AttEPH from a root that means to cover over; hence to be wrapped in darkness, to languish, or faint (Gesenius, p.621). Things are going badly indeed. My spirit (breath) is overshadowed, wrapped in darkness; yet you are there, intimately close to me on my path. As things go from bad to worse, I look everywhere for a friendly face, but there is no one looking after my breathing (life). No one even cares if I die.

HO<u>3I</u>Y.Áh MIMASGÉR NAPHSHIY L:HODOTH .ETH-SH:<u>ME</u>KHÁ BIY
v.7   Bring out from prison my soul (breath, breathing, life)
to give thanks to your Name within me.

Suddenly in the middle of the night I hear a noise; is it outside or inside? Instantly awake, I lie there with every nerve on edge. I try to breathe as quietly as possible so that I can hear. I begin to feel stifled and smothered, there is an unpleasant sensation in my chest. I can't seem to get enough air. After a few minutes of this I begin to sigh and yawn, I am starting to panic. My breath in prison is one way of describing this panicky sensation. I am trying so hard to keep calm and avoid detection that I almost stop breathing.

That awful feeling is more than physical; it seems to penetrate the depths of my being. I feel a profound insecurity, sense of failure, inadequacy. My thoughts go in well-worn circles. What if it is cancer, or fire? What if they have found me out? I know I am a failure, an imposter. Nothing I ever do is right, and no one cares for me. And if they do seem to value me, it is only because they don't yet know, or they are using me.

I have never been in jail, I used to say, and I have never, ever been free. Trying to stay in control, I have created my own prison. Trying to improve myself I have entrapped myself. Now only you, LORD, can set me free. Please, God, bring out my breath from prison, so that I can thank you and praise you. And as I do so all is changed. The righteous begin to gather around me and you begin to "deal bountifully with me."

<u>Suggestions</u>:   Sing refrains to the Tone N:GINOTH (*stringed instruments*). Lift the arms, parallel and close together, palms up, on vv. 1 and 5.

When panic comes, listen for that shallow, ineffective breathing. Inhale sharply, quickly through the nose so that anyone could hear you. Lift up your breathing to God and let him be your refuge. You cannot make yourself safe.

Psalm 142 (KJV)

Tone: N:GINOTH

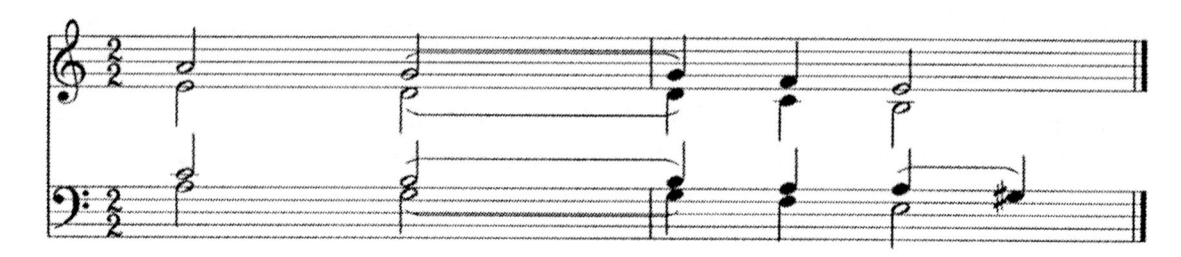

1 **I cried unto the Lord with my | voice;**
   with my voice unto the | Lord did I make my suppli|cation.
2 I poured out my complaint before him *
   I shewed before him my trouble.
3 When my spirit was overwhelmed within me,
   then thou knewest my path. *
   in the way wherein I walked have they privily laid a snare for me.
4 I looked on my right hand, and beheld,
   but there was no man that would know me: *
   refuge failed me; no man cared for my soul.
5 **I cried unto thee, O | Lord;**
   I said, Thou art my | refuge,
   and my portion in the land of the | living.
6 Attend unto my cry; for I am brought very low: *
   deliver me from my persecutors;
   for they are stronger than I.
7 Bring my soul out of prison, that I may praise thy name: *
   the righteous shall compass me about;
   for thou shalt deal bountifully with me.

My Breath From Trouble: Commentary To Psalm 143

Prayer from a dark hour. I think again of those persecuted ones in Psalm 7. The details are not important, only the experience. Here I see the unfolding of that victim experience. Whatever happened, it was too much for this individual.

v.3 For the enemy has pursued my soul (breath, breathing, life) ... crushed to the ground my life ... made me to sit in utter darkness like the eternally dead (Feuer, p. 1671).

WATITH"AttÉPH "ÁLAY RU#IY   B:THOKHIY YISHTOMÉM LIBBIY
v.4 And my spirit (breath) is overshadowed within me, and my heart is astonished, appalled within me, as in 142:3. My coping abilities have been overwhelmed, my sense of control shattered. I cannot relate these events to normal life. In a sense I stop living, trapped in the moment, like the living dead. I will never come home from this war.

ZÁKHARTI YÁMIM MIQQEDEM
v.5 I have remembered the days of old; I have murmured or meditated upon all your deeds; I begin to talk about (muse upon) the work of your hands. A progression of states. The root of ZÁKHAR (*to remember*) is traced to piercing or penetrating, i.e. into the origin of something (Gesenius, p.244). I am learning to think about what happened without re-living it. What really happened? When? Where? How do I cope with it? It is not enough to re-live the suffering over and over, trapped in some awful nightmare. I must learn how to learn about it, talk about it, mourn for what happened to me, and let it go. Can I do this? Not alone. "I spread out my hands to you" [Silence...].

In v.7, I acknowledge my powerlessness. My spirit (what makes me a human breathing, what brings me into relationship) is failing. I plead with God, "Do not hide your face from me." I cannot work my way out of troubles by thinking alone, not by thoughts or emotions. Not by living through it again and again. In v.8, there is a change of tone. Show me your loving-kindness in the morning ... Make me to know this road I begin to walk, for to you I have lifted up my soul (breath, breathing, life). Compare 25, 86. Turning to God, I find that something is changing. I begin to experience trust.

B:3IDQÁTH:KHÁ TO3IY. MI33ÁRÁH NAPHSHIY
v.11 In your righteousness, you will bring out my soul (breath, life) from trouble (from stress, from narrow straits), so that I can breathe again, so that I can live.

<u>Suggestions</u>: Lift the arms, palms up, in a gesture of supplication, on vv. 1 and 6. Lift them again at v.8, go to the heart gesture at "for I put my trust"; extend the right arm on "show me the road" and lift both arms heavenward in a lifting gesture at "for I lift up my soul." Heart gesture again at v.9 ("Deliver me") and praise gesture at "for I flee to you."

Psalm 143 (BCP)

Tone: N:GINOTH *irregular*

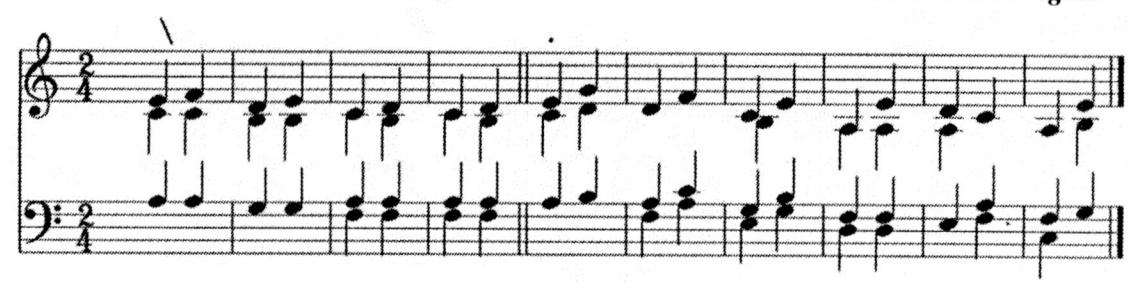

1 LORD, hear my prayer,
    and in your faithfulness heed my supplications; *
    answer me in your righteousness.
2 Enter not into judgment with your servant, *
    for in your sight shall no one living be justified.
3 For my enemy has sought my life;
    he has crushed me to the ground; *
    he has made me live in dark places like those who are long dead.
4 \My spirit faints with\in me;
    my heart within me is \ desolate.
5 I remember the time past;
    I muse upon all your deeds; *
    I consider the works of your hands.
6 I spread out my hands to you; *
    my soul gasps to you like a thirsty land.
              [Silence...]
7 \O LORD, make haste to answer me; my spirit \ fails me;
    do not hide your \ face from me
    or I shall be like those who go \ down to the Pit.

8 .Let me hear of your loving-kindness in the . morning,
    for I put my . trust in you;
    show me the road that I must . walk
    for I lift up my . soul to you.
9 Deliver me from my enemies, O . LORD,
    for I flee to you for . refuge.

10 \Teach me to do what pleases you, for you are my \ God;
    let your good Spirit lead me on \ level ground.
11 Revive me, O LORD, for your \ Name's sake;
    for your righteousness' sake, bring me out of \ trouble.
12 \Of your goodness, destroy my \ enemies
    and bring all my \ foes to naught,
    for truly I am your \ servant.

Teach Me To Fight: Commentary To Psalm 144

January, 1991—war in the Persian Gulf. Our Sunday morning Bible class is struggling with the shock. Everyone is for peace, but each has a different idea how to get there. What about the Palestinians? What about Kuwait? Do we have any business getting involved? Tempers become heated. Some think the war is justified. Others, that war itself is immoral. Voices rise to a shrill edge. There is only one way to look at this, but *they* refuse to see it! Soon enough we might have come to blows—we don't like to think so! We might have had to kill for peace—we refuse to believe it!

Some Christians believe that war has been abolished. It should be enough to pray for our enemies. What Scripture really says is more complicated. Conflict and battles are still with us. We live in a world where the strong still murder the weak and take what they have. To say it should be otherwise sounds moral, but may be prideful. As if to say I am not like those people who make wars.

v.1 Blessed be the LORD my rock!
who teaches my hands for close combat
and my fingers for warfare. What am I to learn here? First, that the LORD is my security and my weapon. Second, he teaches me to fight. How, when, where, how long, on which side. Why, we are not told. Only that he teaches—for close hand-to-hand combat, and for large scale warfare with weapons (Feuer, p. 1678).

v.3 O LORD, what is a human being, yet you intimately know him or her? Human motivation is irrelevant in this battle. Schoolyard concepts of who can push whom around, who is a coward or bully, all are irrelevant. Both we and our enemies are fleeting figures, like a puff of wind. Our days "pass over like a shadow."

v.5 Bow your heavens, O LORD, and come down. God conducts the war and wins the battle. And what is my role? To be willing to learn how to fight—as, if, and when God wants me to fight. To be willing to go to the battle and put my life in danger; to be willing to win or to lose.

Being a Christian does not excuse me from conflict. In every field of life I encounter it. Life should be peace and harmony, I think, but every day I go to work and find battles. Someone has been ill-treated, someone has abused his or her authority, someone is making a complaint about someone who doesn't yet know there is a problem. Someone is rightfully enraged, but the rage is wrongly directed. Every day this happens, and I would like to say, *I don't get into these battles*, or, *I try to consider the source*, or, *I pray for my enemies*. But God has given me enemies and has put me in a world of conflict. God has given me a responsible job and created obstacles to doing it. Do I like this? Of course not! But what can I do? Turn to God.

Teach me how to fight, LORD, in this situation, with this person, now, today. How do you want this handled? And what do you want me to learn from this? Do I defend myself in this matter? Do I lose this one so that I can win a greater one? Am I wrong about this? Unending questions and subtleties. No book of rules with all the answers. All I know is, there is a time to fight. Is it now? Ask God.

Psalm 144 (BCP)

Thirtieth Day: Morning Prayer Tone: "UGÁV

1 Blessed be the LORD my rock! *
   who trains my hands to fight and my fingers to battle;
2 My help and my fortress, my stronghold and my deliverer, *
   my shield in whom I trust,
   who subdues the peoples under me.
3 O LORD, what are we that you should care for us? *
   mere mortals that you should think of us?
4 We are like a puff of wind; *
   our days are like a passing shadow.
5 Bow your heavens, O LORD, and come down; *
   touch the mountains, and they shall smoke.
6 Hurl the lightning and scatter them; *
   shoot out your arrows and rout them.
7 Stretch out your hand from on high;
   rescue me and deliver me from the great | waters,
   from the hand of foreign | peoples,
8 Whose mouths speak de|ceitfully,
   and whose right | hand is raised in | falsehood.
9 O God, I will sing to you a new song; *
   I will play to you on a ten-stringed lyre.
10 You give victory to kings *
   and have rescued David your servant.
11 **Rescue me from the hurtful | sword**
   and deliver me from the hand of foreign | peoples,
12 Whose mouths speak de|ceitfully
   and whose right | hand is raised in | falsehood.
13 May our sons be like plants well nurtured from their youth, *
   and our daughters like sculptured corners of a palace.
14 May our barns be filled to overflowing with all manner of crops; *
   may the flocks in our pastures increase by thousands
   and tens of thousands;
   may our cattle be fat and sleek.
15 May there be no breaching of the walls, no going into exile, *
   no wailing in the public squares.
16 Happy are the people of whom this is so! *
   happy are the people whose God is the LORD!

Alphabet Of Meaning: Commentary To Psalm 145

When a speaker calls for one last question, Robert Fulghum* likes to ask about the meaning of life. Usually he is dismissed with laughter or ignored. *The meaning of life* is not considered a serious question in our time, but a sophomoric one, like *how high is up?* When biblical values are lost, the meaning of life is indeed elusive. Does life, or anything, have meaning beyond what we ourselves read into it? Yet meaning itself is a meaningful concept. To mean is to point to something. The meaning of any thing is what it reminds me of, where it leads my vision. If the meaning of life in general seems nebulous, the meaning of my own life is what it points to; where it leads those who know me. And so this great hymn is about meaning in its profoundest sense: What is creation saying and pointing to? And how do I respond?

DOR L:DOR Y:SHABBA# MA"aSEYKHÁ
v.4 One generation shall praise your works to another.

What always strikes me is the dialogue, those great rolling cadences echoing back and forth. One generation shall praise ... I will ponder ... they shall speak ... I will tell ... they shall publish. The reverential awareness of God is not a new discovery, but an ancient mystery, known in all the universe. Every generation points it out to the next. And I respond with wonder, adding my voice to this great conversation. For the meaning that everything points to is dialogue itself—communion with a cosmic Person!

v.10 All your works continue to praise you, O LORD,
and your faithfully devoted ones continue to bless you.

The dialogue, the telling continues. The works that you have lovingly created speak of you. For the meaning of all things is to point to you, "that the peoples may know of your power." And you LORD, in turn, point to us. You are ever directing your attention to us earth-children—upholding, lifting up, giving, satisfying. Almost as though your meaning were found in us, your creatures.

v.17 You open wide your hand
and satisfy the needs of every living creature. The meaning that everything points to is a God who feeds, a God of bread and wine. He creates the creatures and their needs, and the objects of their needs, and he teaches them to find what they need, what he has given them to need. He created me to need air and water; light, order and meaning; and he gives them to me moment by moment. Most of all, he created me to yearn for him, and he comes to feed me!

Note: Verse 14 is not found in the Masoretic text.

Suggestions: Sing reverentially to the Tone *Alphabet*. Practice the telling of God, not only in words, but in feedings. Nourish everyone you encounter in whatever way you can, and let your living speak of God.

---

*Robert Fulghum: *It Was On Fire When I Lay Down On It*, Ballentine Books, 1988.

Psalm 145 (BCP)

Tone: Alphabet

1 **I will exalt you, O God my | King,**
   and bless your Name for ever and | ever.
2 Every day will I + bless you
   and praise your Name for ever and + ever.
3 Great is the LORD and greatly to be / praised;
   there is no end to his / greatness.
4 One generation shall praise your works to an^other
   and shall declare your ^ power.
5 I will ponder the glorious splendor of your . majesty
   and all your marvelous . works.
6 **They shall speak of the might of your wondrous | acts,**
   and I will tell of your | greatness.
7 They shall publish the remembrance of your great + goodness;
   they shall sing of your righteous + deeds.
8 The LORD is gracious and full of com/passion,
   slow to anger and of great / kindness.
9 The LORD is loving to ^ everyone
   and his compassion is over all his ^ works.
10 All your works praise you, O . LORD,
   and your faithful servants . bless you.
11 \They make known the glory of your \ kingdom
   and \ speak of your \ power;
12 **That the peoples may know of your | power**
   and the glorious splendor of your | kingdom.
13 Your kingdom is an everlasting + kingdom;
   your dominion endures throughout all + ages.
14 The LORD is faithful in all his / words
   and merciful in all his / deeds.
15 The LORD upholds all those who ^ fall;
   he lifts up those who are bowed ^ down.
16 The eyes of all wait upon you, O . LORD,
   and you give them your food in due . season.

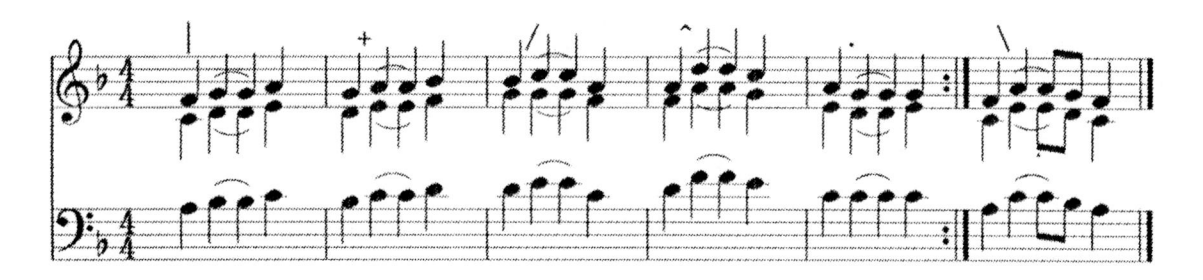

17 **You open wide your | hand**
    and satisfy the needs of every living | creature.
18 The LORD is righteous in all his + ways
    and loving in all his + works.
19 The LORD is near to those who / call upon him
    to all who call upon him / faithfully.
20 He fulfills the desire of those who ^ fear him;
    he hears their cry and ^ helps them.
21 The LORD preserves all those who . love him,
    but he destroys all the . wicked.
22 \My mouth shall speak the praise of the \ LORD;
    let all flesh bless his holy \ Name for ever
    and \ ever.

Cares For The Stranger: Commentary To Psalm 146

HAL:LIY NAPHSHIY .ETH-YHWH

v.1 Praise the LORD, O my soul (breathing, life)!
I will praise the LORD in (or with) my life;
I will sing praises to my God while I still am. There is no contrast here between my soul (breath, breathing, life) and "I" — my thoughts, my sense of self; but as for me. Here as I approach the summit of the climb, I am coming together as one. Praise brings me into harmony as it brings all things. My very breathing praises him; and as for me, I praise him too.

v.2 Put not your trust in rulers (important people). Put not your trust in powerful friends, administrators, or politicians. My boss or the boss of my boss may be sympathetic, they are sure to "look into it" (whatever it is), but they will find there is little they can do. They are but children of red earth, human breathings like myself. Suddenly one day their breath goes out and does not come back in. At that moment all their ambitious plans have perished, and their influence is reduced to zero.

v.4 Happy are they who have the God of Jacob, the God known to our family, for their help. Real happiness. The help of God is contrasted to the help of those friends. What kind of helper is God? In vv. 5-7, he is making the heavens and the earth, the sea(s) and all that is in them. He is preserving truth (what is reliable and constant) to eternity. He is making justice for the oppressed. He is giving bread to the hungry. He is freeing the prisoners.

YHWH .OHÉV 3ADDIQIM   YHWH SHOMÉR .ETH-GÉRIM

v.8 The LORD loves (is loving) the righteous;
the LORD preserves (is guarding) the stranger.
He keeps reaffirming (restoring) the orphan and widow, and frustrating, literally bending or turning aside the road of the wicked.

He is active, creative, involved in the world, reliable, constant, completely righteous, that is, straight. And his righteousness is this: He protects those who have no protector. The stranger passing through town, who doesn't know anyone, and isn't related to anyone. His Daddy and Granddaddy never lived there, and he didn't go to school with anyone who does live there. The righteousness of God — his way, if you would know and do it — is to protect that stranger (orphan, widow, blind person) before taking care of anything else. Compare 61, 72.

<u>Suggestions</u>: Stand, sing to the movement Reverential Praise. The music for 146 and 147 is the same.

Troubles at work or in church? Consult the important people, by all means. The boss or the bishop or top management. But do not look to them for the answers. Look to God. Do not think of this in a sentimental or religious sense. Actually stop in the midst of the troubles, clear your thoughts, listen. Ask God what to do. If you are willing to do whatever he wills, he will show you the way.

Psalm 146 (BCP)

Tone: SHOPHÁR

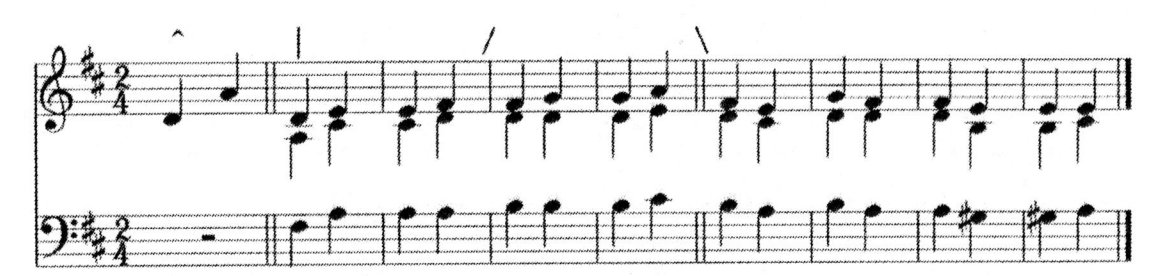

^Hallelu^jah!

1 ^Praise the LORD, O my ^ soul!
   /I will praise the LORD as long as I / live;
   I will sing praises to my God while I have my / being.

2 \Put not your trust in rulers, nor in any child of \ earth,
   for there is no \ help in them.

3 When they breathe their last, they return to \ earth,
   and in that day their thoughts \ perish.

4 **Happy are they who have the God of Jacob for their | help!**
   whose hope is in the LORD their | God;

5 /Who made heaven and earth, the seas, and all that is / in them;
   who keeps his promise for / ever.

6 \Who gives justice to those who are op\pressed,
       and food to those who \ hunger.

7 The LORD sets the prisoners free;
   the LORD opens the eyes of the \ blind;
   the LORD lifts up those who are bowed \ down.

8 **The LORD loves the | righteous;**
   the LORD cares for the | stranger;
   /he sustains the orphan and / widow,
   but frustrates the way of the / wicked.

9 /The LORD shall reign for / ever,
   your God, O Zion, throughout all gene/rations.

^Hallelu^jah!

Respond To The LORD: Commentary To Psalm 147

"eNUW LAYHWH B:THODÁH   ZAMM:RUW LÉ.LOH<u>E</u>YNU V:KHINNOR
v.7 Answer (or respond) to the LORD with thanksgiving;
sing to our God with the harp.

I am reminded that "prayer is responding to God, by thought and by deeds, with or without words" (Prayer Book, p. 856). We are told to respond to him—with praise, thanksgiving, singing, and playing. Respond to the broken-heart healer, the wound-binder, the star-counter.

Responding to God sounds easy. Responding may be easy; responding to God maybe not. The natural way is to do something, almost anything. The worst thing to be accused of is inaction. Responding to God may mean acting or waiting. It may mean living with uncertainty, or taking the blame. Knowing only what I need to know for today, or for the next thirty minutes.

v.3 He heals the broken-hearted
and binds up their wounds.
v.4 He counts the number of the stars
and calls them all by their names.

The healing, saying "Be healed," may be easy. Binding up the wounds maybe not. Healing and praying for healing are not so easy as they sound. Not if I also have to lay hands on the patient or touch the dressings. More important may be calling that patient, like the stars, by name. We pray and make intercession for the sick, not because God needs reminding, but because he asks us to pray for them, because he wants to hear their names!

Many themes come together now as we approach the summit of this mountain. God is actively at work in the broken-hearted, in the wounded, in our broken community where an economic system can no longer care for children. Among those who cannot afford to be sick, or take care of a sick child. In our broken hearts where we long for connection. In the vastness of space, counting the stars and calling them by their names. Respond to him! Not that we should start a movement or a program. What is needed is the response, the willingness. He is calling, calling; and we must find a way to answer.

Even now he is covering the heavens with clouds, preparing the rain, providing food for the animals and the baby birds. He is not impressed as I might be by the physique of a horse or a man. His greatest pleasure is in my response, my willingness.

<u>Suggestions</u>: Stand, sing to the movement Reverential Praise.

Pray for the sick as God leads you. Always begin with silence. Pronounce the sick person's name and ask God what he wants you to do for him or her. Be prepared to do whatever he asks. When the patient is healed, tell no one of your involvement. Never boast about healings.

Psalm 147 (BCP)

Thirtieth Day: Evening Prayer

1 ^Hallelu^jah!
    How good it is to sing praises to our | God!
    how pleasant it is to honor him with | praise!
2 /The LORD rebuilds / Jerusalem;
    he gathers the exiles of / Israel.
3 **He heals the broken | hearted**
    and binds up their | wounds.
4 /He counts the number of the / stars
    and calls them all by their / names.
5 /Great is our LORD and mighty in / power;
    there is no limit to his / wisdom.
6 \The LORD lifts up the \ lowly,
    but casts the wicked to the \ ground.
7 Sing to the LORD with thanks\giving;
    make music to our God upon the \ harp.
8 **He covers the heavens with | clouds**
    and prepares rain for the | earth;
9 /He makes grass to grow upon the / mountains
    and green plants to serve man/kind.
10 /He provides food for flocks and / herds
    and for the young ravens when they / cry.
11 \He is not impressed by the might of a \ horse;
    he has no pleasure in the strength of a \ man;
12 But the LORD has pleasure in those who \ fear him,
    in those who await his gracious \ favor.
13 **Worship the LORD, O Je | rusalem;**
    praise your God, O | Zion;
14 /For he has strengthened the bars of your / gates;
    he has blessed your children with/in you.
15 /He has established peace on your / borders;
    he satisfies you with the finest / wheat.
16 \He sends out his command to the \ earth,
    and his word runs very \ swiftly.

17 He gives snow like \ wool;
 he scatters hoarfrost like \ ashes.
18 \He scatters his hail like \ bread crumbs;
 who can stand against his \ cold?
19 He sends forth his word and \ melts them;
 he blows with his wind, and the \ waters flow.
20 **He declares his word to | Jacob,**
 his statutes and his judgments to | Israel.
21 /He has not done so to any other / nation;
 to them he has not revealed his / judgments.
 ^Hallelu^jah!

At Your Command All Things: Commentary To Psalm 148

At your command all things came to be: the vast expanse of interstellar space, galaxies, suns, the planets in their courses, and this fragile earth, our island home. Prayer Book, p. 370.

    HAL:LUHU KOL-MAL.ÁKHÁW   HAL:LUHU KOL-3:VÁ.ÁW

v.2 Praise him, all his angels (messengers);
Praise him, all his host (armies, forces).

Everything joins in the chorus. All living things: sea-monsters, wild beasts, cattle, creeping things, birds, trees. And all branches of the human family: kings, peoples, princes, rulers, young men and maidens. All fellow singers.

Praise is not limited to words, to prayer, to Christians, or even to mankind. Not even to "life as we know it," for the whole environment is included: the heavens, heights, sun and moon, stars, earth, deeps, fire and hail, snow and fog, mountains and hills. Praise draws it all together, even his angels and his armies. All things, visible and invisible.

Everything, living and non-living, in its own way, praises the LORD. Everything, by its own appointed activity, adds to the stream of affirmation, the creative force, flowing upward to God. So that what we think of as praise is only one tiny stream feeding a great river of praise. What we call praise, even if we include every prayer in every religion, is but a shadow of the real praise.

Praise is the great creative force. God draws it forth from all things toward himself, and it strengthens whatever it is drawn from. We don't understand it at all. Joining in praise we experience it. Following it we begin to be transformed.

Scripture never says "All is One," or, "All this is That." Every thing created is unique, part of a complex and fragile design. Every star has a name. All things are fellow creations, fellow singers. Not to be worshiped, never to be exploited. Fragile and interdependent like a delicate web. Man/woman has been entrusted to care for it, not to own it. For we are fellow singers with angels.

Suggestions: Stand. Sing to the movement Reverential Praise. The same music will be used for Psalm 150.

Read *Prison to Praise* by Merlin Carothers (Escondido, California, 1970). Practice moments of silence and see the world around you. See the actual grasses, flowers, birds, rocks, clouds, every one unique. Practice actually seeing these things, not the idea of grasses, flowers, birds, but the things themselves, without comment, without analysis. Not even "That's beautiful!" And everything you see will begin to strike you with an almost physical impact. For every thing you see is praising God. And when you are silent, you are praising him too!

Psalm 148 (BCP)

Tone: SHOPHÁR

1 ^Hallelu^jah!
   Praise the L<small>ORD</small> from the | heavens;
   praise him in the | heights.
2 /Praise him, all you / angels of his;
   praise him, all his / host.
3 **Praise him, sun and | moon;**
   praise him, all you shining | stars.
4 /Praise him, heaven of / heavens,
   and you waters above the / heavens.
5 **Let them praise the Name of the | L<small>ORD</small>;**
   for he commanded, and they were | created.
6 /He made them stand fast for ever and / ever;
   he gave them a law which shall not pass / away.

7 **Praise the L<small>ORD</small> from the | earth,**
   you sea-monsters and all | deeps;
8 /Fire and hail, snow and / fog,
   tempestuous wind, doing his / will;
9 **Mountains and all | hills,**
   fruit trees and all | cedars;
10 /Wild beasts and all / cattle,
   creeping things and winged / birds;
11 **Kings of the earth and all | peoples,**
   princes and all rulers of the | world;
12 /Young men and / maidens,
   old and young to/gether.
13 **Let them praise the Name of the L<small>ORD</small>,**
   for his Name only is | exalted,
   his splendor is over earth and | heaven.
14 /He has raised up strength for his people
   and praise for all his loyal / servants,
   the children of Israel, a people who are / near him.
   ^Hallelu^jah!

Joyful On Their Beds: Commentary To Psalm 149

v.1 Sing to the LORD a new song;
his praise in the congregation of the faithful.

It is the last "new song" of the Psalter. Compare 33, 96, 98. Sing a new song, yet again. Praise him with de-automatized praise. As though you were singing to Jesus, looking into his eyes! As though you were singing to your spouse, on the night you first knew that you cared. Sing it the way you say, "I love you!"—three words spoken hundreds of times, but each time new.

v.2 Let Israel rejoice in his Maker;
the children of Zion be joyful in their King.

Think of Israel as holy community—the fellowship of all who seek to know and serve God—the communion of saints. Think of Zion as the holy mountain going up to his temple; or as going up itself, the spiritual way, searching and seeking. Let all who seek God and his wisdom rejoice and be glad.

    Y:HAL:LUW SH:MOW V:MÁ#OL   B:TOPH W:KHINNOR Y:ZAMM:RU-LOW

v.3 Let them praise his Name in dance;
with drum and harp let them sing praise to him!

MÁ#OL (*dance*), from a root meaning to twist, turn or turn around, hence to dance in a circle (Gesenius, and see Judges 21:21). Let them gather in a great circle, in community, dancing your praise. With TOPH (*timbrel* or *drum*), beating out rhythm, and KINNOR (the *harp* of David), whose song is healing. Praise him with living music, with rhythm and movement. No one is ever excluded here, no one knows exactly what to do. Let everyone join in. Everyone sing. Everyone dance. Everyone is an expert.

    YA"LZUW #aSIDIM B:KHÁVOD   Y:RAN:NUW "AL-MISHK:VOTHÁM

v.5 Let the faithful exult in glory,
let them rejoice upon their beds.

Let the fiercely devoted ones exult and cry "Aha!" Let them be joyful in their homes, in their beds, in their rest, in their marriages. This too is praise! In battle, too, when battle is the only choice, as in 144. When we must, fight fiercely, fight under heavenly direction, accept the victory. This too is praise!

Notes: (*) Verse 2 is modified by the author for ease of singing.

Suggestions: Sing to the movement Standing Drum. Let your prayer and your meditation be always new, that is renewed, refreshed, open. Let your practice always be open to change, new music, new movement, new understandings. Do you think that God has told you everything? Listen and learn something new!

Psalm 149 (BCP)

Tone: SHOPHÁR

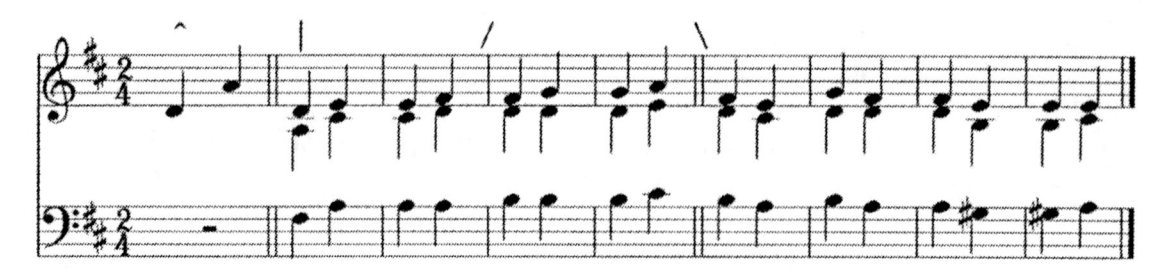

1 **^Hàllelù^jàh!**
   /Sìng to the LÒRD a new / sòng; `
   sing his pràise in the congregàtion of the / fàithful. `
2 **Let Ìsrael rejòice in his | Màker; `**
   the children of Zìon be jòyful in their | Kìng. ` (*)
3 /Let them pràise his Nàme in the / dànce; `
   let them sing pràise to him with tìmbrel and / hàrp. `
4 \For the LORD takes pleasure in his \ people
   and adorns the poor with \ victory.
5 Let the faithful rejoice in \ triumph;
   let them be joyful on their \ beds.
6 **Let the pràises of Gòd be in their | thròat `**
   and a twò-edged swòrd in their | hànd; `
7 /To wreak vèngeance òn the / nàtions `
   And pùnishment òn the / pèoples; `
8 **To bìnd their kìngs in | chàins `**
   and their nòbles with lìnks of | ìron; `
9 /To inflìct on them the jùdgment de/crèed; `
   this is glòry for àll his faithful / pèople.
^Hàllelù^jàh!

The Summit: Commentary To Psalm 150

HAL:LUYÁH'

v.1 Praise the LORD!

One word—the praising and the Praised. One word—the imperative merging with the Name. Arriving at the summit, all flows into that word, a one word prayer. Transcending English and Hebrew, transcending language itself, that prayer encompasses all prayer. Like a sacred circle it encloses praise.

In that circle I see the mystery of existence, a universe converging toward a Person. I see that the secrets of the universe are found not within it, but beyond it, in that Person. All things come together in relation to the One who creates them. And the nature of that relationship is praise.

Praise God, first in his holy place, the place of silence; and in his wide place, heaven and earth; and for his powerful actions upholding creation; and for his greatness, the *abundance* of his greatness. Praise (affirm, bless, thank) him from every level of understanding. Praise him together with all things, join the chorus of praise. For praise is our answer to his love, the most powerful force in the universe.

Praise him with SHOPHÁR (*the ram's-horn*) and NÉVEL (*the lyre*) and KINNOR (*the harp*), with every instrument and faculty. With every state of mind, every emotion. Praise him with joy and anger, grief and reverence, love and hate. Praise him with reading and music, the music in this book and all music, with movements from this book and all movement. Praise him with silence, standing, kneeling, lifting, bowing. Praise him as your own people praise him, and praise him as other people praise him. Say yes to every form of his praise.

KOL-HAN:SHÁMÁH T:HALLÉL YÁH'

v.6 Let all living breath praise YAH!

N:SHÁMÁH is cognate to NEPHESh—the living breath. Not intellect, thoughts, accomplishments, but this: the living breath, the unpredictable, self-organizing complexity that is really me. Even when I sleep, even when I grow old and forgetful. No one will ever again breathe as I breathe or laugh as I laugh. Let the breath of all that is living praise him; and let my own breathing, yes, my breathing, praise him as well.

Hallelujah!

Suggestions: Sing joyfully to the movement Marching Dance. Repeat as often as desired. Form a great circle and march first clockwise, then counter-clockwise. Let different members sing in turn. Breathe deeply, inhaling sharply and deeply through the nose, and let your breathing be praise of God. As you make this your constant practice, you will become ever more awake and alive. Nothing you can do will be more beneficial to your health or more helpful on the spiritual path. Let the echo of this joyful celebration be heard in your praises from now on. Think of it whenever you say *Praise God* or *Hallelujah!*

Psalm 150 (BCP)

Tone: SHOPHÁR

^Hallelu^jah!
1 **Praise God in his | holy place:** praise him in the wide place of his | power!
2 /Praise him for his powerful / deeds; praise him according to his / greatness!
3 **Praise him with the sound of the | ram's-horn:** praise him with lyre and | harp!
4 /Praise him with drum and / dancing: praise him with strings and / organ!
5 /Praise him with cymbals / sounding: praise him with cymbals re/sounding!
6 ^Let all living breath praise ^ YAH –
   ^Hallelu^jah!

Afterword

We began our journey with the image of a walk or path, a path that goes up a hill, through many and varied experiences, to a high and holy place. To a temple, a place of silence. Now we begin to see where the path is taking us. It is a path of liberation from thoughts, words, images; from illusions created by language. In their place we find the voice of God, and we are learning to hear it. The journey is cyclical, never ending. Tomorrow is the first day of the month. Begin with Psalm 1.

Walking the Scriptures is not like analyzing them, boasting of them, debating them, or insisting they are true in some narrow sense. Walking the Word is listening to God himself; listening, listening, and yet more listening. It is giving up control. It is surrender. I cannot tell where the path will take me; I only know it is the path of life.

Suggestions: Continue to meditate daily, going through the psalms each month. Continue even when nothing seems to happen, when it is difficult to be silent. There will be times when meditation seems utterly pointless. Continue to practice faithfully, and let God teach you. Gradually increase your time of silence as the Spirit directs you.

As no psalm is specifically designated for the thirty-first day, you may select whatever psalms appeal to you for this day. You may wish to use selected verses of Psalm 119, or draw on other scriptural songs, such as the Psalm of Jonah (2:2-9) or the Psalm of Habakkuk (3:1-19). Or sing one of the canticles in the Prayer Book, pp. 47-53 and 85-96. Supplement your study with readings from the whole of Scripture and devotional literature. Study the great commentaries. Most of all seek out spiritual companions, those who show fruits of the Spirit in their lives, and learn as much as you can from them.

Continue to study, continue to learn, continue to grow, give no advice, do not engage in religious arguments. In time of trouble, when depressed or anxious or irritable, or when you cannot sleep, or cannot settle down to meditate, use these psalms as medicine. Sing them over and over, any psalms you choose, in any order. Immerse yourself in them, let them comfort you. Practice all you have learned in this book, especially in regard to breathing. May God walk with you on this sacred path, bless you, and keep you in good health.

Appendix (1)
The Tones
KINNOR (*harp*)

This harp is David's. A simple four-note figure (F-G-E-F), with its gentle rise and fall, evokes his music—calming, soothing, even therapeutic. See 1 Samuel 16:26. That rise and fall suggest the hills where he pastured his sheep, or his walking up and down those grassy slopes, sometimes joyful, sometimes weary to the bone. Each hill is balanced by a valley, each exalted moment by a shadow. The spirit of the psalms reflects this balance of highs and lows.

Each measure corresponds to a line of poetry. The first two measures by themselves comprise KINNOR (1), the first four KINNOR (2). The concluding *coda* consists of three sustained notes—for a three-line verse—returning to the original F. This pattern will be found in several of the Tones. I call it the *earth motif,* suggesting surrender and sacrifice, the returning of one's life to its source.

HIGÁYON (*meditation*) is a melancholy variant, based upon the figure F-G-E-D. SHÁRIM (*singers*) is a variant with three musical couplets, for refrains of three lines. Its high-low-higher pattern signifies exaltation or holiness.

Hand movements for KINNOR and HIGÁYON are given below.

N:GINOTH (stringed instruments)

The term is found in the Hebrew titles to several psalms. Long descending tones or a descending series of couplets create a melancholy flavor—themes of persecution, helplessness, the shortness of life. The descending pitch may also suggest a movement from heaven earthward; God reaches down to us when we cannot rise to him. One measure corresponds to one line of poetry. SH:MINITH (*eighth*) is a variant form.

MÁ#OL (*dance*)

The term is explained with Psalm 149. Dance is a form of praise (150:4). This dance has a light-hearted quality, used to denote joy, laughter or irony. It is always associated with the movement Twirling Dance (see below). One measure corresponds to one line of text. Render the three-note ornamental figures slowly, gracefully. The Orders may occur in any sequence and may be repeated.

#ÁLIL (*flute*)

This pipe or flute is found in Isaiah 5:12; the Tone rises and falls in waves, suggesting water; hence, the beauty of creation. It unfolds in four wave-like figures, with two variant forms. Variant A is indicated by the caret marker ^ while in variant B, each stanza begins with boldface type. Each cycle of verses may use one to four Orders, depending on its length. One measure corresponds to one complete verse. The tied notes indicate that a chord is held over from one line to the next. The descending movement of the fifth Order provides contrast and balance. One measure corresponds to one line of the text.

"ÁSOR and NÉVEL

"ÁSOR (*ten-string*) refers to a musical instrument of ten strings, similar or identical to the NÉVEL (33:2, 92:3). The Tone has a cheerful character, signifying blessing, healing, restoration. It rises in two wave-like figures, then descends in two measures of long sustained notes. NÉVEL (*lyre*) has a gentle, repetitive quality, suggesting meditation and wisdom. The first Order is repeated three times, the second, once. It is used for 19:7-13 and all of 119. Each measure corresponds to a line.

GITTITH (*of Gath*)

The obscure word GITTITH (*of Gath*) is found in the titles to 8, 81, and 84. Scholars assign it to a musical instrument or popular melody "of Gath." The Tone carries a sense of exaltation: the presence and power of God in any circumstance. Shining columns of light in hopeless situations. One measure corresponds to one line. There are three Orders, always in sequence.

SHOPHÁR (*ram's-horn*)

A simple two-note fanfare (D-A) represents the actual sound of the ram's-horn trumpet. It is used with *Hallelujah* in a number of psalms. Ascending and descending marches are elaborated out of this simple form to accompany several praise psalms.

#a3O3:ROTH (*trumpets*)

The word signifies trumpets of silver or brass. The Tone is a simple fanfare of four notes (D-A-D-E), suitable for acclamations or shouts of praise. Elaborations of this simple form are composed of ascending and descending couplets of smaller intervals. Either half of the basic fanfare can be repeated, thus D-A-D-A-D-E as in 115, 118.

TOPH (*drum*)

TOPH means a drum or timbrel, beaten in a circle dance or procession, as in 68:25. Such marching and drumming is also mentioned in 150:4. The Tone is a more elaborate fanfare, its march-like beat suggesting triumph and exultation. It is associated with the movement Turning Drum (see below). One measure corresponds to a line of text. The Tone has four Orders which recur in sequence, though not all of them in every sequence.

"UGÁV (*pipe*)

"UGÁV (*pipe*) is a name given to various wind instruments, as a tibia, pipe, reed, or syrinx; or to an organ (Gesenius, p. 610). The character is solemn or sinister, the struggle of light against darkness. The forces of evil are surrounding and besieging me. One measure corresponds to a line of text. Minor variants are suggested for stanzas of irregular length as in 22, 74, and 140.

Alphabet

Alphabet is used for the alphabetic psalms. It is contemplative, sung in a measured and even manner. Several variants will be found. The six Orders in the music represent the twenty-two letters of the Hebrew alphabet. The first five Orders are sung twice through; the sixth functions as a *coda* to each half of the psalm. Each Order consists of four notes, one measure, corresponding to a complete verse. In the short form—for Psalms 111 and 112—each Order consists of two notes.

Selected verses of a long version are found in Psalm 37, while alternate verses are read. The long version of the *coda* only is sung with Psalm 10.

SHO.ÁH (*holocaust*)

The term in Scripture signifies ruin or destruction, as in the dreaded "Day of the LORD." For modern Jews it means the Holocaust, the destruction of European Jews during the Nazi era. The Tone is a variant of *Alphabet*.

Suggestions: Learn the Tones as soon as possible, and incorporate them into your study. Music is an integral part of your psalm walking experience. For the pronunciation of Hebrew terms, see Appendix (3), below.

Appendix (2)

The Movements

For a general overview see the Introduction. What follows is a description of specific movements recommended for the various psalms. Begin movements from a seated position unless otherwise instructed. As with the music, remember the principle of balance—movement contrasting with movement to engage the attention.

Metrical Walking

Recommended for 26, 78, 105 and parts of 101. Marks have been provided to guide you. Walk slowly, keeping a steady, metrical pace. Start each line on the left foot, with one step to each beat (`). Pause at the dash (—). Never rush.

Gestures and Hand Movements

In general, lifting the hands signifies praise, blessing, thankfulness. Lifting the extended hands, palms up, a little higher than the heart, is the praise gesture. It is the starting point for several other movements. Bowing suggests worship; kneeling portrays submission. Folding the arms across the chest, hands clasping the shoulders, signifies heart, comfort, or trust—the heart gesture. The right arm extended straight, as if pointing into the distance, signifies a road or path. Sinking to one knee, head bowed, and touching the earth with the right hand, is the earth movement, suggestive of sacrifice. It generally accompanies two verses, and is concluded on the last line by gracefully rising, the right arm leading the way up.

Movements for KINNOR and HIGÁYON

Begin with the praise gesture on the first musical figure, and maintain this position through the corresponding verse. On the first line of the next verse, second musical figure, lift the hands higher, to about the level of the forehead; on the next line, higher still, to perhaps several inches higher than the head.

The third musical figure will always correspond to three lines of verse. On the first line, lower the hands slightly, to about eye level, and bring them closer together. On the second line, lower the hands to heart level, but bring them close together, almost touching. On the third line, move into the heart gesture. Clasp the shoulders tightly, like a hug. Move back into the praise gesture at the end of the verse. Omit these movements when instructed to stand, bow, or kneel.

The wave gesture for thank offerings is as follows: Beginning with the praise gesture, lift the hands higher and immediately lower them on one line of poetry, move them gracefully leftward and rightward on the next, ending in the original position. The movement recaptures the wave movement of the ancient freewill or thank offering. For a discussion of this and other temple ceremonies, consult Edersheim.*

Jumping

Jump into the air with both feet on the second *Hallelujah*, Psalms 135 and 146 through 150. Always land with arms in the praise gesture.

Reverential Praise

Begin the first Order standing, eyes uplifted, hands extended outward and wide apart, at waist level or slightly above. The palms face up. It is the position of one carrying a long but light tray or basket. On the second line of verse (second measure) bring hands in toward the midline, palms still facing up. On the third line or third measure, lift hands to forehead level. On the fourth line higher still, arms almost vertical.

Whenever the words *bow* or *worship* occur, bow deeply from the waist. Reverential Praise evokes the emotion of reverence; practice the movement until it becomes a worship experience. On *Hallelujah* give arms an additional upward and outward thrust. On the second Order, carry out the earth movement described above. This movement expresses devotion, humility and worship.

Standing Drum

A simple drum made of a tightly stretched animal skin is best. Let one person beat the drum, while the others stand in a large circle. The beat should be slow, steady and powerful. Begin with four beats of the drum before singing, then one beat for each stress in the poetry (`). Except for the drummer, let everyone stand exquisitely motionless. The hands are lifted in front of the face, the palms face each other. One hand is slightly higher than the other and the gaze is directed upward. The dash (—) at the end of a line suggests a brief pause in drumming and singing. On [Silence...] remain motionless for an additional ten to fifteen seconds.

On the second Order, cease drumming, kneel gently in the earth movement. Sing slower, with a looser rhythm. On rising, prepare to resume drumming. Standing Drum can be used for many of the same psalms as Reverential Praise or Marching and Swaying Dance. Use whichever movement feels most suitable at the time.

Turning Drum

The movement also requires a drum. Let everyone form a large circle. On the first line of the first Order verses (boldface type), begin with four beats, then let each dancer turn clockwise in a tight circle. Do the turn with a pronounced stepping or stomping movement, one step or stomp to each beat of the drum. On the second line, reverse direction, turn with the same stepping movement back to the original position.

Otherwise return to the great circle and march in a clockwise direction. Sink slowly into the earth movement on the fourth Order (marked by .). On the upward movement of the second line, you may bring the right hand up with a continuous fluttering movement of the fingers, suggesting the rising smoke of a sacrifice.

Marching and Swaying Dance

The first Order is Marching Dance. Form a great circle and march in a clockwise direction. Begin with four beats of the drum. March briskly, with a light, energetic step, taking three steps forward and one step back. Begin on the left foot, stepping Left—Right—Left—and rock back on the right foot. Left—Right—Left—Back, one beat to each step, one step to each beat (`) in the text. A brief pause in movement and singing is indicated by the dash (—).

The second Order is Swaying Dance, as in Psalm 67.

Twirling Dance

This movement is associated with MÁ#OL (*dance*). Note that the Orders for this Tone are not always in sequence. On the first line of the first Order (boldface), let each dancer spin or twirl in a clockwise direction, with arms outstretched like wings. On the second line, spin or twirl in the reverse direction, coming back to the original position. End with arms in the praise gesture.

On the second Order, walk smoothly around the great circle in a clockwise direction. The movement is slow, gentle, and light, conveying a sense of joy.

At the first line of the third Order, go into the earth movement. Upon returning to the upright position, rock backward on the left foot. Immediately continue walking. Always conclude the dance joyfully, with arms upraised. Although the movement is slow and reflective, the feeling it evokes is joyful and energized.

Warning

Do not attempt these movements, especially Twirling Dance, if you have any doubt about your physical ability to do them safely. If you have any kind of back or knee trouble, or are simply unused to physical activity, do not attempt the movements without obtaining professional advice. Omit or modify any part of the movement that causes even the slightest strain or discomfort.

Appendix (3)

The Sound Of Hebrew

A number of Hebrew words and selected verses have been included in the text so that, if interested, you can experience their actual sounds. The author's system of transliteration is used. Certain words well known in English are also given in their customary spellings, italicized, as *Adonai* and *shalom*. The pronunciation is that of modern Israeli Hebrew.

Hebrew is of course written in the Hebrew alphabet. Hebrew writing presents some difficulties for the Western reader. It is written from left to right, and is mainly a consonantal writing system. The vowels are known by tradition or by the addition of tiny marks above and below the letters. The author's transliteration reflects the Hebrew text accurately, yet is easy to learn. The system used in this book differs from those used by scholars and academics in that it reflects the way Hebrew is actually pronounced—in liturgical reading and in conversation.

In general, and unless otherwise indicated, the vowels are pronounced as in Italian; the consonants as in English; and the accent is on the last syllable.

The word YHWH is not to be pronounced as it is holy. The Jewish people substitute .aDONÁY (*Adonai*). Please, please, please do not say *Jehovah* or *Yahweh*, as these are not real words in Hebrew or any other language.

The vowel Á is a little more rounded than A—halfway between A and O. In modern Israeli Hebrew it is mostly identical to A.

The long vowels—É EY IY OW UW—are slightly longer than E I O U—and always accented.

The half-vowels—a e i o—are fleeting sounds, almost inaudible. The neutral vowel (:) is a fleeting sound like the second e in *telephone* or the a in *among*, barely audible. These vowels never carry the accent.

The dot (.) and ditto mark (") represent silent consonants in modern Hebrew. Their place is noted by the slightest catch in the breath.

The KH and # represent a sound that is not found in standard English, but is well known in the Germanic and Celtic languages—the CH of *Bach* or of *loch*. The 3 corresponds to the Italian Z as in *pizza*. BH is interchangeable with V.

The letter W is also pronounced V except when part of the long vowels OW and UW.

The letters TH and t had special significance in ancient Hebrew but in the modern language are identical to T. Just so, Q is now identical to K.

Certain Hebrew words are accented on the next-to-last syllable. The rules for this are rather complex, so, to make things easier, I have indicated all such accents by underlining. The lower-case h is one indicator of an unstressed final syllable, both after a vowel and in the consonant combinations Bh Kh Ph Sh and Th.

<u>Suggestions</u>: Practice reading the Hebrew verses aloud. If nothing else, try to sense their rhythm and meter. Sing them to the Tones of this book. Reflect on them as you go through the day. If desired, use the Hebrew version for your verse of the day, the verse that you repeat from time to time as you go through the struggles of the day. If you have the opportunity, study Hebrew, and learn to read these psalms in the original.

---

*Alfred Edersheim: *The Temple, Its Ministry and Services*. Updated Edition, Hendrickson Publishers, Peabody MA, 1995.

About the Author

The author is a psychiatrist working with seriously ill patients in a state mental health system. He was raised in the Jewish faith but became a Christian in adult life. Working in a Christian psychiatric practice he discovered the amazing power of the psalms to reach people at every level of illness or health. He spent the next fifteen years developing the method of *walking* the psalms presented in this book. It is a method to go beyond the intellect, beyond words, so that one can begin to listen to the voice of God. Those who have studied with the author report a deepening of spiritual experience and inner peace as they follow this practice. The author lives with his wife in a small but rapidly growing Southern town. They have one daughter.

Printed in the United States
849400003B